THE RIGHTEOUS AND PEOPLE OF CONSCIENCE
OF THE ARMENIAN GENOCIDE

GÉRARD DÉDÉYAN
AGO DEMIRDJIAN
NABIL SALEH

The Righteous and People of Conscience of the Armenian Genocide

Preface by
YVES TERNON

HURST & COMPANY, LONDON

First published in the United Kingdom in 2023 by
C. Hurst & Co. (Publishers) Ltd.,
New Wing, Somerset House, Strand, London, WC2R 1LA
© Gérard Dédéyan, Ago Demirdjian and Nabil Saleh, 2023
Preface © Yves Ternon, 2023
All rights reserved.

Distributed in the United States, Canada and Latin America by
Oxford University Press, 198 Madison Avenue, New York, NY 10016,
United States of America.

The right of Gérard Dédéyan, Ago Demirdjian and Nabil Saleh to be
identified as the authors of this publication is asserted by them in
accordance with the Copyright, Designs and Patents Act, 1988.

Translated from the French by Barbara Mellor.

First published in French in 2021 by Société Nouvelle Librairie
Orientaliste Paul Geuthner as *Les Justes et gens de bien du génocide
des Arméniens*.

A Cataloguing-in-Publication data record for this book
is available from the British Library.

ISBN: 9781805260172

This book is printed using paper from registered sustainable
and managed sources.

www.hurstpublishers.com

Printed by Bell and Bain Ltd, Glasgow

With the collaboration of Héléna Demirdjian, Anna Matevosyan, Nour Saleh

To the memory of all the Righteous, and especially of the Righteous Muslims of the Ottoman Empire, who remained faithful to the duty of *adalet*, and who from 1894 to 1923—before, during and after the genocide—strove to salvage Turkey's honour by offering protection to their Armenian compatriots, at the risk of their careers, their safety, and their lives.

CONTENTS

List of Illustrations	xv
Preface by Yves Ternon	xvii
Authors' Acknowledgements	xxvii
Introduction	1
PRELUDE: THE HISTORICAL BACKGROUND	15
THE HAMIDIAN AND CILICIAN MASSACRES: SOME REMARKABLE INDIVIDUALS	17
1. THE HAMIDIAN MASSACRES	19
2. PIERRE QUILLARD (1864–1912) *Poet and playwright who loved classical culture and sacrificed his work and career for the cause of the Armenians*	21
3. BERNARD LAZARE (1865–1903) *Armenian suffering as a mirror of Jewish persecution*	29
4. JEAN JAURÈS (1859–1914) *Prophet of human rights*	39
5. ALPHONSE CILLIÈRE (1861–1946) *Diplomat enamoured of Turkish culture and passionate about justice for the Armenians*	47
6. ESSAD BEY *Forerunner of the Muslim Righteous of 1915–16*	55
7. ROSE LAMBERT (1878–1974) *Compassionate evangelism*	61
THE OTTOMAN RIGHTEOUS	65
8. THE MUSLIM RIGHTEOUS? *Reflections on a denomination: Religion, compassion and social justice*	67

CONTENTS

9. GOVERNMENT OFFICIALS 75
   Senior Ottoman officials who refused to take part in the annihilation of the Armenians

10. HAMID BEY (D.1919) 79
    Vali of Diyarbekir

11. HÜSEYIN NESIMÎ BEY (1868–1915) 83
    Kaymakam of Lice, faithful to his religion

12. ALI SABIT ES-SÜVEYDI 87
    Deputy kaymakam of Beşiri

13. HILMI BEY (D.1919) 89
    Mutasarrif of Mardin, faithful to his religion

14. ALI SUAD BEY 93
    The 'Armenian Patriarch'

15. FAIK ALI OZANSOY (1876–1950) 97
    Poet and mutasarrif of Kütahya: for the sake of family honour

16. HASAN MAZHAR BEY 99
    Vali of Angora and president of the Mazhar Commission

17. MEHMET CELAL BEY (1863–1926) 105
    The 'Turkish Oskar Schindler'

18. MUSTAFA AGHA AZIZOĞLU (D.1921) 111
    Faithful friend of the German Bethesda Mission for the Blind

TRIBAL CLANS 115

19. THE CHARISMATIC ALEVIS OF DERSIM 117

20. THE KURDS 121
    A rare but valiant defence of the Armenians

21. THE ZAZAS 125
    Protectors of the Armenians

22. THE YAZIDIS OF JABAL SINJAR 127
    A persecuted community who welcomed the Armenians

23. SHEIKH HAMU SHIRU 131
    An exemplary Yazidi protector of the Armenians

24. FAIZ EL-GHUSEIN 135
    The Great Arab Revolt and testimony on the genocide

CONTENTS

25.	TESTIMONY OF GENERAL JEAN-MICHEL BILEMDJIAN *The story of his father Ovhannes and his rescue by a Righteous Arab*	143
26.	ABDUL HALIM ÇELEBI *Compassion among the Sufi*	147

FAMILIES 151

27.	TESTIMONIES REVEALING A RESPECT FOR OR COMPROMISE WITH THE CONCEPT OF ʿADÂLA	153
28.	THE SOMOUNDJIAN FAMILY	163
29.	THE KAZARIAN AND SAKOYAN FAMILIES	167
30.	THE DERDERIAN FAMILY	173
31.	THE DAMLAMIAN FAMILY	177

THE WESTERN RIGHTEOUS 183

32.	HUMANITARIANS *Missionaries, members of religious orders, health workers*	185
33.	MONSIGNOR ANGELO MARIA DOLCI (1867–1939) AND POPE BENEDICT XV (1914–22) *The 'Angel of the Armenians' and the 'Pope of Peace'*	187
34.	PAUL BERRON (1887–1970) *'Action Chrétienne en Orient' (ACO)*	195
35.	CLARENCE USSHER (1870–1955) *American doctor and missionary in Van*	201
36.	TACY ATKINSON (1870–1937) HERBERT ATKINSON (D.1915) *The sacrifice of a life, the testimony of a journal*	207
37.	HENRY H. RIGGS (1875–1943) *Evangelist missionary and witness to the genocide and acts of humanity*	211
38.	BERTHA MORLEY (1878–1973) *Missionary and protector of Armenian girls*	217
39.	RAY TRAVIS (1899–1965) *From the defence of Ayntab to the establishment of the Jbeil orphanage*	221

CONTENTS

40. BEATRICE ROHNER (1876–1947) — 223
    Swiss missionary who tried to negotiate with the Young Turks
41. JAKOB KÜNZLER (1871–1949) AND ELIZABETH KÜNZLER-BENDER — 229
    'In the Land of Blood and Tears'
42. ANNA HEDVIG BÜLL (1887–1981) — 237
    From Haapsalu to St Petersburg
43. MARIA JACOBSEN (1882–1960) KAREN MARIE PETERSEN (1881–?) — 245
    A charitable and effective partnership
44. KAREN JEPPE (1876–1935) — 255
    The 'Danish Mother of the Armenians'
45. BODIL KATHARINE BIØRN — 263
    Healthcare pioneer and witness in words and images
46. JOHANNES LEPSIUS (1858–1926) — 269
    'Guardian angel of the Armenian people'
47. ALEXANDRA TOLSTOY (1884–1979) — 275
    Continuing the humanitarian legacy of Leo Tolstoy
48. AARON AARONSOHN (1876–1919) ALEXANDER AARONSOHN (1888–1948) SARAH AARONSOHNN (1890–1917) — 279
    A genuine empathy with the Armenians

DIPLOMATS — 287

49. FERNAND ROQUE-FERRIER (1859–1909) — 289
    Originator of the right of humanitarian intervention
50. GIACOMO GORRINI (1859–1950) — 297
    A diplomatic mission to support the Armenians
51. HENRY MORGENTHAU (1856–1946) — 301
    Denouncer of Turkey's 'crimes against humanity and civilization'
52. LESLIE A. DAVIS (1876–1960) — 307
    American consul moved by compassion to overcome his preconceptions
53. OSCAR S. HEIZER (1869–1956) — 315
    American consul general and witness to savagery and greed

CONTENTS

54. GERMANY: A SPECIAL CASE 323
    Germany and the Armenian Genocide

55. HARRY STUERMER 329
    Putting ethics before patriotism

56. WALTER RÖSSLER (1871–1929) 333
    German consul who went above and beyond the call of duty

57. ARMIN T. WEGNER (1886–1978) 341
    Righteous on behalf of the Armenians and the Jews

THE MILITARY 349

58. REAR ADMIRAL LOUIS-JOSEPH PIVET (1855–1924) 351
    AND VICE ADMIRAL LOUIS DARTIGE
    DU FOURNET (1856–1940)
    Two men of conscience

59. ABBÉ JULES CHAPERON (1877–1951) 361
    Army chaplain and pioneering humanitarian

JURISTS OF COMMITMENT 369

60. ANDRÉ MANDELSTAM (1869–1949) 371
    Russian Jewish lawyer who championed protection of the Armenians

61. RAPHAEL LEMKIN (1900–59) 377
    Jewish jurist who coined the concept of genocide

THE RIGHTEOUS AT A DISTANCE OF PLACE OR TIME 385

62. LEADING FIGURES IN NEAR EAST RELIEF 387

63. ANTONY KRAFFT-BONNARD (1869–1945) 391
    From humanitarian dedication to political commitment

64. JAMES BRYCE (1838–1922) 397
    'Proof in hand': the reality of genocide

65. ANATOLE FRANCE (1844–1924) 403
    The long struggle for human rights, the Armenian cause and peace

66. JACQUES DE MORGAN (1857–1924) 411
    A dream of Eurasia, a passion for Armenia

CONTENTS

67. AHMET REFIK ALTINAY (1881–1937)   415
    A passion for history and historic truth

68. FRANZ WERFEL (1890–1945)   419
    From Armenian resistance on Musa Dagh to Jewish resistance in the ghettos

69. FRIDTJOF NANSEN (1861–1930)   425
    Polymath who devoted his exceptional talents to aiding survivors of the genocide expelled by Turkey and all stateless peoples

EPILOGUE: THE RIGHTEOUS, AVENGERS AND BRINGERS OF JUSTICE   435

70. THE TRIALS OF THE YOUNG TURKS   437

71. SOGHOMON TEHLIRIAN (1896–1960)   439
    Avenger of the Armenians

CONCLUSION   451

Index   459

LIST OF ILLUSTRATIONS

Fridtjof Nansen in a refugee camp
Van, general view
Adana, the Armenian quarter
Part of a group of 5,000 orphans evacuated from Harput in 1922
Young children waiting to be taken into the Near East Relief orphanage in Yerevan
Maria Jacobsen with a group of orphans
Karen Jeppe, her adoptive son Missak, and Sheikh Hadjim Pasha
Armenian orphans standing in line for their daily bread
Karen Jeppe with her pupils
Bodil Born with a group of orphans
Hamid Bey, Vali of *Diyarbekir*
Faik Ali Ozansoy
Mehmet Celal Bey
Johannes Lepsius
Alexandra Tolstoy
Henry Morgenthau
Armin T. Wegner
Raphael Lemkin
Franz Werfel
Soghomon Tehlirian
Russian soldiers, Sheykhalan, 1915
Map of the Armenian Genocide

PREFACE

Yves Ternon

This important volume, an essential companion to the history of the Armenian genocide, presents a gallery of portraits, including biographical studies, accompanied by photographs, of women and men who at different times and in different places refused passively to accept the mass slaughter of Ottoman Armenians, and who either took action or at the very least bore witness, whether orally or in writing. They were mostly Muslims and Christians as well as some Jews, and all held true to the central tenets of their faiths, even as these were being violated by so many others. Above all, they followed the dictates of their conscience in refusing to collaborate with these crimes, refusing to remain silent, refusing to avert their gaze. Government officials, dignitaries and ordinary subjects of the Ottoman Empire alike put themselves in harm's way, risking punishment or losing their livelihoods, if not their lives. For those foreigners who bore witness to the massacres or the genocide of the Armenian people—diplomats and humanitarians—the risks were on the whole less grave, the most serious sanction being expulsion from the empire. Before, during and after the genocide, journalists, politicians, writers and historians reported the facts and denounced the criminals. Drawn together over a century later and presented in these pages, these lives represent a group of people whose names, for a wide range of reasons, deserve to be commemorated by a memorial. Meanwhile, however, the generous actions of ordinary people from all the different populations of the Ottoman Empire who saved the lives of Armenians out of motives of pure altruism, and asked for no reward, have been forgotten. Unknown and unremembered, these people saved Armenian lives out of the goodness of their hearts, offering to hide their neighbours, their neighbours' families or a lone child, or simply offering a crust of bread to a woman deportee. Standing tall above the mass of collaborators and silent witnesses, they not only ensured that they escaped divine retribution but also behaved in a way that was worthy of humanity. In so doing, they preserved values that had disappeared amid the brutality of genocide. While those who saved Jews during the Second World War are celebrated as the 'Righteous Among the Nations', those who saved Armenians during the genocide have received no such recognition, since successive Turkish governments, locked in denial, have done everything possible to ensure that their names are never invoked.

A brief reminder of the historical background will help to set these actions in the context of their time and place. During the First World War, the Ottoman government, led from January 1913 by the Young Turks of the Committee of Union and Progress (CUP), devised and executed a plan to exterminate the Armenians of the Ottoman Empire. Although drawn up in haste, the operation was carried out with chilling efficiency. First the Armenian soldiers in the Ottoman army were disarmed, and on 24 April 1915 prominent Armenians in Constantinople were arrested. Then the Special Organization, a paramilitary organization made up of criminals, was given orders to carry out the genocide. While the government issued temporary laws to paint the operation as a series of measures to 'transfer' populations and seize the possessions they left behind, on the ground the first phase of the genocide was now unfolding. Following a carefully planned timetable and starting with the Armenians in the eastern provinces, between May and August 1915, the 'secretaries in charge' of the Special Organization, aided by killing squads known as 'butcher battalions' (*çete*), demanded support from government officials, police and gendarmes for their programme, encompassing issuing deportation orders; slaughtering the men and deporting the women, children and old men in convoys; decimating the convoys; and massing the survivors in concentration camps around Aleppo. There they were joined in the autumn by families of Armenians deported from central and western Anatolia, often by train, who had survived massacres carried out in their towns and villages. Finally, in a second phase of the genocide, these deportees were evacuated—in conditions that ensured that most of them perished on the way—to Ras al-Ayn and Der Zor, where the last survivors were murdered. A third group was sent south to concentration camps in Syria, where some 200,000 of them survived. The Genocide Convention, adopted by the UN in December 1948, defines genocide as the crime of killing with the intention of destroying a national, ethnic, racial or religious group and is designated as a breach of international law. Through this act of genocide, the Ottoman government murdered all the Armenians in its eastern provinces and most of those in central and western Anatolia. Nonetheless, a third managed to survive. The Ottoman Empire's borders had been closed since its entry into the war, except for Armenians who sought refuge in Bulgaria, some of the Armenians of Van who followed the Russian army after its retreat in August 1915, and Armenians in Smyrna and Constantinople who were exempt from the deportation order. A section of the survivors in eastern Anatolia—100,000 out of 1 million—therefore owed their lives to the actions of humanitarians, diplomats and Muslim saviours, whether they were Ottoman government officials, Kurds from rebel tribes or simply ordinary people. These government officials knew that the government was enacting a relentless plan for total annihilation, and that the Armenians were condemned to die. The small number of them who refused to carry out these orders were not unaware that their resistance would only be effective if they could count on the support of prominent local figures. They knew and accepted the risks they were running by disobeying orders, but they viewed it as their moral duty to do so. By invoking a higher principle of conscience, that of their 'duty of disobedience', they renounced their obligations to the Ottoman government. For some, this duty was derived from the Islamic concept of justice—*adalet* in Ottoman Turkish—which, as Fatma Müge Göçek explains, 'constitutes the framework within which Muslims judge human conduct as "just" or "unjust"'.

It is not unreasonable to wonder, however, whether these officials were only obeying the precepts of Islam, or whether they were acting out of simple humanity, as did Jews, Christians and nonbelievers. Whatever their motives, they acted on them: these people were the 'people of conscience' of the Armenian genocide. While many Kurdish tribes had been indoctrinated by the Turkish nationalists and took an active part in the genocide, a few tribes who were traditionally rebellious, such as the Kurds of Dersim, took in their Armenian neighbours and protected them throughout the war. Deserving of special mention are the Yazidi Kurds of Sinjar, which became a mountain refuge and enclave of safety for the thousands of Armenians who managed to reach it. In a grim reversal of history, a century later Islamic State forces committed genocide against the Yazidis in the Sinjar region.

The actions of these rescuers are described and documented in this book, in which they are designated as 'The Righteous and People of Conscience of the Armenian Genocide'. It is this crime perpetrated during the First World War that forms the focus of the biographies outlined here. At once actors and witnesses, these were individuals who rose up in the places where mass murders and deportations were carried out, where acts of rescue frequently depended on Turks and foreigners working together.

At Trebizond, the Italian and German consuls confronted the organizers of the genocide: the *vali* (provincial governors) and the leader of the Special Organization. Having witnessed mass drownings in the Black Sea at first hand, they had only been able to save a few children and had been forced to let most of the Armenians they were sheltering leave with the columns of deportees. The *vilayet* of Kharpert (Harput) was a central hub of the deportation process. Rescuers there were mostly American—the consul Leslie Davis, the missionary and doctor couple Tacy and Herbert Atkinson, and the missionary Henry H. (Harry) Riggs—as well as the Danish missionaries Maria Jacobsen and Karen Marie Petersen. They worked together but came up against a wall of intransigence in the *vali*. Having been a presence in the Kharpert province for years, they maintained friendly relations with the Muslim population, who were not hostile to the Armenians. In this way, they managed to save some Armenians and sent a larger number to safety in Dersim, where Kurds and Alevis sheltered Armenians until the end of the war. Harry Riggs was in Kharpert from 1912 to 1917 and bore

PREFACE

witness to the aid given to the Armenians by a number of Turks, including the military governor, Izzet Pasha, and 'a large number of the Muslims in high society'. Defying their government, these Turks gave help to their Armenian neighbours and obtained permission from the *vali* for Armenian artisans to remain in Kharpert. Thanks to their efforts, one-fifth of the Armenian population of the *vilayet* survived. At Marsovan (now Merzifon), the American missionary Bertha Morley noted that a number of Muslim Turks were opposed to the deportation. At Urfa, one of the final stages in the deportation of the Armenians of eastern Anatolia, Jakob Künzler, a Swiss doctor and member of the German Mission who had kept up friendly relations with the Ottoman authorities for some years, managed to save nearly 3,000 Armenians, while his wife took in orphaned children. The Danish teacher Karen Jeppe saved thousands of survivors. In the *vilayet* of Diyarbekir, by contrast, where Hamid Bey was removed from the office of *vali* for being too sympathetic to the Armenians and replaced by the monstrous Mehmed Reshid, Ottoman government officials who refused to obey orders—among whom Hüseyin Nesimî, *kaymakam* or mayor of Lice, was an outstanding example—were murdered at the command of the *vali*. On the other hand, the *mutasarrif* (local governor) in Mardin, Hilmi Bey, was removed and appointed *vali* of Mosul, where he protected the Armenians of the province. In central Anatolia, a number of provincial and local governors, such as Hasan Mazhar Bey, governor of Ankara, and Mustafa Azizoğlu, mayor of Malatya, succeeded in delaying the deportations, and some—like Faik Ali Ozansoy, governor of Kütahya, with the support of the Turks of his *sanjak* (district)—managed to stop them. At Maraş in Cilicia, the Estonian missionary Anna Hedvig Büll saved 2,000 children from deportation.

In the autumn of 1915, the few survivors from the eastern provinces and deportees from the rest of Anatolia were concentrated in Aleppo. The *vali*, Mehmet Celal Bey, who in October 1915 was recalled from his post at Konya, tried to alert the German and American governments to the fate that lay in store for the deportees. The German consul Walter Rössler and his American counterpart Jesse B. Jackson worked actively with him and with German and American missionaries. It was in Aleppo that the greatest number of people were rescued. The rescuers operated on several different fronts, offering refuges, providing money and food, and opening weaving workshops and orphanages. Despite having the support of the Turkish colonel Kemal Bey, the Swiss missionary Beatrice Rohner's joint efforts with the consuls did not yield the results she was looking for. She therefore turned to Djemal Pasha, commander of the Ottoman Empire's Fourth Army, who agreed to accept Armenian orphans in the Turkish orphanage he had set up in Lebanon. In addition, she managed to find hiding places for 4,000 Armenians in Aleppo, and in total she saved nearly 1,000 orphans.

Yet all these rescuers were unable to stop the deportation of 700,000 Armenians to Ras al-Ayn and Der Zor, or southwards to Syria and Lebanon. At Ras al-Ayn and Der Zor, the local governors Yusuf Ziya and Ali Suad were recalled, along with government officials who had aided them in delaying the murder of the Armenian survivors. On his way back to Baghdad in November 1916, the German army medical orderly Armin T. Wegner managed to take photographs of deportees in camps stretching from Der Zor to Maskanah. The sole first-hand witness to the deaths from starvation of hundreds of thousands of Armenians, Wegner later actively resisted the Nazis and was named one of the Righteous Among the Nations at Yad Vashem.

Two men, one American and the other German, and both very well informed about the preparations for the slaughter and its perpetration, each had an interview with one of the architects of the Armenian genocide. The American ambassador Henry Morgenthau met Interior Minister Talaat Pasha, while the German pastor Johannes Lepsius met War Minister Enver Pasha. The two masterminds of the mass murder were quite open about the necessity for the Ottoman Empire to exterminate the Armenians. Having received telegrams from the American consuls, Morgenthau—along with Apostolic Vicar Monsignor Angelo Dolci—was better informed than anyone about the fate of the Armenians. Back in Germany, Lepsius gave numerous talks and wrote a *Secret Report*, published in 1916. This German indictment of the genocide was complemented by the so-called 'Blue Book' compiled by James Bryce and published in Britain in the same year. While the Ottoman government censored the news, Lepsius and Bryce managed to collect together diplomatic dispatches—German and American respectively—some of which had already appeared in the American and Canadian press. The preface to the Blue Book was written by Arnold Toynbee, the first historian to denounce the extermination of the Armenians of 1915. During this period, France was fighting for its life on the Western Front and had no presence left in the Ottoman Empire. Starved of information, the French press barely mentioned the Armenian question, with the sole exception of René Pinon, who published *La suppression des Arméniens: Méthode allemande; Travail turc* in 1916.

The Armenians made attempts at resistance, in acts of heroism that were doomed to failure, overwhelmed by the Turkish military. In one exception, however, some 5,000 Armenians, including women and children, retreated to the heights of Musa Dagh (Mount Moses), where they resisted repeated onslaughts by the Turkish army for over forty days. They were eventually rescued by the French warship *Guichen* and other vessels under the command of Vice Admiral Louis Dartige du Fournet. Nearly thirty years later, this heroic episode helped to inspire resistance fighters in the Warsaw Ghetto.

Twenty years before the genocide of 1915, the Hamidian massacres of 1894–6 had prompted a surge of indignation in France. The country was torn apart at the time by the Dreyfus affair, with support for Alfred Dreyfus spreading from the initial nucleus of Mathieu Dreyfus, Salomon Reinach and Bernard Lazare to include Jean Jaurès, Georges Clemenceau and Émile Zola among others. While the stain of antisemitism pervaded the French army and the reactionary right, France was united in its support for the Armenians massacred in the Ottoman Empire, from the far left (the journalist Séverine) to the antisemitic far right (Édouard Drumond). Members of parliament were also unanimous in their support, ranging from Jaurès to Denys Cochin and Albert de Mun. A pro-Armenian movement—whose supporters, many of whom also supported Dreyfus, were known as *philarmènes*—spread information and stoked the anger directed towards Sultan Abdul Hamid II. This book celebrates the actions of Pierre Quillard, founder of the journal *Pro Armenia*, Jaurès and Lazare. On the ground, it was the French consuls who launched appeals for aid, which were then relayed by the ambassador,

PREFACE

Paul Cambon. Their reports were collected in the *Livres jaunes* published annually by the Ministry of Foreign Affairs, and in books such as those by Victor Bérard and Père Charmetant. It was these diplomats who were the saviours of the Armenians, aided by humanitarians and many unknown Turks and Kurds, government officials and ordinary neighbours in their towns and villages. From the late nineteenth century, the distinguished names who rose to the defence of the Armenians were driven by outrage, like Lepsius in Germany, and Bryce—a friend of William Gladstone, who denounced the massacres in Bulgaria—in Britain.

After the fall of the Young Turk government and the Armistice of Mudros—concluded between Britain and the Ottoman Empire in October 1918—and while the Allies were negotiating the fate of the Ottoman Empire at the Paris Peace Conference in early 1919, and the Kemalist movement in Anatolia was carrying on the work of the CUP by deporting, expelling and murdering the thousands of Greeks who still lived there, the rescue of the Armenian survivors in Syria and Lebanon was getting under way. Funds were provided by Near East Relief, as James Barton's American Committee on Armenian Atrocities was now known. During the First World War, this committee had supplied humanitarian aid of over 100 million dollars, which American rescue workers had used to set up hospitals and orphanages. The rescuers of 1915–16 were still there and were now even more active. The Swiss Jakob Künzler worked with Near East Relief to evacuate 8,000 orphans from Anatolia to Syria and Lebanon, where he set up schools, workshops and sanatoriums. Another Swiss, Pastor Antony Krafft-Bonnard, who had set up an aid committee for the Armenians in 1896, organized foster homes for children up until 1930. Paul Berron, a missionary from Alsace, founded the Association Chrétienne en Orient and worked with the Estonian missionary Anna Hedvig Büll in Aleppo, bringing aid to the 160,000 Armenian refugees in Syria. She set up workshops and a rehabilitation centre, placed children in foster families and built living accommodation in the refugee camps. The Danish missionary Maria Jacobsen managed to extract 110,000 Armenian orphans from the hands of the Kemalists and evacuate them to Syria, Russia, Greece and Lebanon, where she teamed up again with her compatriot Karen

PREFACE

Marie Petersen. The Norwegian missionary and nurse Bodil Katharine Biørn, who spent ten years working in Muş, where she witnessed the extermination of Armenians of the *vilayet* of Bitlis, helped to rescue Anatolian orphans in 1919. If there were a medal of honour, there could be no more deserving recipient than the Danish teacher Karen Jeppe. Appointed commissioner of the League of Nations in 1921, she tracked down between 20,000 and 30,000 women and children who had been abducted during the genocide, notably among the Arabs in Syria, and brought them back home, where they were subsequently settled in agricultural colonies and craft workrooms. To these heroic Scandinavian women should be added the name of the Norwegian Fridtjof Nansen, appointed high commissioner for refugees in 1921 and awarded the Nobel Peace Prize in 1922. In 1924, he was the architect of the first legal instrument of protection for refugees and created the 'Nansen Passport' for stateless refugees, which benefitted the 300,000 surviving Armenians who had been hounded out of Turkey 'with no hope of returning'.

These women and men, humanitarians from neutral countries who arrived during and after the First World War, were—alongside many Ottoman subjects—the true saviours of the Armenians. Forming a separate category are the humanists: the Russian André Mandelstam and the Pole Raphael Lemkin, both jurists; Abbé Chaperon, an army chaplain who witnessed Kemalist attacks in Anatolia; the Dreyfusard and *arménophile* Anatole France, who launched an appeal for Armenia in 1922; and the French archaeologist Jacques de Morgan, a supporter of the Armenians from the 1880s. All of them were unanimous in denouncing the abandonment of the Armenian people by the League of Nations, which could not even bring itself to support a plan for the creation of an Armenian national centre. After the war, in November 1918—during the brief interval between the fall of the Young Turks and the setting up of the Republic of Turkey—Mazhar Bey, former governor of Aleppo, established a committee of inquiry in preparation for the military tribunal in Constantinople. At the beginning of June 1921, the judges of a military tribunal at Berlin-Charlottenburg in Germany, before which Wegner and Lepsius had appeared as witnesses, found Soghomon Tehlirian, who had assassinated Talaat Pasha, not guilty of murder.

PREFACE

The authors of this book and those who have contributed to it have set out to preserve the memory and commemorate the names of those who, during and after the genocide—and in some cases for decades beforehand—helped the Armenian people. Thanks to their work, these individuals—'The Righteous and People of Conscience', as the authors have described them—will no longer be forgotten. I would describe them all, without hesitation, as *Menschen*. In German, the gender-neutral word *Mensch* means simply a human being; in Yiddish, it means something more: a person of honesty and—however extreme the circumstances—of unflinching moral and ethical integrity.

AUTHORS' ACKNOWLEDGEMENTS

The authors would like to express their gratitude to the individuals and institutions who have supported and encouraged them in the creation of this work.

In France, Jean-Marie Carbasse, Professor Emeritus at the University of Montpellier, Rector of Nice Academy, Honorary President of the Société internationale d'Histoire du droit and the Académie des Sciences et Lettres de Montpellier.

Gilles Gudin de Vallerin, Chief Curator of Libraries, of the Académie des Sciences et Lettres de Montpellier.

Roland Andréani, Professor Emeritus, Université Paul-Valéry Montpellier 3.

Carol Iancu, Professor Emeritus, Université Paul-Valéry Montpellier 3, Member of the Académie de Nîmes, Member of the Romanian Academy.

Marc Dumont, Director, Bibliothèque universitaire des Lettres, Université Paul-Valéry Montpellier 3.

Dr Gilles Romieu (Institut du cancer, Montpellier), great-nephew of Colonel Louis Romieu, founder of the Légion arménienne.

Brother Jorel François, O.P., Director of the Centre Lacordaire (Montpellier).

Maître Dominique Bruzy, Honorary President at the Appeal Court, Nîmes, descendant of Alphonse Cillière.

Claire Mouradian, Emeritus Research Director at the Centre national de la Recherche scientifique (CNRS), teacher at the École des Hautes Études en Sciences sociales.

Anaïd Donabédian, Professor at the Institut national des Langues et Civilisations orientales, Member of the Laboratoire 'Structure et Dynamique des Langues', Corresponding Member of the National Academy of Sciences of the Republic of Armenia.

Boris Adjémian, Curator of the Bibliothèque arménienne Nubar (Paris), Meguerditch Basmadjian, Librarian, and Isabelle Ouzounian.

AUTHORS' ACKNOWLEDGEMENTS

Jean-Claude Kuperminc, Director of the Bibliothèque de l'Alliance israélite universelle (Paris).

Hamit Bozarslan, Director of Studies at the École des Hautes Études en Sciences Sociales, Member of the Société asiatique.

Gérard Gauthier, Curator of the Bibliothèque de l'Institut kurde de Paris.

Raymond Kévorkian, Corresponding Member of the National Academy of Sciences of the Republic of Armenia, President of the Armenian Genocide Museum-Institute Foundation (Yerevan).

Claude Mutafian, Research Supervisor, Université Paul-Valéry Montpellier 3, Corresponding Member of the National Academy of Sciences of the Republic of Armenia.

Éric Van Lauwe, Engineer-Cartographer.

Dzovinar Kévonian, Lecturer and Research Supervisor, Institut des Sciences sociales du politique.

Dr Éliane Dabbagh, Michel Chirinian, Gérard Deyrmendjian, Ohan Hékimian, Georges Hérakian, for their assistance with research.

The staff and services of the Médiathèque centrale Émile Zola (Montpellier)

Aurore Bruna, Doctor of History, President of CCAF Sud (Conseil de coordination des organisations arméniennes de France), Marseille City Councillor.

The management and staff of the Centre du Patrimoine arménien, Valence.

Ara Aharonian, Council Member of the Éparchie de Sainte—Croix de Paris des Arméniens catholiques de France.

Pastor Thomas Wild, Director of Action chrétienne en Orient (ACO).

Archag and Vazken Surménian, whose family took in Soghomon Tehlirian and his wife in Morocco.

In Italy, the Very Reverend Father Vahan Ohanian, Vicar-General of the Mkhitarin Congregation at St Lazaro, Venice, and Ara Kétibian, man of letters. Reverend Father Georges-Henri Ruyssen, S.J., Professor at the Pontifical Oriental Institute (Rome).

In Lebanon, Levon Nordiguian, Directeur of the Photographic Library in the Bibliothèque Orientale and founder of the Museum of Prehistory at Saint Joseph University, Beirut.

AUTHORS' ACKNOWLEDGEMENTS

In Armenia, Rouben Safrastyan, Academician, Director of the Institute of Oriental Studies of the National Academy of Sciences of the Republic of Armenia.

Vardan Mkhitaryan, Doctor of History from the Universities of Paul-Valéry Montpellier 3 and Yerevan, Director of the Babken Harutyunyan Laboratory of the History of Armenian Geography and Cartography (Yerevan).

We are especially grateful to the management and staff of the Armenian Genocide Museum-Institute (National Academy of Sciences of the Republic of Armenia), and in particular to Hayk Demoyan, Honorary Director of the Museum-Institute, and his successor, Monsieur Harutyun Marutyan, for allowing us to use most of the images in this book.

We are especially indebted to Professor Jean-Michel Oughourlian, neuropsychiatrist, essayist, Ambassador of the Armenian Order of Malta, for the attention he has given to the present work, as well as to Maria Shammas MBE, President of the British Red Cross, and the Lebanese journalist and writer Selim Nassar.

We offer our thanks to Dr Yves Ternon, Research Supervisor in History at the Université Paul-Valéry Montpellier 3, internationally recognized specialist in twentieth-century genocide, President of the Conseil scientifique pour le Centenaire du génocide des Arméniens (2015).

We are deeply grateful to Myra Prince, Director of Éditions Geuthner, and her colleagues, who, faithful to the traditions of Éditions Geuthner, devoted such care to the production of the original French edition of this book.

A special word of gratitude is due to Barbara Mellor for this translation, and for her dedication and invaluable assistance in completing the English edition of the book and for introducing us to Michael Dwyer, the editor and publisher of the English edition. Thank you to Michael Dwyer and all his team at Hurst Publishers for their hard work, dedication and professionalism, which has made the English edition of this book possible. It has been a privilege to work with you. Thank you to Zoe Jenner, Agathe Vallariello, Patricia Lossignol and Amy Francart for their continuing office support and assistance.

INTRODUCTION

Taking a stand against a criminal campaign orchestrated by a dictatorship may seem like an act of madness that few people would undertake. And yet, when the plan to exterminate the Armenian nation was put into action, there were many—men and women, Westerners and Ottomans, including even some Turks, Kurds and Arabs—who came to the aid of the unfortunate victims, often with limited means and at their own expense.

Paying tribute to the memory of these courageous individuals, whom we call the Righteous and people of conscience—in the sense that they acted in accordance with the principles of justice—does not in any way diminish the barbarity of the crime or the immensity of the injustice. On the contrary, it was precisely this barbarity and this injustice that made it impossible for some individuals to remain silent, to avert their gaze and to carry on with their lives as if nothing had happened.

Only a crime against humanity on this scale could make a senior Turkish government official refuse to obey orders to commit mass murder; could prompt a Kurdish *agha* or Arab chieftain to refuse to submit to the commands of the local governor; or could resolve a *vali* to refuse to carry out a deportation order in the knowledge that it was in fact a death sentence for the deportees.

Christian missionaries and some consuls did all they could to relieve the sufferings of the Armenians, at a time when the carnage of the First World War, in which the Ottoman Empire was fighting alongside Germany and Austria–Hungary, had largely blurred all sense of the distinction between justice and injustice, normality and barbarity. Orders issued by the Ottoman military authorities were to be carried out without question, moreover, with the slightest reluctance to obey being rewarded with the harshest of punishments.

THE RIGHTEOUS AND PEOPLE OF CONSCIENCE

In the years immediately after the genocide, there was little mention of any individuals who might be termed the Righteous or people of conscience, on the side of either the perpetrators or the victims. The reasons for this were clear: those who had organized and carried out the genocide of the Armenian people went out of their way to avoid drawing attention to any humanitarian efforts, since these would only have confirmed the existence of the crime they denied. The victims, meanwhile, could not exonerate the perpetrators of the massacre of an entire population simply because some individual Armenians had been saved by the interventions of a handful of people. Besides, faced with the denial of the genocide by those who were responsible for it, they needed to save all their energies for gathering the evidence.

Before going any further, however, we need to examine why relations between the Armenians and the Ottoman Empire and its leaders had deteriorated to the point where an entire population was massacred.

In 1894–6, under Sultan Abdul Hamid II (ruled 1876–1909), there had already been massacres of Armenians in the wake of Armenian protests against the abduction of their daughters, encroachment on their lands, the plundering of their property by the Kurds and Circassians, the extortionate demands of the fiscal authorities, and the generally unjust treatment to which they were subjected. Some historians view the process of the genocide as a continuum, with its first warning signs pre-dating the Hamidian massacres.

Monstrous as they were, these massacres—perpetrated by a government that included the Young Turks—were outdone in their horror by the genocide of 1915–16, to which the Adana massacres of 1909 formed the prelude. While the Young Turks shared responsibility for the crimes of 1909 with the previous regime, responsibility for the genocide of 1915—when they had been in full power since 1913—lay with them alone.

It is true that during the reign of Abdul Hamid prominent figures came forward to denounce the massacres, including the French socialist deputy Jean Jaurès, who in the Chamber of Deputies, and especially in a speech he gave on 3 November 1896, castigated Europe's failure to protect the Armenians, among other minorities in the Ottoman Empire.

INTRODUCTION

Similarly, British prime minister William Gladstone denounced the Ottoman policy of ill treatment of non-Muslims, and in particular the massacres of Armenians, both in his three ministries (1868–74, 1880–5 and 1892–4) and in opposition, including in his last public speech, delivered in Liverpool in 1896.

Nor should we forget the great French man of letters and Nobel laureate for literature Anatole France, who denounced the first Hamidian massacres as well as all those that followed, including the genocide of 1915–16. He was also one of the editors of the bi-monthly journal *Pro Armenia*, founded in 1900, alongside other prominent figures such as Pierre Quillard, Jean Jaurès and Georges Clemenceau. Later minister of the interior and prime minister, and nicknamed *le Tigre* ('the Tiger') and *Père de la Victoire* ('Father of Victory') during the First World War, Clemenceau was an active supporter of Émile Zola during the Dreyfus affair (but his attitude towards the French mandate in Cilicia in 1918–20 was highly debatable).

Diplomats included Alphonse Cillière, French consul in Trebizond at the time of the Hamidian massacres. Fernand Roque-Ferrier, Cillière's childhood friend from Montpellier, was also then active as French consul in Erzurum, and who died in 1909—when he was French consul in Aleppo—as a result of his fearless intervention in support of the Armenians in Adana.

While we have drawn portraits here of a number of the Righteous and people of conscience from the nineteenth century, the focus of this book is nonetheless on those of the twentieth century, principally during the First World War. For these men and women were courageous enough to stand up against the murderous policies of the Ottoman Empire at a time when it was already at war, and military tribunals were condemning Ottoman subjects found guilty of the most minor of crimes to death.

The massacres under the Young Turk government

The Cilicia massacres (1909)

The genocide of 1915–16 was foreshadowed by massacres in the *vilayet* of Adana, which killed some 30,000 Armenians and left 7,883 widows and 4,072 orphans.

THE RIGHTEOUS AND PEOPLE OF CONSCIENCE

Yet the Armenians, filled with hope, had supported the restoration of the Ottoman constitution in 1876 and had been reassured at that time by the confirmation of the Armenian constitution of 1863, which allowed laymen and clergy to share in the responsibilities of the Armenian patriarch of Constantinople. When equal rights and obligations for all Ottoman subjects were guaranteed following the Young Turk revolution of 1908, the Armenians were filled with real optimism for the future. The massacres in Cilicia in 1909 were to dash their hopes for justice and equality with brutal cruelty.

These promises proved short-lived, in fact, in the face of hostility from the most extremist factions, both among Sultan Abdul Hamid's supporters and among Young Turk revolutionaries. The main target of their resentment was the Armenians, who wanted civil rights and the means to ensure they were respected. The Armenians of Cilicia were economically better off than their Turkish, Kurdish or Arab neighbours, moreover, and thanks to their co-religionists from abroad formed the dominant force in both business and agriculture. The authorities embarked on a massive propaganda campaign accusing the Armenians of wanting to re-establish the kingdom of Cilicia, and in this way the envy felt by local people towards the Armenians combined with religious fanaticism to pave the way for the massacres.

Righteous individuals had already emerged during the Hamidian massacres of 1894-6, just as they appeared in the Adana massacres of 1909. In that year, Sis (present-day Kozan), seat of the Armenian Catholicos of the see of Cilicia, counted 2,000 households, three-quarters of them Armenian. On 14 April, tensions rose, and the following day a mob of Muslim villagers slaughtered the inhabitants of some twenty farms in the environs of Sis, before laying siege to the city for five days. The Armenian population mounted a resistance, supported by the commander of the gendarmerie, the Albanian Haci Mohamed, and with the participation of the military commander, Mehmed Effendi.

Simultaneously, Hadjin (Haçin)—a semi-autonomous Cilician principality until the seventeenth century—was besieged by mobs of Muslim villagers intent on looting and slaughter. As the inhabitants mounted a resistance, troops arrived to assist the city but instead of defending it joined forces with its assailants. Finally, when the city was on its knees, Lütfi Bey came to the rescue. Taking command of a regiment, he promised his soldiers that as soon as he gave the order they could pillage the city at will. As a result of this ploy, he managed to persuade the regiment to liberate Hadjin—and of course he never gave the order to loot it.

In 1909, there were around 1,000 Armenians living in Kars-Bazar, in the north of Osmaniye. This city too was attacked, and the Armenian inhabitants mounted a defence with the aid of Armenians from the surrounding villages. The siege lasted three weeks, during which time the Armenians received assistance from a Turkish gendarme, Ahmed Beşir, and a cavalry officer, Ahmed. Other Turks also came to the aid of the Armenians, including Musa Effendi, Veli Effendi, Husni Effendi (who kept the armed mob at bay with a force of just sixty soldiers), Poyrazoğlu Keussé, Harabanoğlu Mehmed Bey, Gharman Sumbas (who gave food and shelter to 300 Armenians for twenty-six days) and Arif Ağa (son of the mufti of Kars) who saved 600 Armenians.

Many Turks who saved Armenians in this period were dismissed from their posts. Mehmed Effendi, for example, the former military commander who had taken part in the defence of Sis, was rewarded by the government for coming to the aid of the Armenians by being reduced to a state of utter destitution.

The Righteous of this period also included some individuals from the West, and in particular missionaries, who came to the aid of the Armenians at the risk of their own lives. The American missionary Rose Lambert looked after the Armenians of Hadjin. In Adana, American missionaries lost their lives while trying to help the Armenians. During the first massacres in Adana, the Turks put Armenian neighbourhoods to the torch, and the fire threatened to spread to buildings where the Americans were sheltering Armenian women, children and orphans. On Thursday, 15 April, armed only with pails of water, crowbars and an axe, Henry Maurer, Daniel Miner Rogers and Stephen Trowbridge went out to try to control the spread of the fire, under heavy gunfire from both the Muslim attackers and the Armenian defenders. Amid the intense conflagration, they were working frantically to tear down walls when Rogers, who was bringing water from across the street, was suddenly hit by a Muslim bullet. Almost immediately after this, Maurer was struck by a bullet that lodged close to his heart. Heedless of the danger, Trowbridge rushed to where his two fellow missionaries lay in the street, crying out in pain. As he ran back to the mission school to alert the other missionaries, the British vice-consul of Mersin, Colonel Charles Doughty-Wylie, arrived. The wounded men were carried to the school but died minutes later. Trowbridge concluded his account: 'Both men passed peacefully away. They died as good soldiers of Jesus Christ.'

The Armenian genocide

Few were punished for the Hamidian and Adana massacres (in which it is difficult to disentangle the responsibility of the Young Turk government, who shared power from 1908, from that of Abdul Hamid II, who had taken up the reins of the empire again on a very temporary basis). This gave encouragement to the leaders of the Ottoman Empire to push their levels of barbarity yet further, and to solve the Armenian question once and for all by means of the total and systematic extermination of the entire population.

The entry into the First World War of the Ottoman Empire and the Russian Empire, which included eastern Armenia, as well as the presence within the Russian army of a corps of some 5,000 Armenian volunteers, presented the Ottomans with the pretext they wanted for setting their extermination plans into action. Even if the Armenian volunteer corps in the Russian army was weak, its mere existence was enough to aggravate the rift in Turkish–Armenian relations. The Turks had already reproached the leaders of the Armenian Revolutionary Federation (ARF, also known as Dashnaktsutyun, the members of which are referred to as Dashnaks) for refusing to urge Russian Armenians to rise up against their country, and an ARF congress held in Erzurum from late July to 2 August 1914 had indeed concluded that Armenians in both the Ottoman and Russian Empires should offer their loyal service to their home nation.

This series of events resulted in the Ottoman Empire abandoning all restraint in its treatment of the Armenians, viewing them as an enemy within and an extension of the Triple Entente of France, Britain and Russia. When the Allies failed to force a naval route through the Dardanelles in February and March 1915, followed by the heavy setback of their failed landings at Gallipoli from April of that year, the Turks were emboldened to act with merciless savagery.

The failure of the Ottoman offensive in the Caucasus, on the other hand, combined with the resounding defeat of the army led by Enver Pasha at Sarıkamış (Sarikamish)—in the region of the city of Kars, which had belonged to Russia since 1877—in the depths of the winter of 1914–15, meant that the Ottoman leadership was on the hunt for a scapegoat. Without any justification, therefore, they accused the Armenians of collaborating with the Russians and being responsible for the defeat (the Turks had lost nearly 30,000 men in combat, and double that number had succumbed to the Armenian winter, while the Russians also endured heavy losses).

The Armenian genocide of 1915: a summary of key events

When war broke out, the Young Turk government's first response was to expel the two foreign general inspectors who had been appointed to oversee the application of the administrative reforms intended to protect minorities that had been promised by the Ottoman state. This move, which alarmed the Armenians, was followed by others that led them to fear the worst. At the start of the war, all men fit for call-up were conscripted into the armed forces. But after the Battle of Sarıkamış (December 1914–January 1915), Enver Pasha blamed the Armenians for the Ottoman defeat and accused them of collaboration with the Russians. Although Enver had previously praised the bravery of the Armenian troops in the Ottoman army, they were now disarmed, transferred to labour battalions, and ultimately taken into the countryside in groups and put to death. Armenian civilians were then ordered to surrender their weapons, and their homes were searched. Most of the time, there were no weapons to be found, but as the point of the exercise was to incriminate the Armenians, Turkish gendarmes planted them in their houses. Arrests and summary executions followed.

By the winter of 1913, the Special Organization, Teşkilât-i Mahsusa, a paramilitary organization made up of convicted criminals who had been specially released in order to carry out the deportation of the Armenians in convoys, had been set up under the jurisdiction of the minister of war.

In April 1915, the plan for the extermination of the Armenian people was put into practice. On 8 April, the first of the deportations was ordered, at Zeytun in Cilicia. Also in April, as Anahide Ter Minassian notes, the Armenians of Van refused to hand over the full contingent of men whom the *vali*, Cevdet Bey, had ordered them to supply. The governor had demanded 4,000 men from the town; the people offered to give him 500 and to pay the exemption tax for the remainder, as was permitted under Ottoman law. The people of Van were well aware that as soon as the men were handed over to Cevdet they would be killed, since rumours of massacres in the surrounding villages left no room for doubt. But the *vali* turned down their offer, ordering all the men to give themselves up; meanwhile, he surrounded the town with a force of 2,000 regular soldiers and several thousand Kurdish irregulars.

Also at this time, Cevdet had sent a Dashnak leader to negotiate with the inhabitants of a village in the *vilayet* of Van, who had rebelled against the violence they had been subjected to when their houses were searched for weapons, and who were demanding the release of a teacher and five youths. The leader had reached Hirdj (Köklü) on his way to the village, on 16 April 1915, when he was murdered. The forty-six Armenians among the population of Hirdj were subsequently executed. That same day, another Armenian leader, sent by Cevdet to Constantinople, was killed en route. It was at this point that the massacre of the Armenians living around Van was unleashed, and fifty-one Armenian villages were destroyed.

On 20 April 1915, the Armenians of Van began to mount a resistance, but they were few in number and poorly armed. There was intense fighting lasting many days, and compensating for the lack of military means at their disposal called for great ingenuity. Despite their tremendous courage, the Armenians suffered a defeat, which brought about an influx of 500 refugees from Mount Varak (celebrated for its monastery of the Holy Cross). Although the situation appeared hopeless, Van was finally saved by the advance of the Russian army. The Turkish army evacuated the town, taking with it some of the Muslim population. Those who were left behind suffered a terrible vengeance, as the Russians and Armenians looted

INTRODUCTION

Muslim districts and put them to the torch. Fearing encirclement, the Russian army pulled out of the town on 3 August, leaving over 100,000 terrified Armenians to set off into exile, in fear of the revenge of the Turkish troops. The Russians then recaptured the town in the autumn of 1915 and occupied it until the spring of 1918, when the Turks took it back for good.

Taking the defence of Van, dressed up as a rebellion, as a pretext, and alarmed by the presence of Russian troops on its Caucasian frontier and Triple Entente forces at the gates of Constantinople, the Young Turk government decided to put its plan to destroy the Armenian population into action. The anarchic massacres that had already begun in the eastern provinces were now replaced by a plan for total destruction. The speed and efficiency of this plan indicate that it had been worked out well in advance. The first phase of deportations and massacres took place in the six 'Armenian' *vilayets* of Van, Bitlis, Erzurum, Diyarbekir, Kharpert and Sivas, as well as the more recently created Trebizond. The Armenians who were to be deported were put into convoys of between 1,000 and 3,000 people. The man who masterminded these deportations, it appears, was Talaat Pasha, minister of the interior from 1913 and then grand vizier. He was responsible for setting the upper limits beyond which the Armenian population was not to rise: 2 per cent in Aleppo, 5 per cent in the regions of Anatolia and 10 per cent in the desert regions.

On 24 April 1915, the CUP—the governing body of the Young Turks—launched a huge wave of arrests aimed at the heart of the intellectual elite in Constantinople. A massive round-up began in the capital with the arrest of the journalists and editorial staff of the *Azadamart* newspaper, organ of the Dashnak party. During the night of 24–5 April 1915, 270 intellectuals, doctors, lawyers and men of the cloth—the Armenian elite of Constantinople—were arrested. In the days that followed, some 600 individuals were thrown in prison. The resistance at Van, cynically presented as a rebellion, was used as justification for these arrests, the victims of which were transferred far away from Constantinople and, in most cases, murdered.

In their attempts to justify these arrests, the CUP alleged the existence of a huge Armenian plot and set up a kangaroo court that culminated in members of the revolutionary Armenian Hunchak party who had been in prison for over a year being executed by hanging.

The date of 24 April has been officially chosen by descendants of the victims as the annual day of commemoration of the Armenian genocide.

From the spring to the autumn of 1915, the pace of massacres and deportations in the Ottoman Empire intensified. Most of the Armenians in Cilicia were deported in July and August. Those who survived were massacred after the war, in 1918–21, when the French government abandoned its mandate over the region. The eastern *vilayets* were emptied of their populations in June and July, the south-eastern ones in August and September. The fate of the Armenians was widely reported in the Western press, often with information supplied by diplomats in post in the empire or Christian missionaries. In May, Russia, France and Great Britain denounced the massacres of Armenians as 'crimes against humanity and civilization', or 'crimes of *lèse-humanité*'—the first time in history that the expression 'crimes against humanity' had been used.

From the summer of 1915, the genocide entered a second phase. It was now the turn of the Armenian populations in the west of the empire, remote from the battle zones, to be deported. These deportations took place by rail, with deportees being transported to concentration camps that had been set up in Syria, Lebanon and Palestine. Most were deported to the east, to rudimentary camps at Ras al-Ayn and Rakka in the Syrian desert, before being sent on to Der Zor. Between February and December 1916, the 700,000 or so deportees who had survived the death marches and were now in camps were exterminated on the orders of Talaat Pasha.

Following its defeat in 1918, the Ottoman Empire redefined itself around its Turkish dominions, and in 1923 General Mustafa Kemal, who had denounced the sultan's capitulation and, fortified by his victories in Anatolia, proclaimed the Republic, issued a general amnesty for all those responsible for the Armenian massacres, although he had previously denounced them. As a result, the archives for this period were closed to researchers and historians, and no individuals were investigated.

Talaat Pasha did not escape Armenian vengeance, however: on 15 March 1921, he was shot and killed in Berlin at point-blank range

INTRODUCTION

by Soghomon Tehlirian, an Armenian whose family had died in the massacres. Tehlirian was subsequently acquitted by a German court.

Estimates of the number of people killed during the Armenian genocide vary between 1.2 and 1.5 million, out of an Ottoman Armenian population before the genocide of 1.8 to 2.1 million.

The Righteous

Amid this climate of suffering and death, there were some non-Armenians who were moved to offer aid to Armenians in peril, so risking their own lives or careers, without seeking any reward for themselves, financial or otherwise.

Among the Righteous were Turks, Kurds, Yazidis, Zazas, Arabs, Europeans and Americans. We have chosen to study in detail those who appear to us to be most noteworthy. While making no claim to be an exhaustive analysis, which would in any case be an impossible goal, this book sets out to describe the most representative figures of those whose behaviour can with justice be described as righteous. By selecting individuals from each of the nations involved, it explores the broad range of motives that may lead a man or a woman to seriously compromise their careers, or even to put their lives at risk, by intervening in order to save the life of another.

We may wonder what was the deciding factor that resolved these individuals whom we describe as the Righteous to embark on activities that might well have proved fatal—and sometimes did—or that could have led to their losing everything. There was no single motive, but rather a whole range. Humanitarian or religious motives very often played a crucial role, as testified by the actions of American missionaries (it was only in 1917, and then only against Germany and Austro-Hungary, that the United States entered the war) in Kharpert and Van, and by the refusal of some officials to obey orders to deport the Armenians. In other circumstances, the humanitarian motive was further strengthened by a sense of family honour: this was very much the case with Faik Ali Bey, governor of the town of Kütahya, which was home to a large population of Armenian potters. In early 1915, he received a letter from his brother warning him of the atrocities being planned for the Armenians and begging him to take no part in them for the sake of the family's honour. Faik Ali Bey managed to obtain protection from the local Muslims for the Armenians and refused to carry out the order to deport them.

Family ties naturally influenced the actions of some of the Righteous: this was the case with Nureddin Bey, military inspector at Der Zor, who protected the Armenians from deportation and death. That Nureddin Bey was married to an Armenian and had a child with her must undoubtedly have been a determining factor in his decision to disobey the orders of the Ottoman authorities.

In other cases, good neighbourly relations between Turks and Armenians proved the salvation of the latter group. In yet others, as with Haci Halil, it was a resolve to remain faithful to their word. A Turkish businessman and a devout Muslim, Haci Halil had promised his Armenian business partner that he would look after his family if anything happened to him. He kept his promise, giving refuge to seven members of the family in his own house throughout the period of danger, at the risk of his own life.

Zazas, Yazidis from the Sinjar massif, in the *kaza* (canton) of Mosul, and Kurds from Mardin and the *kaza* of Moks also protected the Armenians, in all likelihood motivated by feelings of altruism and of solidarity with the sufferings of a fellow minority population.

Some Muslim women, finally, were doubtless driven by their maternal instincts to save Armenian children.

The first part of this volume is devoted to the Righteous who were active in 1894–6, in order to provide an insight into this period, which provides a form of continuum between the Cilician massacres and the Armenian genocide. The second part is devoted to the Ottomans, whether officials, chiefs of tribal clans or ordinary people, who made a stand against barbarism at the risk of their lives. The third part describes the Righteous from Western countries—missionaries, diplomats and military officers—who saved Armenians. The last section deals with the Righteous who were 'distant in time or place'. While these individuals did not necessarily put their lives in danger, it is important nevertheless to mention those who, while far from the sites where the massacres took place, fought to make the facts known, raise funds, combat indifference or press for recognition of the genocide by Turkey, heir to the Ottoman Empire.

This tribute to the Righteous and the people of conscience seemed to us to be a necessary. It was of course essential to pay

INTRODUCTION

homage to the memory of these women and men. Most of all, however, in a troubled world in which the worst of history all too often repeats itself, and in which a plethora of news and images paradoxically engenders apathy, there seemed to be an urgent need for models of heroism. Our use of the term 'The Righteous' echoes the biblical 'Righteous Among the Nations', now rigorously defined by Yad Vashem as non-Jews who risked their lives to save Jews during the Holocaust. More broadly, we also wanted to include the 'people of conscience' who made sacrifices in a variety of different ways in order to help the Armenians. We leave it up to the reader to decide which of these two titles—'The Righteous' or 'people of conscience'—best describes the heroes and heroines whose commitment and actions we describe in these pages.

Sources and further reading

Sources

Beylerian, Arthur, *Les Grandes Puissances, l'Empire ottoman et les Arméniens dans les Archives françaises* (preface by J.-B. Duroselle), Paris: Université de Paris I, 1983.

Ohanian, Vahan and Ara Ketibian (eds), *The Armenian Genocide: Prelude and Aftermath, as Reported in the U.S. Press (1890–1922)*, 5 vols, n.p.: Mekhitarist Publication, 2018–19.

Poghosyan, Varoujean, *Les massacres hamidiens à travers le prisme des conférences des contemporains français*, Yerevan: Yerevan State University Publishing House, 2013.

Ruyssen, Georges-Henri, S.J., *La questione Armena: 1894–1896, 1908–1925; Documenti degli archivi vaticani*, 7 vols, Rome: Edizioni Orientalia Christiana—Valore Italiano Lilamé, 2013–15.

Svazlian, Verjiné, *Le génocide arménien et la mémoire historique du peuple*, Yerevan: Armenian Academy of Sciences, Éditions Guitoutiun, 2005.

For biographies of missionaries, see *The Vinton Books*, vol. 3, *The Near East (Armenia, Persia, Syria, and Turkey)*, and vol. 4, *Addenda, 1885–1910*, Boston, MA: Congregational Library and Archives, History Matters, 1885–1910.

Studies

Bozarslan, Hamit, Vincent Duclert and Raymond H. Kévorkian,

Comprendre le génocide des Arméniens, 1915 à nos jours, Paris: Tallandier, 2015, pp. 45–68.

Charny, Israel W., *Encyclopedia of Genocide* (prefaces by Simon Wiesenthal and Desmond Tutu), 2 vols, Santa Barbara: ABC-Clio, 2000.

Hassiotis, J. K., *Peuples frères dans la tempête: Arméniens et Grecs pendant la grande crise de la Question d'Orient (1856–1914)/Brothers in the Storm: Armenians and Greeks during the Great Crisis of the Eastern Question* [in Greek, with a synopsis in Armenian], Thessaloniki: University Studio Press, 2015.

Hovannissian, Richard G. 'La Question arménienne, 1878–1923', in Gérard Chaliand (ed.) with Claire Mouradian and Alice Aslanian-Samuelian, *Tribunal permanent des peuples: Le crime de silence; Le génocide des Arméniens* (preface by Pierre Vidal-Naquet), Paris: Flammarion, 1984, pp. 27–65.

PRELUDE

THE HISTORICAL BACKGROUND

THE HAMIDIAN AND CILICIAN MASSACRES
SOME REMARKABLE INDIVIDUALS

1

THE HAMIDIAN MASSACRES

In 1890 and 1895, under the rule of Sultan Abdul Hamid II (1876–1909) and in the wake of the internationalization of the Armenian question under the Treaty of San Stefano in 1878 (the terms of which were to be altered to the detriment of the Armenians at the Congress of Berlin later that year), the Armenian population of Constantinople organized street demonstrations that were brutally put down.

In 1894, the people of Sassoun (Sason) rose up in protest against abuses in levying taxes by Kurdish *aghas* (tribal chieftains), which the Sublime Porte did nothing to control; in 1895–6, it was the turn of the princes of Zeytun in Cilicia to rebel again, after the revolt led by Aghassi (nom de plume of Garabed Toursarkissian) in 1862.

The sultan unleashed a wave of systematic repression that claimed close to 300,000 victims. The Great Powers, who were supposed to be overseeing the application of reforms in the Armenian *vilayets*, contented themselves with verbal protests, even if they were momentarily stirred by the occupation of the Ottoman Bank by a Dashnak party commando in 1896. It was at this point that Abdul Hamid earned the soubriquet *Grand Saigneur* or 'Bloody Sultan' that would rapidly spread among supporters of the Armenians, who—led by Arshag Chobanian, Jean Jaurès and Anatole France among others—were particularly numerous in France.

The National Constitution of 1876 (to which the writer Krikor Odian had contributed, alongside Grand Vizier Midhat Pasha) was suspended until 1908, when it was restored in the wake of the Young Turk revolution. The egalitarian and humanist trappings of the Young Turks, or at least of their dominant nationalist wing, were to prove a tragic deception to the Armenians. Some Armenians leaders were to gloss over the Adana massacres of 1909 and their 10,000 or so victims, unable to spot the signs of the genocide that was looming, planned—in the wake of the Ottoman Empire's entry into the First World War on the side of Germany and Austria–Hungary—by the leaders of the Young Turks.

2

PIERRE QUILLARD (1864–1912)

Poet and playwright who loved classical culture and sacrificed his work and career for the cause of the Armenians

Pierre Quillard, who was born in Paris and died in Neuilly-sur-Seine, is remembered as a distinguished literary figure. He gained a reputation as a Symbolist poet with *La gloire du verbe* (1890); as a playwright with *La fille aux mains coupées*, a 'mystery' dedicated to his friend and fellow poet Lazare Bernard (who later chose to be known as Bernard Lazare), staged at the Théâtre de l'Art in 1891; and as a translator from ancient Greek with, among other works, *Philoktétès* by Sophocles, which he directed at the Théâtre de l'Odéon in 1896. As a political writer, he expounded his anarchist views in *L'anarchie par la littérature* (1892) and declared his commitment to the Armenian cause in *La question d'Orient et la politique personnelle de M. Hanotaux* (Paris, 1897), written with Louis Margery, and *Pour l'Arménie: Mémoire et dossier*, a book-length study commissioned by Charles Péguy for publication in the *Cahiers de la Quinzaine* (1902).

Beyond question the most committed of the French supporters of the Armenians, Quillard was equally—driven by a similar quest for justice—a supporter of Dreyfus when the Dreyfus affair divided French public opinion between 1894 and 1906. The origins of this political and judicial scandal lay in unjust accusations levelled at Captain Alfred Dreyfus, who was Jewish, of spying for Germany. Dreyfus's conviction for treason led to a campaign for a re-trial, lasting from 1897 to 1899, a notable feature of which was Émile Zola's letter *J'accuse!*, aimed at the French government and published in the newspaper *L'Aurore* on 13 January 1898.

THE RIGHTEOUS AND PEOPLE OF CONSCIENCE

Teaching in Constantinople and meetings with Armenian writers

A professor of classical literature and graduate of the École des Chartes (whose many translations attest to his distinguished work as a Hellenistic scholar, which later attracted the attention of the éminence grise in the field and pro-Armenian circles, Victor Bernard), Quillard was invited to Constantinople in 1893 to teach Latin and French at the Armenian Catholic college in Pera. Soon—at the students' request, granted by the administration—he was also teaching philosophy and the history of literature at the Armenian Central College in Galata. In the Ottoman capital, he met contributors to the Armenian daily *Hayrénik'* (Homeland), founded in 1891 by the leading light of Armenian realism, Arpiar Arpiarian, which attracted many writers of progressive views. Their ideas were not to the liking of Sultan Abdul Hamid II, however, and publication of the newspaper was suspended in 1896. Among these writers, Quillard became close to the poet Arshag Chobanian. As Yves Ternon notes, 'these two men, the one French and the other Ottoman Armenian, were to become the twin pillars of the pro-Armenian movement in France'.

At a ceremony presided over by Anatole France on 16 February 1912, days after Quillard's death, by the Ligue des droits de l'homme (Human Rights League), of which Quillard had been a member since 1898 and general secretary since 1911, Chobanian—whom Quillard had introduced into French literary circles after their first meeting—recalled the effects of Quillard's early contacts:

> Quillard's time in Constantinople and the contacts he made with the Armenian people as a teacher in two of our colleges, deserve ... to be mentioned here, for they lay at the origins of the great and generous ties of friendship that bound Quillard throughout his life to the Armenian nation and cause.

Courage in denouncing the Sassoun massacres

As Anatole France recalled at the ceremony organized by the Ligue des droits de l'homme, Quillard was one of the first to battle against the conspiracy of silence that surrounded the Armenian massacres: 'This delicate man of letters, who devoted the finest hours of his life to the alexandrine muses, made his voice heard, amid the shameful silence of the great and the powerful, in order to denounce the slaughter of an enslaved people.'

Quillard was kept closely informed of the earliest massacres committed under the reign of Abdul Hamid in the mountains of Sassoun in August and September 1894, of which the essential events can be summarised as follows. Militants of the Armenian revolutionary Hunchak party (borrowed from the Russian newspaper *Kolokol*, the name meant 'The Bell'), had come to the mountainous region of Sassoun, in south-western Armenia, to organize a small group of partisans, to curtail the extortionate demands of livestock-stealing Kurdish nomads, and to incite some villages to refuse to pay the dual taxes levied by the Sublime Porte and the Kurdish chieftains. In order to put down this tax revolt, the government sent a force of 3,000 men, supported by regiments of Kurdish irregulars, dubbed (after the sultan) Hamadiye, who for the following month and into September 1894 hunted down Armenians and slaughtered them indiscriminately, young and old, men, women and children. They also arrested Murad, the leader of the Hunchak militants. The British ambassador, informed by his local consuls and shocked by the falseness of the Turkish version of events, pressed for the setting up of a commission of inquiry, to be made up of three Turks (two magistrates and a general) and three Europeans (British, French and Russian). Its findings, published halfway through 1895, were contradictory: the Armenian case, which laid the guilt principally at the feet of the Kurds, who had flagrantly exploited the most minor incidents, appeared to be coherent, as opposed to the blatant inconsistencies of the Kurdish–Turkish case. Although the three European delegates could not agree on the numbers of Armenians killed between 12 August and 4 September (which ranged from 900 to 4,000), they concluded—as Paul Cambon, French ambassador in Constantinople, noted in a despatch to Gabriel Hanotaux, minister of foreign affairs—with a 'formal condemnation of the actions of the Turks'.

More than a year after these events, in an article entitled 'Les massacres des Sassounkh', published under the pseudonym of Maurice Leveyre in the 1 September 1895 edition of the highly reputed *Revue de Paris*, then under the editorship of the historian

THE RIGHTEOUS AND PEOPLE OF CONSCIENCE

Ernest Lavisse, Quillard described the events of this appalling tragedy while at the same time underlining the fact that they were far from out of character for the Sublime Porte:

> But it would be very wrong to believe that, their unbridled brutality excepted, there is anything surprising about them. They simply replicate, in more extreme form, the intolerable violence of which the Armenians are perpetually the victims more or less everywhere, and which sooner or later may erupt elsewhere in equally frenzied barbarity.

Quillard had read the report submitted by the combined Ottoman and European (French, British and Russian) commission, whose members had conducted investigations and interrogations. As well as being able, as he wrote, 'to consult documents of unimpeachable authenticity' regarding the Sassoun massacres and the situation of the Armenians in the rest of the Ottoman Empire, he had also 'collected the depositions of three first-hand witnesses who had escaped the slaughter, Khamo Bedrossian, from the village of Gullieh-Guzan, his wife Aaltoun, and Oovig Vartan, from the village of Dalvorik'.

While Quillard was setting out—like all supporters of the Armenians—to elicit an emotional response to the fate of the Armenians in the Ottoman Empire, he also, as Edmond Khayadjian notes, underlined the danger of events such as the Sassoun massacres leading to a wider conflict: 'Specialist studies of the Orient have given me an understanding of the importance of the Armenian movement, and of the degree to which it may pose a threat to peace in Europe.'

Quillard concluded with a somewhat naive appeal to the sultan's understanding: 'Sultan Abdul Hamid Khan, whose intelligence and goodwill are to be admired, will on no account allow himself to be deceived by ill-informed advisors, and will hold it a matter of honour to restore peace and prosperity to a people who have suffered for too long.'

But the Ottoman government was wary of this foreigner who championed the Armenians, who taught exclusively in Armenian establishments, who was frequently to be seen in the company of Armenian friends, and who in their eyes posed a threat to the Hamidian regime. Accusing him of being an 'Armenian agitator', the Turkish police put him in the cells for a few hours, before the French embassy intervened to obtain his release. He was to return to the East to cover the Greco-Turkish War for *L'Illustration*.

Soon, Quillard was to witness at first hand the massacres of Armenians in the Ottoman capital, in reprisal for a peaceful demonstration in the Kumkapı quarter in September 1895, during which, 'for the first time since the entry of the Turks into Constantinople, Ottoman Christians were seen to resist Turkish troops'. Perhaps because of his anger and despair as he shared the anxieties of his Armenian students, as Khayadjian suggests, from then on he was to become 'one of the most active champions of the Armenian cause'.

'The powerful and glorious poem of the fight for justice'

Chobanian gave an eloquent description of the strength of his friend and comrade's commitment to the struggle in the wake of these events: 'Quillard adopted, one might say, something of the Armenian soul. He was interested in our cause not as a foreigner with a big heart, but as though he had Armenian blood in his veins; he shared our suffering at the appalling situation in which our people found themselves.'

As for 'la Bête Rouge'—as Quillard called Abdul Hamid, also known as the Red or Bloody Sultan—Chobanian added: 'No Armenian could surpass Quillard in his hatred of him.' In *À la mémoire de Pierre Quillard*, Chobanian described the self-abnegation of this man of letters who in his early life had 'enhanced the treasure of French poetry with some of its purest jewels' and later devoted his poetic gifts to the 'service of every cause of justice and humanity', and in particular to the Armenians: 'He worked with almost every Armenian propagandist and committee, lending them his support and encouragement.' In Chobanian's view, Quillard 'sought to transform his later life into a lived poem, the powerful and glorious poem of the fight for justice'.

Quillard's life was not put at risk by his support for the Armenians during his time in Constantinople, and he was able to ensure relative safety for himself—and most importantly to avoid seriously compromising the two Armenian educational establishments in which he taught—by writing the pro-Armenian articles he sent to France under a pseudonym. Nevertheless, he sacrificed his considerable talents as a poet—as attested by many anthologies of French poetry—to the demands of his conscience, and for this, in our view, he deserves to be considered as one of the Righteous.

Although Chobanian was uncompromised by any links with Armenian revolutionary groups and able to lead a comfortable life in Constantinople, as Quillard made clear in one of his letters, in 1895 he left for France. While daily life in France was not easy, he was at least able to continue his literary activity, with the encouragement of writers to whom Quillard had already given him introductions or would go on to do so. Armed with a wide circle of political contacts and his own superlative command of the French language, both written and spoken, he became a highly respected ambassador for the Armenian cause.

A year later, realizing he was now under surveillance by the Ottoman police, Quillard followed him. In the literary magazine *Mercure de France* (a forcing ground for Symbolist poets he had helped to found in 1891), under the nom de plume M.-L. Rogre, he reviewed an anthology of first-hand accounts published under the title *Les massacres d'Arménie*, collected by Chobanian and with a preface by Georges Clemenceau (then leader of the radical far left, soon to be champion of Dreyfus and future prime minister).

On his return to France, Quillard also wrote the preface to *L'assassinat du Père Salvatore par les soldats turcs* by Aghassi (nom de plume of Garabed Toursarkissian, who came from a prominent Hadjin family and had fought in the defence of Zeytun against the Turks in 1895), translated from the Armenian by Chobanian and published in 1897. The book told the story of the martyrdom of Father Salvatore Lilli (1853–95), an Italian Franciscan missionary (born in the town of Cappadocia in the province of L'Aquila) who was sent to Marasco. After staying in Marasco during the Hamidian massacres, against the advice of his fellow missionaries (his riposte being, 'Wherever his sheep may be, there the shepherd must stay'), he was arrested by the Ottoman police. When he refused to convert forcibly to Islam, they killed him, together with seven other Armenian Catholics. All were beatified by the Roman Catholic Church in 1982.

PIERRE QUILLARD (1864–1912)

Ardent Dreyfusard and leader of the pro-Armenian movement

In 1898, Quillard joined the Ligue française pour la défense des droits de l'homme et du citoyen, and like many supporters of the Armenian cause he became involved in the Dreyfus affair, alongside Lazare, one of the first Dreyfusards. Only with this wave of anti-semitism that swept through French society, it should be said, did Lazare, who was energetic in his support of the Armenians, reveal that he was himself Jewish and declare his solidarity with all persecuted Jews everywhere.

In October 1900, Quillard and Chobanian founded the fortnightly magazine *Pro Armenia*, published until 1914, with Quillard as editor-in-chief and an editorial committee featuring prestigious names such as Clemenceau, Anatole France, Jean Jaurès, the Protestant pastor and senator Francis de Pressensé and the Russian-born sociologist Eugène de Roberty, with Jean Longuet, grandson of Karl Marx, as subeditor. As one of the earliest and staunchest supporters of the Armenian cause who wanted nothing better than to be able to write about it, Quillard had accepted a proposition from two leaders of the Dashnak party (the Armenian Revolutionary Federation), Dr Jean Loris-Melikov (nephew of the Russian general of Armenian descent Mikhail Loris-Melikov), a research scientist at the Institut Pasteur, and Kristapor Mikayelian, one of the three founders of the Dashnak party, who had come to Paris in 1899. The pair had been mandated by the party's Western bureau to entrust Quillard with setting up and running a journal that would bring together French supporters of the Armenian cause and keep public opinion abreast of developments and that would be funded by the party through the intermediary of Loris-Melkov, its administrative director. Documents published in *Pro Armenia* were subsequently read in the Chamber of Deputies, and members of the editorial committee attended pro-Armenian congresses.

In the words of Vincent Duclert:

> Pierre Quillard sacrificed his career and his own publications in favour of articles and countless documentary accounts concerning the persecution of the Armenians, published in the journal that he founded and edited, *Pro Armenia*. His commitment to two pioneering causes—opposition to the great massacres from 1895, and the

Dreyfus affair from 1897—combined to endow him with an unchallenged position as both leader and prime mover of the 'pro-Armenian party' at the turn of the century.

Sources and further reading

Sources

Duclert, Vincent, *La France face au génocide des Arméniens*, Paris: Fayard, 2015, pp. 157–202.

Poghosyan, *Les massacres hamidiens*, *passim*.

Critical studies

Kharazian, Marat, *De l'illusion à la tragédie: La France et la question arménienne (1894–1908)* (preface by Jean-Pierre Mahé), Paris: Éditeur Rouben Kharazian, 2004, *passim*.

Khayadjian, Edmond, *Archag Tchobanian et le mouvement arménophile en France*, 2nd edn, Alfortville: SIGEST, 2001, part 1, chapter 4, 'Tchobanian et Pierre Quillard à Constantinople, au temps des massacres hamidiens', and chapter 6, 'Tchobanian et les arménophiles de la première heure, Séverine, Henri Rochefort et Pierre Quillard'.

Minassian, Anahide Ter, 'XII. L'Arménie et l'éveil des nationalités (1800–1914)', in Gérard Dédéyan (ed.), *Histoire du peuple arménien*, Toulouse: Privat, 2007, pp. 475–521.

Mutafian, Claude, 'Les Arméniens et la France. 9', in Claude Mutafian, *France–Arménie: Des relations séculaires* (bilingual Armenian–French), exhibition catalogue, Yerevan: Matenadaran, 2018.

Vahramian, Agnès, 'De l'Affaire Dreyfus au mouvement arménophile: Pierre Quillard et Pro Armenia', *Revue d'histoire de la Shoah*, 177–8 (January–August 2003), pp. 35–55.

3

BERNARD LAZARE (1865–1903)

Armenian suffering as a mirror of Jewish persecution

Playwright turned dramatist

Born in Nîmes into a Jewish family who were observant on occasion and who had become prosperous and well established through their successful textile mill producing cloth and passementeries, Lazare Bernard reversed his first and last names to create his nom de plume when he abandoned his scientific training in favour of literature. In 1886, encouraged by his friend Ephraïm Mikhaël (1866–90), born in Toulouse and also Jewish, he joined him in Paris, where Ephraïm had won a place at the École des Chartes. Also in that year, Édouard Drumont, a prominent polemicist and antisemitic propagandist under the Third Republic (who was nevertheless to become a supporter of the Armenian cause), published *La France juive.* Wanting to train as a historian, Lazare gained a place at the École pratique des Hautes Études, where he met the Symbolist poet Pierre Quillard—a pro-Armenian and Dreyfusard with whom he would form an enduring friendship—and studied under Monseigneur Louis Duchesne, who was considered suspect by the Catholic hierarchy for his modernist views. Lazare wrote and staged plays including *La fiancée de Corinthe* in 1888 with Mikhaël, and his friend's untimely death at the age of just twenty-three marked a turning point in Lazare's early career. It was at this point that he 'entered into anarchy', like Quillard, a pillar of the pro-Armenian movement, with whom he published *La Révolte* from 1887 to 1895, and subsequently *Les temps nouveaux,* which replaced *La Révolte* as the main focus of his journalistic activities. He distinguished himself with his news reporting and articles of both literary and social criticism, including his coverage of the Carmaux miners' strikes and their champion Jean Jaurès.

From relative indifference to militant support of Dreyfus

Active support of Dreyfus frequently went hand in hand with support for the Armenian cause. Within a few months of the arrest of Captain Alfred Dreyfus in 1894, Lazare published *L'Antisémitisme, son histoire et ses causes* (Paris, 1894; published in English translation as *Antisemitism, Its History and Causes* in 1903). After being approached by Dreyfus's brother Mathieu, whom he met in February 1895, Lazare then published a second version of this text, with the title *La vérité sur L'Affaire Dreyfus: Une erreur judiciaire; Deuxième mémoire avec des expertises d'écriture* (Brussels, November 1896), so paving the way for Émile Zola's interventions and especially his famous *J'accuse!* One of the consequences of the Dreyfus affair was the setting up in 1898, by former Minister of Justice Ludovic Trarieux, of the Ligue des droits de l'homme (Human Rights League). Many of the same figures were to be found among the ranks of both the Dreyfusards and the pro-Armenians. As Yves Ternon points out, however, Lazare—unlike Quillard—was not a member of the Franco-Armenian committee founded in 1897 by the writer and militant pro-Armenian Arshag Chobanian, one of the major figures of western Armenian literature (who also wrote in French). Lazare also lagged behind his friend Charles Péguy in becoming involved in the Armenian question. Yet he was just as well informed as the most committed of pro-Armenians, including his friend Quillard. The explanation for this, Ternon argues, lay in Lazare's stand on Zionism. The movement had come into being in 1878 with the creation of a first agricultural colony but became active towards the end of the century when the writings of Theodor Herzl, notably *The Jewish State* of 1896 and articles in *Die Welt*, the newspaper he founded, paved the way for the First Zionist Congress in Basel in 1897.

Growing awareness of Jewish persecution

As he stood up in defence of oppressed peoples, Lazare became increasingly conscious of the persecution of Jews. He had originally been very reticent about the people he called 'Jews', who lived in Central and Eastern Europe, as opposed to the 'Israelites', or at least those living in France, whom he considered as 'fine people' (*braves gens*), along with the rest of the French population. It was after a journey to Romania, an Orthodox Christian kingdom where in the late nineteenth century, Jews, as Carol Iancu notes, were—despite the terms laid down in the Treaty of Berlin (1878)—subject to 'legal alienation': deprived of their civil rights although obliged to do military service, they were excluded from public service and from many economic activities.

Won over to a veritable 'Jewish nationalism', in his talks and writings Lazare invoked the case of other nationalities—including the Armenians—in order to find a solution that would answer the aspirations of the Jews. In *Le fumier de Job* (Job's Dungheap), a manuscript that remained unpublished at his death in 1903, he examined the socialist position with regard to various nationalisms, to which he added Jewish nationalism, with the following questions: 'Besides, are the majority of socialists, even internationalists, consistent with themselves; do their actions match their doctrines? Are they not now, quite rightly, demanding autonomy for the Cubans, the Cretans and the Armenians?' So why, he asked, 'would they not do the same for the Jews?'

Having seen for himself the sufferings of the Jews in Romania (and soon of those in the Russian Empire), in his articles in *L'Aurore* (the newspaper published by Clemenceau, a prominent pro-Armenian), Lazare castigated the attitude of the Christian world towards the persecuted Christian populations, and *a fortiori* towards the Jews:

> Certainly, in raising my voice on behalf of my brothers in Romania I felt no hope that I would be heard by the civilized world. Anyone who has not heard the voice of the Armenians, anyone who has remained indifferent to Cuba, Finland and the Philippines, will not hear the voice of the Jews.

Defence of the Armenians: Bernard Lazare versus Theodor Herzl

Overwhelmed by the tragedy of the Armenians, Lazare would allow no compromise with Abdul Hamid II. Now that he had become a champion of 'Jewish nationalism', it was inevitable that

Lazare's path would cross with that of Theodor Herzl (1860–1904), a Hungarian Jew whose commitment, bolstered by the persecution of Jews in Europe and the extremism of the anti-Dreyfusards, formed part of the 'awakening of nationalities' by which the whole of the nineteenth century was shaken. After meeting Herzl in Paris in July 1896, Lazare took part in the Second Zionist Congress in Basel, from 28 to 31 August 1898, and wrote for various Zionist periodicals. But less than a year later, on 24 March 1899, Lazare sent a letter of resignation to the Zionist Action Committee. This move was in fact motivated, as Iancu notes, by Herzl's diplomatic approaches to controversial figures such as Wilhelm II, king of Prussia and emperor of Germany (ruled 1888–1918), warmonger and proponent of Pan-Germanism, whom he dubbed 'the mystic warrior', and—even worse—Abdul Hamid II (1876–1909), the 'Red Sultan' who had perpetrated the Armenian massacres of 1894–6.

Following an audience with Abdul Hamid, Herzl nursed hopes, as Ternon notes, that the sultan would favour the creation of a Jewish homeland in Palestine; and on 26 December 1901, he told the Fifth Zionist Congress in Basel that Abdul Hamid had authorized him to declare him publicly as the friend and benefactor of the Jewish people. Lazare responded initially with an indignant article in *L'Aurore* on 3 January 1902, in which he declared that 'Zionists and Armenians denounce the making of advances to the cut-throat sultan.' But he reserved the full force of his outrage for a piece in *Pro Armenia*, the journal founded in 1900 by Quillard, in which, as quoted by Ternon, he roundly condemned Herzl's position as an insult to oppressed Jews: 'The representatives—or those who claim to be—of the most ancient of persecuted peoples, whose history can only be written in blood, send their greetings to the most heinous of murderers.' In Lazare's view, the 'men of Basel' did not in any way represent the mass of Jews, who were everywhere persecuted, and who 'fulfil the true and living image of the Jesus of legend, and like him, sadly, forgive their executioners instead of rising up against them'. These 'men of Basel' should be told: 'You have no right to dishonour your people.' The Jews of Poland and Russia, crushed by their poverty and wretchedness, knew nothing of the 'Red Sultan, of the massacred Armenians, of all the oppressed populations of the Ottoman Empire.'

BERNARD LAZARE (1865–1903)

In addition to the Armenian massacres, Lazare was fearless in his denunciation of all barbaric persecutions, including those perpetrated by Christian populations. He was also admirably clear in his thinking and courageous in his political views. On 17–18 July 1902, he took part in the first major European Pro-Armenia Congress in Brussels, alongside Jaurès, Pressensé, Quillard and other supporters of the Armenian cause. Invited to an event in support of Armenia and Macedonia at the Théâtre du Château-d'Eau in Paris on 15 February 1903, with other prominent pro-Armenians including Jaurès, Ernest Lavisse and Anatole Leroy-Beaulieu, he was unable to attend as he was convalescing in Grasse. In a letter to Leroy-Beaulieu three days later, he had no hesitation in reminding him that barbarism was not the exclusive preserve of Muslim states:

> I have always been one of those who have protested against the oppression that Armenia has suffered and who have deplored the massacres. Alongside Jaurès and Pressensé, I took part in the Pro-Armenian Congress in Brussels. Turkish barbarism—or Muslim, as it is too often described—has always found a determined adversary in me, but I would not want it to be used to make us forget Christian barbarism.

He had in mind the unrelieved torments visited—with the complicity of European nations—upon the Jewish population of Romania by their government.

A demand for justice: Bernard Lazare, inspirational figure for Charles Péguy

Lazare was also an inspirational force behind the *Cahiers de la Quinzaine*. In 1900, he became friends with Charles Péguy (1873–1914)—École normale supérieure graduate, Dreyfusard, pro-Armenian and (from 1908) Catholic—who founded the *Cahiers de la Quinzaine* that same year. In the first issue, Péguy published a motion by the Ligue des droits de l'homme in support of the Armenians, and in 1902 he commissioned Quillard to contribute a special edition entitled *Pour l'Arménie: Mémoire et dossier*. While in the final years of his life he travelled through Central Europe several times to plead the cause of oppressed Jews—as personified in the emblematic figure of human misery in *Job's Dungheap*, published posthumously in 1934—when Lazare described the obstacle put in the way of the immigration of Romanian Jews, in an article published in *L'Aurore* on 9 August 1900, cited by Ternon, it was with his customary reference to the Armenians, among other oppressed peoples, of whom the Jews were the most persecuted:

> Anyone who has not heard the voice of the Armenians, anyone who has remained indifferent to Cuba, Finland and the Philippines, will not hear the voice of the Jews. ... No nation has yet closed its doors to the Armenians, however, nor will they close them tomorrow to the Finns, while America has granted lands to the Boers, but the Jew is doubtless excluded from humanity.

In the article for *Cahier de la Quinzaine*, entitled 'L'oppression des Juifs dans l'Europe orientale: Les Juifs de Roumanie', published in 1902, Lazare provides the key to his unwavering support of the Armenians, though without adopting too controversial a position:

> To ask Europe which, in violation of the Treaty of Berlin has allowed the massacre of thousands of Armenian Christians by Muslims and has not been able to stay the hand of the Assassin, to ask Europe now to prevent a Christian population from making 100,000 Jews perish from poverty and hunger, that would be too great an irony.

As Iancu points out: 'Like Charles Péguy, Bernard Lazare demanded justice and truth; it was he who was the "inspiration" and *éminence grise* behind the *Cahiers de la Quinzaine*, and he was also the driving force behind the series devoted to oppressed peoples.'

When Péguy published *Notre Jeunesse* in 1910, in refutation of nationalist attacks on the sincerity of his support for Dreyfus, he described the spiritual nature of his relationship with Lazare, 'a friendship that death cannot sever', and paid tribute to his friend's role in the genesis of the *Cahiers de la Quinzaine*, to which he remained 'the most confidential friend, the hidden inspiration, and I would say, without the slightest hesitation or exaggeration, the *patron*'.

In Lazare, Péguy saw a man of a prophetic vocation that was rooted in his feelings of belonging to the Jewish people, who inspired him to refer to the prophet Isaiah, whose lips were touched with a burning coal by one of the seraphim before he was invested

BERNARD LAZARE (1865–1903)

with his mission as a prophet by Yahweh. Endowing Lazare with the attributes of sainthood, Péguy was specific: 'And when I speak of a saint, I should not be suspected of speaking in metaphors.' For Péguy, the Catholic poet par excellence, Lazare was also a 'martyr', since his defiance of power and military authority had cost him his career as a journalist. But 'this atheist bathed in the word of God', in Péguy's words, could also, according to Matthieu Giroux, claim to be 'the safekeeper of the authentic republican mystique'.

The compassion of the Jewish elite for the Armenians

In the late nineteenth and early twentieth centuries, an emancipated elite among the Jewish community showed compassion in their response to the sufferings of the Armenians. As we have seen, pro-Armenians and Dreyfusards often fought shoulder to shoulder. Standing alongside Quillard and Péguy were not only Lazare but also other figures of the French 'Israelite' elite, who since their emancipation in French civil society in the late eighteenth century had flourished in the nation's political, economic and cultural arenas. The members of this elite (as well as their counterparts in the United States, also emancipated at this time) were quick to view the Armenians massacred under the regime of the 'Red Sultan' as their brothers in suffering. In addition to undoubtedly serving to prompt some Jews to actively support Armenia through Near East Relief, this must also have accounted partly for the robustness of American ambassador Henry Morgenthau's denunciation of the Armenian genocide, as well as inspiring the Austrian novelist Franz Werfel, a Jew imbued with the Christian faith, to write his epic novel *The Forty Days of Musa Dagh*, which helped to inspire the resistance fighters of the Warsaw Ghetto. It comes as no surprise that the Natanson brothers, sons of a modest Jewish banker who emigrated from Warsaw to Paris, where they founded *La revue blanche* (1889–1903), a literary and artistic view of anarchist persuasion, were champions not merely of new artistic trends but also spearheaded political struggles in support of indigenous peoples exploited by European colonialism, of Dreyfus and of the Armenians. As Vincent Duclert notes, once alerted by Quillard—who was the best-informed about events in Armenia—Lazare immediately involved *La revue blanche*, which made reference to them in late 1895 in a column by Georges Dalbert entitled 'Questions d'Orient'. In the next issue, it went on to introduce Chobanian's translation of a medieval chronicle that detailed the ravages wrought by the Turkomans in Armenia in the mid-eleventh century with a dramatic description of the position of the Armenians in the late nineteenth century, penned by its sub-editor Félix Fénéon.

On the subject of solidarity with the persecuted, we should not forget either the great poet, precursor of Surrealism, art critic and painter Max Jacob (1876–1944), who converted to Catholicism in 1915 but in 1944 was arrested by the Gestapo for his Ashkenazi origins and imprisoned in the internment camp at Drancy, where he perished. In 1918, inspired by his great friend the antiquarian Jean Altounian, he published a long poem in free verse in the form of a small volume entitled *Les Alliés sont en Arménie*, a raw and moving reflection on the Armenian massacres of 1894–6 more than the genocide of 1915 (when he, like Péguy, was in the trenches): 'This report says nothing! The facts are appalling! / People are tortured with red-hot irons, boiled alive; / Chalices are filled with excrement; / Every holy object is defiled / And to abuse God the altar is abused.'

Lazare was therefore not the only intellectual of Jewish descent to be stirred by centuries of persecution to feel a profound empathy with the Armenians.

From this perspective, he can certainly be considered as one of the Righteous of the Armenian genocide. But the last word should go to Ternon, expert on genocide in general and the Armenian genocide in particular: 'Thus through his humanism, rigour, humility and immense compassion, Bernard Lazare too was a champion, even if through the mirror of Jewish suffering, of the persecuted Armenians.'

Sources and further reading

Studies

Giroux, Matthieu, 'Bernard Lazare, un précurseur du lien judéo-arménien', *Arméniens, Juifs vieilles connaissances, Israël, Arménie, le rendez-vous manqué, Résonances*, special edition of *Nouvelles d'Arménie Magazine*, 3 (2021), pp. 46–52; Giroux, 'Notre Jeunesse, de Charles Péguy: Une apologie de Bernard Lazare', *Philitt (Philosophie, littérature et cinéma)*, Newsletter, 10 July 2014.

BERNARD LAZARE (1865–1903)

Iancu, Carol, 'Charles Péguy, Bernard Lazare, l'Affaire Dreyfus et les Arméniens', in Annick Asso, Héléna Demirdjian and Patrick Louvier (eds), *Exprimer le génocide des Arméniens: Connaissances, Arts, Engagements* (preface by Vincent Duclert), Rennes: PUR, 2016.

Khayadjian, *Archag Tchobanian et le mouvement arménophile*, part 2, chapter 9, '"Les Alliés sont en Arménie", poème de Max Jacob'.

Leroy, Géraldi, 'L'Arménie dans l'œuvre et la pensée de Charles Péguy', *Ailleurs, hier, autrement: connaissance et reconnaissance du génocide des Arméniens, Revue d'histoire de la Shoah*, 177–8 (January–August 2003), pp. 356–67.

Oriol, Philippe, *Bernard Lazare*, Paris: Stock, 2003.

Ternon, Yves, '1916: Max Jacob, un poète au secours de l'Arménie martyre', *Archives juives*, 48 (Paris, 2015), pp. 10–27; Ternon, 'Pierre Quillard, Bernard Lazare et les Arméniens', in D. Delmaire, L.-Z. Herscovici and F. Waldman (eds), *Roumanie, Israël, France: Parcours juif*, Paris: Champion, pp. 309–29.

4

JEAN JAURÈS (1859–1914)

Prophet of human rights

Academic, journalist and politician from a bourgeois provincial background

An unconditional champion of the rights of the poor, the powerless and the oppressed—whose struggle was the direct heir to the evangelical message of the Declaration of the Rights of Man and the Citizen of 1789—Jean Jaurès himself came from a well-to-do background. He was born in Castres, to a family who were descended from agricultural workers but had prospered to become part of a local bourgeoisie and to find success in the liberal professions, as well as producing two admirals: Jean's cousin Benjamin, who also became minister for the navy, and his brother Louis.

Initially, Jaurès distinguished himself as an academic, journalist and local politician. After being spotted by a school inspector in his last year of secondary education in Castres, at the age of nineteen he took first place in the fiercely competitive entrance examination to the École Normale Supérieure, beating another candidate in philosophy, Henri Bergson, who three years later would in turn beat him—by a narrow margin—in the philosophy *agrégation*. Jaurès taught in the Faculty of Literature at the University of Toulouse, before entering politics and being elected as a Republican deputy to the National Assembly from 1885 to 1889, which did not prevent him from publishing two theses (the main one entitled *De la réalité du monde sensible*) in 1881. But his vocation as a politician was becoming clear: a contributor to *La Dépêche de Toulouse* (a radical socialist newspaper founded in 1870, which also published Georges

Clemenceau before he moved on to *L'Aurore*), he was elected as deputy mayor of Toulouse (with responsibility for public education, taking into account his academic background) from 1890 to 1893.

The Carmaux strikes: Jaurès as standard-bearer for socialism

The Carmaux coal strikes of 1892–5 marked a turning point for Jaurès. Prompted by the actions of the miners of Carmaux in solidarity with their mayor, Jean-Baptiste Calvignac, also a miner, who had been sacked for absenteeism after being elected as mayor, and the brutal reaction of the government, which seemed to go out of its way to protect the interests of capitalism, Jaurès took an uncompromising stand against the employers and their actions and wrote a series of articles that appeared in *La Dépêche de Toulouse* (in which Clemenceau also gave his support to the miners). The resignation in 1893 of the son-in-law of the president of the 'Compagnie des mines' (the most influential family on the right in the Tarn *département*), following government arbitration that found itself obliged to uphold the mayor against accusations of absenteeism, resulted in Jaurès' election to the Chamber of Deputies, where he was to be a staunch supporter of the workers of Carmaux. Through his contacts with the workers' movement, which was supported by socialist militants, Jaurès was to become a standard-bearer for socialism.

During his first mandate as a socialist deputy, in 1893–8, Jaurès championed workers' rights, supported the Carmaux glass-workers' strike of 1895 (sparked by the sacking of two union members) and waged a campaign against the *lois scélérates* ('villainous laws') passed in the wake of attacks by anarchists (particularly the bombings carried out by Ravachol), which flouted the principles of law and stirred up a general 'witch hunt' involving agents provocateurs, preventive arrests and denunciations. Some Catholics, including Albert de Mun, also denounced the effects of these laws, but their attacks were treated with greater tolerance by the government.

Jaurès' speech in the Chamber of Deputies

The speech Jaurès delivered in the Chamber of Deputies on 3 November 1896 marked a turning point in the championing of the

JEAN JAURÈS (1859–1914)

Armenian cause by the French humanitarian elite, as noted by Vincent Duclert in his article 'Jean Jaurès et la défense des Arméniens', published in the *Cahiers Jaurès* in 2015, the centenary of the genocide. Up to that time, Jaurès had been fully occupied by his militant socialism, but now he rose to speak after conservative Catholic deputies including Denys Cochin and Albert de Mun, who denounced the massacres ordered by Sultan Abdul Hamid II in 1894–6 and condemned the support for the sultan shown by the minister for foreign affairs, Gabriel Hanotaux. Wilfully ignoring reports he had received from the French ambassador in Constantinople, Paul Cambon, and seduced by the economic prospects that the 'Red Sultan' (whose agents had acquired the major Paris newspapers) appeared to be opening up for France, Hanotaux painted a rosy picture of the situation faced by Armenians in the Ottoman Empire. Jaurès' heroic speech, delivered by this deputy who was very much of the left but seemed also to be driven from within by a compelling urgency, was immortalized by Marcel Proust through the character of Couzon in his novel *Jean Santeuil*. The most telling phrase of this critical intervention was highlighted by Jean-Marie Carzou in his pioneering book *Arménie 1915: Un génocide exemplaire*: 'We have reached the point where humanity can no longer live with the corpse of a murdered people buried in its cellar.'

Building his case on the consular reports among other documents, Jaurès started by denouncing what was nothing less than a 'war of extermination', in a term pertaining to the language of genocide. He then came close to a definition of genocide, outlining how this 'war' had been deliberately planned by a potentate who was panic-stricken by the Ottoman Empire's territorial losses and British control of Cyprus; and finally he denounced the passive stance adopted by the European powers, in contravention of the terms of the Treaty of Berlin, signed on 13 July 1878, and castigated a British diplomatic policy 'consisting solely of a quest for imperial power' (making an exception for Gladstone and George Campbell, 8th Duke of Argyll) while condemning the silence of French diplomacy and public opinion, manipulated by the press. The government's protestations served only to redouble the vehemence of his accusations.

Jaurès reiterated the accusations he had levelled at the French government in his second speech in the Chamber of Deputies, on

22 February 1897, on the 'Cretan war of independence', criticizing it again for not listening to the protests of its ambassador Paul Cambon. For him, this was an opportunity to ascribe to the proletariat a quest for justice that was founded on the ideals of 1789, in the face of the 'moral bankruptcy of the old Europe of Christianity and capitalism'. In his appeal to 'the proletariat', which he broadened to include intellectuals and the people, Jaurès went further than the Catholic deputy Mun, who before him had invoked the obligation to save a Christian minority in the East. But far from seeking to start a revolution, he wanted to entrust these 'new agents' with the defence of justice, peace and truth. He also hoped to bring about a democratization of the Ottoman Empire (as he was under the illusion had come to pass when the Young Turks came to power in 1908), to whose crimes under Abdul Hamid II the tsarist government, through fear of revolutionary movements in the Russian Empire, had closed its eyes.

The defence of the oppressed—Armenians and Jews—as a moral principle of republicanism

Jaurès was a non-violent optimist, a champion of 'persecuted humanity' (*l'humanité victime*). The concluding section of his speech of 3 November 1896 (which would be rejected by an overwhelming majority) contained two central ideas: first that the democratization of the Ottoman Empire would be sufficient in itself to put an end to the inter-ethnic and inter-religious conflicts generated by the Hamidian tyranny; and secondly that the intervention of the proletariat, far from seeking to unleash a revolution, was aimed solely at 'constraining the nations of Europe to alter their diplomatic policy and to insist on the rights of persecuted humanity'.

Expanding on his speech in *La Dépêche de Toulouse* of 7 November 1896, the socialist deputy gave socialists—and first and foremost French socialists—a mission: to champion a diplomatic approach worthy of the Republic's values, embedded in public debate and excluding any diktat from foreign powers such as the Russian Empire. It was during this time that Clemenceau and his friends founded the Société des droits de l'homme to fight against the extreme, anti-German nationalism of boulangism. The notion of

JEAN JAURÈS (1859–1914)

republican citizenship, espousing the ideals of democracy, had just been given fresh impetus when the first large-scale massacres were committed. The rights of man and the citizen were no mere abstract ideals. The Armenians should be defended because they were part of suffering humanity. Whether a persecuted population happened to be Christian or Jewish was irrelevant.

As France and Europe remained unmoved by the crimes being committed in the Ottoman Empire, the ideals invoked by the majority of pro-Armenians, from laicist and internationalist circles and ranging from liberals to socialists and anarchists, were strictly democratic.

In a speech on 22 February 1897, Jaurès—who had taken stock of the limited progress that had been achieved by his own commitment and that of other people of goodwill—described the diplomacy that would have been worthy of France: 'Our system is to make heard the voice of humanity, and the voice of France, which should be indistinguishable from the voice of humanity, and to make it heard in time.'

As so often in this context, Jaurès' career also featured an overlap between pro-Armenians and supporters of Dreyfus. It was only natural that in 1898, along with other pro-Armenians including Anatole France, Pierre Quillard and Clemenceau, he should stand with Émile Zola (whose *J'accuse!*, addressed to the French president Félix Faure, was published in the newspaper *L'Aurore* on 13 January that year) in supporting Captain Alfred Dreyfus, a Jew unjustly accused of spying for the Germans. The victory of the Dreyfusards bolstered the pro-Armenian cause in France, which took tangible form in the founding of the journal *Pro Armenia*. Both Jaurès and Clemenceau were involved in this venture, with support from Armenians exiled in France including the poet Arshag Chobanian and Dr Jean Loris-Melikov, nephew of Mikhail Loris-Melikov, general and reforming minister under Tsar Alexander II.

After the massacres at Adana in Cilicia in 1909, for which the Young Turks bore the major responsibility, Jaurès' own newspaper, *L'Humanité*—and particularly Francis de Pressensé, who was the president of the Ligue des droits de l'homme, and Jean Longuet, a specialist on international questions in the socialist party— denounced the nationalist violence of a party that affected to adopt

European ideals, so bolstering hopes for the democratization of the empire. Jaurès himself, however, did not rush to condemn the party that would go on to plan and perpetrate the Armenian genocide.

Posthumous victory for Jaurès

In the end, Jaurès' victory came posthumously. Although he died prematurely, assassinated for his militant pacifism by a Catholic nationalist in Paris on 31 July 1914, on the eve of the First World War, his ideas lived on. When the massacres began again, under cover of the Ottoman Empire's entry into the First World War (denounced by Pressensé), there were vehement protests from Jean Longuet and Marcel Cachin, who, following the appearance of the writer Avedis Aharonian (future representative of the Republic of Armenia at the negotiations that would culminate in the Treaty of Versailles) before the Foreign Affairs Committee of the Chamber of Deputies, proposed a motion that was adopted unanimously condemning massacres aimed at 'the disappearance of the Armenian people'. Through the heirs to Jaurès, this was the voice of France being raised at last, clearly and unequivocally.

The stand taken by Jaurès and other pro-Armenians undoubtedly contributed, as Duclert notes, to the declaration by the Entente powers (France, Great Britain and Russia) on 24 May 1915—a month after the Armenian genocide had been unleashed in Constantinople with the arrest and deportation of Armenian intellectuals on 24 April 1915—that the Ottoman government was guilty of a 'crime against humanity and civilization', and that after the war the perpetrators would be brought to justice. But after the war there was 'no Nuremberg trial, no recognition, no reparation'. Instead, the Kemalist forces went on to finish off the genocide, notably targeting the Armenian population after the capture of Smyrna in 1922.

But Jaurès and his allies had opened up a split in the pro-Turkish positions adopted by the French government at the time of the Hamidian massacres. The campaign Jaurès waged in support of the Armenians was only one aspect of his fight for human rights, which embraced the workers of Carmaux, bullied by their bosses; Alfred Dreyfus, falsely accused by antisemites; and the whole of humanity, threatened by the war. It was with good reason that, on Sunday, 23 November 1924, the mortal remains of this lay prophet and campaigner for human rights—for the miners of Carmaux, Dreyfus and persecuted Armenians alike—were transferred to the Panthéon.

Sources and further reading

Sources

Jaurès, Jean, *L'intégrale des articles publiés dans 'La Dépêche' de 1887 à 1914*, ed. Rémy Pech and Rémy Cazals, Toulouse: Éditions Privat, 2009.

Studies

Bozarslan, Duclert and Kévorkian, *Comprendre le génocide des Arméniens*, pp. 266–72.

Candar, Gilles and Vincent Duclert, *Jean Jaurès*, Paris: Fayard, 2014.

Duclert, *La France face au génocide des Arméniens*, pp. 45–7, 51–5, 107–10, 142–8, 153–7, 173–5, 178–9, 196–202, 218–22, *et passim*; Vincent Duclert (ed.), *Jaurès contemporain*, Toulouse: Éditions Privat (with the support of the Fondation Jaurès), 2018; Duclert, 'Jean Jaurès et la défense des Arméniens: Le tournant du discours du 3 novembre 1896', *Cahiers Jaurès*, 217, no. 3 (2015), pp. 63–88.

Minassian, 'XII. L'Arménie et l'éveil des nationalités', pp. 475–521.

Ternon, Yves, *Les Arméniens: Histoire d'un génocide*, 2nd edn, revised and updated by the author, Paris: Éditions du Seuil, 1996 [1977], pp. 139–43.

5

ALPHONSE CILLIÈRE (1861–1946)

Diplomat enamoured of Turkish culture and passionate about justice for the Armenians

Alphonse Cillière was a French diplomat who had just been posted to Trebizond when the massacres of 8 October 1895 took place. One of the most ancient cities in Asia Minor and the administrative centre of a *vilayet* that would later be created out of six *vilayets* with a strong Armenian community, Trebizond was also one of the biggest of the Black Sea ports. When Cillière arrived, he discovered a city that he would later describe in his reports as 'one of the most peaceful in Turkey'. Armenians were a small minority within the city itself, but other Christian communities lived side by side and respected each other's customs and ways of life. While the prosperity of the Armenians doubtless gave rise to envy, their presence nonetheless ensured stability for the community as a whole.

Cillière was French consul in Trebizond from 1894 to 1897, serving under Paul Cambon, the ambassador in Constantinople, whom he lauded for his integrity. Anyone reading Cillière's reports cannot fail to be impressed by the rigour, subtlety and commitment, both professional and ethical, that he displayed during his tour of duty, and especially by his resourcefulness in protecting an Armenian population that was powerless in the face of Turkish state repression.

Orientalist and diplomat

Cillière was born in Sète in 1861 into a distinguished family who soon afterwards moved to Montpellier. There he obtained his bachelor's degree in 1880, before leaving for postgraduate studies at the École des Langues Orientales in Paris, from which he emerged two years later with a degree in Turkish, Arabic and Persian. He then enrolled for a year at the École Libre des Sciences Politiques, followed by the École Pratique des Hautes Études. In July 1883, he qualified in law, and in 1887 he entered the diplomatic service. In the same year, he was nominated as a member of the Société Asiatique by the orientalist Charles Barbier de Meynard, translator of the Persian poet Ferdowsi and of Arabic geographical and historical works. In 1889, he was posted as deputy ambassador to Constantinople, under the reign of the 'Bloody Sultan', Abdul Hamid II. His duties running the consular court there doubtless nurtured the administrative and organizational skills that he made such efforts to deploy during the massacres of 8 October 1895 and that later led to him being made responsible for the legal department of the French High Commission. His reports, which have since passed to his great-great-nephew Dominique Bruzy, leave no doubt as to his great literary, linguistic and stylistic gifts.

Alphonse Cillière's reports

The structure that Cillière gave to his reports, which he intended to publish under the title *Vêpres arméniennes: Les massacres de Trébizonde de 1895* (Armenian vespers: the Trebizond massacres of 1895), consisted of a foreword giving the background to his situation, a detailed and critical narrative of the events of Abdul Hamid's planned massacres, and what he called a 'retrospective counter-inquiry', putting these events in perspective. They demonstrate a modern feeling for narrative, both in the time sequencing, which respects the logic of the first-hand accounts, and in the vivid and arresting descriptions of the setting and especially a gallery of individual character portraits. He describes the governor general or *vali* of Trebizond, Kadri Bey, for example, as 'looking like a man of authority, but devoid of any airs and graces, who in the simplicity of his manners stood in stark contrast to the ceremonious vanity of many Muslim high officials ... [and who] possessed a quality that is rare everywhere, and especially in the Orient: decisiveness'.

In addition to the gentle humour of his description, he paints a portrait of a man of action who enjoyed a close relationship with his

ALPHONSE CILLIÈRE (1861–1946)

fellow citizens, and who was strong enough to ensure that he was not shadowed by the spies who were generally planted in the corridors of power. Subsequent events were to show not only the careerist ends to which Kadri Bey put his decisive turn of mind, but also the degree of cynicism that on 8 October 1895 could impel a man who had spent years as leader of a peaceful local administration to turn a blind eye—and even to facilitate—the annihilation of the city's Armenian community. The raw power that lay in his hands and the way he chose to use it form a striking contrast with Cillière's unrelenting efforts to provide effective protection for as many as he could of the intended victims of a massacre that no one was meant to survive. He offers a subtle account of the machinations involved, describes events as they are witnessed and foreseen, and pushes this inquest into events to its conclusion with denunciations of the parts played by each individual in the massacres.

The massacres

Cillière's reports detail the events he was involved with on a daily basis from 1894 to 1896. During this period, the massacres still had as their goal the subjugation of the Armenians in the Ottoman Empire in order to avoid any intrusion by foreign powers. But they also signalled the start of the Armenian genocide that was to culminate in the attempt at total extermination in eastern Anatolia in 1915. In his narrative, Cillière dissects the manner in which events unfolded and analyses the sustained and coordinated policy aimed at eliminating the Armenians, based on the pretext of enacting the reforms they had demanded and the international community supported. In Constantinople, people were beaten to death with sticks. In the region of Van, 350 villages were put to the torch. Near Trebizond, rumours of the planned reforms in favour of the Armenians were cunningly manipulated by those in power to gradually inflame the Muslim population's hostility and feelings of being duped, so preparing public opinion for the massacre.

At the beginning of 1895, news of the Sassoun massacres spread throughout Europe, and in France there were protests against government policy. In the wake of reports from consuls in the field, Cambon declared his active support for the Armenians, so clearing the way for the consuls to take action. Cillière took full advantage of this. On 2 October 1895, Bahri Pasha, a visitor to the city, was involved in a minor incident with an unknown assailant, who was immediately marked out as an Armenian. Rather than opting to play for time, Kadri Bey applied the full authority of the law, in so doing unleashing an irreversible process that would serve as a pretext for the massacres. On 4 October, Armenian houses were attacked. Cillière, who would later detail the machinations of this ploy, was tireless in his efforts and met repeatedly with the *vali* to obtain promises of protection that, it transpired, would deliberately not be put into effect until it was too late: 'The different undertakings made to the consuls by the *vali* were not generally adhered to. The Rizé regiment, which was meant to arrive the following day, did not enter the city until 11 October, three days after the massacres.'

Defence of the Armenians

When the *vali* threatened to further inflame the tensions in the community by requesting the help of prominent figures in the police investigation into the attack of 2 October, Cillière was unable—despite his efforts at both official and personal levels—to stop him. Suspicious marks appeared on some Christian houses, with a cholera epidemic used as an excuse. Menacing gangs of outsiders began to form. Cillière demanded an inquiry, to no effect. On the night of 8 October, the slaughter took place. Cillière was in the city when the massacre began. As the scale of the disaster dawned on him, he paced the city's streets amid the general panic and violent bloodshed, searching at the risk of his own life for a refuge that was secure enough to withstand the attacks. The only places he could now depend on to offer shelter and sustenance to survivors of the massacre were a handful of religious institutions, and in particular the Capuchin monastery. He used the few means available to him to raise the alert outside the city, and to send a warning to his friend Fernand Roque-Ferrier, who was also in Trebizond at the time. It is impossible to read his reports without wondering how he found the courage to rush through the city streets knocking on any door that might open, or to interpret the indications of an unfolding massacre in a context that was clearly designed to terrorize the

ALPHONSE CILLIÈRE (1861–1946)

Armenians and generate panic on all sides. Within the space of a few hours that day, out of an Armenian community of 6,000 and a total city population of 35,000, nearly 2,000 people were massacred.

A warning to civil society

On his return to France in 1925, Cillière retired to Aix-en-Provence, where he devoted himself to writing up, or more precisely rewriting, the notes he had made at the time of the massacres. In 1929, on the 'advice of wise friends', he decided to type up all his reports under the title *Vêpres arméniennes: Les massacres de Trébizonde de 1895*. As he notes in his foreword, these friends had 'impressed upon me the interest there would be in shedding as much light as possible on an event the consequences of which, both immediate and far-reaching, continue to intensify its gravity, and that for the Armenian nation marked the beginning of an era of tremendous sufferings'.

Cillière also published the memoirs of Pierre Loti (in fact his collected unpublished letters) in the *Revue de France* in 1934 and wrote an unpublished article on Roque-Ferrier, his childhood friend from Montpellier who initiated the law enshrining the 'right to intervene'. His only other writings were translations of two Turkish comedies by Mirza Feth-Ali Akhond-Zadé, which showed the depth of his interest in Turkish culture and its humanist expressions.

Anyone reading his reports today might wonder why he waited so long—thirty-five years—to bear witness. He justified the long delay by the fact that the protagonists were now dead, and he could therefore speak freely, since his hands were no longer tied by either his official role or the implications for the individuals involved. More than just an explanation of the events, they form a political narrative that offers a subtle analysis of the effects of international vacillations on a regime in decline, battling against reforms imposed from outside in order to hang on to its own crumbling power. Further, he describes the collapse of a community and the overthrow of a stable, organized and established world in a killing frenzy that utterly destroyed the prosperity of a city and an entire region: 'Although the truth may now be known in its broad outlines, it is still useful to shed more light on it, to clarify many points, to highlight certain individuals.'

Indeed, Cillière did not hesitate to draw attention to the duplicity of Kadri Bey, governor general of Trebizond, 'who could and should have prevented the massacres' but did not, while at the same time citing the courage of Essad Bey, president of the criminal court, who paid for his bravery with his career. In his conclusion, he was clear that responsibility lay with Abdul Hamid II, whose policies 'unleashed the massacres', but also personally with Kadri Bey.

After serving as French consul in Trebizond from 1894 to 1897, Cillière had a long career in the Ottoman Empire until it entered the First World War on the side of the Triple Alliance in late 1914: he was French consul in Salonica in 1897 and in Constantinople in 1898, before being promoted to the rank of consul general in 1902. In 1912, he was posted to Port-au-Prince in Haiti as minister plenipotentiary and envoy extraordinary. In 1914, he was seconded to the finance department of the Ottoman government. From December 1918 to October 1925, he was president of the Inter-Allied Commission. For his contribution to the drawing up of texts defining the status of Allied nationals and confirming the repeal of the Turkish Capitulations, he was promoted to officer of the Légion d'Honneur in 1909 and commander in 1925.

Sources and further reading

Sources

Cillière, Alphonse, 'Vêpres arméniennes: Les massacres de Trébizonde du 8 octobre 1895; Notes et impressions d'un témoin', in Gérard Dédéyan, Claire Mouradian and Yves Ternon (eds), *1895, Massacre des Arméniens*, Toulouse: Éditions Privat, 2010.

Dossier no. 358, Archives du ministère des Affaires étrangères, personnel, 2e série, concerning Alphonse Cillière.

Studies

Dédéyan, Gérard, 'Un aperçu des contacts arméno-languedociens début XIVe–début XXe siècle)', in Asso, Demirdjian and Louvier, *Exprimer le génocide des Arméniens*, pp. 27–50; Dédéyan, 'Introduction', in Dédéyan, Mouradian and Ternon, *1895, Massacre des Arméniens*, pp. 13–24.

Duclert, Vincent, 'Aux sources du premier génocide contemporain: Nouveaux documents sur les grands massacres arméniens dans l'Empire ottoman (1894–1896)', *Problèmes internationaux*, *Cahiers Jaurès*, 3–4, nos. 201–2 (2011), pp. 197–218.

Ternon, Yves, 'La politique du sultan', in Dédéyan, Mouradian and Ternon, *1895, Massacre des Arméniens*, pp. 25–35.

6

ESSAD BEY

Forerunner of the Muslim righteous of 1915–16

Since the only known source on Essad Bey is Alphonse Cillière's *Vêpres arméniennes: Les massacres de Trébizonde du 8 octobre 1895; Notes et impressions d'un témoin*, this entry follows Cillière's text very closely and in places summarizes it.

A Caucasian exile

At the time of the Hamidian massacres of the Armenians in the Ottoman Empire, Essad Bey was president of the criminal court in Trebizond. His full name and life story remain unknown. The first-hand accounts we have of this magistrate are essentially those of Cillière, who knew him when he was French consul in Trebizond, but his descriptions of this 'impartial' and 'cultivated' individual are confirmed by Armenian sources.

Essad Bey—possibly a Dagestani—was born in what is now Shamakhi (then in the Russian Caucasus, now in Azerbaijan) and emigrated to Turkey when the tsarist empire conquered the region. Like many other Caucasian Muslim exiles, he entered the service of the sultan, working his way up through the magistracy. It is possible that he mixed with Armenians—who had their own local dialect—in his native city. But because of his forced exile it would have been equally possible for him to have nursed deep feelings of resentment towards Christians of all persuasions.

A man of learning, he had a wide-ranging knowledge of oriental cultures, although Russian was his only European language. 'A devout Muslim as well as a liberal', he sympathized with the Christian population. A man of integrity, he supported the principle of an impartial and independent judiciary. More than once he had to deal with attempts at interference in cases he was hearing by prominent Muslims, local governors and the Yıldız Palace of Abdul Hamid. On such occasions, modest but rigorous, he would always persist in carrying out his duties as a magistrate. This quiet persistence was to cost him his career.

A fair and honest magistrate

In the spirit of his customary humanity and benevolence, during the Trebizond massacres of October 1895, Essad Bey gave refuge to a number of Armenians in his own house, so saving them from certain death.

During his career as a magistrate, Essad Bey was president of the criminal court in Trebizond for four years and was then posted to Adrianople (present-day Edirne) before being sent back to Trebizond. This second posting, which already had a hint of exile about it, came to an abrupt end when he was arrested a few years later. A few examples from contemporary reports attest to the honesty and fair-mindedness with which he exercised his judicial powers.

During his first appointment as president of the criminal court in Trebizond, Essad Bey was called on to give a ruling in a case involving an extremely wealthy Turkish dignitary and an Armenian merchant. Despite 'the most vigorous approaches and attempts at influence', he displayed his usual impartiality and ruled in favour of the Armenian merchant, so earning the hostility of the Turkish dignitary and the annoyance of the authorities. Whenever funds in the *vilayet* were low, it transpired, the *vali* Kadri Bey was in the habit of appealing to the wealthy Turk, who would regularly advance him large sums of money. This fair and honest magistrate was a nuisance. A few years later, this affair was to spawn the shameless machinations that were to put an end to Essad Bey's career.

At Adrianople, Essad Bey presided over a case in which the accused were Armenians. At the behest of the palace, pressure was brought to bear on him by the *vali*, Abdur Rahman Pasha, to hand down a judgement that 'went against his conscience'. Recalled to

Constantinople, he lodged a protest against this infringement of the law and put in a request for retirement. His request fell on deaf ears; instead, he was sent back to Trebizond to take up 'an office that he had already occupied once before', in 'a roundabout and hypocritical rebuke' that he had no choice but to endure.

The sensitive trial of the Sassoun accused

In June 1894, when Essad Bey had succeeded Hamdi Bey as president of the criminal court at Trebizond, a highly sensitive case came up before the court. A few months earlier, seventeen Armenians had been arrested in Sassoun and charged with belonging to a revolutionary secret society. Set against a highly volatile background (there had been massacres of Armenians in Anatolia that summer), the trial took on a particularly grave significance.

The prosecution of the case, handled in Sassoun, was aggressive: the witnesses called during the hearing appeared to be 'agents provocateurs' who 'played into the hands of the police'. In this tense atmosphere, Essad Bey courageously gave the accused the freedom to defend themselves and testify to the torture they had suffered at the hands of the police. At the same time, the court also heard the testimony of the *zaptieh* (gendarmes) who were accused of this brutality. Although there was not enough material evidence to ensure the police were punished in any way, the defendants' testimony made a powerful impression. Given the context of the times, the final verdict was relatively lenient towards the Armenians: twelve of them were acquitted, while the remaining five were sentenced to prison terms of between five and fifteen years. 'It was impossible to acquit them all, in the light of the limited but specific confession of the principal accused', Adom Aslanian, but nonetheless the decision tended in principle towards a spirit of reconciliation.

The Trebizond massacres: 'a duty of humanity'

In late 1894 and during the course of 1895, a number of events shook the relative calm enjoyed hitherto by the people of Trebizond. Here and throughout Anatolia, feelings of resentment among the Muslim population were whipped up and inflamed by the Ottoman authorities, culminating in premeditated and orchestrated massacres in the 'Armenian' *vilayets* in late 1895.

During the slaughter of the Armenians of Trebizond on 8 October 1895, 'a handful of Muslims, all too rare but all the more worthy of praise', came to the aid of the victims. Cillière gave a moving account of Essad Bey's response to these tragic events:

> It was the president of the criminal court, Essad Bey, who showed most nobility in carrying out the duty of humanity. He did so in all simplicity, as he did everything. Elderly and then in poor health, he went out into the street to drag wretched Armenians from the hands of their assailants and take them to his house. Others he took to the monks, to whom he made repeated visits, lavishing consolations and encouragement on the refugees.

On the afternoon of that day of bloodshed, the *vali* sent Essad Bey to present his apologies to Cillière. This was the first proper discussion between the two men. In recalling his conversation with Essad Bey, Cillière was struck by 'the clarity with which he condemned the shameful events' and 'the sincerity that emanated from his words and his presence'.

Essad Bey's integrity and honesty earned him enemies who were to cost him his career. On the feast of the Epiphany in January 1896, he was getting ready to visit some Christians (who were among the friendships he maintained in both the Greek and the Armenian communities) when a strange figure in a mullah's robes appeared at his door. Reproaching him for his friendships with 'the infidel', the man accused him of blaspheming against Islam. News of the accusation was carried to Constantinople. It was in fact a plot, fomented by the wealthy Turk who regularly bailed out the *vilayet*'s finances, and covered up by the *vali* Kadri Bey:

> Essad Bey stood in the way of interests that were of the greatest importance to the *vali*. He was sacrificed. The consular staff, who held Essad Bey in the highest regard, made interventions at ambassadorial level in defence of the magistrate. The affair was referred to the court of appeal, and while awaiting the court's verdict Essad Bey was not recalled to Constantinople.

Soon after this, however, more false and grotesque accusations were levelled at him, when he was accused of spreading panic and alarm among the Christian community. Clearly nothing could have been further from the truth, as he did everything he could to reassure them. One morning, the news spread that Essad Bey had been arrested and sent by sea to Constantinople. The circumstances of his arrest were shameful: 'An officer of the gendarmerie of the most abhorrent reputation' was arrested and expelled from the city at the same time as him, and 'this measure that struck equally at two men who had nothing in common had something appalling and offensive about it'.

This coup against him had a profound effect on Essad Bey, who now wanted only to retire. Once again, the consular staff who had just intervened in his support came to Constantinople to support him 'with an intervention that was at once discreet and powerful'.

Cillière, who met Essad Bey again a few years later when he was posted to Constantinople, described him as a 'simple, honest and courageous' man for whom he had a 'high and most affectionate regard'. An exemplary magistrate who during the Hamidian massacres put his own life at risk and fatally compromised his career, Essad Bey appears to us to be a true forerunner of the Righteous Muslims of the Armenian genocide.

Sources and further reading

Sources

Cillière, Alphonse, reports in Dédéyan, Mouradian and Ternon, *1895, Massacre des Arméniens*, pp. 37–226.

Studies

Dédéyan, Gérard, 'Introduction', in Dédéyan, Mouradian and Ternon, *1895, Massacre des Arméniens*, pp. 13–24.
Duclert, 'Aux sources du premier génocide contemporain', pp. 197–218.
'Notes d'Alphonse Cillière et de Claire Mouradian', in Dédéyan, Mouradian and Ternon, *1895, Massacre des Arméniens*, pp. 235–65.
Ternon, Yves, 'Contre-enquête', in Dédéyan, Mouradian and Ternon, *1895, Massacre des Arméniens*, pp. 229–33; Ternon, 'La politique du Sultan', in Dédéyan, Mouradian and Ternon, *1895, Massacre des Arméniens*, pp. 25–35.

7

ROSE LAMBERT (1878–1974)

Compassionate evangelism

Rose Lambert was born on 8 September 1878 in Pennsylvania, where her father was a Mennonite Brethren minister. After working briefly as a teacher in Indiana, she was inspired by her faith and her desire to help others to become a missionary working among the Armenians of the Ottoman Empire. In 1898, she left America for Hadjin in Cilicia, to look after children orphaned by the Hamidian massacres.

From Mersin, where her ship docked, she endured a gruelling journey inland to Hadjin, on which her caravan of missionaries was escorted by a Turkish guard in order to deter the robbers that infested the region. Although the Americans were considered as honoured guests in the khans where they made overnight stops, conditions on the journey were harsh. Lambert recalled that their bedding was invariably 'thickly populated with the contemptible little flea', so that rising well before dawn came as a relief. On the way to Hadjin, she and her companions met some Armenians, and she very quickly gained an idea of the scale of the discrimination they were forced to endure.

On her arrival in Hadjin, she found 'an Armenian town with a population of about 20,000', where 'the Turkish population consists of only about sixty families beside the officials and the standing army'. She helped to set up the orphanage there, and ten years later, in 1908, many of the young men were able to support themselves and many of the girls were married. But 'at this time still nearly 300 orphans were being fed, clothed and educated', a mission to which she devoted herself tirelessly.

THE RIGHTEOUS AND PEOPLE OF CONSCIENCE

The Armenians were subjected to a regime that was unjust in the extreme: 'The Turkish officers treated ... the Armenians always as inferiors and the poorest Mohammedan beggar thanked "Allah" (God) that he was one of those who were "resigned to God" and not an unbelieving "Ghavour" (Christian).'

On 26 July 1908, news reached Hadjin that liberty, justice, equality and fraternity had been proclaimed. The Armenian population, suddenly sensing freedom, rushed to do everything that had hitherto been forbidden to them, which caused alarm among some of the Turkish leaders, who were used to considering them as *dhimmi* (protected) and hence of inferior status. The harvest had been bad that year, and between 3,000 and 5,000 men left the town to work on the plain, many of them taking their families with them and so setting up numerous Armenian villages in the environs of Hadjin.

A few months later, in April 1909, news of the Adana massacres reached Hadjin. Although the town was peaceful, it was attacked and besieged by the local villagers but managed to resist. Lambert devoted herself to helping the people, using every means at her disposal to alert the outside world and get help. She also learned of the massacre of a large delegation of her missionary colleagues on the way to a conference at Adana. More or less impregnable because of its geographical position, the town was saved in extremis by a Turkish regiment under the command of Lütfi Bey, who in order to persuade his soldiers to follow his orders promised them that once they had lifted the siege they could loot the town, a promise that this humane commander failed to keep.

With the regiment came appalling news from the plain:

> Scarcely had the regiment arrived when news reached us of the awful massacre on the plain. Many Christian villages were completely wiped out and not one Armenian left alive. ... Widows and orphans by the hundreds came flocking back to Hadjin and the villages about us, from the plain, bereft of beloved ones, many of whom had been brutally massacred before their eyes. They were penniless, ragged, barefooted, sick, pale and almost beyond recognition, the mothers, wives, sisters and daughters of the three thousand Hadjin men who had been massacred on the plain.

ROSE LAMBERT (1878–1974)

It was to the missionaries that the widows and orphans came to seek help and to tell of the atrocities they had witnessed. Following the massacres, martial law was declared. According to Lambert's account, the killers had little trouble securing pardons, whereas seventy of the defenders of Hadjin were imprisoned and some were tortured.

Lambert continued her missionary work until 1910, when she returned to America. The following year, she married a Texas rancher, with whom she had five children. She died in 1974, at the age of ninety-six.

In addition to her work with the widows and children, Lambert's account also sheds light on the unfolding of the Cilician massacres, and clearly shows that—contrary to the official account seeking to indemnify the killers—there were no Armenian uprisings.

In a letter to Lambert, the Armenian patriarch of Constantinople, Yeghishe Tourian, paid tribute to her: 'You helped in such a way as to endanger your own life, and by so doing have comforted thousands of the unfortunate ones during their bitter and hard affliction. ... Your name and nobility will ever remain unforgotten in our annals.'

Sources and further reading

Sources

Lambert, Rose, *Hadjin and the Armenian Massacres*, New York: Fleming H. Revell Co., 1911.

The Vinton Books, vol. 4, *Addenda 1885–1910*, Boston, MA: Congregational Library and Archives, History Matters, 1910.

Studies

Demirdjian, Héléna (trans.), preface to Rose Lambert, *Hadjine et le massacre des Arméniens*, Chamigny: Le cercle d'écrits caucasiens, 2009.

THE OTTOMAN RIGHTEOUS

8

THE MUSLIM RIGHTEOUS?

Reflections on a denomination: Religion, compassion and social justice

Among those who came to the aid of the Armenians during the genocide of 1915 were a number of Muslims, whether Ottoman, Turkish or of other nationalities. Here we shall look at some of them in detail. The Turks and non-Turks who tried to alleviate the sufferings of the Armenians did so for a variety of different motives. In many cases, Muslim subjects of the Ottoman Empire found that their moral conscience could not accept the barbarity inflicted on their Armenian fellow citizens, with whom many of them were linked by ties of friendship or good neighbourliness. Admittedly, they may also have been tempted by the financial or economic advantage they could expect from saving the Armenians, the criteria of humanitarianism and of personal interest frequently being closely intertwined, and possibly especially so in the relatively unsophisticated culture of the empire's tribes and clans.

Studies of the sufferings of the Armenians tend to focus on these motivating factors. Yet there is another one that was crucial on a different level and that is often overlooked: respect for the tenets of Islam, to which most Turks retained an attachment, despite the lack of belief and even atheism among the Young Turks and the lengths to which they went to foster antagonism between Turks and Armenians. Islam advocated social justice—*'adâla*—in relations between the inhabitants of *Dar al-Islâm* (lands in which Islam and Islamic law prevailed). In its strictest legal definition, as noted by the great Lebanese jurist Émile Tyan, *'adâla* is 'a state of religious and moral perfection'. On a more modest level, it 'simply describes someone who is generally obedient to moral and religious law'. The Young Turks did nothing to take into account the codification of the law carried out in the Ottoman Empire around the mid-nineteenth century, under Sultan Abdülaziz (ruled 1861–76), in the midst of the period of reforms (Tanzimat) enacted from 1839 to 1876. 'The *'adl* individual is one whose good actions prevail over the bad', or a 'person of good morals', according to Article 1705 of the Mecelle, the monumental civil code of Islamic law drawn up by a team of legal scholars headed by the distinguished jurist Cevdet Pasha, which set out to codify the Sharia-based law of the Islamic empire. According to the historian Paul Dumont, the civil code it created formed a 'worthy Islamic pendant to the Napoleonic Code and its various avatars'.

Faced with the scale of the persecutions inflicted on them with the underlying agenda of denying them the right to Ottoman citizenship, Armenians could in principle invoke their status as *dhimmi*. A *dhimmi* (from the word *dhimma*, meaning a contract to protect) was a 'protected person', usually from the monotheistic religions of Judaism and Christianity, or 'People of the Book'. In return for being granted freedom of worship and a degree of autonomy in their institutions, *dhimmi* were required to pay taxes from which Muslims were exempt and to accept a range of restrictions in their daily lives. As a 'protected people', they were entitled to protection against attacks on their rights within the Ottoman Empire. Every good Muslim knew the words of the hadith of the Prophet Muhammad, as reported by his Companions, which declares: 'Whosoever shall kill a *Mu'ahid* [a person who is granted the pledge of protection by the Muslims] shall not smell the fragrance of Paradise, though its fragrance may be scented from forty years' walk away.'

The right of *dhimmi* to protection implied, in the unanimous opinion of Islamic legal scholars, the protection of their persons, their property and their honour. The American missionary Henry H. Riggs observed this belief in action:

> There were many Moslems, however, of a very different type. A large part of the better class looked with genuine horror at the treatment accorded to the Armenians, and when it came to enriching themselves as a result of the sufferings of the poor victims, they would not do it. Many Turks at the time refused to have even a

legitimate share in the booty, and made it their boast afterwards that they had not a single article in their homes that had belonged to the Armenians. They regarded such goods, however legitimately bought, as 'Haram' (Forbidden) and considered that they would bring them a curse instead of a blessing.

Another American missionary, Bertha Morley, wrote in her *Diaries* that in the face of the massacres that accompanied the deportations, many Turks were adamant that neither they nor their religion could be the instigators of such appalling deeds, and that responsibility could lie only with Germany and Christianity. Apparently, these Turks were unmoved by the official campaign to demonize the Armenians at the time, remaining stubbornly attached to the teachings of their religion despite all the Young Turks' efforts to lure them away.

The Danish missionary Maria Jacobsen reported in her own *Diaries* that an elderly sheikh in Kharpert threw himself at the feet of the provincial governor, begging him to end the persecution of the Armenians and protesting that enough was enough, the innocent should be freed, and that the Koran forbade such cruelty. The *vali* declared solemnly that this was true and that the persecutions should stop, but took no action to ensure that they did.

Of the officers in the Turkish army and officials of the Ottoman administration who helped the Armenians, many did so without seeking any personal benefit of any kind. While some accepted bribes to allow Armenians to slip through the net during round-ups, sooner or later the victims would be sent to their deaths, having run out of means to buy off their executioners.

While some corrupt officials made false claims to have rescued Armenians, this should not detract in any way from the altruism and courage of those who dared to come to the aid of their Armenian fellow citizens, so sacrificing their careers and putting their lives in peril. Since very few of them left written accounts of their actions, in most cases we know of them only through the accounts of those whom they saved, either at first hand or through their descendants.

One important consideration, as Raymond Kévorkian demonstrates, was the fact that a large section of the Muslim population discovered that their immediate interests were adversely affected by the deportation of the Armenians, since they were suddenly deprived of the services of doctors, pharmacists, artisans and the like, and they were concerned about the collapse of economic activity in their regions. Some provincial dignitaries were apparently aware that the eradication of the Armenians would unleash a major economic crisis and complained about the fact. This led some to react by protecting the Armenians, either because they were neighbours or friends, or to ensure economic stability. The hostile attitude of some Muslims to the CUP directives prompted Mahmud Kâmil, commander of the Third Army, to send a coded telegram from his headquarters at Tortum on 10 July 1915, which was circulated to the governors of the *vilayets* of Sivas, Trebizond, Van, Mamuret ul-Aziz, Diyarbekir and Bitlis. As Kévorkian emphasizes, the text of the telegram was of critical importance:

> We have learned that, in certain villages the population of which has been sent to the interior, certain [elements] of the Muslim population have given Armenians shelter in their homes. Since this is a violation of government orders, heads of households who shelter or protect Armenians are to be executed in front of their houses and it is imperative that their houses be burned down. This order shall be transmitted in appropriate fashion and communicated to whom it may concern. See to it that no as yet undeported Armenian remains behind and inform us of the action you have taken.

In her deeply considered contribution to *Resisting Genocide: The Multiple Forms of Rescue*, published in English in 2011, Fatma Müge Göçek, Turkish-born professor of history at the University of Michigan, argued that although the science and rationalism of the Enlightenment had taken the place of the sacred, the origin of the idea of the 'Righteous', as it has emerged in the West, is grounded in the Judeo-Christian religious tradition. She argues that the refusal of Turkish (or Kurdish or Arab) Muslims to kill Armenians who had not failed to fulfil their obligations to the Ottoman state was justified by the concept of Islamic (and Ottoman) justice, *'adâla* in Arabic, or *adalet* in Ottoman or modern Turkish:

> This concept differs from the Judeo-Christian concept of 'righteousness'. Governance of the Ottoman Empire and its entire judicial system was based on the Muslim notion of *'adâla*, which constitutes

the framework within which Muslims judge human conduct as 'just' or 'unjust'. This was the frame of reference within which Ottoman subjects acted benevolently towards the Armenians and resisted the destructive, 'unjust' orders of the CUP. A difference from the Judeo-Christian notion of 'righteous conduct' is that Muslims do not act in accordance with the principle of the supreme value of humanity but in accordance with the principles of Islam.

By these principles Allah commanded them to respect the duty of protection towards the *dhimmis*, as long as the latter fulfilled their obligations towards the state. This, in principle, provided the foundation for the actions of the Muslim Righteous who opposed the massacres of the Armenians. An alternative concept—a corruption of the spirit of the Enlightenment—emerged in 1915, according to which true justice was embodied by the interests of the state.

It thus took Ottoman subjects a great deal of courage and religious conviction to make an open stand against the government policy of exterminating the Armenians, especially in wartime, when even minor breaches of the law were punishable by death.

Göçek's assessment of the protection that their *dhimmi* status afforded the Christians of the Ottoman Empire requires some qualification, however. In recruiting leading Ottoman clerics to support their plan to annihilate the Armenians, the Young Turks predicated the project, as Igor Dorfmann-Lazarev has shown, on the notion of holy war, or jihad (a term originally used to signify an internal striving towards moral and religious perfection, or a form of asceticism), and in an empire in which over three-quarters of the Muslim population was illiterate, this could only rekindle—and distort—religious zeal.

Upon the outbreak of war against Russia in November 1915, Sheikh-ul-Islam Mustafa Hayri Bey, advisor to Sultan Mehmet V (ruled 1909–18) and the highest authority on the interpretation of Islamic law within the Ottoman Empire, proclaimed a jihad against 'enemies who had committed acts of aggression against Islam and Muslim territories' and who 'were holding the Muslim populations of these lands prisoner'. The fatwa (the precise interpretation by an Islamic jurist of the law in a specific case) identified these enemies, who, as Dorfmann-Lazarev explains, were described as adversaries of Islam, as Russia, Great Britain and France. Muslims who refused to take part in the jihad were threatened with divine punishment. On 23 November 1915, the proclamation of the jihad was ratified by the sultan—closely controlled by the CUP—who was also caliph, and by the Senior Council of Ulema (Council of Senior Scholars). The call—all the more urgent now that the Ottoman Empire had lost most of its Balkan possessions to the Christian powers—was also addressed to the Muslims of the Caucasus, Iran and Central Asia. All of these regions had Armenian populations.

While Armenians living in *Dar al-Islam* and benefitting from *dhimmi* status were not in principle involved in the war, very soon they were brought into it by a legal sleight of hand. The regions in which they lived were declared frontier zones (*al-thoughoûr*), a legal definition that for Muslims involved obeying the legal duty of 'defensive jihad' and permitted the use of any means to defend them, however extreme. To the great cost of the Armenians, these means included totally unfounded accusations of collusion with the enemy.

The holy war was proclaimed from every mosque and in all the various languages of the Ottoman Empire, even including French. The notion of a jihad was strengthened by the fact that many recruits to the Special Organization were *muhajirs* (émigrés) who had returned from regions of the Balkans and the Caucasus that had just been conquered by Christian powers. This concept of the Hijra, or emigration, had its origins in the Hegira or journey of the Prophet Muhammad and his followers to Medina in 622, there to wage a holy war against the enemies of the new religion of Islam, and in particular against the dignitaries of Mecca.

Following this logic of the jihad, all the Christians of the Ottoman Empire were targeted, without exception. Thus a genocide that had initially been aimed only at the Armenians—whose huge presence in both Ottoman and Russian Armenia presented an obstacle to the racial project of Pan-Turkism, uniting the Turks in Anatolia, the Caucasus and Central Asia—spread to include Syriacs of all faiths, and later Greeks.

Sources and further reading

Sources

Jacobsen, Marie, *Diaries of a Danish Missionary, Harpout 1907–1919*, Ann Arbor: Taderon Press, Gomidas Institute, 2001, pp. 76, 88.

THE MUSLIM RIGHTEOUS?

Morley, Bertha, *Marsovan 1915: The Diaries of Bertha Morley*, ed. Hilmar Kaiser, Ann Arbor, MI: Taderon Press, Gomidas Institute, 2000, p. 24.

Riggs, Henry H., *Days of Tragedy in Armenia*, Ann Arbor, MI: Gomidas Institute, 1997, pp. 85–6.

Studies

Donikian, Denis, 'Justes et attitudes justes (1), (2)', in Denis Donikian, *Petite encyclopédie du génocide arménien (Medz Yeghern)* (preface by Ragip Zarakolu), Paris: Geuthner, 2021, pp. 264–5.

Dorfmann-Lazarev, Igor, 'Le génocide des Arméniens dans l'empire ottoman', *Istina*, 1 (January–March 2001), pp. 32–47; Dorfmann-Lazarev, 'Nazionalismo e religione nelle dinamica del genocidio degli Armeni (1915–1016)', in F. Berti and F. Cortese (eds), *Il crimine dei crimini: Stermini di massa nel Novecento*, Milan: Franco Angeli Edizioni, 2008, pp. 64–84.

Dumont, Paul, 'La période des Tanzîmât (1839–1878)', in Robert Mantran (ed.), *Histoire de l'Empire ottoman*, Paris: Fayard, 1989, pp. 459–522.

Göçek, Fatma Müge, 'In Search of the "Righteous People": The Case of the Armenian Massacres of 1915', in Claire Andrieu, Sarah Gensburger and Jacques Sémelin (eds), *Resisting Genocide: The Multiple Forms of Rescue*, London: Hurst and CERI/Sciences Po, 2011, pp. 33–50.

Kévorkian, Raymond, 'Ottoman Officials against the Armenian Genocide: A Comparative Approach to Turkish Towns', in Andrieu, Gensburger and Sémelin, *Resisting Genocide*, pp. 183–200.

9

GOVERNMENT OFFICIALS

Senior Ottoman officials who refused to take part in the annihilation of the Armenians

Ottoman subjects who came to the aid of the Armenians during the genocide, whether senior government officials or ordinary citizens, were shamed and treated as traitors by their fellow citizens both before and after the Armistice, and subsequently under Mustafa Kemal Atatürk as president of the Republic of Turkey from 1923 to 1938. They left few traces, and the little that was published about them was in Turkish and so remained virtually unknown in the West.

This all changed in 2015 with the publication by the International Raoul Wallenberg Foundation of a report entitled 'Turkish Rescuers: Turks Who Reached Out to Armenians in 1915', written and researched by Burçin Gerçek under the supervision of the historian Taner Akçam, with transcription of Ottoman archive documents by Ömer Türkoglu. The report not only lists the names of those who were courageous enough to come to the aid of the Armenians but also shines a bright light on the lives of the Righteous and of the men and women in the Ottoman Empire who acted according to their conscience at the time of the Armenian genocide.

The assassination of Archduke Franz Ferdinand in Sarajevo on 28 June 1914 stoked acute international tensions and prompted a flurry of alliances among the Great Powers in anticipation of the war that now seemed unavoidable. On 28 July, the day that Austria–Hungary declared war on Serbia, Germany and the Ottoman Empire embarked on a round of intense negotiations that culminated a few days later in a written accord. Now the Ottoman Empire was officially at war with Russia, Great Britain and France. And so the Armenians of the empire lost potential friends.

During the nineteenth century, the Ottoman Empire had been divided into provinces called *vilayets*. The six easternmost *vilayets*—Sivas, Trebizond, Van, Mamuret-ul-Aziz, Diyarbekir and Bitlis—were together known as the 'Armenian provinces' because of the size of their Armenian populations, who dwelt side by side with Muslims and sometimes Syriacs (who were Christians of various confessions). Each *vilayet* was governed by a *vali* and was subdivided into districts called *sanjaks*, each *sanjak* being governed by a district chief or *mutasarrif*. Sanjaks were further subdivided into cantons or *kaza*, each *kaza* being under the authority of a *kaymakam*. The *kaza*, finally, was divided into *nahiye* (communes) under the leadership of a *müdir*.

The members of the CUP, who believed that a war might be a way of ending the endemic weaknesses of the empire, were prepared for a general conflagration in the expectation of being able to turn it to their own advantage. First they cast a general suspicion of collective disloyalty over the Ottoman Armenian community and placed its leaders under police surveillance. Then, following mobilization, requisitions and looting, they set up gangs of thugs and criminals under the orders of Dr Bahaeddin Şakir, whose job was to perpetrate the crimes that the CUP wanted done but that army officers might be reluctant to carry out. Among the criminals recruited to carry out this dirty work were Alo, a brigand from the Zaza people, who spoke their own language related to Iranian, and a Chechen from the North Caucasus called Hamid, both of whom were to play a notorious part in the deportations.

Everything was now in place: all the CUP were waiting for were the right circumstances that would allow them to unleash their plan to slaughter the Armenians and get rid of them for good. The required pretext came with Russia's victory over Turkey at the Battle of Sarikamiş (22 December 1914–16 January 1915) and the British, Australian, New Zealand and French naval offensive in the Dardanelles from February 1915. Armenian police officers and government employees in the provinces of Erzurum, Bitlis and Van, the frontier zone with the Russian Empire, were dismissed from their posts.

GOVERNMENT OFFICIALS

In February 1915, the homes of Christians were searched, and Armenian and other Christian soldiers were disarmed and forced into hard labour battalions. Other Armenians were imprisoned and tortured. Armenian newspapers were banned and printing works confiscated.

Everything was now ready for sending the Armenians to certain death. Those who did not die of starvation or thirst on the marches to their purported exile, or who managed to survive the massacres carried out by gangs of armed thugs, would find when they reached their destination that they were condemned to perish for lack of the basic means of survival.

10

HAMID BEY (d.1919)

Vali of Diyarbekir

Among those who presented unexpected obstacles to this murderous plan was Hamid Bey, *vali* of Diyarbekir, who was fearless in making his position uncompromisingly clear: 'I will have no part in this lawlessness.'

Appointed to the governorship of Diyarbekir on 7 October 1914, Hamid Bey remained in post until March 1915, when he was replaced by Dr Mehmed Reshid. A graduate of the Imperial Military School of Medicine and one of the original founders of the CUP, Reshid was hostile to the Armenians and ruthless in exterminating them.

Hamid arrived in Diyarbekir with a reputation for scrupulous honesty in his previous posts. Following his appointment as *vali*, he lost no time in addressing the case of a fire that had broken out in a grain market and that had been followed by general looting, as Muslim merchants ransacked Christian-owned shops with impunity before setting fire to them. A huge blaze ensued, and no genuine attempts were made to fight it.

Hamid Bey was convinced that Memduh Bey, the chief of police and a CUP loyalist, had cleared the way for the looters and incited the fire in the bazaar. He dismissed him from his post, so sending a clear signal that he would have no part in the deportations, the prelude to the massacres. But Memduh Bey was soon reinstated, following the intervention of the parliamentary deputy Feyzi. The uncle of Ziya Gökalp, champion of pan-Turanism, Feyzi viewed the prospect of the annihilation of the Armenians with equanimity and hoped to regain all the regions lost by the Ottoman Empire since the early nineteenth century. On 25 March 1915, Hamid Bey was removed from office in his turn, to be replaced by Reshid. Once the war was over, Reshid was arrested and imprisoned in Istanbul. Managing to escape from prison, he lived as a fugitive, moving from one hiding place to another until 1919, when he was tracked down by the police. On the verge of being recaptured, he committed suicide.

During his brief term as *vali* of Diyarbekir, from October 1914 to March 1915, Hamid Bey endeavoured to achieve the impossible in mitigating the violent attacks against Christians committed by Young Turks in the city. Under ferocious attack from Turkish extremists, he was forced to play down his efforts to protect the Armenians, declaring in his memoirs, 'I was neither friendly nor hostile towards the Armenians.' Made in response to the ultra-nationalist politics of the time, this statement is contradicted by letters and memoirs written by prominent Armenians, which testify that Hamid Bey saw the storm approaching and did everything in his power to protect the Armenians.

Ordered by Dr Reshid and carried out by his henchmen, the murders in June 1915 of two senior Ottoman government officials who had refused to obey orders to deport the Armenians, Ali Sabit Es-Süveydi, deputy *kaymakam* of Beşiri, and Hüseyin Nesimî, *kaymakam* of Lice, were proof—if proof were needed—of the ruthless cruelty of the CUP. Like the Young Turks who formed its membership, the CUP was not a government but, in Morgenthau's words, 'an irresponsible party, a kind of secret society, which, by intrigue, intimidation, and assassination, had obtained most of the offices of state'. When Dr Reshid and the other CUP leaders were brought to justice after the First World War, the murders of Nesimî and Es-Süveydi were high on the list of crimes of which they were accused.

Hamid Bey gave evidence at their trial, testifying that the two *kaymakams* had been slaughtered because they were opposed to the deportation of the Armenians. After the Armistice, Hamid Bey found himself in opposition to Mustafa Kemal, at which point he attempted, as we have seen, to minimize his role in the inquiry into the murders. The only safety at this period lay in discretion, as was demonstrated by the case of Astik Effendi, a young Armenian graduate of the Ottoman School of Administration who had worked with

HAMID BEY (d.1919)

Hamid Bey and gained his highest respect. He had arrived in Diyarbekir in a pitiful condition in 1914, and to save him from deportation Hamid Bey had given him an administrative post. Once Hamid Bey had been dismissed from office, however, Astik Effendi was sent to Van, where he perished in 1915, aged twenty-six.

Sources and further reading

Studies

Kévorkian, Raymond, *The Armenian Genocide: A Complete History*, London: I. B. Tauris, 2011, pp. 320, 357.

Suny, Ronald Grigor, Fatma Müge Göçek and Norman M. Naimark, *A Question of Genocide: Armenians and Turks at the End of the Ottoman Empire*, Oxford: Oxford University Press, 2012, pp. 136–40.

11

HÜSEYIN NESIMÎ BEY (1868–1915)

Kaymakam of Lice, faithful to his religion

Hüseyin Nesimî Bey was born in 1868 at Girit in the province of Sivas. Imbued with the humanist principles of the Bektashi Sufi dervish order, which seem to have foreshadowed the Declaration of the Rights of Man, he himself prefigured the Turkish Righteous. Sufi philosophy was central to his life, and in it he saw a solution to the decline of the Ottoman Empire. Involved in revolutionary activities during his student days, he then distanced himself from politics before returning to favour and active politics once again. After a modest posting as a government official, he worked for himself in Constantinople.

In January 1915, he became mayor of Lice, the administrative centre of the *kaza* of the same name, a small town not far from Diyarbekir that counted among its population nearly 3,000 Armenians and some 2,000 Jacobite Syrian Christians. Another 3,000 or so Armenians were scattered throughout the mountains and valleys of the *kaza*. Hüseyin Nesimi's politics, always tinged with humanism, brought him into rapid and inevitable conflict with Dr Reshid Bey, who was appointed *vali* of Diyarbekir on 25 March 1915. When he received orders from Dr Reshid to exterminate the Armenians, he responded: 'I will have no part in this sin.' He then demanded a written order, meanwhile persisting in keeping the Armenian population in the town. In Nesimi's view, religious law allowed the killing only of those who were disloyal to the state and gave no sanction under any circumstances to the massacre of innocents. Initially, therefore, he felt in a position to delay the departure of the deportation convoys. Having been unable to prevent the departure of the first convoy, he even went so far as to accompany it in person in order to protect the Armenians from attacks by armed gangs. He also managed to save some of the Armenian women from deportation by arranging sham marriages with elderly Muslim men.

Nesimi's vision was very different from the secular and nationalist agenda of the Young Turks, who put the nation above all else. In his correspondence with Dr Reshid, he accused him of being as cruel as Genghis Khan. In response to Nesimi's refusal to carry out his orders, Reshid—who was known to be one of those responsible for the Special Organization, which not only oversaw the extermination of the Armenians but also the murders of Muslim officials who refused to obey government orders—summoned him to appear before him. He then dispatched his notoriously loyal Circassian bodyguard, Harun, to intercept Nesimî en route and kill him. Obeying his orders, on 15 June 1915, Harun threw Nesimi's lifeless body into a ditch near the village of Karaz. The spot subsequently became known as *Türbe-i-kaymakam*, or 'the mayor's grave'. Nesimi's body was never returned to his family.

Nesimi's fate is emblematic of that of the handful of Turkish government officials whose refusal to obey inhumane orders cost them their lives. In the Diyarbekir region, the mayors of Çermik, Savur, Silvan, Mardin, Midyat, Derik and Beşiri were dismissed from their posts, and the latter two were murdered. It also demonstrates how government denial of responsibility for the crimes went hand in glove with the murders themselves, as state propaganda accused Armenian rebels of committing the murder. Following Nesimi's death, the Armenians of Lice were deported and massacred.

Nesimî was not alone in putting up resistance to Reshid: there were many officials in the province who refused to obey his orders. But Reshid would stop at nothing to ensure the plan to exterminate the Armenians was carried out, including the elimination of officials who refused to cooperate. Following the murder of Nesimî, he sent another of his loyal henchmen, Ibrahim Bedreddin, to Lice to 'supervise' the massacre of the Armenians, starting with the massacre of the elite of the community and moving on to the decimation of the deportation convoys. In November 1918, as we have seen,

HÜSEYIN NESIMÎ BEY (1868–1915)

Reshid was arrested and imprisoned. While awaiting charges brought by the special tribunal set up after the Armistice, he managed to escape and go into hiding. He committed suicide in February 1919, when he was on the verge of being recaptured.

Following the proclamation of the Turkish Republic by Mustafa Kemal in 1923, Reshid was rehabilitated and declared a 'martyr'.

During preparations for the commemoration of the centenary of the Armenian genocide at the Free University of Brussels, a tribute was due to be paid to Hüseyin Nesimî Bey. The lawyer Grégoire Jakhian (son of Maître Édouard Jakhian, president of the Brussels Bar, whose dream it had been to give due credit to the Muslim Righteous who had protected Armenians during the genocide, many of them at the cost of their own lives) planned to arrange a meeting between the son of a woman saved by Hüseyin Nesimî Bey, to whom she had recently revealed the name of her rescuer, and Nesimi's grandson, who lived in Istanbul; at the last minute, unfortunately, the latter was forced to cancel his travel plans.

Sources and further reading

Sources

Nesimî, Abidin, *Yillarin Içinden*, Istanbul: Gözlem, 1977.

Studies

Göcek, Fatma Müge, 'In Search of the "Righteous People": The Case of the Armenian Massacres of 1915', in Andrieu, Gensburger and Sémelin, *Resisting Genocide*, pp. 61–9.

Kévorkian, *Armenian Genocide*, pp. 363, 368.

12

ALI SABIT ES-SÜVEYDI

Deputy kaymakam of Beşiri

Ali Sabit Es-Süveydi was appointed to serve as a member of the administration of Diyarbekir as a young graduate of twenty-one. In 1915, he was deputy *kaymakam* of Beşiri when the deportation of the Armenians was at its height. When he refused to have any part in this crime, Dr Reshid gave orders for his execution. The murder was carried out by Aziz the Circassian; the victim was just twenty-five.

When the authorities proved unwilling to carry out a proper investigation of the murder, it fell to the victim's brother Naci to investigate. For similar reasons, after the murder of the *kaymakam* of Lice, Hüseyin Nesimî, it was the victim's son, Abidin Nesimî, who led his own investigation. In both cases, the evidence pointed to Dr Reshid, *vali* of Diyarbekir.

When the CUP leaders were brought to justice in 1919, following the Armistice, the murder of Ali Sabit was among the crimes cited by the prosecution.

Sources and further reading

Gerçek, Burçin, 'Turkish Rescuers', The International Raoul Wallenberg Foundation, https://www.raoulwallenberg.net/wp-content/files_mf/1435335304ReportTurkishrescuerscomplete.pdf
Göçek, Fatma Müge, *Denial of Violence: Ottoman Past, Turkish Present, and Collective Violence against the Armenians; 1789–2009*, New York: Oxford University Press, 2015, *passim*.

13

HILMI BEY (d.1919)

Mutasarrif of Mardin, faithful to his religion

In 1914, on the eve of the genocide, the town of Mardin, in the heart of the Syriac region, counted among its population 12,609 Syrian Jacobite Christians and 7,692 Armenians, who were Arabic-speaking and mostly Catholic. Dr Mehmed Reshid, *vali* of Diyarbekir, was certain that Hilmi Bey, *mutasarrif* of Mardin from 30 November 1914, would refuse to obey his orders. He was all the more convinced when Hilmi Bey's deputy released several prominent Assyrians whom Reshid had accused of crimes that he knew they had not committed. Hilmi Bey himself had made contact with the Christians of Mardin, promising to help them when the storm that he saw approaching broke. It was thus clear that Hilmi Bey would prove to be an obstacle to the execution of Reshid's murderous plans.

In May 1915, Hilmi Bey refused to obey Reshid's orders to arrest and liquidate prominent members of Mardin's Christian community, declaring: 'I am not sufficiently lacking in conscience to be able to take part in the massacre of Ottoman citizens who, to the best of my knowledge, are innocent and loyal to the state.'

In response, Reshid sent a request to the authorities in Constantinople to dismiss Hilmi Bey. When he did not receive an immediate response, he ordered the chief of the Diyarbekir police to fabricate a witness statement accusing the Armenian Catholic archbishop of Mardin, Monsignor Ignatius Maloyan, of concealing weapons. While Hilmi Bey was absent on a journey, he used this false testimony as an excuse to arrest the archbishop and other prominent Christians. When Hilmi Bey returned, he was ordered to a new post at Hakkari, south-east of Lake Van. There was therefore nothing he could do. Two days later, Monsignor Maloyan and 410 Armenians were sent under escort to Diyarbekir and massacred on the way. Before he was killed, the archbishop cried out to his persecutors: 'We have never been disloyal to the state ... but if you want to force us to forsake our religion, that we will never do. Never!' He was beatified by Pope John Paul II on 7 October 2001.

Hilmi Bey could not countenance standing by and allowing Reshid to wipe out the Christians of Mardin. He decided to contact the German vice-consul in Mosul, Walter Holstein, and inform him that Reshid was attacking the Christians, and that 700 of them, including Archbishop Maloyan, had been massacred in a single night.

Holstein passed this information on to the German diplomatic mission in Constantinople, mentioning Hilmi Bey by name. The German ambassador, Hans von Wangenheim, in turn presented a note to Talaat Pasha, minister of the interior, in which Hilmi Bey's name and the charges of which he accused Dr Reshid were clearly spelt out. The persecution of the Armenians continued unabated, and Hilmi Bey was now even more of a thorn in the flesh to the CUP and other extremists.

After being dismissed from his post on 25 May 1915, Hilmi Bey served as *vali* of various eastern provinces before being appointed as governor of Eskişehir province in August 1919, then under British army control. After a brief period of conflict with Mustafa Kemal and his entourage, he was assassinated on 4 October 1919.

An inquiry was set up to investigate who was responsible for his murder and on whose orders; such was the lack of zeal on the part of its members, however, that it was not long before it was wound up.

Sources and further reading

Sources

de Courtois, Sébastien, *The Forgotten Genocide: Eastern Christians, the Last Arameans*, trans. Vincent Aurora, Piscataway, NJ: Gorgias Press, 2004, *passim*.

Studies

Kévorkian, *Armenian Genocide*, pp. 443–4, 454–6; Kévorkian, 'Ottoman

HILMI BEY (d.1919)

Officials against the Armenian Genocide', in Andrieu, Gensburger and Sémelin, *Resisting Genocide*, pp. 183–201.

Kiuciukian, Pietro, *I disobbedienti, Viaggio tra i giusti ottomani del genocido armeno* (preface by Marcello Flores), Milan: Guerini e associati, 2020, pp. 108–10.

Ternon, Yves, 'The Impossible Rescue of the Armenians of Mardin: The Sinjar Safe Haven', in Andrieu, Gensburger and Sémelin, *Resisting Genocide*, pp. 383–95; Ternon, *Mardin 1915: Anatomie pathologique d'une destruction*, Paris: Éditions Geuthner, 2007, *passim*.

14

ALI SUAD BEY

The 'Armenian Patriarch'

Mutasarrif Ali Suad was a man of both conscience and good education. As sub-prefect of Der Zor, he was responsible for the Euphrates region where the principal concentration camps lay: Meskene, Dipsi, Rakka/Sebka and Der Zor/Marat. Before civil war broke out in Syria in 2011, visitors to Der Zor could still see the traces of Ali Suad's benevolent actions there, most of which have now been swept away by the war. The memorial to the Armenian genocide was dynamited by Islamic State in 2014. Nonetheless, material vestiges of his actions had survived for nearly a century. Travellers to Syria could visit his home, which he turned into an orphanage for Armenian children. And he was not alone in supporting the region's Armenians, since his actions inspired others around him. As Pietro Kuciukian notes, for instance, with Ali Suad's encouragement, Yusuf Ziya Bey, sub-prefect of Ras al-Ayn, allowed deportees who had the means to do so to farm the land or practise their trades, as well as organizing protection for the camp against attacks by Arab gangs.

This state of affairs lasted until 1916. Up to that time, 13,000 deportees had perished, a relatively small number in the circumstances. The deportees were well treated and were not subjected to the brutality that was habitually meted out by Turkish officials. But radical changes were to take place with the arrival of Ali Suad Bey's successor, Salih Zeki, in July 1916.

In an article entitled 'The Extermination of Ottoman Armenian Deportees in the Concentration Camps of Syria-Mesopotamia

(1915–1916)', cited by Kuciukian, Raymond Kévorkian reports a conversation between Zia Bey and Ali Suad Bey that sheds light on the latter's motivation. In the orders he gave to Zia Bey, Ali Suad explained in substance that there was no rhyme or reason behind the deportation of the Armenians; that the officials were at liberty to do absolutely anything with them, including exterminating them; but that they would do nothing of the sort. Instead, he ordered Zia Bey to do everything to ensure the deportees' survival, and to ensure that Turkish officials did not abuse them in any way. In fact, he was genuinely convinced that if he saved the Armenians they would succeed in growing crops and transforming the parched desert by the sweat of their brows.

Under Ali Suad's administration, Armenians were granted real protection. Although their situation remained difficult, they were given the right to buy and sell goods freely. A particular threat came from gangs of Arab thieves, as shown by the first-hand account of an Armenian deportee, Karekin Hovhannessian, quoted by Kévorkian in the *Mémorial du génocide des Arméniens*: 'On the way, we were attacked once again by more Arabs who, finding we had nothing to steal, made us strip off all our clothes, even our undergarments, and made off with them.' To prevent nocturnal attacks on the Armenians, Ali Suad resolved to make an example of an Arab attacker and offered a reward to the first official who could bring him the head of an Arab bandit. When, a few days later, a Turk killed one of the attackers, his severed head was mounted on a pike and displayed outside the camp—a brutal tactic that proved to be an effective deterrent.

The deportees had absolutely nothing: there was not enough bread, and illness and disease were rife. Ali Suad therefore ordered the construction of sixty ovens and a large hospital, giving the work to Armenian craftsmen who were paid with food. The deportees also needed shelters. For this, Ali Suad came up with an ingenious scheme that was of benefit both to the deportees and to the Turkish nation. He picked 120 families from Hadjin and asked them to construct barrack-like buildings as dwellings, his idea being that if the deportees were allowed to return home one day, the buildings would be useful to the Turkish state. Ali Suad Bey was not merely a great humanitarian but also an intelligent patriot. Realizing that the Armenians had a great deal to offer the empire, instead of setting out to annihilate them he gave them protection and encouraged their skills in such a way as to serve the collective interest.

When Ali Suad received orders to 'make room' for new convoys of deportees by emptying the camp at Der Zor of its existing inmates, he did everything in his power to make sure they stayed where they were. When at last he was forced to send some convoys of deportees away, he attempted to mitigate their conditions as far as possible, arranging for pack animals to carry the children and the weak (in stark contrast to the monstrous conditions in which the deportations habitually took place). Neither he nor Ziya Bey had a moment's hesitation in falsifying documents and changing the deportees' dates of arrival.

On receiving orders to send the Armenians into the desert, Ali Suad refused and was dismissed from his post. In early July 1916, he was replaced by Salih Zeki, who had already wiped out the Armenians of Everek and now proceeded to massacre the Armenians in the camp without mercy.

For his actions, Ali Suad Bey was dubbed the 'Armenian Patriarch' by the Turks. Under his administration, as described by Kévorkian, other men also acted benevolently towards the Armenians. Colonel Nureddin Bey, military inspector, and Naki Bey, naval commander, supported Ali Suad in his efforts to keep as many deportees as possible at Der Zor; Hadji Faroz and Ayial, from the same family native to Der Zor, also distinguished themselves by their actions, the former being given great credit by the tribes on the route from Der Zor to Aleppo and enjoying good relations with all the sheikhs in the region. Kaymakam Haci Fadil, civil inspector, gave aid to many Armenians, while Naki Bey and Nureddin Bey managed to keep a large number of Armenians at Der Zor. Nureddin Bey married an Armenian woman from Bilecik in the *vilayet* of Bursa and they had a child together.

Sources and further reading

Sources

Ternon, Yves, *Enquête sur la négation d'un génocide*, Roquevaire: Éditions Parenthèses, 1989, pp. 98–9, 112–13.

THE RIGHTEOUS AND PEOPLE OF CONSCIENCE

Studies

Akçam, Taner, *Killing Orders: Talat Pasha's Telegrams and the Armenian Genocide*, Palgrave Studies in the History of Genocide, Basingstoke: Palgrave, 2018, pp. 258–61.

Kévorkian, Raymond, 'L'extermination des déportés arméniens dans les camps de concentration de Syrie-Mésopotamie (1915–1916): La deuxième phase du génocide', *Revue d'histoire arménienne contemporaine*, 2 (1998), p. 191; Kévorkian, 'Ottoman Officials against the Armenian Genocide', in Andrieu, Gensburger and Sémelin, *Resisting Genocide*, pp. 183–201; Kévorkian, 'Pour une typologie des "Justes" dans l'Empire ottoman', in *There Is Always an Option to Say 'Yes' or 'No': The Righteous against the Genocides of Armenians and Jews, Padua, 30 November–2 December 2000* [conference proceedings], Padua: Cleup, 2001, pp. 71–4.

Kuciukian, *I disobbedienti*, pp. 151–8; Pietro Kuciukian, *Voci nel Deserto*, Milan: Guerini, 2000, pp. 209–22.

15

FAIK ALI OZANSOY (1876–1950)

Poet and mutasarrif of Kütahya: for the sake of family honour

Over the course of a highly unusual career, Faik Ali Ozansoy served as a senior official in the Ottoman administration while also pursuing a distinguished vocation as a poet, like his brother Süleyman Nazif. Writing in Turkish, he explored romantic themes, tinged with a contemplative mysticism, a love of nature and patriotism. During the First World War, he served as governor of Kütahya, roughly halfway between Constantinople and Angora (Ankara). It was during this time that a man who might have been remembered merely as a civil servant with a passion for poetry distinguished himself by both his integrity and his courage.

When he received orders from Constantinople to send the Armenians in his region away to certain death, he refused to obey, his resolve stiffened by his brother who urged him to refuse 'for the sake of our family honour'. He instead chose to protect not only the Armenians of Kütahya but also those who poured into his province after hearing that the local governor had refused to obey the expulsion order.

When summoned by Talaat Pasha to explain why he had not sent the Armenians arriving in Kütahya to Aleppo, Faik Ali offered a plethora of excuses, the details of which are now lost, as the telegrams have vanished from the archives. In the end, Constantinople simply gave up asking him to explain. The governor went so far as to offer his resignation to Talaat—one of the Young Turk triumvirate together with Enver Pasha and Kemal Pasha, the de facto rulers of the Ottoman Empire at the time—who was adamant that the deportation policy had to be applied to all Armenians, saying, 'I am not a murderer, please accept my resignation and appoint someone else who is willing to carry out this policy.' Talaat responded: 'Take your Armenians and stay in post.'

While Faik Ali was away from Kütahya, the chief of police, Kamal Bey, gave the Armenians a choice between being deported or converting to Islam, resulting in a mass conversion. When Faik Ali discovered this on his return, he dismissed Kamal Bey on the spot and questioned the Armenians as to whether they genuinely wanted to convert to Islam. All but one of them recanted and chose to revert to Christianity.

After the persecutions, the Armenians presented Faik Ali with 500 gold pieces as a token of their gratitude. He in turn used the gold to help the Armenians by setting up a communal kitchen and a school.

Faik Ali was able to ignore multiple orders from Constantinople with relative impunity partly because of the staunch support he received from prominent local Turks, especially the Kermiyanzade family and Hocazade Rasik Effendi.

After the war, Ali Ozansoy continued to serve in senior administrative posts, becoming governor of Diyarbekir and undersecretary in the Ministry of the Interior before eventually retiring. He died in Istanbul on 1 October 1950.

Sources and further reading

Bedrosyan, Raffi, 'The Real Turkish Heroes of 1915', *Armenian Reporter*, 29 July 2015.

Gerçek, 'Turkish Rescuers'.

Kévorkian, *Armenian Genocide*, pp. 564, 754; Kévorkian, 'Ottoman Officials against the Armenian Genocide', in Andrieu, Gensburger and Sémelin, *Resisting Genocide*, pp. 183–201.

Kuciukian, *I disobbedienti*, pp. 35–9.

16

HASAN MAZHAR BEY

Vali of Angora and president of the Mazhar Commission

When Hasan Mazhar Bey, governor of Angora (Ankara) from 18 June 1914, received the order to deport the Armenians, he initially pretended not to understand it. He was well aware, in fact, that the true goal of the deportations was to exterminate the Armenians, but he did not believe that the Armenian population were disloyal to their country. Furthermore, he knew that they made an essential contribution to the region's economy, and that they took little interest in questions of politics and lived in harmony with the other communities in the province. It was a view that was shared by the local chief of police. According to Vahakn Dadrian, Hasan Mazhar drew up a declaration affirming that the Armenian population was not disloyal, had it signed by prominent local Turks and sent it to Talaat Pasha, minister of the interior. In July 1915, after the secretary of the CUP in Angora had tried and failed to influence him, the central committee of the Young Turks sent Atif Bey, who was prominent in the Special Organization, to the city. When Atif Bey tried to bring Hasan Mazhar Bey to heel, the governor responded: 'I am not a thug without scruples; I am the *vali*. I am unable to do this. You will have to take my place and do it yourself.'

At first, the Young Turks proposed to Hasan Mazhar that he should return to Aleppo, where he had already served, and exchange his post with Celal Bey. The unspoken aim of this manoeuvre involving two high-ranking officials who were both refusing to obey orders was to take advantage of the period when they would be travelling to their new posts to carry out the plan to exterminate the

THE RIGHTEOUS AND PEOPLE OF CONSCIENCE

Armenians. Hasan Mazhar saw through this subterfuge and refused to leave Angora for Aleppo, even when Talaat Pasha sent him a personal telegram insisting on it. He and his chief of police were dismissed from their posts immediately, on 8 July 1915. Hazan Mazhar was replaced by the notoriously cruel and ruthless Atif Bey, who lost no time in carrying out the plan to exterminate the Armenians, starting with the community's elite. A non-Armenian traveller who was passing through Angora at this time testified:

> The *vali* of Angora, a man of true courage, refused to carry out his orders from Constantinople to deport the Armenians of Angora; the commander of military forces and the chief of police were in agreement with him and gave him their support. The prominent Turks in Angora, including the religious leaders, were all of the same opinion. They all knew that the Christians in the city were loyal and useful subjects of the empire. The Armenians here were mostly Catholic and loyal to the Turkish government. They had no sympathy with nationalist aspirations. ... There were also between 200 and 400 families belonging to the national Gregorian church. ... Armenian homes and shops were searched during the month of July 1915, and no weapons or compromising documents were found. But the central authorities in Constantinople had decreed that they should be exterminated, and since the *vali* refused to obey, both he and the chief of police were dismissed from their posts. Their successors made themselves the instruments of the government in carrying out its orders, and they succeeded in deporting all the Armenians from Angora.

Once the *vali* had been relieved of his duties, the genocide proceeded in the same way as in the other provinces of eastern Anatolia, and the majority of the 72,000 Armenians of the *sanjak* of Angora were massacred.

The reign of the Young Turks came to an end on 7 October 1918 with the resignation of the second war government, led by Talaat Pasha since February 1917. With German assistance, Ahmed Izzet Pasha, appointed grand vizier by Sultan Mehmet VI, shielded the flight of the triumvirate of Talaat, Enver and Cemal, along with four of the other chief architects of the Armenian genocide, to Berlin. The triumvirate was then replaced with a cabinet under Tewfik

Pasha. It was this new cabinet—with the support of a public and media who were motivated less by the horror of the crimes committed (the scale of which was now emerging) than the political consequences that might ensue—that set up a parliamentary commission to investigate. At the request of the Council of State, meanwhile, the sultan established a commission of inquiry by special decree—and entrusted it to the former governor of Angora.

In the aftermath of defeat, Turkey was forced to name those responsible for the Armenian genocide or else risk the Turkish people as a whole being accused of the crime. While most of the population had done nothing to stop the massacres and looting or had actively taken part in them, and relatively few people had actually helped the Armenians, men of integrity among state officials were even rarer. Hasan Mazhar's record was unsullied, however, and so he was appointed to head the commission of inquiry that was to bear his name—the Mazhar Commission. Set up by imperial decree on 21 November 1918 within the Office of General Security, the commission's brief was to gather testimonies and documents that would establish the extent of the guilt of the government officials involved in the massacre of the Armenians. It also set out to establish who was responsible, so that the new Turkish government could not be held accountable for crimes committed by the CUP during the war. Chairing the commission was not without risk for Mazhar, since most Turks looked askance at this 'clean hands' operation, and in any case were at a loss to see anything reprehensible in the fate that had befallen the Armenians. The commission was granted some latitude in its actions, and Hasan Mazhar was thus able to circulate a request to every prefect and sub-prefect for documents pertaining to the orders received. Witnesses were also questioned, and within three months the commission had built up 150 dossiers, which were referred to courts martial. For a period of eighteen months, the massacres of the Armenians were freely discussed in the Turkish press. There was no question at this point of denying the crimes, but rather of settling scores as everyone scrambled to put themselves in the clear, claiming that they were only obeying orders. Nonetheless, the crime was recognized and acknowledged, as noted by Ali Kemal Bey, editor-in-chief of the newspaper *Sabah*, on 28 January 1919: 'Four or five years ago, a crime unique in history, a crime to make the world tremble, was committed in our land.'

The trial of the CUP leaders in Constantinople ended with Talaat Pasha, Enver Pasha, Cemal Pasha and Mehmed Nazim being sentenced to death in absentia. The courts martial held in other regions of the Ottoman Empire resulted in similar verdicts, often in absentia, as the criminals had fled, frequently with the help of the German government. In 1920, with the rise of Kemalism, the courts martial were suspended indefinitely. When Mustafa Kemal came to power, Hasan Mazhar was accused of treason and forced to flee the country. Intending to make a radical break with the past, the Turkish Republic reinvented the nation's history, notably through the lens of the Turkish Historical Society founded by Mustafa Kemal Atatürk. The Armenian genocide and the commissions of inquiry and the trials that ensued were thus erased from the national memory. Insidiously, denial of the Armenian genocide became an intrinsic part of Turkish national identity.

All this notwithstanding, the documentation that Hasan Mazhar had managed to assemble forms an overwhelming body of evidence that is invaluable for informing our understanding of how the Armenian genocide unfolded and identifying those responsible.

The creation of the Mazhar Commission, reporting to the Ministry of the Interior, was not dictated by ethical considerations. This product of the Ottoman judicial system was imposed on the Allies by the government in Constantinople, which was anxious to present itself in the best possible light at the Paris Peace Conference, held from January 1919 to August 1920. This they would achieve by laying all responsibility for the genocide at the door of the central committee of the CUP and its network of 'secretaries in charge' and by absolving civilian and military personnel who had been party to the crime against their will. But the proceedings of the main trial, held in Constantinople, produced such a wealth of evidence that the reality of this deliberate policy of mass extermination, meticulously planned by a central power (and later defined by the Polish jurist Raphael Lemkin as 'genocide'), now seemed irrefutable. This is why successive Turkish governments have endeavoured to ensure the disappearance of most of the evidence used at this trial.

Hasan Mazhar Bey stands out among the Righteous for two reasons: first, he was a high-ranking official who refused to obey CUP orders, at the expense of his own career; and second, he put together an extensive body of evidence and eyewitness accounts of the crime, which resulted in the conviction of many of its perpetrators.

Sources and further reading

Sources

Chaliand, Gérard and Yves Ternon, *The Armenians: From Genocide to Resistance*, trans. Tony Berrett, London: Zed Books, 1983, pp. 121–34.

Kévorkian, Raymond H. and Yves Ternon, *Mémorial du génocide des Arméniens*, Paris: Editions du Seuil, 2014, pp. 469–95.

Ternon, *Enquête sur la négation d'un génocide*, pp. 117–24.

Studies

Dadrian, Vahakn, *The History of the Armenian Genocide*, New York: Berghahn Books, 1995, pp. 502–46.

Gerçek, 'Turkish Rescuers'.

Nichanian, Mikaël, 'Le procès des responsables du génocide arménien à Constantinople (1919–1920)', in Conseil scientifique international pour l'étude du génocide des Arméniens, *Le génocide des Arméniens*, Paris: Armand Colin, 2015, pp. 166–77.

Safrastyan, Ruben, 'Mustafa Kemal in Constantinople', in *The Struggle of Mustafa Kemal against the Republic of Armenia (1919–1921)* [in Armenian], Yerevan: Tir Publishing House, 2019, pp. 12–34.

Ternon, Yves, *The Armenians: History of a Genocide*, New York: Caravan Books, 2004, pp. 278–9, 329–33; Ternon, *Empire ottoman: Le déclin, la chute, l'effacement*, Paris: Le Félin Poche, Éditions Michel de Maule, 2005, pp. 342–9; Ternon, *Enquête sur la négation d'un génocide*, pp. 35–48.

17

MEHMET CELAL BEY (1863–1926)

The 'Turkish Oskar Schindler'

Mehmet Celal Bey, known as the 'Turkish Oskar Schindler', was born into a distinguished family in the suburbs of Constantinople in 1863; his father was a government official in the Ministry of Finance, and his grandmother was the daughter of Sultan Abdul Hamid. After a good education at the Mekteb-i Mülkiye-i (now the Faculty of Political Science, University of Ankara) and in Germany, he occupied a string of very senior positions: *vali* of Erzurum (1910–11), *vali* of Aydin (1911–12), minister of the interior (1911–12) and minister of agriculture (1913). On 11 August 1913, he was appointed *vali* of Aleppo, before being transferred to Konya on 4 June 1915 for refusing to obey his orders to deport the Armenians. In October 1915, he was once again dismissed from his post for the same reason.

When the Armenian genocide began, Celal Bey was in post in Aleppo. He immediately realized that the deportations were part of a programme to exterminate the Armenians. Aware too that their annihilation ran counter to the interests of the Ottoman Empire, he was tireless in his denunciations of this senseless plan while also attempting to mitigate the extremity of the orders he received. He notably refused to deport the Armenians of Antioch (Antakya) and did everything in his power to save his Armenian friends Krikor Zohrab and Vartkes Serengülian, managing to secure temporary reprieves for them. When these two Armenian members of the Ottoman Parliament (the former also being one of the greatest writers in the Western Armenian language) were arrested and sent to

Aleppo, Celal Bey refused to put them in prison and instead housed them in a hotel, where he allowed them to receive visitors. When he received orders to transfer them to Diyarbekir, where certain death awaited them, he refused to do so and instead arranged to keep them in Aleppo. After Celal Bey was forced to resign his post in Aleppo, the two deputies were ordered to be transferred to Urfa (Edessa), but they were murdered on the journey. Krikor Zohrab was bludgeoned with stones, shattering his skull.

Celal Bey's actions in coming to the aid of the Armenians were prompted by more than one motive. First and foremost, even if the aim of eliminating everyone who was not Turkish by birth was viewed by a large number of high-ranking Ottomans as an end that justified any means, his own conscience would not allow him to support the massacre of innocent people, 'I cannot go against my conscience', as he later wrote in his *Memoirs* (published in 1918 in the Turkish-language journal *Vakit*).

Convinced as he was that the Young Turk leaders were impervious to the spirit of justice and immune to any feelings of compassion and would never change their views, he also endeavoured to impress on them the serious harm that their policy towards the Armenians would inflict on the nation. He wrote a personal and confidential letter to Talaat Pasha containing a passage that he reproduced in his *Memoirs*:

> Working towards the destruction of the Armenians will bring a loss to the country that it would be impossible to make up for in the years to come. Were all our enemies to consult with each other for months to find the best way to inflict damage upon us, they would not be able to conceive of a greater calamity.

While in post at Aleppo, Celal Bey also tried to alert the foreign diplomats there—especially the Italian and American consuls—to the urgency of the situation, urging them to push their governments to intercede on the Armenians' behalf. For this, he was accused of 'betraying his country' by the local branch of the CUP, before being exonerated by an inquiry. When he was removed from his post and ordered to transfer to Konya in June 1915, he declared that if the Armenians in Konya were due to be deported, he would not accept the new post. The government gave him an assurance that the

Armenians in the city would not be touched, but he soon realized that these were mere empty words. Konya occupied a key position in the organization of the deportations, as it lay on the route between Adapazarı and Bozantı: its railway station thus became a transit or regrouping centre for the deportees, and all the deportation marches from western Anatolia and Thrace converged there.

Before Celal Bey was appointed, the Armenians of the province had endured the regime of Azmi Bey (formerly chief of the Istanbul police), who extorted money from them, organized searches and refused to allow medics or missionaries to dispense any aid to the deportees. He even claimed that local Armenians should count themselves fortunate: 'The policies adopted with regard to the Armenians cannot now be modified. The Armenians of Konya should consider themselves lucky because they have been deported no further than to a neighbouring province.'

Celal Bey's appointment to Konya was therefore a relief for the Armenians: he refused to allow them to be deported and grasped every opportunity to try to save them, sending regular demands to the authorities to provide shelters for the deportees, writing letters denouncing the inhuman cruelty of the policy and delaying the departure of the convoys. His frustration was now intolerable, as he described in his *Memoirs*:

> My position at Konya was that of a man sitting on the bank of a river without any means of saving anyone from its waters. Blood flowed like water, and thousands of innocent children, blameless old men, defenceless women and strong young men were borne away to oblivion on those currents. Anyone I could save with my hands and fingernails I did save, the rest vanished never to return.

It did not take long for Celal Bey to realize that the aim of the deportations was the liquidation of the Armenians. He shared these fears with the Italian and American consuls in Aleppo, with whom he had formed firm friendships. In confidence, he informed them that he had received secret directives ordering him to destroy the Armenian population, and that this went against his conscience. He was convinced that the only way of tempering the savagery of these orders was to warn the German and Austrian empires (which with the kingdom of Italy formed the Triple

THE RIGHTEOUS AND PEOPLE OF CONSCIENCE

Alliance). The hectoring, peremptory tone of the telegrams he received from Talaat Pasha clearly indicates the risks he was running in refusing to obey orders. After finally dismissing him from office, the minister of the interior wrote:

> How many local Armenians remain who have not been deported and are being held in situ, in accordance with my latest instructions, and how many have arrived from other regions and have been temporarily detained, also according to my instructions? And how many Armenians are there intended for other destinations? Supply me with detailed answers within three days.

Pointing out to Celal Bey that state censorship was likely to hinder the delivery of his messages, the Italian consul offered to take them to Constantinople himself with a letter of trust.

In August 1915, Celal Bey left Konya to travel to Istanbul for medical treatment. In his absence, the local CUP members deported some 3,000 local Armenians. A second convoy was about to leave when Celal Bey returned and halted it, so providing temporary rescue for the Armenian families, whom he allowed to return to their homes, most of which had already been looted. For as long as Celal Bey remained in post, the Armenians of Konya stayed there, but after he was dismissed from office in October 1915, they were all deported. Even when still in office, Celal Bey had little room for manoeuvre, and despite his opposition some Armenian men were in fact deported. Dr William S. Dodd, chief physician of the American Red Cross Hospital in Konya, noted:

> All reports that the Government are providing food are absolutely false, those who have money can buy, those who have none beg or starve ... How many can survive it? ... The *vali* is a good man but almost powerless. The Ittihad Committee and the Salonika Clique rule all. The Chief of Police seems to be the real head.

Celal Bey had sent a number of telegrams to the Sublime Porte criticizing the treatment of the Armenians. As has been seen, he stated that the destruction of the Armenians would be an irreparable loss for the country as the reason for his opposition to these atrocities, and declared that a simple sense of civic duty prevented him from taking part in an action that he believed was fundamentally damaging to the interests of his country:

MEHMET CELAL BEY (1863–1926)

Scarcely could I have imagined that a government would ever be capable of exterminating its subjects in such a way, its human capital which must be considered as the nation's greatest wealth. I believed that these measures derived from the desire to temporarily remove the Armenians from the field of operations, necessitated by military considerations. This was the reason behind my telegrams to the Minister of the Interior asking for funds to build camps to house the deported Armenians. By way of funds, I was sent an individual bearing the title of 'immigrant settlement agent', whose mission was in fact to deport the Armenians en masse.

In halting the deportations and allaying the sufferings of the deportees, Celal Bey achieved the impossible, contriving to avoid the forced departure of some 30,000 Armenians from Konya. His dismissal on 3 October 1915 put an abrupt end to his actions, however. He was replaced by Ferid Bey, known as Hamal Ferid (Ferid 'the Porter'), the secretary in charge of the CUP in Konya, who with the support of the most prominent party members in the city applied the deportation policy with extreme ruthlessness.

The close links between the deportation of the Armenians and the confiscation of their possessions cannot be over-emphasized. With Celal Bey gone, Konya became, as Raymond Kévorkian notes, a marketplace in which Turks would go round Armenian houses and tell the owners that they should hand over their belongings, since soon they would no longer need them as they would be dead. When the Armenians were deported, a commission for 'abandoned property' seized their houses and bank accounts. An appeal by Karekin I Khachadourian, archbishop of Konya, to the commanding officer of the German troops stationed in the city had no effect.

In the years after these events, Celal Bey and his family faced considerable financial difficulties. In 1918, he and a German partner set up a modern farm project in the Eskişehir region, but the machinery they imported from abroad was confiscated by the Turkish authorities. He later started an insurance company. At the end of the war, a new era opened up for him. While the CUP were accused of leading the country into the abyss, Celal Bey, who had done everything to oppose them, was appointed governor of Adana, then under French control (Cilicia was under the French mandate from 1919 to 1921). Once in post, he made contact with Mustafa

Kemal to lend him his support in his struggle against the Allied occupation of Turkey. This did not prevent him from offering his continuing support to the Armenians, writing to Mustafa Kemal to ask him to be merciful to the Armenians of Cilicia so as not to provide them with a pretext for supporting the French.

Celal Bey subsequently became mayor of Istanbul, occupying the post from July 1921 to March 1922. He died on 11 February 1926; his funeral cortege in Istanbul was followed by a large crowd made up of both Armenians and Turks.

A man of wide education, liberal values and high morals, Mehmet Celal Bey obeyed his conscience, acting with unimpeachable honour throughout his country's darkest years.

Sources and further reading

Sources

Gerçek, 'Turkish Rescuers'.

Studies

Kévorkian, *Armenian Genocide*, pp. 710–15; Kévorkian, 'Ottoman Officials against the Armenian Genocide', in Andrieu, Gensburger and Sémelin, *Resisting Genocide*, pp. 183–201.
Kuciukian, *I disobbedienti*, pp. 165–71.
Ternon, *Enquête sur la négation d'un génocide, passim*.

18

MUSTAFA AGHA AZIZOĞLU (d.1921)

Faithful friend of the German Bethesda Mission for the Blind

Born into a family who came originally from Baghdad but had lived in Turkey for generations, Mustafa Agha Azizoğlu was mayor of Malatya when the genocide began in 1915. A man of courage, he sheltered Armenian families in his home and did everything in his power to oppose acts of violence and investigate organized killings. His involvement in the defence of the Armenians was to cost him his life. His position as mayor meant that he had a good understanding of the population of Malatya, who were predominantly Kurdish, but according to accounts of the massacres it offered him little scope to stand up against the *vali*, who was responsible for organizing the extermination of the Armenians.

The German Protestant pastor Ernst Christoffel described him as an old friend of the Bethesda Mission for the Blind, a German foundation that lay outside the city:

> Mustafa Agha was a longstanding friend of 'Bethesda'. He was a patron of the mission from the beginning of his work. He worked on our behalf in many difficult circumstances, especially at the time of the Adana massacre in 1909. At Malatya, too, Christians and missionaries were to be massacred. At that point, Mustafa Agha told me: 'As long as I live, nothing will happen to you.' Yet, as we later discovered, his name was on the list of people to be murdered before the general massacre, even before us. The relatively smooth growth of 'Bethesda' until the outbreak of the world war would have been impossible to imagine without his active benevolence, and we have always considered such friends in our work as a gift from God.

Mustafa Agha himself left no written accounts of his actions; it was Ernst Bauernfeind, the joint director of the Bethesda Mission, who related events at Malatya in his notebooks. These were not a spontaneous record made at the time, however; rather, Bauernfeind had been entrusted by the organization with making a record of events at Malatya to be handed down to future generations. Written in diary form, the notebooks are quoted at length in *The Armenian Genocide* by Kévorkian, who explains that the pastor initially took a sceptical view of the mayor who was his contact, because he did not believe that such organized atrocities could be the work of the CUP. They saw each other regularly, nonetheless, either for discussions with the prefect or to entrust Armenians who had been saved from the massacres of 1915 to the care of the mission.

On the eve of the First World War, Malatya had a population of 35,000, a third of whom were Armenian. In February 1915, the government used the desertion of Kurdish, Armenian and Turkish troops as a pretext for introducing new disciplinary measures targeting the Armenians. These were gradually followed by a widespread operation to disarm the Armenian population and pressgang the men into forced labour on the roads to the north and west of Malatya, with a view to systematically removing them from their communities.

On 4 May 1915, Bauernfeind wrote: 'The government has lost all trust in the Armenians.' Their homes were searched for letters, newspapers or leaflets that would provide evidence of plots against the government. The process was always the same: the government would fabricate an accusation and use the press to wage a campaign aimed at whipping up tensions in the community. As an example, the Ottoman bureau claimed that Armenian insurgents had sabotaged the mountain passes to hinder troop movements. So effective was this campaign of blame and incrimination that any protests against it were in vain. On 20 May, a state decree was proclaimed forcing Armenians to surrender their weapons to the authorities on the pretext of national defence. This was followed by a second wave of searches and arrests. On 22 May, all Armenian officials were thrown into prison, along with members of the general council, leaders of political parties and men of substance. No one with the power or influence to lead or fund a rebellion of any sort was now left.

MUSTAFA AGHA AZIZOĞLU (d.1921)

The ground was laid for the city to become a transit centre for convoys of deportees from all over eastern Turkey. When a new *mutasarrif* or sub-prefect, Rashid Bey, was appointed by the government, his predecessor was dismissed to make room for him, and he was given lodgings in the home of a Young Turk party member. On 20 June 1915, a new prefect was also appointed. Rashid Bey set up all the arrangements for the slaughter in the next phase of the genocide, which lasted from June to September 1915. On 6 June, common criminals were freed and formed into armed *çete* squads, who were to massacre the men who had been sent out to mend the roads. On 11 June, on the orders of Nasim Mehmed, 12,000 soldier-labourers were massacred at Çiftlik on the Euphrates by these newly formed death squads. On 2 July, the rest of the men were slaughtered.

Mustafa Agha Azizoğlu stood up against the atrocities perpetrated against the Armenians. Tireless in his denunciations of the crimes committed by the authorities, he also disseminated information about them in the hope of prompting reactions from abroad. It was he who arranged for the bodies to be buried, so feeding the rumours of the massacres that the authorities denied. It was he too who, thanks to his regular work with the German Mission, put in place all the arrangements necessary for offering shelter and care to the refugees. And it was he, finally, who gathered accurate information about the deportations, the massacres and the movements of the convoys.

It was certainly no coincidence that a commission of inquiry was set up that led to his being court-martialled for dissidence on 25 November 1915 and dismissed from his post by the authorities. In 1921, his son Ekrem, a young nationalist who had recently returned from the war, murdered him for having refused to obey government orders.

Sources and further reading

Sources

Bauernfeind, Hans, 'Journal de Malatya 1915', ed. Méliné Pehlivanian and Tessa Hofmann, in Raymond Kévorkian, 'L'Extermination des déportés ottomans dans les camps de concentration de Syrie-

Mésopotamie (1915–1916), la deuxième phase du génocide', *Revue d'histoire arménienne contemporaine*, 2 (Paris, 1998), pp. 245–325.

Christoffel, Ernst, 'Des profondeurs obscures: L'expérience d'un missionnaire allemand au Kurdistan turc pendant les années de guerre 1916–1918' [extracts], *Revue d'histoire arménienne contemporaine*, 2 (Paris, 1998), part 4, 'Ernst Christoffel, témoignages 1916–1919'.

Studies

Donikian, Denis, Malatya 1915: Le Journal de Hans Bauernfeind (1), (2), (3)' 'Malatya 1915: Les observations de Ernst Christoffel', in *Petite encyclopédie du génocide Arménien*, pp. 195, 196, 197; pp. 195–8.

Hofmann, Tessa and Méliné Péhlivanian, 'Malatia 1915: Carrefour des convois de déportés d'après le Journal du missionnaire allemand Hans Bauernfeind', http://web.archive.org/web/20051220011018/ http://www.aga-online.org/fr/malatia/index.php

Kévorkian, *Armenian Genocide*, pp. 411, 412.

Kuciukian, *I disobbedienti*, pp. 61–7.

'Mustafa Aga Azizoglu', Padovanet, http://www.padovanet.it/informazione/mustafa-aga-Azizoğlu

TRIBAL CLANS

The population of the Ottoman Empire included many tribes or clans, whose attitudes towards the Armenians varied. This section therefore offers a tour of the regions of the empire that, despite all attempts at modernization, remained structured along largely feudal lines.

19

THE CHARISMATIC ALEVIS OF DERSIM

The population of the province of Dersim, renamed the province of Tunceli (also the name of its prefecture) in 1937, was largely Kurdish and Alevi. Followers of Ali, son-in-law and cousin of Muhammad, Alevis are Muslims but follow a less strict religious practice than Sunni Muslims. Their interpretation of Islam is more spiritual, and they are not obliged to pray five times a day or to go on pilgrimage to Mecca, as they believe that pilgrimage is an internal journey. Alevis do not enter mosques, as they believe that Ali was assassinated while at prayer in a mosque, instead worshipping in *cemevi*, in which men and women—who do not wear the veil—are unsegregated. Alevis believe that God lies within us, and that every individual should awaken the holy within themselves by loving their neighbour. Originally, the Alevis were Turks, but many Kurds and Zazas also follow the faith.

The people of Dersim, who were mostly Alevis, were generally benevolent in their attitude towards the Armenians, who, fleeing the terrible death that awaited them, took refuge in the mountains there. Many first-hand accounts by survivors of the Armenian genocide bear witness to the nobility and humanity of the Alevis of the Dersim province, large numbers of whom paid with their lives for rescuing the Armenians.

A few of the names of the rescuers in Dersim have come down to us. Mutullah Bey (not to be confused with Murtula Beg of the *kaza* of Moks), for example, the Kurdish *agha* of Shatakh, forbade the Kurdish population of Dersim from taking part in the massacres, so making it possible for nearly 20,000 Armenians to seek refuge in his region. Another *agha*, Yusuf Khan, saved and protected Armenians by allowing them to seek shelter on his lands.

According to some researchers, many Alevis are of Armenian descent. Before the genocide, it is believed that Armenians accounted for around a third of the population of Dersim province, and although never very concentrated they were well organized. Here as elsewhere, Armenians were regular victims of robberies, and their *dhimmi* (protected) status afforded them only slight protection in law and little standing in society. Many Armenians had emigrated from the province over the centuries, so reducing their numbers, while others adopted the Alevi faith. Mass conversions began in the seventeenth century, to the point where it became impossible to distinguish the Armenian converts from other Alevis. Nonetheless, many retained the memory of their Armenian origins, and some maintained links with other Armenians who had not converted.

Eventually, entire villages in this region converted to Alevism, and as a result the Armenian converts and the Alevis mingled their traditions over the course of the centuries. During the 1890 massacres carried out by Kurdish-Sunni Hamidiye cavalry regiments in Dersim, several Alevi-Kizilbashi tribes adopted an anti-Sunni position and refused to take part in the crimes committed against the Armenians. The Young Turks accused Armenian 'propaganda' of sowing the idea of the difference between the Sunnis and the Alevis. Young Turk policy was to abolish the differences between populations and unite all peoples of the empire under a single Turkish identity. In 1915, the Alevis feared that they too would be forced to give up their identity or be slaughtered and began to suppress the Armenian side of their identity.

Long after the Armenian genocide, in 1937–8, a terrible massacre was perpetrated in Dersim province. The region had long been under surveillance by the Turkish authorities, and Mustafa Kemal chose this moment to launch a vast ethnic cleansing operation, believed to have been planned as early as 1925. The monastery of Surp Garabed at Halvor, holy ground for both Alevis and Christians, was blown up as a signal for the start of the massacres. The eighty-one-year-old leader of the armed resistance in Dersim province was executed, and the Alevi population suffered at least 13,000 deaths, in addition to torture and disappearances. A small number of Armenians had survived in the province until 1938, but after the massacres the surviving Armenians renounced their Armenian identity, although some Armenian cultural practices have survived.

Sources and further reading

Donikian, Denis, 'Les Alévis durant le génocide des Arméniens', in *Petite encyclopédie du génocide Arménien*, p. 266.

Kerivel, Erwan, *Fils du Soleil, Arméniens et Alévis du Dersim*, Paris: Sigest, 2013.

Kuciukian, *I disobbedienti*, pp. 132–40.

Terrasse, H. "Alawīs', in P. Bearman, Th. Bianquis, C. E. Bosworth, E. van Donzel and W. P. Heinrichs (eds), *Encyclopaedia of Islam*, 2nd edn, Leiden: Brill, 1991, https://referenceworks.brillonline.com/entries/encyclopaedia-of-islam-2/alawis-COM_0043?s.num=0&s.f.s2_parent=s.f.book.encyclopaedia-of-islam-2&s.q=alawis

20

THE KURDS

A rare but valiant defence of the Armenians

The Kurds are an Iranian ethnic group who believe they are descended from the Medes. In his account of the Greek mercenary army's great retreat across Asia Minor around 401–399 BCE, Xenophon described the Carduchians (another name for the Kurds) as 'ferocious defenders of their mountainous lands'. Despite their struggle for independence, the Kurds still have no nation state (although the Iraqi constitution recognized the Kurdistan Region in the north of the country as an autonomous political entity in 2005), and most of the Kurdish population is divided between Turkey, Iraq, Syria and Iran. Nearly 40,000 Kurds live in Armenia and follow the Yazidi faith. There is also a wide Kurdish diaspora in the West as a result of economic migration. In Turkey, Kurds have historically inhabited the country's eastern regions, although many have now settled in Istanbul in order to escape the sporadic conflict between the PKK (Kurdistan Workers' Party) and the Turkish army. The two principal Kurdish languages are Kurmanji, spoken by an estimated 15 to 20 million Kurds, and Sorani, spoken by some 6 to 7 million. Most Kurds are Sunni Muslim by faith, while many are Alevis or Yazidis, and a few are Jewish or Christian. Although the last Kurdish principalities in Turkey disappeared in the nineteenth century, the Kurds nevertheless preserved their identity and their tribal system. The Ottoman authorities endeavoured to use the Kurds to impose their policies, alternating between benevolence and repression. The nineteenth century saw a number of Kurdish revolts, and in the early twentieth century the Kurdish tribes strove to recover their lost autonomy.

THE RIGHTEOUS AND PEOPLE OF CONSCIENCE

In general, the Kurds behaved as oppressors towards the Armenians, with the support of the central Ottoman power. In his novel *The Fool*, the Armenian author Hakob Melik Hakobian, better known by his pen name Raffi (1835–88), described the abuses committed by the Kurdish *aghas*, including the ransacking of Armenian farms and the abduction of young girls. During the Armenian genocide, many Kurds formed the armed wing of the Young Turk government. Nonetheless, according to eyewitness accounts, some *aghas* opposed the massacres and gave protection to the Armenians. Some of their names have come down to us, largely through the work of Pietro Kuciukian:

> Mehmet Agha, of the Khatabash tribe, rescued nearly five hundred young Armenian men and seven or eight hundred women and children. Haci Agha, of the Pilvank tribe, saved another five hundred; the authorities had ordered him to hand over the Armenians, but he fought the order for twenty days, setting fifteen Turkish villages ablaze. It appears that the Armenians remained at his side permanently. A Kurd by the name of Matkhutsi Pasha protected nearly seven hundred Armenians, resisting government orders, setting fire to fifty Turkish villages in the Çarsancak district of Kharpert province and refusing to hand over the Armenians to the Turks. According to one first-hand account, there are still Armenians living in his village today. The aghas Zeynal and Sleyman of Kozan gave refuge to four hundred Armenians, resisting official pressure and taking up arms against the gendarmes. Sleyman and his son were killed. A Kurd called Mze Agha gave hospitality to fifty Armenians in his village.

One of the most celebrated Kurdish protectors of the Armenians was Murtula Beg, *agha* of the *kaza* of Moks in Van province. The forty-five villages in the *kaza* and an estimated population of 4,459 Armenians escaped the massacres thanks to this Kurdish chief, who refused to carry out the orders of the provincial governor, Cevdet, and continued to resist until the arrival of the Russian army.

Sources and further reading

Sources

Raffi, *The Fool*, trans. Jane S. Wingate, n.p.: Indo-European Publishing, 2009.

Studies

Bozarslan, Hamit, 'Les relations kurdo-arméniennes 1894–1996', *Revue du monde arménien moderne et contemporain*, 4 (1998), pp. 23–33; Bozarslan, *La question kurde: États et minorités au Moyen-Orient*, Paris: Presses de Sciences-Po, 1997.

Chaliand, Gérard (ed.), *A People without a Country: The Kurds and Kurdistan*, London: Zed Books, 1992.

Kuciukian, *I disobbedienti*, *passim*.

Ternon, Yves, *The Armenian Cause*, Delmar, NY: Caravan Books, 1985, pp. 117–19.

21

THE ZAZAS

Protectors of the Armenians

The Zazas are an Anatolian people who speak the Zaza language, an Indo-European language of the Iranian group. Possibly originating from Daylam, a region that lay to the south of the Caspian Sea, and so sharing roots with the Persian-speaking Daylamites, the Zazas now live mostly in the eastern Anatolian regions of Erzincan, Siverek and Varto. Their numbers in this region are estimated at between 1.5 and 2 million, with a similar number in western Anatolia and Europe. Many Zazas have become assimilated with their Turkish and Kurdish neighbours and no longer speak the Zaza language. The Zazas are of the Muslim faith, including some Alevis and Sunnis. The Zaza language was for a long time considered to be a Kurdish dialect, but it is now known to be a distinct language forming part of the Iranian group, like Kurdish, although similarities with Kurdish are tenuous. In general, the Zazas believe they belong to a separate ethnic group from the Kurds. The Zazas of Dersim province, who were mostly Alevis, frequently displayed a benevolent attitude towards the Armenians during the period of the genocide.

Sources and further reading

Andrews, Peter Alford (with Rüdiger Benninghaus), *Ethnic Groups in the Republic of Turkey*, Beihefte zum Tübinger Atlas des vorderen Orients, Wiesbaden: Dr Ludwig Reichert, 1989, pp. 121–5.

'Zazas', in Bearman et al., *Encyclopaedia of Islam*.

22

THE YAZIDIS OF JABAL SINJAR

A persecuted community who welcomed the Armenians

Jabal (Mount) Sinjar is part of a range of mountain peaks rising in the desert region between the Rivers Tigris and Khabur. Most of the range lies in present-day Iraq, while the western part lies in Syria. In 1916, the whole of the range was part of the Ottoman Empire and formed a *kaza* in the *vilayet* of Mosul. Here and there, the valley is clothed with woods and vegetation, and some of the mountain slopes are irrigated to make cultivation possible. The town of Sinjar lies to the south of Mount Sinjar. The mountains have frequently provided refuge for persecuted ethnic and religious minorities, especially the Yazidi Kurds. The name 'Yazidi' derives from the Persian *ized*, meaning 'angel' or 'divinity'. While Yazidis define themselves as worshippers of God, they have unjustly been accused of worshipping the devil. Although ethnically Kurdish, their persecution by Kurdish Sunni Muslims has led them to identify as Yazidi rather than Kurdish. Some historians have suggested that the Yazidis may have intermarried with the Armenians of Van, but this remains unverified.

As a rule, however, the Yazidis do not intermarry with other ethnic groups or religions but marry only within their community. It is not possible to convert to the Yazidi religion, only to be born into it. Yazidi women do not wear the veil, and Yazidis in general are renowned—even among their enemies—for their great loyalty and for keeping their word. Socially, they are organized in tribes, like the Kurds, under an emir or chief, with every family having its own hierarchy. During the Ottoman period, the Sinjar Mountains were initially part of the *vilayet* of Diyarbekir, before becoming included in the *vilayet* of Mosul. The Yazidi community on Mount Sinjar were longstanding rebels against the Ottoman regime and posed a threat to travellers through the region, whom they would attack. Yazidi uprisings in 1850 and 1864 were violently repressed by the Ottoman government. It was only after lengthy negotiations that Midhat Pasha, the reforming grand vizier of the Ottoman Empire (assassinated on Abdul Hamid II's orders in 1883), managed to introduce taxation to the Sinjar region.

Some mistakenly believe that the name 'Yazidi' (*yazîdiya* in Arabic) refers to Yazid ibn Muawiya, the second caliph of the Umayyad dynasty in 680–3, who was in power when the second son of Ali, Husayn, was killed at Karbala, a holy city for Shi'ite Muslims south-west of Baghdad. Subsequently, it is believed, pro-Umayyad political and religious feeling crystallized around the figure of Yazid, in a movement that had its origins in Iraq and spread through southern Kurdistan. Later, it is claimed, it was taken up by Sheikh Adi, a descendant of the Umayyad dynasty who lived among the Kurds in the Hakkari Mountains in the early twelfth century, whose teachings so changed and developed its original spiritual principles that Yadizism moved away from its Islamic origins to incorporate anti-Islamic elements.

The Yazidis themselves trace the origins of their faith to ancient Persia and Mithraism, while claiming that in order to adapt to their environment they were obliged to adopt elements of Sufism. Whether Yazidism is a branch of Islam that has become autonomous or is an ancient belief system incorporating elements of Sufism is a complex question to which there is no clear answer. Whatever the case, it has also absorbed many other influences, from paganism, Zoroastrianism (Persian dualism), Manichaeism (Persian Gnosticism), Judaism (dietary laws), Nestorian Christianity (baptism, a form of eucharist, breaking of bread, drinking of wine), Islam (circumcision, sacrifices, pilgrimages, Islamic grave inscriptions), Sufism (doctrinal secrecy, ecstasy, respect for many Sufi sheikhs) and shamanism (burial, interpretation of dreams, dancing). The Yazidis pray five times a day, facing towards the sun.

The largest population of Yazidi Kurds is found in Iraq, but there are also populations in the former Soviet Union, in Armenia, Russia and Georgia. Later immigration has led to the establishment of communities in Western countries. Yazidism is a monotheistic religion, believing in a single god and creator. As in many early religions, however, this god was a *deus otiosus*, a neutral god who stood back and handed responsibility for watching over the world to an intermediary, in this case the peacock angel Tawûsê Melek, his alter ego. The Yazidi believe Sheikh Adi, the Sufi 'reformer' who raised himself to the level of the divine, to be the latter's avatar. The peacock angel was originally a disgraced, fallen angel who earned the Creator's forgiveness through repentance and extinguished the flames of hell with his tears. The Yazidi do not believe in the devil or the existence of hell but in the progressive purification or redemption of the soul through successive reincarnations.

Although it has two holy books, as well as a hymn dedicated to Sheikh Adi (who is buried in the principal Yazidi holy town of Lalish in Iraqi Kurdistan) that is also revered as a sacred text, the Yazidi faith remains an essentially oral tradition. The development of the Yazidi faith towards a spirituality marked by principles that may be described as humanist, or even humanitarian, may account for the attitude adopted towards the Armenians by the Yazidi of Mount Sinjar.

23

SHEIKH HAMU SHIRU

An exemplary Yazidi protector of the Armenians

At the time of the Armenian genocide, Yazidis represented over half of the 18,000 inhabitants of the Sinjar region, with some fifty tribes cultivating crops and raising animals in pockets of greenery around villages scattered among the steep and rocky hillsides.

Then as now, the Yazidi were governed by two sheikhs, one with responsibility for civil affairs and the other for religious matters, including the safeguarding and maintenance of their sanctuary, named after their most venerated saint, Sheikh Adi.

In 1915, Sheikh Hamu Shiru was virtually the absolute ruler of Mount Sinjar, although he made a show of consulting the Yazidi tribal chiefs before taking important decisions. His actions in saving thousands of Christians, including Armenians who had found refuge on Mount Sinjar when the massacres started, have been reported by some of those he rescued.

As early as July 1915, escape networks were set up from Mardin and Ras al-Ayn to Mount Sinjar. It is hard to imagine the physical and mental sufferings of the unfortunate refugees who had to entrust their fate to people smugglers who belonged to the same religion as those who were slaughtering their people, or to conceive of the terror of not knowing—supposing they ever succeeded in reaching the refuge they had been promised—whether they would be given sanctuary by the Yazidi.

As long as they were paid, most of these smugglers—Arabs, Circassians and Chechens—honoured their promises, guiding Armenians to Mount Sinjar in convoys of 400 or 500, with the complicity of gendarmes who had been bribed in advance. When the refugees reached Mount Sinjar, Sheikh Hamu Shiru gave them tents as temporary shelters and land on which to build more permanent dwellings, and ensured they were fed until they could find work. The Armenians who had experience of working the land went to work in the orchards, while others resumed their previous trades and businesses. Before the war, they had already traded with the Yazidi, and once settled on Mount Sinjar they resumed these activities and managed to arrange deliveries from Mardin of sugar and small manufactured items that could not be bought in the region. Travelling from village to village, they then exchanged these goods for local agricultural produce.

Sheikh Hamu Shiru's protection of the Armenians was particularly conspicuous on two occasions. In the first case, during an epidemic of typhus that broke out in October 1915, the Yazidi chiefs wanted to throw the Armenians out of their houses. Sheikh Shiru opposed this, proposing instead that those who were ill should be put in isolation until they were better—a plan that was to prove effective. The second case offers even clearer evidence of his humanity and independence of spirit, which embraced everyone who lived on the mountain, whether Yazidi or from an ethnic minority living among them. In March 1918, a Turkish expeditionary corps mounted an assault on the mountain with orders to destroy the Yazidi enclave, which the authorities accused of staging an uprising. The Turkish commander demanded that Sheikh Shiru hand over his weapons and the Christians he was protecting. Summoning the tribal chiefs, Hamu Shiru informed them of the Turkish commander's orders, saying that they should refuse to obey them. Opinions in the meeting were divided, and lengthy discussions ensued. Meanwhile, Shiru set off with a group of his men and attacked and killed some of the Turkish troops. In retaliation, the Turks overran the mountain and, overcoming heroic resistance, managed to reach Sheikh Shiru's village, which they looted and put to the torch. Yazidi and Christians alike retreated to the highest slopes of the mountain, and some of them succeeded in reaching its southern face.

Because the troops were needed on other fronts, most of the Turkish force was withdrawn from Mount Sinjar soon afterwards. The Yazidi, who had been waiting for this development, now unleashed guerrilla attacks on those who were left behind. Their harrying forced the Turkish military to abandon the mountain entirely, with the result that the Christians were able to return and live there until the end of the war. One of the most outstanding guerrilla fighters was the Yazidi hero Jahangir Agha, whose exceptional courage won praise from the Armenian military leader and statesman General Andranik; he went on to help win victory for the Armenians at Bash Abaran in 1918, which played a crucial part in the creation of the First Republic of Armenia (1918–20).

If any individual deserves to be named as one of the Righteous, it is Sheikh Hamu Shiru. Putting his own safety in peril and risking his life, he gave food and shelter to the Armenians until they could fend for themselves, protected them during an epidemic of typhus and defended them against attacks by the Turkish army. In all these ways, it is estimated that his help enabled several thousand Armenians to survive the genocide.

Sources and further reading

Studies

Kuciukian, *I disobbedienti*, pp. 133–40.

'Sindjar' and 'Yâzîdî', in Bearman et al., *Encyclopaedia of Islam*.

Ternon, Yves, 'L'impossible sauvetage des Arméniens de Mardin', in Jacques Sémelin, Claire Andrieu and Sarah Gensburger (eds), *La résistance aux génocides: De la pluralité des actes de sauvetage*, Paris: Presses de Sciences Po, 2008, pp. 399–409; Ternon, *Mardin 1915*, pp. 230–6.

'Yezidis', in Dominique Sourdel and Janine Sourdel-Thomine (eds), *A Glossary of Islam*, trans. Caroline Higgitt, Edinburgh: Edinburgh University Press, 2007.

24

FAIZ EL-GHUSEIN

The Great Arab Revolt and testimony on the genocide

It was at the request of British Indian Army officer Sir Percy Cox (Colonial Office administrator in the Middle East and later high commissioner of Iraq and ambassador to Baghdad) and Gertrude Bell (archaeologist, writer, traveller, political officer and intelligence agent), both of whom played a crucial role in the creation of the state of Iraq, that in 1916 Faiz El-Ghusein published a pamphlet that was translated into English the following year under the title *Martyred Armenia*. Originally written in Arabic, the document was an indictment of the Turkish authorities for their inhumane and criminal treatment of the Armenians, their fellow Ottoman citizens. The testimony it offers is all the more valuable for being contemporary with the annihilation of the Armenians.

From service under the Ottomans to Arab nationalist opposition

In the preface to *Martyred Armenia*, El-Ghusein describes himself as a Bedouin, the son of one of the heads of the Sulut tribe who lived in the Hauran region in what is now southern Syria. He was educated at the Tribal School in Constantinople (set up for the sons of grand sheikh families) and at the Royal College. He then joined the staff of the *vali* of Syria for a lengthy period, before being appointed *kaymakam* of the canton of Mamuret ul-Aziz. After three and a half years as a modest subordinate of the *vali*, he resigned his post in order to practise law in Damascus while continuing to represent Hauran in a variety of official capacities.

THE RIGHTEOUS AND PEOPLE OF CONSCIENCE

At the outbreak of war in 1914, he was ordered to take up the duties of *kaymakam* once more but refused, as practising law was more lucrative, offering a plethora of excuses for his decision. The truth of the matter was that he had developed close links with Arab nationalists who wanted to cast off the Ottoman yoke, and he was even accused of being a member of one of the secret societies that then proliferated in Syria and Lebanon, probably Sûriyya al-Fatât.

On 23 July 1915, he was arrested by the government and sent to the military prison at Aley in Lebanon for trial by a military tribunal. His fellow defendants were a large number of Syrians and Lebanese, some of whom were found guilty and condemned to execution in Damascus and Beirut on 6 May 1916, on the orders of Cemal Pasha. Although El-Ghusein was found innocent, the verdict was not recognized by the Ottoman government, which sent him into exile in Erzurum, the administrative centre of the *vilayet* of Erzurum, in north-eastern Anatolia, on the eastern frontier of the empire.

Unable to reach Erzurum because of the Russian offensive, he was detained in Diyarbekir for six and a half months, until he managed to escape on 27 February 1916. After crossing the Syrian desert on foot and horseback for seventy days, through Kurdish and Bedouin lands, he finally reached Basra in Iraq, on the Persian Gulf.

Involvement in the Great Arab Revolt of 1916–18

The objective of the Great Arab Revolt—led by Hussein bin Ali (1854–1931), sharif of Mecca, guardian of the holy places of Islam, of the Hashemite dynasty and therefore a descendant of Muhammad—was to free Arabia from almost total domination by the Ottoman Empire. The revolt was declared following the arrival of emissaries from the Allies: on the British side, Colonel T. E. Lawrence (1888–1935), archaeologist, intelligence officer and political agent, later to be celebrated as Lawrence of Arabia; and on the French side, Lieutenant-Colonel Édouard Brémond, commanding officer of the military mission to Egypt and the Hejaz, and later administrator-in-chief in Armenia and Cilicia. The turning points in the campaign were the capture of Aqaba in June 1917, followed by that of Damascus in September 1918 by forces led by Prince Faisal, and General Edmund Allenby's victorious Palestine campaign in November–December 1917. The Armenian volunteers of the Légion d'Orient (which also included Syrian volunteers), the kernel of the future Armenian Legion, were congratulated by Allenby and Commandant Louis Romieu, the legion's founder, for their outstanding contribution to the French and British victory at the Battle of Arara, north of Jerusalem, in September 1918.

The lands that were to be granted to the Arabs in recognition of their support for the Allies had already been designated under the secret Sykes–Picot Agreement, signed by the British and French in March 1916, which broke some of their promises in advance. Under the terms of the Armistice of Mudros, which ended hostilities between the Allied powers and the Ottoman Empire in October 1918, the latter was allowed to keep only a small part of Anatolia, though this would soon be swept aside by the spectacular victory of General Mustafa Kemal.

El-Ghusein's attitude towards the Armenians—like that of Prince Faisal—was consonant with Sharia, the religious law of Islam. A *firman* (edict) issued in 1917 by Faisal's father, Sharif Hussein, required Arab princes to defend the Armenians living within their borders and among their tribes, by virtue of their protected status, enshrined in the Koran, as *dhimmi*. In Basra, El-Ghusein was given a warm welcome by Sir Percy Cox and Gertrude Bell, who urged him to join the Arab revolt. He did so after discussions with T. E. Lawrence in late October 1916. The future author of *The Seven Pillars of Wisdom* (published in 1926), who was then central to the organization of the Arab revolt against the Ottomans, spotted huge potential for his plan in the person of El-Ghusein and encouraged him to write to Prince Faisal to canvass him for the post of secretary. El-Ghusein's petition was successful, and he became—as Lawrence described him in *The Seven Pillars*—a 'friend at court'.

Eyewitness accounts: his own and others'

It is not El-Ghusein's role in the Arab Revolt that most concerns us here, however, but rather his testimony to the Armenian genocide. A witness—both direct and indirect—to the unfolding tragedy, he collected reliable first-hand accounts from individuals who had participated in the extermination of the Armenians of

Diyarbekir and the surrounding villages and hamlets. On reaching Basra, he was determined to publish this testimony, not just for the sake of exposing the truth but also, as he himself wrote, to defend Islam against the accusations of fanaticism that Europe would be sure to level at it.

There are several respects in which *Martyred Armenia* stands out among other eyewitness accounts of Ottoman atrocities against the Armenians written and published at this time. First and foremost, it was the work of an educated Arab who spoke Turkish as well as his native language and who had been appointed *kaymakam* of Mamuret ul-Aziz by the Ottoman authorities, staying in post there for two and a half years. Armed with these credentials, El-Ghusein could inspire the trust of the Turkish witnesses to whom he spoke and encourage them to confide in him in harrowing detail, as with the officer who described how the authorities in the *vilayet* of Bitlis had rounded up Armenians and herded them into barns before piling straw against the doors and setting it on fire 'so that they perished in the smoke'. Or the doctor by the name of Aziz Bey in the *vilayet* of Sivas who volunteered to oversee butchers hand-picked by himself as they slit the throats of the Armenians. Thus El-Ghusein was able to draw up a macabre inventory of the methods used to slaughter the Armenians, including binding women and children together and casting them down from a great height; throwing men and women into wells and caves and blocking up the entrances, abandoning them to die of thirst and starvation; or stripping them of their possessions and clothes and throwing them into the Tigris or the Euphrates to drown. This information came from reliable witnesses, and sometimes from the mouths of the executioners themselves, who were so convinced that the elimination of the Armenians was in the natural order of things, since the sultan had willed it so, that they were happy to boast about their crimes. On his journey to Diyarbekir, El-Ghusein had himself become an eyewitness to these events, as he encountered hundreds of dead and dying abandoned on the sites where massacres had taken place.

Another remarkable factor was the circumstance by which El-Ghusein was sent back to the *vilayet* where had had been *kaymakam*, but this time as a prisoner on the way to exile, together with five Armenians who had been imprisoned by the Turkish authorities but whom he did not identify by name, for fear that they would be mistreated or worse when *Martyred Armenia* was published. When the prisoners arrived at Diyarbekir, they were unable to continue their journey to Erzurum because of the Russian military presence; at this point, El-Ghusein was imprisoned without any legal justification. When he was released, he rented a house in Diyarbekir where he lived for six and a half months before managing to escape. This period was of critical importance, as it enabled him to observe at close quarters the methods used by the Turkish authorities to exterminate the Armenians.

Does Faiz El-Ghusein therefore merit inclusion as one of the Righteous? While it is true that he did not save any Armenians from death, it is also true that he did not have the power to do so, since he himself was under close guard on the journey into exile. Nor did he gather up any orphans or open any schools. But he nevertheless bore witness, loudly and clearly, to the atrocities committed by the Ottoman government. He had to engineer his escape from Diyarbekir and face innumerable dangers before he reached safety, there to publish his indictment of the executioners and a searingly raw description of the barbaric methods they used to slaughter their victims.

His testimony is especially valuable for being contemporaneous with the events he describes, which he witnessed at first hand or gathered accounts of from eyewitnesses, who in turn were either survivors who had escaped the terrible fate that awaited them or killers who were happy to boast about their murderous crimes.

The attitude adopted towards the Armenians by Arabs varied according to their education and social standing. Many ordinary people refused to hand over the Armenian women and children they had taken in to the Turkish troops. Sometimes this was motivated by simple humanity and solidarity, since the Turks were hostile to the Arabs as well as the Armenians; sometimes it was prompted by more material concerns, such as wanting help with domestic tasks and gardening, or more women in the household, or even because they intended to sell them in slave markets; and sometimes there was a combination of both these motives.

As for the women and children held by Bedouin chiefs in the Arabic Near East, it is possible, as Raymond Kévorkian points out, to draw up a typical profile using the lists of Armenians drawn up by the British intelligence service and identified by name, along with the names of the Bedouin chiefs who refused to give them up: 'They were, for the most part, young women around twenty years old, held in the Wadi Musa, Maan, or elsewhere, who served as objects of a lucrative trade that went beyond the bounds of Transjordan. Thus, these young women were often sold in the slave markets in Arabia.'

Reconnaissance groups were set up under the supervision of the Egyptian Armenians. While some of these, like the one led by Levon Yotnakhparian, benefitted from the support of Prince Faisal of the Hashemite dynasty and of the British General Staff in 1918 and afterwards, others came up against the undisguised reluctance of the Bedouin chiefs. Rupen Herian, nicknamed the *Mufettish el-Ermen* or 'Inspector of the Armenians' by the local people, was sometimes forced to use strong-arm tactics to encourage tribal chiefs to give up their Armenian 'protégés'. In the summer of 1919, Herian succeeded in sending over 500 women and children back to Aleppo.

During that year, the French authorities sent Armenian investigators into Upper Mesopotamia, and their findings have now been studied by Vahé Tachjian. In July 1920, the Armenian Patriarchate in Constantinople estimated that nearly 6,000 children were still scattered among the Arab tribes living in the deserts of Syria and Mesopotamia. The number of young women still held there remained unknown.

Arab respect for Sharia law

The American Near East Relief and Armenian institutions such as the Armenian General Benevolent Union—which helped survivors, set up reconnaissance groups, and created shelters for young women and their children as well as orphanages, dispensaries and schools— were committed to rehabilitating these thousands upon thousands of deeply traumatized people. While the picture of the Armenian 'protégés' in Arab lands offers areas of both light and darkness, it can nevertheless be said that the Arabs were unwilling to carry out massacres, and that unlike the Young Turks, who held Sharia law in contempt, they refused to transgress against its precepts on the *dhimmi*, the protected. This reluctance was further entrenched by Ottoman oppression, which induced feelings of solidarity between

Armenians and Arabs. Prominent figures of high standing in the Arab Muslim world, such as the sharif of Mecca and his son Prince Faisal, the future Iraqi king, were scrupulous in their respect for the teachings of the Koran. Sheikh Faiz El-Ghusein of the Sulut tribe, meanwhile, embodied all that was best in the Bedouin tradition. While it seems probable that he received support from the British and French intelligence services, this in no way diminishes his courage as a patriotic Arab unable to remain silent in the face of the massacres of innocents, and who is emblematic of so many other Arabs who shared his attitude but lacked the means to communicate their own experiences. By virtue of all this, there can be no doubt that he deserves to be included among the Righteous.

In 2004, a group representing the Union of Armenians in Italy, including Pietro Kuciukian, travelled to Syria to meet the family of El-Ghusein. A year later, earth from his grave was placed in the Memorial to the Armenian Genocide at Tsitsernakaberd. El-Ghusein was already considered as *giusto per gli Armeni* (one of the Righteous among the Armenians).

Sources and further reading

Sources

El-Ghusein, Faiz, *Martyred Armenia*, London: C. Arthur Pearson, 1917.

Studies

'Fayez El Ghossein (1883–1938)', Gariwo (Gardens of the Righteous Worldwide), https://it.gariwo.net/giusti/biografie-dei-giusti/metz-yeghern/giusti-del-muro-della-memoria-di-yerevan/fayez-el-ghossein-173.html

Kévorkian, *Armenian Genocide*, p. 367.

Kévorkian, Raymond H. et al., *The Armenian General Benevolent Union: One Hundred Years of History*, vol. 1, *1906–1940*, n.p.: Armenian General Benevolent Union, 2006, pp. 54–9.

Kuciukian, *I disobbedienti*, pp. 197–202.

Tachjian, Vahé, 'Femmes et enfants arméniens: Les rescapés du génocide', *Histoire du christianisme magazine*, 65 (March–April 2013), pp. 24–46.

25

TESTIMONY OF GENERAL JEAN-MICHEL BILEMDJIAN

The story of his father Ovhannes and his rescue by a Righteous Arab

Ovhannes, son of Agop and Vartouhi Bilemdjian, was born in Aintab (now Gaziantep), eastern Cilicia, in 1907. Until 1915, he lived happily with his family and numerous cousins in Aintab's Armenian quarter, beneath the walls of its medieval castle.

In early 1915, Ovhannes' father and one of his uncles, both *fedayeen* (members of an armed group prepared to sacrifice their lives for a wider cause), received orders to mount an assault on a Turkish gendarmerie guardhouse and to kill as many gendarmes as possible in retaliation for the gendarmes' violent attacks on Armenians living on the outskirts of the town. After successfully completing their mission, the two men were hunted down in a Turkish cemetery, surrounded by gendarmes and killed when they ran out of bullets. Their bodies were then tied behind horses and dragged through the streets of the Armenian quarter as a demonstration to the *fedayeen* in general, and to the Bilemdjian family in particular, that they were not invincible. The young Ovhannes was a witness to this macabre spectacle, the painful memories of which left an enduring mark.

Ovhannes was nearly eight in July 1915, when columns of deportees from the north halted at Aintab. He watched as his mother prepared fruit, bread and cheese and put it all into a large basket. Understanding that this was food for the deportees, he filled his pockets with pistachios from the tin in which he carefully stored them and went with his mother and other women relatives to distribute handfuls of them to the children. It is possible that these included Karnig Panian, who would be Ovhannes' companion in misfortune at the orphanage in Antoura, and who would later publish a memoir of his experiences. A few weeks later, at the very end of July, it was the turn of Ovhannes, his mother and his two younger sisters to join a column of deportees. The convoy headed for Aleppo, then the concentration camp at Meskeneh, and ultimately—for those who survived—the camp at Der Zor, some 300 kilometres east of Aleppo.

One morning after the convoy had left Aleppo, Ovhannes woke to find his mother had gone. He would never know what happened to her, whether she was abducted by a Turkish, Bedouin or Kurdish gendarme, and he was never to see her again. Now the full weight of responsibility for his two young sisters fell on his eight-year-old shoulders.

At Meskeneh, both his sisters perished for lack of basic supplies, carried off by the epidemics of disease that ravaged the camp. With the help of other orphans of his own age, Ovhannes piled little heaps of stones over their bodies to prevent them from being eaten by jackals or packs of wild dogs.

Ovhannes survived in the camp as best he could, until one day a senior officer in the Syrian Arab police took ownership of him. This took place in front of one of the gendarmes guarding the camp, who may have sold him. Ovhannes would never know, but he remembered that the two men talked at length, and then the gendarme walked away. The police officer took him by the hand and led him away.

They travelled by horse-drawn carriage to Aleppo, some 60 kilometres away. When they reached his house, the police officer introduced the boy to his elderly mother and told him that they would keep him safe and give him board and food, and that in return he was to carry out household tasks that the officer's mother could no longer do and look after the kitchen garden.

A few weeks later, two gendarmes came to the house and arrested the police officer. Soon afterwards, they took him to the prison at Daraa, 400 kilometres south of Aleppo and close to the Jordanian border. Ovhannes would never know whether he had been denounced for committing an act that was forbidden under Turkish law or whether he had previously shown hostility to the Ottoman government. His arrest was deeply worrying for the boy.

Some weeks after the officer was taken away, the officer's mother wound a wide bandage round the boy's leg and hid some money in it. She asked him to take it to her son in prison and gave him instructions to ensure the stratagem's success. She was well aware that corruption was rife among the gendarmes, especially among the prison guards.

Travelling by train and on foot, Ovhannes reached Daraa. Once there—thanks to a few Turkish expressions that he already knew and some phrases that the old lady had made him learn by heart—he managed to visit his protector in prison:

> Hello Ovhannes. What are you doing here? Do you bring me good news or bad?
>
> Good news, effendi! Mayrig [Mother] has hidden money in this bandage for you.
>
> Thank you, Ovhannes, for making this long journey for me, but keep the money for yourself. It won't be any use to me. Tomorrow, I am to be hanged on the square outside the prison. I ask one last thing of you: stay and watch my execution, then go back and tell my mother that I died with great courage. That will be some consolation for her.

After hugging Ovhannes tightly, the police officer asked him to leave the prison so as not to make the guard suspicious. The boy found an abandoned house on the square and spent the night in it. At daybreak, three gallows stood on the square. Ovhannes watched as his protector and two other condemned men were hanged.

Distraught, the boy set off back to Aleppo, reaching the city late the following night. There he imparted the tragic news to the frail old lady, who for a brief period would continue to give him shelter and food.

A few weeks later, a patrol of Turkish gendarmes stopped Ovhannes in the street and questioned him. They would not let him go back to the house but took him straight to an abandoned school, where another dozen or so Armenian orphans were already waiting.

Several days later, two gendarmes escorted all the children on the train journey to the orphanage at Antoura, where Karnig Panian and around 200 orphans, mostly from the camp at Hama, had already been taken.

THE RIGHTEOUS AND PEOPLE OF CONSCIENCE

Sources and further reading

General Jean-Michel Bilemdjian is a graduate of Saint-Cyr Military Academy and officer of the Légion d'Honneur and the Ordre nationale du Mérite. As a young officer, he served in the Parachute Engineer Regiment and in French army mechanized units in Germany. As a senior officer, he was commanding officer of a regiment and then at the École du Génie in Angers, before being appointed second-in-command of the United Nations Interim Force in Lebanon in 1985–6 and commanding officer of UN operations in southern Iraq in 1995–6.

No direct information about this righteous Arab is available. Remarkable light is shed on the experiences of Ovhannes Bilemdjian and his family in the memoirs of Karnig Panian, who shared his fate: Panian, Karnig, *Goodbye, Antoura: A Memoir of the Armenian Genocide*, Stanford: Stanford University Press, 2015.

Lutfieh Bilemdjian, the sole survivor of the immediate family of Ovhannes, came from Ayntab and was deported to Der Zor. She was rescued from slavery—during which she was tattooed—in 1926, as part of an official operation by the Danish missionary Karen Jeppe with the support of Arab chiefs.

26

ABDUL HALIM ÇELEBI

Compassion among the Sufi

Sufism in medieval Anatolia

Sufism—the most introspective aspect of Islam, drawing on an esoteric reading of the Koran—has a long tradition of mystics who strive to go beyond the quest for *haqiqa* (eternal spiritual truth) and the narrow application of Sharia (the letter of divine law) to discover the deeper meaning hidden within Islam's sacred text. According to its followers, the origins of Sufism stretch back almost as far as those of Islam itself, and the Traditions of the Prophet are rich in mysticism.

With its less stringent approach to some precepts of the Koran and their application, Sufism has attracted large numbers of Muslims in quest of a spiritual inner life that they believe a literal interpretation of the Koran would be unable to provide.

The practice of Sufism rests on a hadith that draws parallels between the 'minor jihad', as practised on the battlefield, and the 'major jihad', or the believer's struggle against the darkness of the inner self. Only mastery of the soul (*nafs*) can make room for God in the believer's heart and open a dialogue with him.

Spreading gradually throughout the Islamic world, Sufism began to be structured into different orders from the twelfth century onwards. One of these orders was the Mevlevi, founded in Konya, Turkey, in the Seljuk Sultanate of Rum. The founders of the order were the successors of Jalal ad-Din Muhammad Rumi (1207–73), known as Mevlana ('our master'), and its members are often called 'whirling dervishes'—a reference to their sacred dance (*samâ*), in which the dancers revolve slowly before whirling faster and faster, until they reach a trance-like state of immersion in God. Nowadays, the *samâ* is often viewed as a spectacle rather than a form of prayer leading to God.

Conflict between Sheikh Abdul Halim Çelebi and the Young Turks

In 1910, the leader of the Mevlevi order was Abdul Halim Çelebi, a man of holiness whose profound tolerance and openness of spirit earned him considerable unpopularity among the Young Turks. On 24 May 1910, he was dismissed as sheikh and replaced by Veled Çelebi. In response, the dignitaries of Konya showered Constantinople with telegrams protesting against his removal, all of which had no effect.

With the obliging Veled Çelebi in post, the CUP resumed its deportation policy. But Abdul Halim implored the local population to protect their Armenian fellow citizens and not to allow a single drop of their blood to be shed. Powerless to stop the deportations, he urged the people of Konya to do what they could to help the suffering victims.

In the years leading up to the deportations and the massacres at Konya in 1915, Abdul Halim Çelebi had observed the deteriorating situation with mounting anxiety. On 13 April 1909, two men who preached in the mosque at Konya, dressed as *hodja* (wise men), had incited the people to attack the local Christians. Panic had spread through the town, and the governor of Konya had taken no action to calm the situation. While hundreds of Armenians sought refuge in the British consulate, Abdul Halim made conciliatory speeches in an effort to restore calm. His intervention was successful in preventing a massacre.

His attitude could hardly fail to attract the attention of the Young Turk government. Although he had worked with them to oust Abdul Hamid from the throne, the gulf between him and the Unionists grew ever wider, and eventually he accused them of following a 'policy of madness'. Meanwhile, by appealing to the new sultan, Mehmed Reshad V (ruled 1909–18), son of Abdul Hamid II, who had been installed on the throne by the Unionists, he had managed to save several individuals whom he knew to be innocent from the gallows. The new rulers did not look favourably on all this.

In May 1910, Abdul Halim was dismissed from his position and replaced by Veled Çelebi. Although he now had no official standing, he continued to follow the actions of the CUP closely, launching scathing attacks on them and describing them as a 'cruel organization' as they began to implement their policy of destroying the Christian community.

In his memoirs, the Armenian Catholic bishop of Trebizond, Monsignor Jean Naslian, published a collection of accounts by Armenians who had survived the massacres, all of which concur in bearing witness to Abdul Halim Çelebi's demands that the people of Konya should protect their Christian fellow citizens.

The relationship between the Mevlevi sheikhs and the Ottoman sultans

The Mevlevi order consolidated its relationship with the Ottoman sultans from the fourteenth century, when Devlet Hatun, descended from the eldest son of Jalal ad-Din Muhammad Rumi, married Sultan Bayezid I (ruled 1389–1403). Among other functions attributed to the Mevlevi, the sheikhs enjoyed the privilege of taking part in the sultans' enthronement ceremony, in which the new sultan would be girded with the Sword of Osman by the sheikh of the Mevlevi order. Abdul Halim was the last sheikh of the order to take part in this ceremony, carrying out this duty for the last sultan, Mehmed Reshad V. With the weakening of Unionist power that accompanied the defeat of the empire, his high rank was restored to him.

In 1925, he was dismissed from office once again, and in the same year the Mevlevi order was declared illegal and its holy places shut down. The order's Mevlevihane, or lodge, was turned into the Mevlevi Museum.

Abdul Halim Çelebi left Konya and moved into a hotel in Constantinople. He died on 12 November 1925. The cause of his death is disputed: some reports state that he fell or jumped from his hotel balcony, while others claim that he died in hospital from complications of diabetes.

THE RIGHTEOUS AND PEOPLE OF CONSCIENCE

Sources and further reading

Élias, 'Le Soufisme ou l'humanisme de l'Islam', *La Tribune d'octobre*, 19 (*El-Badil*, Montreuil 25 March 1990).

Hoffner, Anna-Bénedicte, 'Le soufisme, langue des mystiques musulmans', *La Croix*, 18 December 2013.

Massignon, Louis, 'Taşawwuf', in *E. J. Brill's First Encyclopaedia of Islam 1913–1936*, reprint edn, Leiden: Brill, 1993, vol. 8, cols. 681–5.

Sourdel, Dominique and Janine Sourdel-Thomine, 'Sufism', in Sourdel and Sourdel-Thomine, *Glossary of Islam*.

FAMILIES

27

TESTIMONIES REVEALING A RESPECT FOR OR COMPROMISE WITH THE CONCEPT OF *'ADÂLA*

Armenians who escaped the genocide were able to do so for a variety of different reasons, as the historian Hasmik Tevosyan has documented. Many of the Armenians of Smyrna and Constantinople were saved by the presence of foreign diplomatic missions in the cities. Some Armenians were spared because they possessed valuable skills that the Young Turks did not want to lose. Some women married Muslims, most of them against their will, and converted to Islam, while children were placed in Turkish families as slaves or were adopted by couples who were unable to have children. Some Armenians escaped under the protection of the Russian army (notably in Van) or the French navy (at Musa Dagh). Some, for the most part orphans, were taken in and rescued by missionary organizations. And others, more rarely, survived the massacres thanks to their Kurdish or Turkish neighbours, who hid them at the risk of their own lives. Many of these cases involve rescuers whose names have not come down to us. And not all of them were disinterested. Given the dangers involved and the religious differences between the Armenians, Turks and Kurds, which were widely exploited by Young Turk propaganda, there were few people prepared to take the risk of saving the Armenians.

Yet there were still instances of rescues for humanitarian motives. In the town of Bayburt, the Turkish townspeople were generally opposed to the deportations, to the point where Mehmet Nusret Bey, *kaymakam* of the *kaza* of Bayburt, felt obliged to execute three Turks, so making an example of them and encouraging a more cooperative attitude. In May 1915, the elite of the town's Armenian community were arrested and hanged, while the first convoy of deportees left the town on 4 June, to be followed by others throughout the month. Despite local opposition to the deportations, the deportees were massacred, and very few Armenians survived.

Some Armenian families entrusted one or more of their children to Kurdish or Turkish families before they were deported. The missionary Henry H. Riggs, a witness to the genocide, described the attitude of many Turks towards the Armenians with whom they had lived side by side:

> Their Moslem neighbours were inclined to side with them rather than with the government, in spite of all the efforts of the government to inflame the minds of the Turk, the more intelligent Turks for the most part remained either indifferent or positively friendly to the Armenians. Some were very outspoken in their condemnation of the government and expressed their sympathy with the Armenians. There were plenty of Turks, of course, who gladly took advantage of this opportunity to clear up old scores with their Armenian rivals, or of enriching themselves at their expense. But there was no outbreak of popular fanaticism on the part of the Turks. In fact, we who had lived all our lives among the Turks and knew something of their ways said again and again at the time, 'This is not a Turkish outbreak.' It was altogether too cold, too calculating, too efficient. The common people liked it not.
>
> So it happened that the Turks individually did much to help their friends and rescue them from their fate. Some did it from real neighbourly kindness, some from motives of cupidity or worse. At first, a large number of Armenians took refuge in the homes of their Turkish neighbours hoping thus to be overlooked in the general search. Soon, however, it became apparent that the government officials would not tolerate this. Threats of severe punishment and the systematic searching of suspected Muslim houses by the police soon brought most of the Turks to terms, and all but a few of the Armenians so sheltered fell into the hands of the police. Some were directly betrayed by their protectors, but more were secretly turned out to shift for themselves, which was little better.
>
> There were some few Turks, however, who were either fearless enough or influential enough to defy the threats of the government.

THE CONCEPT OF 'ADÂLA

In spite of repeated commands and threats, they kept the Armenians whom they were sheltering out of sight of the police, and refused to reveal their hiding places.

The historian Taner Akçam, a professor at Clark University, Massachusetts, dedicated his remarkable study *A Shameful Act: The Armenian Genocide and the Question of Turkish Responsibility* to the memory of the Turkish businessman Haji Halil, 'a devout Muslim Turk who saved the members of an Armenian family from deportation and death by keeping them safely hidden for over half a year, risking his own life'. He first heard this story from Greg Sarkissian, president of the Zoryan Institute (a registered charity in the United States and Canada that promotes the study and recognition of genocide, with particular reference to the Armenian genocide), whose own family had been saved by Haji Halil, who hid the eight members of his mother's family in his home for some six months. Halil had promised his Armenian business partner that if anything should happen to him, he would take care of his family. He kept his promise, hiding the family in his home and taking on the responsibility of feeding eight extra mouths, which was no easy feat in wartime. It was vital to avoid getting caught, moreover, as he and his family were risking their lives. To avoid suspicion, he smuggled extra food into the house at night. When two of the Armenian children died, he buried them in secret. His servants knew that he was sheltering Armenians, but none of them betrayed him. In risking his life to protect the family, he thus honoured his promise to his Armenian friend.

The accounts collected from survivors and eyewitnesses of the genocide by the ethnologist Verjine Svazlian shed light on stories of Turks who rescued Armenians, and their mixed reasons for doing so. Armand Arapian bore witness to the way in which his grandfather Armenak Arapian was saved:

> Armenak must have been born in 1875. His father used to call him Artin. He had five brothers and one sister. The whole family lived in Akşehir in central Turkey. They had grown wealthy importing and exporting furs and opium, which it was not yet illegal to grow. According to family legend, when you came out of Akşehir railway station there were three immense warehouses that belonged to our

family. Armenak was the accountant for the family business. In 1912, he married Myriam Mesdjian, my grandmother, who was then sixteen. The celebrations lasted for a whole week, as was the tradition among wealthy families. In 1913, my aunt, Verkine, was born, followed in June 1915 by my father, Movsês. It was with these two tiny children that the family was deported across Turkey to Der Zor. During this first exodus, Myriam's brother died of typhus. On the journey, Armenak managed to save his family by hiding in the basement of a house belonging to a Turkish family. History does not relate whether or not their protectors were Righteous people.

This story demonstrates the difficulty that so often surrounds the designation of 'Righteous'. It is not always easy to determine whether the motivations of rescuers were purely altruistic, or whether there was an element of self-interest at work.

Taron Khachatrian describes how a Kurdish woman promised her Armenian neighbours that she would save their seven-year-old son. She was true to her word. When officials came knocking at her door, she claimed that she had killed all the Armenians who had crossed her path with her own hands. In fact, she kept the child with her for a year.

One unnamed witness told how a Turkish soldier, whose name is now forgotten, saved an entire Armenian family in Smyrna. He went to warn them of the danger of a massacre, mounted the children on donkeys and led the family to the port, where they were able to board a ship to Greece and so avoid the massacres. The Armenian family later learned that their Turkish rescuer and all his family had been executed for helping the Armenians flee.

Mariam Karatchian, born in 1903 in Adıyaman, had been left under a tree with her little brother while their mother went to beg for a crust of bread, when a Turkish gendarme found them and killed the little boy by crushing him with a rock. A Kurdish woman who witnessed the scene took pity on the little girl, leading her away in case she suffered the same fate as her brother. Hiding the girl in her tent, she managed to heal her wounds by applying a salve and took care of her until the Americans arrived and took her to the orphanage in Aleppo.

THE CONCEPT OF 'ADÂLA

Hagop Mourad Mouradian, born at Fertek in 1903, was entrusted by his mother to a Kurdish family, which was to prove his salvation. All the Armenians in the village were massacred, with the exception of a few who were also sheltered by Kurds. When he grew up, Hagop married a young Kurdish woman, and together they had three children.

Born in Kessab, also in 1903, Kioulinia Dzerouni Moussoyan recounted how she and her family were deported in 1915. On the march, her elderly grandfather was struggling to walk when a Turkish gendarme approached and struck him. Kioulinia's mother screamed at the gendarme, asking him if he had no shame in hitting an old man. Suddenly seized by remorse, the gendarme went to find camels for the family to ride on, but the grandfather died of thirst on the way. The rest of the family did not reach Der Zor but stopped in the town of Hama, where a Turk offered them shelter in his house and did all he could to help them. It was thanks to the goodness of this family that Kioulinia's family survived.

In addition to the children who were saved in this way, some Turks showed their gratitude to Armenians who had previously helped them by saving Armenian lives in return during the genocide and so running all the attendant risks. We know little about a man named Hac Halil Boum, for instance, except that he rescued an Armenian who had previously saved his own life in prison. One of the torments inflicted on the Armenians by the Turks was to entomb them in ancient Persian underground water cisterns, where they were forced to try to survive among the decomposing bodies of their compatriots. One man, Elias Djerdji Nasri Nazarian, was able to survive thanks to Hac Halil Boum, who managed to get him out of the cistern in which he was imprisoned.

Yeghya Demirdjian recounted how her father Haroutioun and his younger brother Hayk were rescued in Mamahatun (present-day Tercan). The two boys, then fourteen and twelve, had already lost their father, a man of good reputation who had gone to a political meeting and never returned, probably having been killed on his way there or on the way back. When the deportation order was posted on the walls of the town, the family's Kurdish neighbours, grateful for the many kind deeds the father had done for them, went to find his widow and offered to hide her family with them. She chose to leave the town with her fellow Armenians, taking her two youngest children with her, as she thought that her skills as a nurse would be useful and ensure her survival. But realizing that Haroutioun and Hayk, being older boys, would be killed as soon as they left the town, she decided to entrust them to the Kurds and left them to live with them. One day, while the boys were watching the cows with the family's daughter, the girl's cousin, a gendarme, came and told her to hand over the children to him. She refused and gave him a slap. When she told her father about the altercation that evening, he went to see his brother and complained about his son the gendarme's attitude. When the son came home, his father beat him with a stick and forbade him ever again to dare ask for the Armenian children whom his uncle had taken in. Never again did he do so, for in these regions the respect commanded by the father of a household outweighed all other considerations. After the Armistice, the boys left for Malatya before going on to the refugee camps in Aleppo. The family later settled in France, where Haroutioun's granddaughter would meet and marry a young Kurd who was as distinguished in his character as he was in his lineage.

Antranig Tchachikian told how his family was saved by a Turkish gardener. Born in Tripoli to a German father, a civil engineer who specialized in building bridges, and an Armenian mother, Archalouys, Antranig was caught up in the full horror of the genocide. Despite being German, his father was killed, along with his brother, and the rest of the family was sent into exile. They were saved by their Turkish gardener, who had been well treated by the family and felt gratitude and loyalty towards them. When the massacres began, he hid Archalouys, Antranig and his sister in the long grass under one of the bridges that his father had built, and despite all the risks smuggled food to them. When the Americans reached Tripoli, the family were able to sail for Greece, safe and sound, thanks to the Turkish gardener who had saved their lives.

In Smyrna, the family of Antranig Semerdjian also owed their lives to the kindness of a Turkish neighbour. In 1918, the family lived in a quarter of the city that was too close to the French consulate for the Turkish army to be able to perpetrate a massacre there. So the Turks ordered the Armenians not to leave their houses, in the hope that they would die of starvation. The three Semerdjian children, Antranig, Khatoun and Vartivar, the eldest of whom was just thirteen, remembered writhing on the floor, tortured by hunger pangs, when a Turkish neighbour knocked on their door and brought them food. Despite the risks, she continued to feed the family for several months. Eventually, the family were able to board a French ship bound for Athens, where they arrived unharmed.

Similarly, Assadour Hovsep Menetchian, born in Afyonkarahisar in 1907, was saved thanks to a Turkish neighbour who came to see his mother and asked her to leave her door open and come and take refuge with her. When the police knocked on the Turkish neighbour's door, she pretended that a high-ranking official lived there. The police believed her, and thanks to her goodness and presence of mind the family was saved.

The story told by Jean Kujumgian is particularly remarkable. When a convoy of deportees left Adana for the terrible fate that awaited them at Der Zor, the gendarmes who were escorting the march, knowing that the deportees would be massacred when they arrived at their destination, diverted the convoy in a different direction, thus saving large numbers of Armenians from certain death. Afterwards, they could never go back to their homes in Adana, since if they did so they risked being hanged for disobeying orders.

After the genocide, there were some Turks who showed kindness to the survivors. At this stage, they were not running the same risks as those who had intervened during the genocide, but their good deeds were not forgotten by the survivors. As a young woman, Esther Armine Zerahian recalled how the director of the orphanage at Samsun, whom she called 'Müdür Effendi' ('Mr Director') and about whom she knew nothing except that he was Bulgarian, was kind to the orphans. It was to him, she testified, that she owed her life.

These Righteous and people of conscience were driven by a variety of motives. Some risked their lives out of friendship, others out of compassion, others again out of gratitude towards Armenians who had been their benefactors, and some because they were doubtless unable to stifle the instinct to save a child. Sometimes the Islamic faith also played a part. The Islamic concept of 'adâla or justice, as we are reminded by Fatma Müge Goçek, forbade the massacre of innocents, echoing the hadith describing how Muhammad put the Jewish Ben-i Kureysh tribe to the sword for rebelling against him but spared the innocents and children. Hence

Muslims with a true understanding of Islam could be prompted to undertake good actions by their religious sentiments.

There were also some Turks and Kurds, finally, who might have enabled some Armenians to survive, but who could not by any means be described as Righteous. Some officials and gendarmes agreed to help Armenians escape deportation in return for money. The father of Serop Chloyan, born in Kharpert in 1903, gave a sum of money to a high-ranking Turk in the hope that he would help. This proved to be of no avail, however, since several members of the family were deported all the same, and those who remained were reduced to slavery. Other Armenians did manage to escape the death marches by paying, but it was not unusual, nevertheless, for people who had been paid to save Armenians in this way to fail to honour their promises once the deal had been done. Rescuing Armenians was a punishable offence, after all, with sanctions that grew in severity as the genocide unfolded. Whether or not they demanded money from them, the rescuers of Armenians were risking their lives.

The fate of Selim Agha, the Kurdish chief of a small village in Sassoun province who bribed a Turkish officer, hoping to save several Armenian families by declaring they worked for him, is testimony to the gravity of the danger. While Selim Agha was genuinely one of the Righteous, the Turkish officer who took his bribe had no intention of honouring his word. A few days later, Selim Agha was beheaded for helping the Armenians, and his severed head was sent to Muş as a warning to other Kurds who might be tempted to act as rescuers.

Papken Injarabian related how as a child, after seeing a number of his family perish during the genocide, he was abducted by a Kurd and reduced to slavery as the man's goatherd, ill-fed and barefoot. In four years of captivity, he had nine different masters. He eventually managed to escape, despite the threats of his last master, and reached the orphanage at Urfa.

A young Turkish woman called Sevim told how her Armenian grandmother had seen her entire family killed in front of her. The man who had massacred her family then forced her to marry him and convert to Islam, changing her name to Ayse. She was terrorized by her husband throughout her marriage, and only when close to death did she dare speak Armenian again.

THE CONCEPT OF 'ADÂLA

Zepur Medznakian recounted how, surrounded by corpses, she had cried out that she would convert to Islam. A Kurd tossed her a blood-soaked chemise and took her away with her seriously wounded sister. When he saw how serious their wounds were, he abandoned the girls on a riverbank. They hid in a wheat field and early next morning spotted some Kurds who had been sleeping in the open, as was customary in the summer. The Kurds gave the girls some food, then made them work for them. When Zepur caught typhus, the girls were handed over to the government, who put them in prison. There they were forced to convert to Islam and given Turkish names, Zubideh and Zelkha.

While these forced marriages and conversions may have enabled some Armenians to survive, they contributed to the annihilation of their identity. As Ugur Ümit Üngör points out, 'what was saved was merely the physical existence of this or that individual. The self was stripped of all its Armenian characteristics, including Armenian names, and these were buried deep in private memories and banished from the public memory.'

In the considerable research work that remains to be done in identifying the Righteous of the Armenian genocide, distinguishing between Righteous people who acted purely out of humanitarian and altruistic concerns, rescuers who were motivated by self-interest, and slave masters who preserved Armenian lives while contributing to the destruction of their identity thus presents a challenge, the resolution of which is as difficult as it is necessary.

Sources and further reading

Sources

'Arménak', http://www.imprescriptible.fr/dossiers/arapian/armenak

Asso, Annick, *Le Cantique des larmes: Arménie 1915*, Paris: La Table ronde, 2005, *passim*.

'Extraits de Témoignages de survivants, Témoins Oculaires du génocide des Arméniens', http://www.imprescriptible.fr/pedagogie/pedagogie/temoignage-svazlian.htm

Orfalian, Sonia, *Paroles d'enfants arméniens, 1915–1922* [with contributions by Joël Kotek, Yves Ternon, Gérard Chaliand], Paris: Gallimard, 2021.

Riggs, *Days of Tragedy in Armenia*, pp. 96–7.

THE RIGHTEOUS AND PEOPLE OF CONSCIENCE

'Sevim, femme turque à la recherche de ses racines arméniennes', https://www.imprescriptible.fr/dossiers/sevim/racines

'Témoignage devant le Tribunal des Peuples', http://www.imprescriptible.fr/dossiers/tribunal/injarabian

Studies

Göçek, 'In Search of the "Righteous People": The Case of the Armenian Massacres of 1915', in Andrieu, Gensburger and Sémelin, *Resisting Genocide*, pp. 33–50.

'Honoring "Turkish Schindlers": Forgotten Heroes of the Armenian Genocide', Worldcrunch, https://worldcrunch.com/world-affairs/honoring-turkish-schindlers-forgotten-heroes-of-the-armenian-genocide

Kévorkian, 'Ottoman Officials against the Armenian Genocide', in Andrieu, Gensburger and Sémelin, *Resisting Genocide*, pp. 183–201.

'The Story of Haji Khalil', Zoryan Institute, https://zoryaninstitute.org/wp-content/uploads/2017/04/The-Story-of-Haji-Khalil.pdf

Tevosyan, Hasmik, 'Rescue Practices during the Armenian Genocide', in Andrieu, Gensburger and Sémelin, *Resisting Genocide*, pp. 163–82.

Üngör, Ugur Ümit, 'Conversion and Rescue: Survival Strategies in the Armenian Genocide', in Andrieu, Gensburger and Sémelin, *Resisting Genocide*, pp. 201–18.

28

THE SOMOUNDJIAN FAMILY

Narrative of the family's deportation from Turkey and exile in Greece, collected by Jean-Claude Parcot from the accounts of his mother-in-law Chaké Derderian, née Somoundjian, mother of Hermine and survivor of the Armenian genocide.

The Somoundjian family originated from Bardizag, a small town on the heights overlooking the Sea of Marmara, some 40 kilometres from İzmit, known in ancient times as Nicomedia. A farming town, it was also a religious and intellectual centre, with three churches, eight Armenian schools and an American college.

In August 1915, Garabed and Zarouhi Somoundjian, with five of their children, their two sons-in-law and their five grandchildren, were forced to leave their homes, with all the other Armenians of Bardizag, and join a march to İzmit. There they were to board a train to Adana, where, they were told, they would be safe. Worried by this order from the gendarmerie, Garabed snatched time to go to the post office to send a telegram to their son Ohannes, a medical officer who was away in Berlin on a training course, to warn him about what was happening to his family.

Exhausted after the march, the family reached the railway station at İzmit. There they were forced into a railway carriage on a train heading for Adana, relieved to be together. On the way, the train stopped at towns including Eskişehir and Afyonkarahisar, where more and more distressed and suffering families boarded it. When the train stopped at Konya station, they heard a loudspeaker announcement ordering the Somoundjian family to get off. Was it a lucky chance or a trap? Garabed and Zarouhi decided to obey the order, taking their family with them and leaving the space they had occupied to be filled by more families dragging their bundles of belongings. As they left the station, they passed a window, where an officer in the gendarmerie explained to his subordinate that they had to let this family through because he had received an order from Berlin. It was then that the family realized that the telegram Garabed had sent in desperation had borne fruit. And to think that he had been reluctant to let his son study medicine in Constantinople for fear he would be tempted to get involved in politics and be active in the Dashnak party.

In Konya, Garabed and Zarouhi knocked on the door of the Greek Orthodox church to ask for shelter. This proved a wise choice, as the Greek family the priest recommended welcomed them with open arms, accommodating them in two well-appointed barns belonging to their business. The men—Garabed, his son Khatchig and his sons-in-law—soon set to work doing manual labour in their hosts' business, treating animal skins and cleaning and sorting sheep intestines to pay for their keep. Meanwhile, the Greek and Armenian women helped each other out in countless different ways, sharing the cooking, sewing, gardening and household chores. In this way, the Greek family sheltered the Somoundjians from August 1915 to October 1918. They ran considerable risks in doing so, since only Muslims were allowed to take in Armenians, and even then only for forced conversion to Islam, to exploit them for work or, if they were young and female, for sexual gratification. The Greek *dhimmis* (protected people) of the empire were forbidden from giving any aid to them whatsoever.

Once the Armistice of Mudros was signed between the Ottoman Empire and Great Britain (representing the Allied powers) in October 1918, and the Three Pashas—Talaat, Enver and Cemal—had fled to Germany, Garabed, Zarouhi and their children wanted to go back to Bardizag, since the political situation seemed to have returned to normal. For were their house and garden not under the protection of the Turkish state? Leaving the Greek family was heart-rending, and the journey back to Bardizag was an epic ordeal, but the worst was yet to come when they discovered that all the Armenian houses in the village were now occupied by Turks. In the circumstances, it was impossible to get their house back or to fight the Turkish law requisitioning all Armenian possessions. It was then that Garabed, Zarouhi and the children decided to leave Bardizag. Garabed paid a Turkish peasant he knew through his wholesale business to drive them hidden in a covered wagon to the nearest port, on the Sea of Marmara. There, by a stroke of luck for which they could never have dared to hope, they were able to jump on a Greek ship that took them to the port of Volos. By an irony of geography, they had travelled from one shore of the Aegean to the other.

Following the advice of the Greek people they met in Volos, the family immigrated to the north-west of Greece, settling in the Thracian town of Komotini, where there was work on farms and in the disinfection of malarial regions. Then, one day in the spring of 1919, the whole family rejoiced at the most wonderful news. Ohannes, the doctor in Berlin, had discovered from the Red Cross in Aleppo, where he had gone to work with the British army, that his parents, brother and sisters had survived the genocide and settled in Komotini. A new life now began for the family, reunited after their extraordinary experiences. Ohannes soon opened a medical practice that proved to be a godsend both for the region, which was then suffering an epidemic of malaria, and for his younger sister Chaké, who became his medical secretary.

Jean-Claude Pacot is a retired history and geography teacher and former deputy mayor (2001–14) of the fifth arrondissement of Lyon, with responsibility for education, memory and military veterans. He is married to Ermine Derderian, former Italian teacher and daughter of Chaké Derderian. He is the author of *Survivre à la mort de ses enfants* (Saint-Denis: Société des Écrivains, 2017), inspired by a family tragedy, and *Odyssées arméniennes* (Saint-Denis: Société des Écrivains, 2021), an imagined history of the Somoundjian and Derderian families in the medieval period, followed by the true story of their deportation and exile.

29

THE KAZARIAN AND SAKOYAN FAMILIES

Testimonies related by Archpriest Pierre Kazarian, Orthodox Church of Sainte-Philothée d'Athènes, Domaine de Grammont, Montpellier

A few aspects of the history the Armenian community in the *sanjak* of Yozgat in the *vilayet* of Angora (Ankara), in Central Anatolia, established with the help of specialists in the field, will help to put the events in this narrative in context.

Lying at an altitude of over 1,300 metres on the Anatolian Plateau, the district had a large Armenian population as well as a few Greek communities, who together were slightly outnumbered by the Muslim population. The Armenian population was largely rural and scattered among over fifty villages, mostly in the southern part of the district, over half of which were exclusively Armenian. According to Greek sources, there were Armenian-speaking Greek Orthodox communities in Anatolia from the eleventh century, which endured despite being marginalized by the official Armenian church and would later be included in the exchange of population between Greece and Turkey in 1923.

The city of Yozgat, the administrative centre of the *sanjak* and capital of the *kaza* of the same name, was founded in the early eighteenth century by the chief of a Turkmen tribe, when the Armenian craftsmen who helped build it settled there. The principal Armenian place of worship was the cathedral of the Holy Mother of God, attached to which were buildings housing the Armenian Apostolic Bishopric, itself attached juridically to the Armenian Catholicosate of Cilicia with its seat at Sis. Armenians also worshipped at the church of the Holy Trinity. Three Armenian schools were set up in the 1870s, and it has been estimated that in 1872–3 the city counted 1,220 Armenian households, 200 Greek and 2,500 Turkish. On the eve of the genocide in 1915, the total population of the *sanjak* was 38,000, of whom 12,000 were Armenian. The Armenians of the city, like the Greeks, were mostly tradespeople and artisans (including large numbers of blacksmiths and tailors). With its stone-built houses with tiled roofs surrounded by orchards where its famous apricots grew, the settlement was a handsome city. By 1931, in the wake of the genocide, the Armenian population had been reduced to a mere 500.

This was the background against which the tragic and heroic odyssey of the Kazarian and Sakoyan families unfolded, as recalled by myself and my older cousin Éliane Sakoyan. This was not an easy process, as the only testimonies I have are oral accounts heard in my early youth. My family drew a veil over the subject of the genocide and put their hopes in a better future.

My great-grandfather on my mother's side, Father Ohannes Der Sakoyan, was the priest of an Armenian parish in Yozgat, and because he had received an education he was also the local teacher. As he also held a number of other positions, he was a prominent figure locally. He was married to Tourvanda Alexandrian, and they had five children.

During the first phase of the genocide, from April to October 1915, the couple fell victim to the brutality meted out by thugs of the Special Organization. Their house was seized, and the couple were arrested and tortured; Tourvanda's breasts were cut off, they were both hanged and their bodies burned. Two of their children died on a deportation march. The surviving children, two girls— seventeen-year-old Gulnar and her younger sister Zarouhi—and their brother Ohannes were watched over throughout their painful wanderings, from Yozgat to Beirut, by the Greek priest of Yozgat. This priest must have taken considerable risks, for it was forbidden for *dhimmis* to take in Armenians or help them in any way, on pain of severe punishment.

The two girls had been involved in resistance activities even before the genocide, in the face of the growing danger posed by the rise to power of the Young Turks (partial in 1908, just before the Adana massacres, and completed in 1913). In 1915, Gulnar had just married Samuel Indjeyan, aged twenty-five, whose exploits as a *fida'i* ('those who willingly risk their lives', as the Armenian partisans were called) earned him the nom de guerre of Samuel 'Tchavouch' (meaning sergeant in Turkish), and together the couple went underground. When their first baby was born, Gulnar smothered him rather than let him be killed by the Turks, who speared baby Armenian boys on their bayonets. They had a second baby, born in the forest, another boy whom they called Penon. The formidable Samuel Tchavouch was hunted down relentlessly by the Turks and eventually killed. The two sisters, now seasoned fighters, fought on tenaciously, killing many enemies of the Armenian people. Their feats of arms were to live on in the memories of the Armenians of Décines-Charpieu, the commune outside Lyon where the family eventually settled. A book relating the history of this struggle, written in Armenian and published in Marseille in 1952, contains a photograph of a group of armed *fedayeen* including Samuel Indjeyan, with a portrait photograph of the 'incomparable heroine' Gulnar inset. Another photograph shows Gulnar on horseback, holding a rifle and with cartridge belts strapped across her chest. (Later on, after the family moved to Lyon, Gulnar, who was renowned as a crack shot, would sometimes display her skills on the Place Garibaldi, near the barracks. There she was spotted by an officer who asked her if she would train the soldiers in sharpshooting. She refused.)

Eventually, Gulnar and her son Penon, Zarouhi and Ohannes were deported and, accompanied by the courageous Greek priest from Yozgat, reached Syria. From Damascus—on the initiative of their Greek priest protector, it would seem—they were sent on to a Greek orphanage in Beirut, Lebanon.

In the 1950s, the great American film director Rouben Mamoulian heard about this extraordinary family odyssey and asked Gulnar's permission to make a film about it, but she refused.

Various disparate episodes were to remain vivid in the family's memories. Ohannes recalled an Armenian prima donna coming to the orphanage to sing for the children and shattering a crystal glass with her piercing high notes; he also remembered that an American family wanted to adopt him, but, not wanting to have him separated from her, Gulnar refused; and it was also in the orphanage that

Zarouhi met Anton Kazarian, originally from Brousse, whom she would later marry. When the couple were living in Beirut, they had a daughter, Juliette, who was my aunt.

Eventually, all these survivors made their way to France. After arriving at Marseille, they settled first at Aubenas in the Ardèche, where the men worked in the coalmines (including Ohannes, who was too young but did so illegally to help the family to survive) as well as gathering silkworms for the silk industry in Lyon. While they were in Aubenas, Zarouhi and Anton had a son whom they named Hayk, after an ancient Armenian hero (*Hayk* in ancient Armenian means 'the Armenians', while *Hayastan* was 'the land of Hayk', or Armenia). Another Armenian offered to take Hayk with him to Australia, but they refused. In the end, the whole extended family moved to Lyon, where Anton died of the injuries he had sustained during the deportation.

Ohannes subsequently followed in the family tradition of heroism. In 1935, at Trévoux in the Ain department, at the request of the prefect, the Carnegie Foundation presented him with a bronze plaque, a diploma and an allowance. On the obverse, the plaque bore a portrait of Andrew Carnegie and the inscription, 'Fondation Carnegie 1909. Libéralité du Citoyen Américain pour Récompenser les Actes de Courage Accomplis en France' (A generous reward from the citizens of America in recognition of acts of courage undertaken in France), while the reverse bore the figure of Victory crowning a kneeling 'Hero of Civilization', with the inscription 'Sakoyan 1935'. A letter addressed to Ohannes by the prefect on 5 November 1935 evokes 'the act of courage undertaken by you on 30 June of this year' but gives no details of the incident involved. This distinction enabled Ohannes to become a naturalized French citizen in 1936. Called up in 1937, he saw active service in the Second World War and was decorated with the Croix de Guerre in 1940. Although he wanted, prompted by feelings of patriotism, to respond to Stalin's call to return to his country—the source of so much disillusionment—he was turned down on the grounds that he had no male children.

In 1941, Ohannes married Carzouhie Findiklian, daughter of a stone carver, originally from Tokat, who had been well treated by the Turks, who liked to decorate their graves with sculptures.

THE KAZARIAN AND SAKOYAN FAMILIES

These are the stories of the families from which I am descended, who have produced their fair share of heroes and martyrs for their faith.

Sources and further reading

Sources

On the treatment of Armenians of the Greek Orthodox faith in the early Kemalist period, see Deirmendjian, Navassart, *History of an Armenian Village, Kendjelar: Ethnographical, Topographical, Social and Political* [in Armenian], Beirut: Imprimerie Sevan, 1960, *passim*.

Studies

For oral testimonies, see Hovanessian, Martine, 'Anthropologie du témoignage et de l'histoire orale: Traversées des lieux de l'exil et de l'appartenance', in Catherine Coquio (ed.), *L'Histoire trouée: Négation et témoignage*, Nantes: L'Atalante, 2004.

On a key period in Armenian–Greek relations, see Hassiotis, Ioannes K., *Brother Peoples in the Storm: Armenians and Greeks in the Great Crisis of the Eastern Question (1856–1914)* [in Greek, synopsis in Armenian], Thessaloniki: University of Thessaloniki Press, 2015.

30

THE DERDERIAN FAMILY

Account of the deportation of the Derderian family, from the testimony of Chaké Derderian, née Somoundjian, wife of Hapet Derderian

The Derderian family—Missak and Nazeli and their children Hapet, Mihran, Vartan, Setrak and Marie—came from the village of Pakaridj, north of Kamakh/Kemah, administrative centre of this district in the province of Yerznka/Erzincan. Like most Armenians who were not farmers or stock breeders in the small towns and villages of Anatolia, they gravitated towards larger urban centres in search of work to support their families; and so the Derderian family became scattered geographically.

In 1915, Hapet was in Constantinople, where he owned a coffee roastery that his father had opened. Mihran was a shopkeeper at Drama in Greece and was planning to send for his wife and children, who had stayed behind in Pakaridj. Setrak and his wife and children were in Tekirdağ (Rodosto) in Thrace, on the shores of the Sea of Marmara, where the couple ran a food shop. Missak and Nazeli were still in Pakaridj with their invalid son Vartan, their daughter Marie and her husband Sevan, together with Mihran's wife and children.

In May 1915, Turkish soldiers backed up by Kurds from Yerznka came for the Armenians of Pakaridj. Caught unawares, Missak, Nazeli, Vartan and Mihran's wife and children were taken away by force in horse-drawn carts. According to an Armenian from Kamakh whom Hapet later encountered in Aleppo, they were massacred and thrown in the Euphrates.

Hapet was deported to the Der Zor region and then to the camp at Karlık, where he managed to escape. After several narrow escapes, he reached Aleppo, liberated from the Turks by Sharif Faisal ibn Hussein and the British general Edmund Allenby in October 1918. After working for some Arabs in Aleppo, he took the opportunity to go to Beirut where he again found work and so was able to save enough money to travel to Athens in 1920. From there, it was easy to make his way to Drama, where he expected to find his brother Mihran.

Mihran was not in Drama, however. After learning that his wife, children and parents in Pakaridj had been killed, he joined up with the Greek army to fight the Turks in 1918. He was never heard of again.

Serak and his family were living in eastern Thrace in 1920, but when the region was handed to Mustafa Kemal's Turkey under the terms of the Treaty of Lausanne in 1923, they sought refuge in Drama.

How did Marie succeed in slipping through the Turkish net to become the only member of the family still in Pakaridj to survive? When the soldiers came, she and her husband Sevan had time to hide in the barn attached to the house. When evening fell, they decided to spend the night in the forest, in a hut that Sevan knew. Next morning, Sevan went to scout out some paths that would be safe for them to take. Some time later, when Marie was starting to worry that he hadn't returned, a distressed Kurdish peasant suddenly appeared and informed her that her husband had been attacked and killed by two Turks. At the sight of Marie's tears, he invited her to come home with him, saying that his wife, mother, two daughters and son would welcome her. At Marie's request, he willingly went to find Sevan's body, laid it across the back of a donkey and took it to a burial vault in the Armenian cemetery.

From May 1915 to January 1919, Marie was given shelter by this Kurdish family, who lived in a hamlet just a few kilometres from Pakaridj. Whenever visitors came to call, she would pretend to be a Muslim. There was no language difficulty, as they all spoke Turkish. For three years, Marie worked on their small farm, tended the vegetable garden, cooked and cleaned in the kitchen and looked after the house and outbuildings. Everyone in the Kurdish family treated her with respect, and the parents considered her as their daughter. As Marie related, their generosity and kindness could be attributed in part—but not completely—to the fact that an Armenian doctor in Kamakh had saved their son's life when he was a baby. More importantly, however, the family all practised their Muslim faith with the utmost respect. The men played cards just like Armenian men, moreover, and the women cooked just like Armenian women. When Marie asked the son and one of the daughters to go with her to the Armenian cemetery, they willingly did so. As Marie would often stress, this Kurdish family treated her with the greatest humanity.

In January 1919, when she knew that the country was no longer being ravaged by slaughter and devastation, Marie announced to the Kurdish family that she wanted to find her family. The Kurdish couple completely understood. Although it was painful to them to part with her and they were concerned about her travelling on her own to Constantinople, where she hoped to find her Armenian family, they gave her a small sum of money for the journey.

By giving shelter to an Armenian woman for four years, the Kurdish family risked losing not only all their possessions but also their lives, so earning their place among the Righteous.

Further reading

On the memory of deported children, see Altourian, Janine, *De la cure à l'écriture: L'élaboration d'un héritage traumatique*, Paris: PUF, 2012.

31

THE DAMLAMIAN FAMILY

Testimonies of Rosine Biron and Christine Badémian, daughters of Haroutioun Damlamian, and Christine's sons Jean-Jacques and Alain Damlamian, presented by Jean-Jacques and Alain Damlamian

According to our family bibles (which escaped the genocide), the family tree of the Damlamian (or Damlamyan) family of Kayseri (Caesarea) in Cappadocia stretches back at least as far as Khatchadour, born in 1765. In 1910, one of his grandsons, Ghazar, announced that he was making six of his seven sons partners in the family business in Kayseri, which imported building materials. To this end, his sons Hagop and Setrak settled with their families in Samsun. Garabed went to live in Sivas, while Parsegh went to Constantinople. The seventh son, also called Khatchadour, a graduate of the French University in Beirut, was a doctor.

In 1915, Khatchadour was in the French town of Clamart, where he was acting as locum for French doctors who had been called up to the front. Meanwhile, in Asia Minor, the deportations of Armenians were beginning.

In 1987, our father, Stépan, wrote a 'Letter to My Two Sons', in which he described the origins and history of our family. In it, he detailed in particular how during the deportation the life of Setrak's son Haroutioun, born in September 1914, was saved by a Greek couple. The baby's parents, Setrak and Esther, had refused to convert to Islam and had been sent away on a deportation march, but his mother Mariam had left Haroutioun behind, knowing that he would quickly perish on the road to exile. In his autobiography, entitled *Potoric* ('Storm' in Armenian), written in 1990 and dedicated

THE RIGHTEOUS AND PEOPLE OF CONSCIENCE

to his grandchildren, Haroutioun himself returned to this episode in his early life:

> At last the dark day arrived, 15 July 1915, when the deportation order came that was to signal the start of the sufferings of an entire nation. I was just nine months old. My mother and father, grandparents and uncle Serope (who was seventeen) prepared to set off on the road to the exodus and the unknown. Because I was so young, my parents entrusted me to the care of my uncle Hagop and Mariam Mayrig, who were going to remain behind for the moment, thanks to their friendship with the prefect, who advised them to change their religion.
>
> Naturally the men were separated off and exterminated, while the women went on with their ordeal in the most dreadful conditions and suffered every sort of assault, both physical and moral. Two months later, my uncle and all his family also set off on the road to the exodus. On the way, being still an infant, I suffered more and more from the lack of nourishment and care. The whole family sacrificed themselves for me.

Our father now takes up the narrative:

> We had little Haroutioun with us and he was growing weaker by the day. He was looked after by Hadji Maïrig [our father's maternal grandmother], who took care of feeding him when we stopped for the night (our convoy did not walk at night). She would prepare a bottle for him with Nestlé condensed milk, of which we had bought large quantities before leaving Samsun, using an alcohol heater. On the journey, it was Nichan [Hadji Maïrig's son] who carried him on his back, while I rode on a donkey.
>
> Our next stop was the town of Niksar [Neocaesarea]. It took us two or three days to get there. The gendarmes made us go through the town as fast as we could until we reached the banks of the River Iris [Yeşilırmak]. There we were to spend the night. The entire Armenian population of Niksar had been massacred there and thrown in the river. I remember going upstream to fetch water and seeing human bones. Mama hurried me straight back to the camp as fast as she could so that I (then nine years old) shouldn't see such sights. We spent two nights and a day there.

THE DAMLAMIAN FAMILY

The most urgent problem was the baby's health: my father had found a *yayle* [cart] to hire, with the gendarmes' consent. Hadji Maïrig, Yevkine (our father's older sister), Haroutioun and one of my mother's cousins who was pregnant got in and set off towards Tokat, the next stop. The driver took them to a khan (caravanserai) that had belonged to a wealthy Armenian woman who had been deported. When we arrived there with mules and donkeys, the gendarmes took us to another khan, so the family was split in two. Another problem to solve. A very difficult problem unless our gendarmes were plied with gold coins. Which is what my father did in order to get the rest of the family brought to our khan.

But since he had managed to get out, he took advantage of this to go and see one of his Greek clients, and to ask him whether he knew any childless Greek couples who would like to take little Haroutioun. Since there was little chance of our coming back alive, in that case the child would be theirs; in the unlikely event of our returning, we would take him back. The client found a couple who answered this description. When he got back to the khan, my father called my mother to him and explained what he had decided; given the state of the baby's health, it was clearly the best solution.

And thus it was no sooner said than done, despite the tears of the children (us).

You could say that the baby was saved four times over:

1. By my mother Mariam, who would not let his mother Esther leave Samsun with him, but instead kept him with us.
2. By my grandmother Hadji Maïrig, who fed him in difficult conditions on the journey from Fatsa to Tokat, through rain, storms, thunder and lightning.
3. By my Uncle Nichan, who carried him on his back all the way.
4. By my father, above all, who had the foresight and presence of mind to leave him with the Greek couple in Tokat.

In his autobiography, Haroutioun confirms these harrowing events and their aftermath:

When we reached Tokat, my Uncle Hagop finally decided, despite his wife begging him not to, to entrust me to a Greek family (clients and friends of our business in Samsun). Since they had no children,

THE RIGHTEOUS AND PEOPLE OF CONSCIENCE

I was given a royal welcome by this family: Monsieur and Madame Stavros Ismirlioglou (a broker in Tokat), the patronym meaning 'son of the Smyrniote' (İzmir being the Turkish name for Smyrna).

The next day, the Turkish authorities in the town came knocking at my adoptive parents' door, ordering them to hand me over to share the fate of the rest of my generation. But Monsieur Ismirlioglou went to the prefecture and defended himself like a lion, insisting that he had found me in the street and, being childless, had taken me in. That same day, I was baptized for a second time in the Greek Orthodox church and given the name Yorgo (Georges). Naturally Uncle Parsegh and the Mendikian family in Constantinople were told about my adoption.

I was entrusted to this family on two conditions: if my mother returned from the exodus, I would go back with her; otherwise I would remain their son. For four years I was looked after and pampered like a little prince, spending the winter in Tokat and the summer at their vineyards. My parents taught me to say, 'These vineyards belong to Yorgo.'

After the very painful and difficult period of the exodus, my mother and grandmother managed to survive and arrived in Constantinople (Istanbul from 1930). Naturally, the first thing she wanted to do was to find her son. She boarded a boat to Samsun. I hardly need describe the state of mind in which she found the family. As soon as my adoptive parents heard that my mother was alive, they got ready to take me to Samsun to give me back to my natural mother. The first meeting with her was deeply poignant. Following confirmation from the Armenian religious authorities that she really was my mother, they [my adoptive parents] handed me over to her, asking her never to forget them, something that she always impressed on me.

A month later, we left for Istanbul on the steamer *Alte Aï*: our parting with the family who stayed behind in Samsun was highly emotional. And for the first time, alone with my mother on the steamer, I threw my arms round her neck and called her 'Mama', a moment that was doubly poignant for her.

After a tempestuous voyage, we arrived in Istanbul. On the quayside, my mother's cousins were awaiting the return of the prodigal son. 'Millet' came and took me in her arms, and Uncle Parsegh and

THE DAMLAMIAN FAMILY

Jiraïr were also there. All this side of the family set off for Sisli and the Mendikian house (my grandmother's sister). Another moment of high emotion was my grandmother meeting her grandson. She had lost her husband, her son-in-law and her seventeen-year-old son, so now she lavished all her love on me. Naturally she spent the rest of her life pampering me.

I was like a little savage. The first thing to think about was my education, and my grandmother took care of this with a patience and kindness that became legendary. A month later, my adoptive parents came to see me in Istanbul. That first meeting with them was very difficult, I was angry and screamed at them, 'Why did you leave me with these strangers?'

In his letter, our father returned to the way in which the family found little Haroutioun again and the events that followed. Haroutioun's father, Setrak, had been killed in a massacre during the deportations, but his mother, Esther, had been deported to Der Zor and survived:

> To go back a little: at Tokat, we saw Haroutioun's adoptive parents, who were charming. But in the conditions in which we were living, there was no question of asking to have him back. And anyway, he lived for 'Papaka' and 'Mamaka' and had become a little savage. I went once or twice and got punched and kicked. He spoke only Greek.
>
> In late November 1918, Armenian life was organizing itself in Samsun. The schools were open, and there were also orphanages run by the American organization Near East Relief, since the motherless and fatherless children whom the Turks could not keep were flooding into our town from the Anatolian interior.
>
> The church was open for worship with a priest, a good peasant from the *tebirs* [clerics], of whom I was one although I was only thirteen (the church had been used to store hay throughout the deportation).
>
> My mother was enormously active. Above all, although she was not very strong, she looked after the orphans, who called her 'Maïrig' [mother]; she managed to obtain the maximum aid possible from the employees of the Near East Relief, who had boundless confidence in my mother. The numbers of orphans arriving from Anatolia

were growing daily, and they had to be sent on to the Armenian Patriarchate in Constantinople. Mother went to see the Turkish shipowners 'Nemli Zade' and got them to agree to take a large proportion of them on their boats for free.

The political situation between the Turks and the Greeks was deteriorating, meanwhile, and in 1923, Haroutioun notes, 'my Greek father suffered the same fate as my Armenian father':

> Our paternal grandmother, her mother, her three daughters and her son (our father Stépan) survived the genocide and deportations under difficult conditions. When peace returned, they went back to Samsun for a while, before Uncle Parsegh brought them to Istanbul.

> Meanwhile, Uncle Khatchadour, the doctor, had settled for good in Clamart, south-west of Paris, after a period in Yerevan during the first Armenian Republic.

> In 1923, Uncle Parsegh sent his sixteen-year-old son Jiraïr and our father, aged seventeen, to their uncle in France to start their training as electrical engineers at the elite École Violet in Paris. Soon afterwards they were joined by the rest of our father's family and Uncle Parsegh's family too.

> Haroutioun, his mother Esther and his grandmother, meanwhile, left for Romania in 1924, to join the family of Esther's uncle in Galatz. In September 1932, when Haroutioun was sixteen, the two uncles brought him to Paris, also to study electrical engineering at the École Violet. He would later be joined in Clamart by his mother and grandmother.

The stories of the rest of their eventful lives are continued in Stépan's 'Letter to My Sons' and Haroutioun's *Potoric*.

THE WESTERN RIGHTEOUS

32

HUMANITARIANS

Missionaries, members of religious orders, health workers

With the Tanzimat—the period of reforms lasting from 1839 to 1876—the Ottomans hoped to modernize the empire. In the beginning, they viewed the arrival of Western Christian missions as a means of accelerating this process of modernization and therefore adopted a relatively benevolent attitude towards their presence.

In America in 1806, a meeting of five students had led to the founding of the American Board of Commissioners for Foreign Missions, which sent Protestant missionaries out to Asia, Africa and the Middle East. Not content with converting the local populations, American missions in the Ottoman Empire set up a wide network of schools, hospitals and universities for the local Christian population. And while doing so, they also endeavoured to export the ideal of liberty, as espoused by the United States.

Other Western countries also sent missionaries. In 1915, missionaries from countries that were not at war with the Ottoman Empire found themselves caught up in the turmoil of the genocide and did what they could to come to the aid of the Armenians. In addition to the actions they undertook, which were often heroic, the eyewitness accounts left by some of them form an invaluable resource for understanding the Armenian genocide.

33

MONSIGNOR ANGELO MARIA DOLCI (1867–1939) AND POPE BENEDICT XV (1914–22)

The 'Angel of the Armenians' and the 'Pope of Peace'

Born in the Lazio region of Italy and ordained in the priesthood at the age of twenty-three, Angelo Dolci was appointed bishop of Gubbio in Umbria less than ten years later, when he was thirty-two. A man of outstanding humanity and intellectual ability, he was to carve out a remarkable career in the diplomatic corps of the Holy See. After being sent as apostolic delegate to Latin American countries, he became titular archbishop of Nazianza in Cappadocia and afterwards archbishop of Amalfi in Umbria. In 1914, under the papacy of Benedict XV (1914–22), he was appointed vicar apostolic of Constantinople and brought face to face with the Armenian question. He was subsequently appointed as apostolic nuncio to Belgium in 1922 and nuncio to Romania in 1923. He was made a cardinal in 1933 by Pope Pius XI (1922–39).

While his presence on the ground guaranteed a certain amount of autonomy, Monsignor Dolci's policy towards the Armenians was in principle closely aligned with that of Benedict XV. Benedict condemned the Modernist scholars and promoted traditional social values, and he took a particular interest in those who bore witness to their faith at the risk of their safety and their lives. In 1920 (the year of Joan of Arc's canonization), he beatified Charles Lwanga and his twenty-one companions, the 'Ugandan martyrs' who had fallen victim to the wave of persecution unleashed by King Mwanga of Buganda in 1885–7. During the First World War, he initially took a cautious approach to Austria–Hungary's alliance with Germany, since it was a bastion of Catholicism, while Russia, although one of the Entente powers, was viewed as schismatic. In 1917—the year in which America entered the war on the initiative of President Woodrow Wilson (in office 1913–21)—he issued an appeal for peace to the belligerent nations, which he accompanied with concrete proposals that demonstrated a laudable conviction that arbitration offered a way forward:

> The same spirit of equity and justice must guide the examination of other territorial and political questions, and notably those relating to Armenia, the Balkan states and the territories of the former kingdom of Poland, towards whom its noble historic traditions and the sufferings it has endured, particularly during the present war, must rightly arouse the special sympathies of all nations.

As Jean-Marie Mayeur has stressed, Benedict XV showed no hesitation in inviting the Great Powers to create a new international order founded upon gradual disarmament and arbitration. It was a positive and courageously argued basis for discussions, but it found little favour with the belligerent nations. Paradoxically, Benedict's views echoed the proposals that had been put forward in Europe for some time by pacifists on the left, who favoured the creation of a 'League of Nations'. His views would also converge with those of Woodrow Wilson, who was sensitive to the realities of international relations. Benedict XV was clear that the resolution of questions regarding Armenia should be considered on an equal footing with those relating to the Balkan states and Poland.

During the First World War, Dolci was the only figure in the Vatican to be in permanent contact with both the Holy See and the Ottoman government, and he was one of the first diplomats to protest to the latter about the atrocities that were being perpetrated. Within a couple of days of 24 April 1915 and the deportation of 300–400 Armenians from Constantinople—the elite of the capital's Armenian community—he sent a telegram to the Vatican to inform them of the fact. In May that year, he was informed of the massacres at Trebizond by the Capuchin monk Hofen, then by the Protestant mission at Sivas, and finally by the Armenian patriarch of Constantinople, Zaven I Der Yeghiayan (1913–22), who begged him to intercede on behalf of his congregation. The Catholicos of

All Armenians, Gevorg V Soureniants (1911–30), then sounded the alarm to the Entente powers. Around mid-June 1915, rumours of the massacres (after Monsignor Ignatius Maloyan, Armenian Catholic archbishop of Mardin, had been killed on a deportation march on 11 June) prompted Dolci to send another telegram to the Holy See. A few days later, he received confirmation that widespread measures aimed at eliminating the Armenians had been put into effect, which subsequently led Benedict XV to address his first missive to Sultan Mehmet V on 10 September, and to appeal to international opinion. In late August, the order to carry out the massacre of the Armenian Catholic men of Angora—some 1,500 individuals, including the bishop and seventeen priests—was rescinded, almost certainly, as Raymond Kévorkian describes, thanks to the intervention of Dolci and Johann von Pallavicini, Austro-Hungarian ambassador to the Ottoman Empire. However, by the time this counter-order came through, the men had already been stripped and forced to march for eighteen hours, and only a little over a tenth of their number were to reach Aleppo alive. In reality, unless he went through the intermediary of European diplomats from the Central Powers (the German, Austro-Hungarian and Ottoman Empires), the results that Dolci managed to obtain were negligible. Though his dedication was absolute, he was overcredulous and too ready to be taken in by the more lenient measures applied following Benedict's letter to the sultan, as Francis Latour has pointed out. On 12 December 1915, while the genocide was still under way, he wrote to Cardinal Gasparri: 'The results ... have been highly effective. Not only has an immediate amelioration in [the Armenians'] situation been obtained, but the barbaric persecution, as such, has stopped almost completely.' He would have been wise to recall the advice given to the disciples in St Matthew's Gospel: those sent out like sheep among wolves needed to be innocent as doves but shrewd as serpents.

In April 1916, *L'Osservatore Romano* reported that a million Armenians had been massacred. Dolci set up the first orphanage for Armenian children, in Benedict XV's name. The orphans were later taken to the papal palace at Castel Gandolfo, before being transferred to Turin under the auspices of a humanitarian programme to which the pope was closely attached. At that time, Eugenio Pacelli, later Pius XII, was responsible for a service to provide assistance to the wounded and prisoners of war in Western Europe. As part of this service—as recalled in a 2015 interview with Father Georges-Henri Ruyssen, S.J., to whom we owe information on the pope's humanitarian actions—ration distributions were planned for children from countries involved in the world war.

In a second letter, sent to Mehmet V on 12 March 1918, soon after the signing of the Treaty of Brest-Litovsk, under which the Russians abandoned Kars, Ardahan and Batoum to the Turks, the pope was to express his concerns regarding the Christian minorities. The sultan responded that in fact it was bands of Armenians who were attacking the Muslims.

A report sent by Dolci to the Vatican on 5–8 June 1915 indicates that the scales had by this time fallen from his eyes, and he was now aware of the full scale of the tragedy:

> The plan to exterminate the Armenian population in Turkey is still being implemented with full force. Every week, on a variety of pretexts, many Armenians are still being sent into exile from the capital. The Armenian exiles in Eskişehir, Angora, Afyonkarahisar and Konya have been expelled from these cities without mercy and dispersed among the Muslim villages in their environs and even further afield. The Armenian exiles in Aleppo and its environs—Bah, Mumbuc, Mârra, etc—are driven out towards the deserts or deprived of all means of survival. They perish wretchedly from hunger, diseases of every variety and the harshness of the climate. Every type of violence is inflicted on the Armenian families who remain in various cities, whose breadwinners are serving in the army, to force them to embrace Islam.

In his 'Proposals to the [Ottoman] Government in Favour of the Persecuted Armenians' of August 1916, Dolci wrote:

> It is essential that the Ottoman government, as a civilized power, should take into consideration the following proposals in order to make amends, at least in part, for the harsh measures to which the Armenians in Turkey have been subjected for over a year.
>
> 1. Issue orders to the provincial powers with a view to changing their policy of persecution of the Armenians in their area. The latest news from Kastamonu, Angora, Yozgat, Caesarea,

Andrinopolis, Brousse, etc. informs us that some families without their menfolk—even the families of soldiers—have been dispersed among the surrounding villages without any means of support or sufficient bread to eat.
2. Issue orders to the authorities in the provinces to which Armenians have been transferred urging them to treat these unfortunate people with humanity and allow them to settle where they are, so that they may rest and earn a living: we have been told that Armenians transferred to Mesopotamia and in particular the *vilayet* of Aleppo have been forced to change their place of exile frequently, and to settle in places where, unable to live, they die of hunger.

The description of the Ottoman government as a 'civilized power' was somewhat belied by the reality of the situation: by this time, the genocide was virtually a fait accompli.

There followed a strong convergence of views between the Holy See and the American president. On 8 November 1918, the pope sent a letter to President Woodrow Wilson, who had brought his country into the war alongside the Entente powers and who was attached to the principle of national self-determination (as cited by Marcel Launay), in which he made an impassioned plea on behalf of the Armenians. Urging Wilson to 'become the champion of peace and of a just and lasting peace', and expressing profound gratitude for his recognition of the independence of Poland, he wrote:

> In addition to Poland, there has been and is still another nation that merits the sympathies of Your Excellency and all men of feeling. We refer to Armenia. No reminder is needed of the scale of the sufferings of this unfortunate nation, particularly in recent years! While the great majority of the Armenian population does not belong to the Catholic religion, the Holy See has on several occasions come to its defence, whether in the special mention made in its note to the belligerent powers of 1 August 1917; in writing to the Sultan to obtain, on behalf of the wretched Armenians, a halt to the massacres; or in sending material aid to mitigate their sufferings a little. But all this is of no use if Armenia is not granted the full independence that it merits besides, from every point of view. This is why the whole of humanity is fixing its gaze on the great President of the greatest democracy in the world.

THE RIGHTEOUS AND PEOPLE OF CONSCIENCE

This letter clearly influenced the role played by Wilson (the son of a Presbyterian minister) as arbitrator in Armenia's favour. It has also been suggested, not without justification, that the Fourteen Points of the Principles for Peace that he laid out before Congress on 8 January 1918 were influenced by Benedict XV's appeal to the belligerent nations in 1917. It comes as no surprise that Wilson advocated the creation of the League of Nations (established by the Treaty of Versailles on 28 June 1919), and that he was awarded the Nobel Peace Prize in 1919.

Alongside the pro-Armenian position of the pope and his apostolic delegate, due credit is also due to the support and steadfast commitment to the Armenian cause of a number of Jesuit priests. When the Légion d'Orient—later to become the Légion arménienne—was set up by the French government, Major Louis Romieu was sent out to recruit most of its number from among the Armenian refugees in Egypt (most of whom had fought in the resistance at Musa Dagh). He was accompanied by two Jesuit priests, Joannes Gransault and Guillaume de Jerphanion, both of whom were familiar with Asia Minor. De Jerphanion was also the first to document the rock-cut churches of Cappadocia. Spurred on by the idea of fighting within the French army (of which they were to be the principal representatives during the French mandate in Cilicia, from 1918 to 1921), and by the prospect of creating an Armenian nation state, many of the Armenians signed up.

Another Jesuit, Father Antoine Poidebard (renowned as the pioneer of aerial archaeology in the Levant), played a part of fundamental importance as representative of the French army mission in the defence of the First Armenian Republic of 1918–20. As a reserve cavalry captain, he travelled the length and breadth of the region on horseback and was able to observe both the catastrophic humanitarian situation and—through his links with Generals Nazarbekian and Korganoff and with Andranik, commander of the Armenian volunteers—the strength of the spirit of resistance. Advocating that Armenia should be viewed as a true ally in any peace negotiations, he argued for its viability as an independent state.

The Jesuits' links with the Armenians continued: the twenty-ninth superior general of the Society of Jesus, from 1989 to 2008, was Peter Hans Kolvenbach, a highly distinguished Orientalist who had been ordained in the Armenian Catholic Church.

MONSIGNOR DOLCI & POPE BENEDICT XV

The 'Angel of the Armenians'

Despite a certain initial naivety—rooted in his faith both in Christianity and in humanity—as apostolic delegate from the Vatican to Constantinople, Monsignor Angelo Dolci undeniably deserved the soubriquet 'Angel of the Armenians' through his denunciation of the genocide; through his pressing interventions in favour of the Armenians, which furthered the petitions made by Benedict XV; and through his commitment to charitable works, in accordance with the pope's will.

Benedict XV, meanwhile, overcame his initial cautiousness to become fully committed to the Armenian cause. Wilson's humanitarian principles, in particular, were fortified by the pope's missives, which underlined the necessity—since he was so resolutely in favour of Armenian independence—of making reparations to the Armenians, at least at the political level. Sharing a belief with the American president in the principle—enshrined by the French Revolution—of the right of populations to self-determination, Benedict XV has been dubbed by contemporary historians the 'Pope of Peace'.

Sources and further reading

Sources

Kévorkian, 'L'extermination des déportés arméniens', pp. 240–2.
Ruyssen, Georges-Henri, S.J., *La questione Armena: 1894–1896, 1908–1925; Documenti degli archivi vaticani*, 7 vols, Rome: Edizioni Orientalia Christiana—Valore Italiano Lilamé, 2013–15, *passim*.
Yeghiayan, Zaven Der [Armenian patriarch of Constantinople], *My Patriarchal Memoirs*, Barrington: Mayreni, 2014.

Studies

Chiron, Yves, *Benoît XV: Le pape de la paix*, Paris: Perrin, 2014.
Dédéyan, Gérard, 'Le colonel Louis Romieu (1872–1943), la Légion arménienne et le mandat français sur la Cilicie (1918–1921)' [session of 26 March 2018], *Bulletin de l'Académie des Sciences et Lettres de Montpellier*.
Durand, Bernard, 'Le mandat sur l'Arménie n'aura pas lieu? Un drame au cœur de la Turquie, de la Cilicie et de la Syrie (1915–1920)', *Revue*

historique de droit français et étranger, 3 (July–September 2017), pp. 393–410.

Latour, Francis, 'Les relations entre le Saint-Siège et la Sublime Porte à l'épreuve du génocide des chrétiens d'Orient pendant la Grande Guerre', *Guerres mondiales et conflit contemporains*, 3, no. 19 (2005), pp. 31–43.

Launay, Marcel, *Benoît XV (1914–1922), un pape pour la paix*, Paris: Éditions du Cerf, 2014.

Mayeur, Jean-Marie, 'Trois papes: Benoît XV, Pie XI, Pie XII', in Jean-Marie Mayeur (ed.), *Histoire du christianisme des origines à nos jours*, vol. 12, *Guerres mondiales et totalitarisme (1914–1958)*, Paris: Desclée-Fayard, 1990, *passim*.

Minassian, Anahide Ter, 'Les combats de Kévork V l'Affligé: Le Catholicos Kévork V Vechtali (1911–1930) et l'Arménie' and 'Antoine Poidebard et l'Arménie', in *L'échiquier arménien entre guerres et révolutions, 1878–1920*, Paris: Karthala, 2015, pp. 89–122; pp. 175–211.

Ruyssen, Georges-Henri, S.J., 'Le Saint-Siège et le début du génocide arménien de 1915 à la lumière des Archives vaticanes', *Relations internationales*, 1, no. 177 (2018), pp. 75–8.

34

PAUL BERRON (1887–1970)

'Action Chrétienne en Orient' (ACO)

Paul Berron addressed his book *Souvenirs de jours sombres* primarily to the 'small circle of friends of the Alsatian mission to the Orient', while hoping that it would be 'received with a degree of interest in Alsace'. In justifying the publication of his journal, he invoked the notion of destiny—not so much his own as that of the Armenian nation during the Great War. Interweaving his reflections on faith and the international upheavals of the time, he offered his book as the work of a missionary, a personal and highly committed response to the spiritual and military challenges of his era, and to the fate of the Christians in the Orient.

Born in Alsace in 1887 into a family of Protestant pastors who were very active in the community and deeply devout, Berron wanted to become a missionary from an early age and was committed to helping his fellow men. Imbued with the colonialist ethos of the age, he wanted to travel and—determined to lend his life a clear direction beyond merely crossing borders—to set up Protestant missions in the East. He also displayed a talent for adapting to all the turmoil of the period, so managing to build bridges between Alsace and places further afield. In his writings, he would stress the parallels between the destinies of Alsace and Armenia, two lands that had both suffered from national conflicts and been subjected to treaties, violent upheavals and migrations. After completing his studies in Halle-sur-Saale in Germany, he returned to Strasbourg, where he founded a student missionary society similar to an association he had joined in Germany, so setting the direction of his future path.

THE RIGHTEOUS AND PEOPLE OF CONSCIENCE

In the summer of 1914, he applied to join the Frankfurt-based 'Deutscher Hilfsbund für christliches Liebeswerk im Orient' in a mission to Muslims in Aleppo (as an Alsatian, he was still a German citizen at this time, hence the publication of his works in German and French). He declared that he had decided to take this step into 'the unknown' because he was still determined to convert Muslims to Christianity, and that he knew nothing yet of the massacres perpetrated against the Armenians since the nineteenth century.

This German mission was to be a guiding thread, through the journal *Sonnenaufgang* (Sunrise), and a permanent operating base for dealing with the difficulties caused on the one hand by changes in nationality associated with the special status of Alsace, which was to become French after the defeat of Germany, and on the other by the post-war changes in territorial boundaries in the East that were to make his work more complicated.

But the outbreak of war put paid to all Berron's plans, and he became seriously ill. After his recovery, he ascribed his ability to overcome these setbacks, and to leave for Aleppo at last in 1916, to his faith and his ideological commitment. He went to Aleppo to supervise the mess rooms of 'German and Austrian troops in Syria, Lebanon and Palestine'. Having been ordained as a minister in 1914, in 1915–16 he was appointed assistant pastor to the religious establishment of the Diaconesses de Strasbourg and chaplain to the military hospitals. It was in this capacity that he was now able to take action.

Sent with his wife to Turkey to open mess halls for German and Austrian troops, he immediately encountered missionaries who had come from Maraş, including Beatrice Rohner, who had set up an orphanage for Armenian children in Aleppo. The children were now once again the victims of Turkish persecutions and had been deported, the aim of the government being not merely to send the whole of the Armenian population out of what was then known as Asia Minor and into exile but to annihilate them completely in the desert. Rohner was illicitly organizing aid for the Armenians in an attempt to supply their most basic needs, and Berron decided that he too would help these people in their 'immense wretchedness', both in Strasbourg, where he organized collections and talks to inform people of the situation, and in Aleppo, where he established a network to protect them. But above all, he wanted to 'unite with these Armenian Christians in order to accomplish the great task of announcing the gospel to the Turks', a plan that was to lay the ground for the future 'Action Chrétienne en Orient' (ACO), still active today. It was a remarkable position based entirely on action and mutual respect; this was very clearly not a question of charity but rather of a joint and concerted long-term action to prevent the disappearance of Christianity in the East while also supporting the rebuilding of a population.

The defeat of Germany and Turkey eventually forced Berron to leave Aleppo and return to Alsace. The collapse of empires and upheavals among nations, provoking more massacres, prompted what was to become his life's work, however: the creation in 1922 of the ACO, which would later work in Syria, Lebanon and Algeria.

What most interested Berron were individuals and his encounters with them. Rather than dwelling on misery and suffering, his writings focus on descriptions of constructive meetings and exchanges that went beyond the vagaries of politics and the cynicism and short-term interests that went with them. He spoke with a strikingly wide range of people, both in terms of their nationality and their social status, and it was through his reliance on and interest in them that his work was so effective and just. And it is for this reason, too, that he may be called one of the Righteous. In describing the foundation of the ACO, he referred to 'friends of the Armenian cause' and described a full church on the day he registered its articles of association as an 'encouragement'. He also cited his Armenian co-workers, in particular Hovannes Ghazarossian, who were to be his future representatives as ministers in France, revealing the efforts they had made and the difficulties they had encountered, as well as the support he had received from them.

On his return to France, Berron set to work helping to settle Armenian refugees in Alsace and Marseille. Thanks to the strength of the refugees' determination to rebuild their culture on French soil, welcoming Armenians of the Apostolic Church and respecting the traditions and languages of their native lands, the evangelical parishes grew in size. Berron referred more than once to the spiritual strength and vitality of these communities, as demonstrated by the newspaper they published, *Panpère*, the places of worship they built and the holiday homes they ran.

THE RIGHTEOUS AND PEOPLE OF CONSCIENCE

The ACO became established in numerous countries in Europe in addition to France, which enabled its revival after being dissolved during the Second World War and also broadened the opportunities for Armenian refugees to find a welcome and financial support in traditionally Protestant countries, in particular Holland and Switzerland. Berron described this period as one of modest but structured progress in association with other active Protestant communities. It provided an essential foundation to develop their work in the East, not only in Aleppo but also in Beirut, where they worked especially with fatherless children and set up sponsorship links with Europe to supply their material needs. There were many discussions and offers of help, and as in Europe the focus was on building a pragmatic organization to provide for the essentials in terms of care, work and education, as well as spiritual needs. By virtue of its geographical and cultural position, Aleppo was an important reception centre for the Armenians, as well as being a place of special significance 'because of its situation at the frontier between the Turkish and Arab worlds and its large number of evangelical Christians'.

Subsequently, the activities of the ACO, relying particularly on its Armenian pastors, spread to the Arabic-speaking populations of Syria, the former Mesopotamia and Lebanon. Here again they not only relieved material distress but also spread the Christian Gospel, so following Berron's original aim as a missionary, as he wrote in his book *Une oeuvre missionnaire en Orient*, published in 1957:

> The Armenian question, which for years has been in the foreground of our concerns, is known to many people in our country only for its political aspects, while to others it is known for its philanthropical aspects. As for us, we have always striven to present it from the religious point of view.

Berron was to remain director of the ACO until 1961. After retiring in 1950, he developed, under the auspices of the ACO in Strasbourg, a service to provide assistance to North African migrant workers. A question that he posed in his *Souvenirs des jours sombres* encapsulates the essence of his commitment: 'What meaning can this small group of Christians have within such a large Muslim city [referring to Aleppo]? Time will tell.'

PAUL BERRON (1887–1970)

Sources and further reading

Sources

Berron, Paul, *Une œuvre missionnaire en Orient et en Occident, origine et développement de l'Action Chrétienne en Orient*, Strasbourg: Oberlin, 1950; Berron, *Une œuvre missionnaire ...*, ed. Cécile and Francis Bezler, Paris: L'Harmattan, 2015; Berron, *Souvenir de jours sombres: Un pasteur alsacien témoigne*, Paris: L'Harmattan, 2015.

Studies

Wild, Thomas, *L'appel de l'Orient, Sept visages du protestantisme*, Lyon: Éditions Olivetan, 2009.

35

CLARENCE USSHER (1870–1955)

American doctor and missionary in Van

Born in Illinois in 1870, Clarence Ussher, medical doctor and Episcopalian missionary, studied at the Reformed Episcopal Seminary in West Philadelphia and subsequently at the University Medical College in Kansas City. He subsequently built up a flourishing medical practice in the city, but when the American Board of Commissioners for Foreign Missions offered him a mission in Turkey, at a greatly reduced salary, he accepted this opportunity to tend to people's spiritual needs in addition to their physical health.

When he arrived in Constantinople in June 1898, after setting sail from Boston the previous month, he was forced to negotiate a great deal of Ottoman bureaucratic red tape before he was able to practise medicine within the empire. Ironically, especially since he had sailed there on the Leyland Line cargo liner SS *Armenian*, put into service in 1895, the maps in his Bible were torn out because they contained the name 'Armenia'.

After spending a year in Harput, Ussher was sent to Van in response to an appeal from the resident physician, who wanted to offload his medical duties in order to concentrate on missionary work. In 1899, after a gruelling journey, the new missionary doctor arrived in Van, as he described in his book *An American Physician in Turkey*:

> We were in a great plain, the summit of a plateau fifty-five hundred feet above sea-level, bordered by mountains twelve thousand to fourteen thousand feet high. The city lay before us, its suburbs

called Aikesdan [Aygestan] (Garden City), with their orchards and vineyards, stretching greenly eastward from the old walled city for four miles.

Of Van's 50,000 inhabitants, three-fifths were Armenian and the rest Turkish. Barely had Ussher settled in than he was obliged to return to Erzurum in order to escort another missionary, Elizabeth Barrows, sent by the Woman's Board of Missions to run the girls' school in Van. On 26 June the following year, Dr Ussher and Elizabeth Barrows were married in a church in Van, the first American marriage to be celebrated in the region.

The American compound at Van lay at a low elevation in the southern suburbs, and after many years of struggles and wrangling with the administration consisted of a church, two very large schools and two smaller ones, a lace-making workshop, a hospital, a dispensary and four houses for the missionaries. The staff of the American mission in 1914–15 comprised Dr G. C. Raynolds, the most senior; Dr Clarence Ussher, in charge of the hospital; Elizabeth Barrows Ussher, in charge of the lace-making workshop; Ernest Yarrow and his wife Jane (née Tuckley), in charge of the boys' school and day-to-day running of the mission; Gertrude Rogers, in charge of the girls' school; Caroline Silliman, in charge of the primary school; the Usshers' daughter, Eleanor, in charge of the music department; Louise Bond, matron of the hospital; and Grisell McLaren, touring missionary. There were also two Armenians and a Turk who helped look after the youngest children.

On 2 July 1914, Turkey signed a treaty of military alliance with Germany and against Russia, which led to the Triple Entente powers (Russia, France and Britain) declaring war on 2 November. As a result, diplomats and citizens of the Triple Entente had to withdraw from the Ottoman Empire, so depriving the Armenians of some of their most powerful protectors. This role now fell to America, which was not to enter the war—and then only against Germany and Austria–Hungary—until 6 April 1917.

The American mission in Van was therefore well placed to witness the massacres of the Armenians that were planned and systematically carried out in 1914–15. A treaty concluded between the United States and Turkey granted to America all the rights that had accompanied the designation of 'most favoured nation' under the

Ottoman government. Even when the Turkish Capitulations favouring the Europeans were abolished on 1 October 1914, the most favoured nation clause remained in force until America's entry into the war. Under the terms of this treaty, American citizens and their possessions were inviolable, but in wartime this immunity was frequently disregarded. A good deal of courage—both moral and physical—was therefore needed for Ussher and his team to stand up to the recently appointed governor of Van, and to continue to take care of the orphans and treat the inhabitants of Van.

The new governor, Cevdet Bey, was none other than the brother-in-law of Enver Pasha, minister of war and member of the Turkish wartime ruling triumvirate. Both were merciless in using their public office to persecute the Armenians. Cevdet Bey exploited every possible pretext, however minor, to disarm and exterminate the Armenians who lived in the villages around Van. In response, the Armenians in the city armed themselves as best they could in expectation of the worst. This was not long in coming.

Before sunrise on 20 April 1915, as Ussher later wrote,

> Turkish troops had occupied a line of trenches about the Armenian quarter of Aikesdan ... Two of them had seized a beautiful young woman, one of our former orphan girls fleeing with her two children to the city ... Two Armenian men running up to rescue the woman were fired at and killed.

A general fusillade ensued, and Cevdet Bey gave orders to open artillery fire on the Armenian quarters in the old town and the Aygestan.

The events of the defence of Van have already been outlined at the beginning of this book, but the narrative is complemented here by the invaluable support and dedication of the American mission. Once the lines of defence were established, Ernest Yarrow 'organized a government with a mayor, judges, police, and board of health'. Meanwhile, a housing committee assigned accommodation to an influx of thousands of refugees, and a supply committee 'bought and requisitioned provisions ... started a soup-kitchen and issued bread-tickets and soup-tickets. Miss Rogers and Miss Silliman secured a daily supply of milk, and set their school-girls the task of sterilizing and distributing it to the babies who needed food.' The

Usshers' thirteen-year-old son Neville 'translated the Scout Law into Armenian and induced ten boys of his own age to join him; ... [they] secured a book on First Aid and studied it together. These Boy Scouts now became the sanitary police and fire patrol ... and brought patients on litters to our hospitals.'

It became clear to Ussher that Cevdet Bey's criminal plan had been intended to culminate with a 'massacre of all the Armenians in the *vilayet*' on 19 April. Only the determined resistance of the Armenian fighters and Ussher's refusal to allow Turkish soldiers to occupy a dominant position within the mission compound, where thousands of Armenians had sought refuge and the hospital was working flat out, had prevented it. Enraged, Cevdet Bey turned his ire on areas of Van that could make little or no resistance. 'We have absolute proof,' wrote Ussher, 'that fifty-five thousand people were killed.' Many thousands more fled to the mountains and hid in caves. Thousands of wounded and starving Armenians began streaming into the compound, where temporary hospitals were staffed by Armenians whom Ussher had earlier trained up as Red Cross workers.

When America entered the war against Turkey, on 6 April 1917, the American mission withdrew from Van. By their presence during those terrible years, Dr Ussher and his companions had prevented the wholesale massacre of the region's Armenian population. In addition, they had taken care of the physical health of the inhabitants of Van and its region during epidemics of typhus and cholera, had helped to save the population from starvation, and had provided a refuge for hundreds of orphans. All these humanitarian activities were of inestimable value at the time and remained so afterwards. But the most singular feature of Ussher's work is his first-hand and disinterested account of the events he experienced. He was a witness to Cevdet Bey's false promises, and to the stratagems with which he attempted to end the Armenians' resistance. And as well as reporting the stories of survivors, he was also an eyewitness to the massacres perpetrated by the Turks and their acolytes.

At a point when they had been abandoned on all sides, the Armenians of Van were in desperate need of protection. This they found in Clarence Ussher and his companions, men and women moved by a combination of humanity, faith and extreme courage.

CLARENCE USSHER (1870–1955)

Elizabeth Barrows Ussher succumbed to typhus on 14 July 1915, the victim of her own devotion to duty. Clarence Ussher died in Los Angeles on 20 September 1955.

Sources and further reading

Sources

Ussher, Clarence D. and Grace H. Knapp, *An American Physician in Turkey: A Narrative of Adventures in Peace and War*, n.p.: Kessinger Publishing, 2010, [1917].

Studies

Balakian, Peter, *The Burning Tigris: The Armenian Genocide and America's Response*, New York: HarperCollins, 2003, *passim*.
Kévorkian, *Armenian Genocide*, pp. 233, 320, 326.
Minassian, Anahide Ter, 'Van 1915', in *L'échiquier arménien entre guerres et révolutions*, pp. 123–49.

36

TACY ATKINSON (1870–1937)
HERBERT ATKINSON (d.1915)

The sacrifice of a life, the testimony of a journal

Tacy Atkinson, née Tacy Adelia Wilkson, was born in Salem, Nebraska, on 3 July 1870. Her parents were farmers, and she became a teacher. When she was thirty, she was diagnosed with a breast tumour, and while in hospital she met Henry Herbert Atkinson, a medical intern. They were married in San Rafael, California, on 7 July 1901. Born in India, Herbert Atkinson came from a family of Christian missionaries; the couple both became missionaries and in 1902 arrived in Harput, where Herbert served as mission doctor. In August 1908, they went back to America for Tacy's health, before returning to Harput on 23 October 1909. Like other missionaries before them, they were struck by the beauty of the city in its commanding position overlooking a fertile plain. The mighty Euphrates River flowed through the region, making its soil fertile. The 350 or so villages that flourished on the plain were inhabited largely by Armenians, who farmed the land and raised livestock to make a living.

Before the genocide, at least 165,000 Armenians lived in the province, many of them concentrated around Harput, where they formed half the population, alongside Kurds and Turks. The area was ringed by the Taurus Mountains, where the missionaries liked to go and relax beside the sources of the Tigris, a day's walk from the city.

Herbert and Tacy Atkinson spoke very good Armenian and Turkish, and despite their insistence that at home the family should speak English, their children grew up speaking Armenian more fluently than English. Immediately after their marriage, Tacy started to keep a diary, following the example of her mother-in-law, who methodically recorded her experiences as a missionary in India. Tacy's journal is particularly valuable because, apart from her innate powers of observation, her husband's privileged position gave her access to every sphere of society. In 1915, she realized that a terrible tragedy was unfolding and was determined to set down the facts, though constantly haunted by the fear that her diary might be discovered by the Turkish authorities.

During the genocide of 1915, both Tacy and Herbert worked courageously to help the deportees, striving to relieve their sufferings as best they could, and to save their lives whenever possible. Bravely, Tacy went several times to see the governor of the province to demand the release of Armenian prisoners, although even if they were released there was no guarantee they would not be recaptured. Through the summer and autumn of 1915, Herbert Atkinson devoted himself body and soul to the Armenians, immersing himself in their tragedy, until—like Elizabeth Barrows Ussher—he contracted typhus. He died on 25 December 1915, leaving Tacy and their three children. For two years, Tacy carried on their work by herself, running the hospital and courageously confronting the Turkish military commander in her attempts to save lives. She finally left Turkey in 1917, after America entered the war. Since the Turkish authorities prohibited any written records from being taken out of the country, she left her journal behind, sealed in a trunk in her house in Harput. Nine years later, the trunk was sent to her, still locked, in the United States.

Once back in America, she struggled financially for the rest of her life. She ran a modest lodging house for other missionaries, sometimes sleeping on the floor herself when she ran out of beds for them. Despite several offers of marriage, she remained single. The scars of the Armenian genocide were to live with her for the rest of her years. Though still a believer, she struggled to understand how such horrors could take place in God's world. She never ceased to talk to her friends about what she had seen in Harput, and she toured America giving talks on the fate of the Armenians and trying to raise funds for them. Never able to forget the horrors she had witnessed, and profoundly affected by her tragic experiences, she died on 1 December 1937, aged sixty-seven.

Sources and further reading

Sources

Atkinson, Tacy, *The German, the Turk and the Devil Made a Triple Alliance: The Harpoot Diaries, 1908–1917*, Princeton: Taderon Press, 2000.

Studies

Winter, Jay (ed.), *America and the Armenian Genocide of 1915*, Cambridge: Cambridge University Press, 2003.

37

HENRY H. RIGGS (1875–1943)

Evangelist missionary and witness to the genocide and acts of humanity

Born into a family of Christian missionaries in Sivas, Turkey, on 2 March 1875, Henry H. Riggs received his education in the United States, at Carleton College in Minnesota and Auburn Theological Seminary in New York. He was posted to Harput as a missionary in 1912 and remained there until 1917, when he returned to America. When he went back to Harput in May 1919, he was expelled by the authorities for no valid reason. On 22 December 1920, he arrived in Constantinople, before being transferred to Beirut in September 1923 and continuing his missionary work among Armenian refugees in Lebanon and Syria. In June 1940, he returned to the United States, before travelling out to Beirut in May 1943. He died in Jerusalem on 17 August 1943. He was married three times (his first two wives died prematurely, in 1905 and 1917), to Annie C. Tracy, Emma M. Barnum and Annie M. Denison.

The genocide carried out against the Armenians by the Young Turks is documented by a number of written accounts, not only in Armenian but also in English, French, German and Arabic, among other languages. Many of these accounts were written by individuals whose occupations meant they were living and working in the places where the atrocities ordered by the Ottoman authorities were perpetrated, and who therefore became eyewitnesses to them. Their reports of the events are faithful in their detail and concur with each other so consistently that it is impossible in good faith to dispute their veracity, as some continue to do to this day. Among these accounts, Henry Riggs' *Days of Tragedy in Armenia: Personal Experiences in Harpoot, 1915–1917* stands out for a number of reasons.

THE RIGHTEOUS AND PEOPLE OF CONSCIENCE

First and foremost, Riggs was a sharp and clear-eyed observer, who early on deduced the true motive for the war that was being waged against the Armenians: 'The attack on the Armenian people, which soon developed into a systematic attempt to exterminate the race, was a cold-blooded, unprovoked, deliberate act, planned and carried out without popular approval, by the military masters of Turkey' (p. 46).

He also returned several times to the subject of the feelings of the Turkish population:

> As a matter of fact, so far as local conditions in Harpoot were concerned, the Armenian atrocities of 1915 had no historical setting. In other periods of massacre ... there have been certain conditions that have presaged the coming storm. Not only were all these conditions lacking in 1915, but the relationship of the Armenian to his Moslem neighbor was more friendly and sympathetic than ever before. (p. 45)

At the same time, measured and impartial as he invariably was, he recognized that in their secret hearts, the Armenians had no affection for 'the government that has always oppressed and outraged them'. But, he added, 'Whatever their secret longings, the Armenians comported themselves with great propriety at that time' (p. 46).

Riggs drew a clear distinction between the Turks who were the perpetrators of the atrocities and their fellow countrymen and women who came to the aid of the victims. In the former camp, he gave pride of place to the governor of the province, Sabit Bey, who made promises that he had no intention of keeping, and who sent the deportees into the desert to a certain death, without bread or water. In the region of Diyarbekir, the Turks proceeded to liquidate the Armenians without any preliminaries, drowning 2,000 in the River Tigris. In the city of Çüngüs, 5,000 residents were massacred. But, Riggs was careful to point out, 'There were many Moslems, however, of a very different type. A large part of the better class looked with genuine horror at the treatment accorded to the Armenians, and when it came to enriching themselves as a result of the sufferings of the poor victims, they would not do it. Many Turks at the time refused to have even a legitimate share in the booty' (p. 85).

HENRY H. RIGGS (1875–1943)

He later returned to this subject in more detail:

> One fact, however, gave some hope to the Armenians. Their Moslem neighbors were inclined to side with them rather than with the government. In spite of all the efforts of the government to inflame the minds of the Turk, the more intelligent Turks for the most part remained either indifferent or positively friendly to the Armenians. Some were very outspoken in their condemnation of the government and expressed their sympathy with the Armenians. ... So it happened that the Turks individually did much to help their friends and rescue them from their fate. ... There were some few Turks ... who were either fearless enough or influential enough to defy the threats of the government. (pp. 95–7)

And he went on:

> It may not be well to scrutinize too closely the motives for such courageous loyalty on the part of Moslem friends. In the few cases where it was successful, the effort to protect an Armenian family usually appeared to be justified by some very tangible gain to the man who took the risk. In some cases it was outright bribery; in other cases the Armenian was kept to act as a business agent of the Turk, an exceedingly profitable arrangement, as the Turks are notoriously poor in business dealings, and the saving of an Armenian assistant meant the saving of their business. But even this hope of gain is not sufficient to entirely discount the real generosity and courage of the Turks who did, first and last, save the lives of quite a number of Armenian men.

In fact, Riggs explained, if the Armenians were eradicated, civilization in all its forms would necessarily be set back 100 years or more, not to speak of the harm to the economy and business that would ensue:

> The Turks of Harpoot therefore took matters in their own hands. They made strenuous representations to the local officials, with the result that a list was prepared of the Armenian craftsmen whose presence was considered essential to the comfort of the Turks, and the list having been duly revised and scrutinized by the Vali, the men whose names were on the list were notified that they and their families might remain in Harpoot. (pp. 100–1)

THE RIGHTEOUS AND PEOPLE OF CONSCIENCE

In a few cases, Riggs identified Turks who came to the aid of the Armenians by name. More often, however, he did not, since he knew that he might be putting the individuals concerned in danger. But when it came to the Kurds, he was more comfortable, as they had their own region, the Dersim, where they could take refuge from the murderous fury of the Turks. Riggs would send on funds that had been left in trust with him to the Armenians who had sought safety in the Dersim, and he testified to the honesty of the Kurds who transported the gold. He also bore witness to the courage and integrity of the Kurds who would escort defenceless Armenian women and girls into the Kurdish regions.

Riggs mentioned these instances of compassion in order to make it clear that the Turks did not unanimously support the policy of deportation, a cruel stratagem that plunged the Armenians into agonies of uncertainty as they awaited their forced departure. This was then frequently postponed, so resulting in a few days' reprieve filled with mounting anguish.

Another ubiquitous feature of the deportations was the selling off at any price, no matter how derisory, of anything belonging to the people who were about to be sent into exile. Particularly noteworthy among the cases cited by Riggs were a group of Armenians who testified that their guards had taken good care of them, procuring food for them and protecting them (albeit for payment); and another group who testified that the officers who had been ordered to escort them to the village of Huseynig fulfilled their duties to the letter, so saving them from the cruelties inflicted on other deportees.

Riggs told the story of a well-known Turkish baker in Harput who sold him bread at a very reasonable price, so that he was then able to issue coupons to the Armenian population, which they in turn could exchange for several days' rations of bread. The case of another Muslim neighbour is also edifying. When the baker could no longer supply all the bread that was needed, the missionaries opened their own bakery. To begin with, Armenians worked there; since they were arrested one after another, however, soon no more Armenians were willing to work in such a public place. So the missionaries turned to a Muslim neighbour who had done everything he could to save the Armenians from deportation, and who was to prove indispensable when it came to feeding them.

Subsequently, with one or two other men, he would tour the villages to buy up wheat.

One scene reported by Riggs clearly illustrates the refusal of some of the Turkish elite to take part in the eradication of the Armenians. Orders came from Constantinople to the effect that all the Armenians in the city who had so far escaped deportation were to be rounded up and brought before the governor and the chief of police, who would decide their fate. The two senior officials sent virtually all of them back to their homes and, as Riggs reports, 'while they were sitting there sending away one after another those people who had been arrested, the Governor was heard to say to the Chief of Police, "You will lose your job for this, so will I, but no matter"' (p. 172).

The survival of the Armenians in any given region depended on the presence of a benevolent local Turkish official. In Harput, the military governor was replaced by Izzet Pasha, described by Riggs as 'a man of remarkable refinement and a man of kindly and sympathetic temperament'. When the order came from Constantinople to deport all the remaining Armenians, he replied: 'There are no Armenians in Harpoot except a few widows and orphans, and it is not necessary to deport them.' At the same time, as Riggs pointed out, 'in other regions, the order was carried out with great vigor. Thousands of Armenians were not simply deported but actually massacred wholesale.'

He concluded:

> There is no doubt that those who sent the order from Constantinople had determined on the absolute extermination of the Armenians. … It is quite possible that one-fifth of the population of the depopulated areas still survive either in exile or in their homes due to the kindness of the local officials. (p. 175)

In addition to the testimony he left to the atrocities perpetrated on the Armenians by the Young Turk government, and to his refusal to lay the responsibility for them at the feet of the Turkish people as a whole, Riggs was also tireless in his personal efforts to help the Armenians, intervening with the authorities and demanding delays to deportations in order to allow the unfortunate victims more time to prepare for their departure. The governor, Sabit Bey, was determined to execute his orders from Constantinople to the letter, however, and Riggs' appeals fell on deaf ears.

When Riggs realized that he would be unable to gain more time, he decided to do what he could to help on a financial level. As he was now prohibited from accepting money in trust, he found a way of getting round this by taking the sums of money that the Armenians gave him and sending them to family members in America, asking the relatives to promise in return that they would do everything in their power to give it to those who survived deportation.

When the Armenians in his region were starving, Riggs gave them bread and—even better—set up a bakery to distribute bread to the ever-growing numbers of refugees who were being sent to the city.

With his customary succinctness, Riggs summed up the casual brutality of the Young Turks: '[M]any thousands were ... massacred at the last moment, when apparently the Turkish government had tired of the pretense of carrying out the theory of deportation.'

Sources and further reading

Sources

Riggs, *Days of Tragedy in Armenia*.

Studies

Kieser, Hans-Lukas, *Nearest East: American Millennialism and Mission to the Middle East*, Philadelphia: Temple University Press, 2010.

Tevosyan, Hasmik, 'Rescue Practices during the Armenian Genocide', in Andrieu, Gensburger and Sémelin, *Resisting Genocide*, pp. 196–7.

38

BERTHA MORLEY (1878–1973)

Missionary and protector of Armenian girls

The American missionary Bertha B. Morley was born in Mentor, Ohio, in 1878. In 1895, she entered Oberlin College, Ohio, to study music, but she was unable to graduate owing to ill health. She subsequently became a music teacher.

In 1911, she visited her sister Lucy and her husband in the provincial Turkish town of Marsovan (Merzifon), in the province of Amasya in the Black Sea region. She then took up a teaching post at the American School in Constantinople, where she stayed for two years. After this, she worked with the American Board of Commissioners for Foreign Missions, and so became a powerless witness to the systematic persecution and extermination of the Armenians in the region, which she related in her journal.

Although the diary she kept during her mission at Marsovan covers only five months, from 29 April to 14 September 1915, it is of great importance. Some lines added on 21 April 1916 also presaged further sufferings for the Armenians. The diary reveals her overarching determination to save the souls of faithful Protestants, which led her to urge the Armenians to choose deportation rather than convert to Islam, even though in theory this would have saved them from deportation.

At the time when Morley was writing, the Ottoman authorities had cut off communications between the interior of the empire and the world outside, so it was no longer possible to send messages to Constantinople or to diplomats still in post to inform them of the scale of the persecution of the Armenians. Tales of massacres and disappearances reached the ears of the missionaries in Marsovan, but the atrocities described were so horrific that they struggled to believe them; they were also obliged to give the benefit of the doubt to the Ottoman authorities in order to continue their work. The extermination of the Armenians in Turkey was now well under way, but the local Ottoman officials consistently lied about the crimes being committed. Even so, there came a time when it was no longer possible to lend them any credibility.

In her diary, Morley described the climate of anguish and terror the authorities cultivated in order to subjugate the Armenians while they awaited their deaths. The Armenians in Marsovan and all the surrounding towns and villages lived in constant fear, waiting for the knock on the door in the early hours as the soldiers came to get them. This was the moment when the men and women would be separated from each other to be sent off on death marches.

Morley and her fellow missionaries lived through these harrowing days with their faithful followers. The Armenians were ordered to be ready to leave their houses the instant the order was given. The mission's workshop made bags and blankets for them, and a little money and some provisions were distributed among the Armenian members of the mission and their congregation to help them survive on the marches, which for some of them would end barely a few kilometres from their starting place. Morley told the story of an Armenian woman who went to buy bread for the journey, only to be told by the shopkeeper, with a sarcastic laugh that made his meaning all too clear, 'You won't be needing as much bread as that.'

The diary was not intended for publication, during the war at least, and was more of an aide-mémoire in which Morley jotted down the details of the everyday life of a missionary, juxtaposed with the relentless persecution of the Armenians. Thus she begins her entry for 29 April 1915 by relating how thirteen Armenian men were seized from their houses between midnight and four o'clock the night before, and then adds details of a 'very good' theatrical performance, with tickets at 1, 3 or 5 piastres. A month later, on 29 May, she writes that she has heard that Dr Tabebian has been beaten in Amasya, that all the Armenians who have been arrested have been put in a single cell together, and that some of them have

BERTHA MORLEY (1878–1973)

typhus. She then adds that the children have put on a play written by Enid and called 'Perseverance Rewarded', which everyone enjoyed. These juxtapositions seem incongruous but are perhaps understandable in such troubled times, when it had become impossible to distinguish between the true and the false, between the monstrous and the ordinary.

The diary offers a litany of the ordeals suffered by the Armenians, of men arrested and then released, and of others who disappeared never to return; of women and children lying awake, night after night, awaiting the blows of rifle butts on their doors and windows; of endless nights that merged into one.

In this harrowing atmosphere, the wives of some of the Turkish officers, and some of the officers themselves, would visit the houses of well-off Armenians and display no compunction in taking any items they took a fancy to, paying a fraction of their true value in sham transactions agreed between the parties. When the Armenians offered them their possessions at a derisory price, the Turks would reply, 'No need for us to buy them, soon they'll be ours.'

Throughout this time, Morley and her fellow missionaries employed every possible subterfuge to save the girls in their charge from the abductions and forced marriages from which they were constantly under threat. Although she devoted most of her diary to the persecution of the Armenians, she was also happy to record examples of the kindness shown by some Turks. She notes, for instance, an offer by a family of devout Turks to shelter a certain Isgouhi Manoukian and his family. She also relates an episode in which some gendarmes displayed a benevolent attitude, in contrast to the vicious treatment usually handed out by their colleagues. And she mentions the sympathy and affection shown by a woman called Nejebe Hanum to the Armenians, with whom she had always lived. But she was mortified, by contrast, by the treachery of an Armenian man, who betrayed twenty boys who were in hiding from the authorities.

In 1916, the Turkish authorities closed the mission and its institutions in Marsovan, and Morley went back to America. After the Ottoman Empire's defeat, she spent some time in Lebanon, where she took over the running of the orphanage at Antura near Beirut, where the children had been subjected to many different sorts of ill treatment under the Young Turks. In 1919, she returned to Marsovan to run the Anatolia Girls' School. When the school was shut down by the Turkish authorities two years later, she went to teach at the American Collegiate Institute in Smyrna, then under Greek control. In 1922, she witnessed the Turkish occupation of the city and massacres of its Christian population, during which she managed to save a large number of children and elderly people who had sought refuge in the city's American institutions. She subsequently continued her work as a teacher and missionary in Salonika and then afterwards in Marsovan once more. She retired in 1945 and died in 1973 in Clairemont, California.

Bertha Morley's career shows how the life of an individual dedicated to music and the spreading of her faith was turned upside down by unforeseen events. Throughout all the many different challenges she faced, she never failed to rise to the occasion and took every opportunity to come to the aid of people who otherwise faced certain death.

Sources and further reading

Sources

Morley, Bertha, *Marsovan 1915: The Diaries of Bertha Morley*, ed. Hilmar Kaiser, Princeton: Gomidas Institute, 2000.

39

RAY TRAVIS (1899–1965)

From the defence of Ayntab to the establishment of the Jbeil orphanage

Born in New York State in 1899, Ray Travis volunteered to serve during the First World War and was sent to France, where he was promoted to the rank of sergeant and served as a quartermaster. After the war, instead of going back to America, he went to work with the American missionary organizations in their launch of a wide-ranging operation to find and collect the Armenian orphans who had been scattered all over the Near East. In the autumn of 1919, he went to Beirut, then to Aleppo, and finally to Ayntab, where he was installed as the director of a new orphanage set up by Near East Relief.

Travis was tireless in his efforts to improve conditions for the orphans, and from April 1920, when heavy fighting broke out between Turkish nationalists and the French occupying forces, he did everything in his power to shield them from the armed clashes and bloodshed that erupted in the city. From 1 April to 30 May, he kept a daily diary in which he detailed the main events in a period that was fraught with danger. While he singled out the military leader of the Armenian self-defence, Adour Levonian, for praise, he made no mention of his own involvement in the armed defence of the orphanage; however, a number of witnesses, including Karnig Panian, who later published his memoirs, reported on the intensity of his engagement. Travis also took numerous photographs of the Armenian refugees who had returned to Ayntab engaged in their everyday tasks. All these documents were later preserved in the Yates County History Center in New York State.

In June 1920, Travis took the 800 or so orphans in his charge back to Beirut, where he was in charge of running a large tented camp set up to provide temporary shelter for the orphans in the Karantina (Quarantine) neighbourhood. Eventually he managed to find some buildings that had formerly housed a silk factory in Jbeil, which, although partially ruined, enabled him to house all his orphans safely, and left them with indelible memories.

With this new and irreversible exodus, not only of the orphans but also of tens of thousands of refugees, the rupture between the Armenian people and Turkey became final and permanent. The political activists of the diaspora, supported by Armenian intellectuals and teachers, now aimed to rebuild an Armenian nation that would be founded on the Armenian language (expunged of any borrowings from Turkish), culture and traditions.

As director of the Jbeil orphanage, Travis lent this programme his full support. He invited deeply committed teachers to work at the orphanage, built up a large library of Armenian books, set up clubs for sports, cultural activities and the arts, and encouraged the orphans to publish a newspaper. He also invited prominent figures in the Armenian community to come and speak at the orphanage, including Yervant Odian, Vahan Tekeyan, Nigol Aghpalian and Yervant Khatanasian, among many others. Even Sahak II, Catholicos of Cilicia of the Armenian Apostolic Church, came to visit the orphans and their 'father' (who was to remain unmarried until the end of his life).

Also at this time, however, the directors of Near East Relief were attempting to impose a culture in all their orphanages that was based on Protestant religious teaching, which would be more compatible with the new diplomatic engagement of the United States in the Near East. To this end, they dismissed some of the teachers who had been recruited by Travis, which sparked a mutiny among the orphans and vehement protests in the Armenian nationalist press. Near East Relief's ultimate response to this deeply entrenched difference of opinion was to close the Jbeil orphanage in 1925 and to blackball Ray Travis for life.

Further reading

Tachjian, Vahé, 'American Missionary Ray Travis and His Armenian Legacy', https://www.houshamadyan.org/en/mapottomanempire/vilayetaleppo/ayntab/religion/missionaries.html

40

BEATRICE ROHNER (1876–1947)

Swiss missionary who tried to negotiate with the Young Turks

The Swiss missionary Beatrice Rohner worked for the German Protestant Hülfsbund für christliches Liebeswerk im Orient (Aid Association for Christian Charity in the East), founded in Frankfurt in 1896 as part of the aid campaign launched in the wake of the massacres perpetrated against the Armenians in 1895. The charity was embedded in the pietistic tradition that had emerged in German Protestant circles in the seventeenth century and enjoyed a revival in the nineteenth; with its emphasis on personal faith, hope and prayer and close learning of the Gospels, it had a profound influence on the young missionary.

In 1900, Rohner was sent out to take care of the mission and orphanage in Maraş, where she was followed by her mother in 1908 and her sister in 1913. Vartan Bilezikian, an Armenian author who had lived in Maraş, described her as 'a woman of gentleness and humility, full of compassion and tender solicitude toward the needy and weak, and generous with things entrusted to her care'. Fluent in Turkish, French, German, English and Armenian, and with the rudiments of Arabic, she was able to communicate directly with a wide range of officials and ordinary people, and through sheer perseverance often succeeded in improving the lot of those for whom she was responsible.

The province of Maraş, where Rohner had begun her mission, formed a corridor between Cilicia, Cappadocia and the Armenian plateau and was an enclave between the Taurus and Anti-Taurus mountain ranges. In the early twentieth century, 70,000 Armenians lived there, in sixty-four towns and villages. A highly active presence in the region, the Armenians had come to exercise a virtual monopoly over local trades and businesses, so fuelling the jealousy of local non-Armenians.

With the outbreak of the First World War, the Young Turks put their criminal plan to deport and massacre the Armenians into action, with the aim of exterminating a population that was regarded with suspicion and jealousy. The first operations in what was to become a genocide took place in the *kazas* of Zeytun, Göksun and Elbistan, and in the regions of Maraş and Pazarcık. The Armenian population fell to 22,500, most of them living in Maraş, which in 1914 had had a population that was 50 per cent Armenian.

Rohner was thus a witness to a tragedy that unfolded before her eyes and that affected her deeply. Unlike some other Europeans who remained in Turkey, she refused to act as a mere spectator, or at most as a provider of body counts of the massacred Armenians. Instead, she focused her attention on individuals who were in a position to offer help. She implored the two who first sprang to mind— the American and German consuls in Aleppo, Jesse B. Jackson and Walter Rössler—to intervene in order to stop the deportations, or otherwise to supply aid to the deportees. The German consul's measured if sincere intervention did nothing to change the Ottoman authorities' policy of extermination, and the American consul was no more successful. So determined were the authorities to press ahead with the plan that when the governor of Aleppo, Celal Bey, tried to resist the order to deport the city's Armenians, he was replaced by a more amenable official.

Eventually, Jackson came to the realization that the aim of the plan was to bring about the annihilation of the Armenians. Rohner, meanwhile, became increasingly convinced that she needed to speak directly with Cemal Pasha, one of the triumvirate of the Three Pashas who ruled the Ottoman Empire during the war. Cemal Pasha had full military and civil powers over the Arab nations and was a sort of proconsul in Syria; he had also been appointed as commander-in-chief of the Fourth Army, which was to suffer two defeats during their offensives on the Suez Canal.

Rohner made careful preparations for the journey to Aleppo, which necessitated obtaining a permit to enter the city. She was in possession of several advantages: she was Swiss, and therefore neutral; she was employed by a German charity, which was viewed favourably by the Turks; she was multilingual and could therefore communicate with a wide range of people; and finally, she was a woman, and therefore to contemporary eyes did not pose a threat. Soon she was to gain an additional advantage, as America, Germany and Switzerland became united in the realization that she was the only person who was in a position to make practical use of the funds raised by their respective countries to provide aid to the Armenians. They duly placed all their funds in her hands.

Accompanied by her 'mission sister' Paula Schäffer, Rohner set off for Aleppo, the Syrian city that had become the gathering point for Armenian deportees. The two women hoped to obtain official permission from Cemal Pasha to bring aid to the Armenians who had been herded into concentration camps on the outskirts of Aleppo while they waited to be sent on to Der Zor and Ras al-Ayn in the Syrian desert. However, the two women had not reckoned with the strength of Cemal Pasha's dogged support for the extermination policy, nor with the stalwart collusion of the local authorities in this criminal plan.

Rohner met Cemal Pasha twice but failed to obtain what she wanted. At their second meeting, he made her an offer. Although it is not known for certain where this meeting took place, it was more than likely at the Hotel Baron, recently built by the Armenian Mazloumian brothers. Aleppo boasted no other hotel of such standing, and it had become the meeting place of choice both of the Turkish authorities and of the Germans in the city. The Swiss missionary would thus have made her pleas for the survival of the Armenians in an Armenian venue.

Cemal Pasha refused to give her permission to visit or take aid to the concentration camps, where thousands of Armenians were dying of hunger and disease. This did not deter her from sending messengers—courageous young Armenian men—into the camps to help keep the prisoners' hopes alive. Among the deportees at Der Zor, they found a young woman called Araxia who had been a protégée of Rohner, and who sent back a message about conditions in this death camp: 'I have no words to describe the misery to you ... We live God's presence as never before; the prayers are fervent and all separations have disappeared.'

THE RIGHTEOUS AND PEOPLE OF CONSCIENCE

What Cemal Bey did offer Rohner was responsibility for the running of the Armenian orphanages in Aleppo, which—following pressure from the city's German community—had been placed under German protection. This step had been taken in order to protect the orphans from being sent to Turkish orphanages to be assimilated and stripped of their identity and religion. Rohner accepted this offer, which meant that she could stay in Aleppo. But she had not given up on her initial determination to bring aid to the Armenians who were perishing on the outskirts of the town and in the desert.

She now turned to the Armenian community in Aleppo, and more particularly to the Armenian pastor of the evangelical church there, Hovhannes Eskidjian. Eskidjian was an excellent organizer who had helped to set up an aid fund for the Armenians, to which local communities of all faiths contributed, and which he distributed with Father Haroutioun Yayian of the Armenian Apostolic Church. Other Armenians also worked with them, including the courageous volunteer messengers who left the city to take aid to the deportees, and at the same time gathered information on the atrocities they had suffered.

One of the messengers, Hagop Halebian, spoke Arabic and Kurdish fluently, and transformed his appearance and had his face and body tattooed so that he could pass as a Kurd or an Arab. Using connections that he had contrived to make, Halebian was able to smuggle letters and money out of Aleppo. Rohner and Schäfer thus managed to send a large proportion of the money that had been entrusted to them out to the concentration camps where the Armenians were dying.

Meanwhile, wave after wave of deportations were taking place, and the threat that the orphans in Rohner's care might be sent to other orphanages, where they would be assimilated among Turkish orphans, grew very real once again. Pastor Eskidjian contracted typhus and died on 25 March 1916. His widow worked with Rohner to carry on their aid mission, but their activities had aroused the suspicions of the local authorities, who had carried out a secret and probing investigation to identify who was supplying and distributing these funds. The official funds for the orphans had virtually run out, and the Turkish authorities had stopped supplying Beatrice with the provisions promised by Cemal Pasha. She could no longer feed the

Fridtjof Nansen in a refugee camp near Alexandropol, tasting an orphan's meal, © Armenian Genocide Museum-Institute Foundation, Yerevan

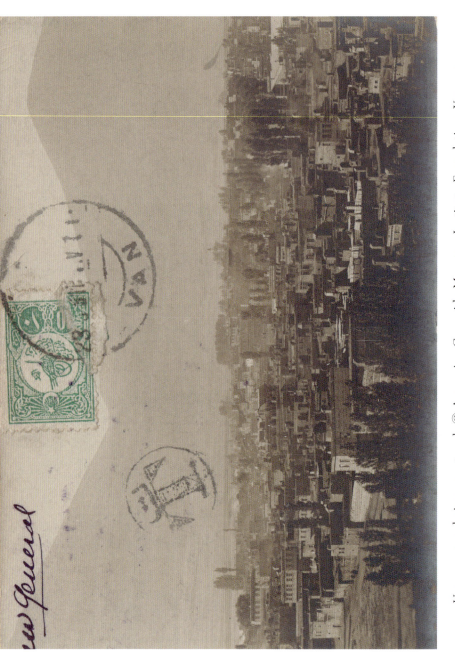

Van, a general view, postcard, © Armenian Genocide Museum-Institute Foundation, Yerevan

Adana, the Armenian quarter, French postcard, early twentieth century, © Armenian Genocide Museum-Institute Foundation, Yerevan

Orphans evacuated from Malatia to Syria and Lebanon, 1922, © Armenian Genocide Museum-Institute Foundation, Yerevan

Young children waiting to be taken into the Near East Relief orphanage in Yerevan, 1920s, © Armenian Genocide Museum-Institute Foundation, Yerevan

Maria Jacobsen with a group of orphans at the Bird's Nest orphanage, Lebanon, 1950s, © Armenian Genocide Museum-Institute Foundation, Yerevan

Karen Jeppe with her adoptive son Missak and Sheikh Hadjim Pasha, Danish postcard, © Armenian Genocide Museum-Institute Foundation, Yerevan

Armenian orphans standing in line for their daily bread, Aleppo, 1920s, © Armenian Genocide Museum-Institute Foundation, Yerevan

Karen Jeppe with her pupils at the Ourfa handicraft workshop, Aleppo, 1920s, Danish postcard, © Armenian Genocide Museum-Institute Foundation, Yerevan

Bodil Katharine Biørn with her Armenian pupils, Mush, 1906, © Armenian Genocide Museum-Institute Foundation, Yerevan

Hamid Bey, *vali* of Diyarbekir (source, Wikimedia Commons)

Faik Ali Ozansoy (source, Wikimedia Commons)

Mehmet Celal Bey (source, Wikimedia Commons)

Johannes Lepsius (source, Wikimedia Commons)

Alexandra Tolstoy (source, Wikimedia Commons)

Henry Morgenthau (source, Wikimedia Commons)

Armin T. Wegner (source, Wikimedia Commons)

Raphael Lemkin (source, Wikimedia Commons)

Franz Werfel (source, Wikimedia Commons)

Soghomon Tehlirian (source, Wikimedia Commons)

Russian soldiers in the Armenian village of Sheykhalan, 1915 (source, Wikimedia Commons)

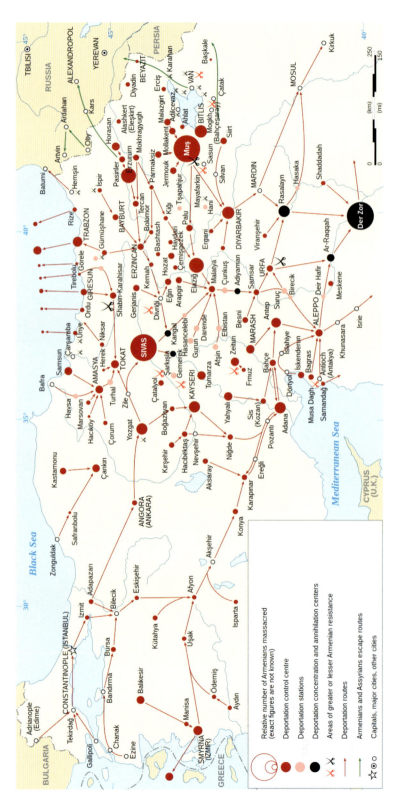

Map of the Armenian Genocide (source, Wikimedia Commons)

4,000 or so Armenians who were in hiding in Aleppo. In addition, the Armenian pupils in the German schools in Aleppo were under threat of deportation, which would mean almost certain death. Meanwhile, the rare scraps of information that arrived from the camps painted a picture of indescribable horror. Massacres and famine created an atmosphere of fear that left the surviving Armenians in little doubt that their days were numbered.

On 27 June 1916, the governor of Aleppo ordered Rohner to hand over all orphans over thirteen years of age to the local authorities, and to dismiss all the Armenian women who worked for her. One of the messengers smuggling money for the Armenians had been arrested by the police and under torture had revealed everything, including Beatrice Rohner's name. In an attempt to limit the danger, she relinquished her involvement in the aid effort, handing it over to Jesse B. Jackson.

In February 1917, the Ottoman government took steps to close Rohner's orphanage. Seventy boys were to be taken from Aleppo to a Turkish orphanage in Lebanon, where they would be assimilated. Sixty more were too ill to be transported, and 370 had already fled. Under pressure from the authorities, 400 other orphans whom Rohner had fed and clothed were sent to Turkish orphanages.

Faced with the collapse of her little world and its young charges, whom she had managed to save and protect so far, and the certain knowledge that she could no longer do anything to help survivors of the concentration camps, Rohner sank into depression. She left Aleppo for Maraş, and after a while returned to Germany.

She was to return to Aleppo in 1919, and to Maraş, Ayntab and Syria in 1928–9. The two memoirs that she wrote were tributes to the Armenians who had helped her in her mission. But she could not bring herself to describe all the horrors she had witnessed and that had undermined her health.

Fragile but fortified by her faith and her humanity, Beatrice Rohner had stood up against a destructive machine of terrifying proportions. She had succeeded in saving close to 1,000 orphans, who with other survivors would be the driving force behind the post-war survival of the Armenian nation. In particular, she had helped hundreds of deportees who would have perished without the funds smuggled to them by her courageous messengers.

THE RIGHTEOUS AND PEOPLE OF CONSCIENCE

The reports she sent to the German and American consuls and to the directors of the charity for which she worked are contemporary documents that demonstrate the existence of a premeditated campaign to exterminate the Armenians.

In 1933–4, as the Nazis rose to power, she found the strength to write a memoir of her experiences in 1915–16, entitled *Pfade in grossen Wassern* (Paths through wide waters). This account of her struggle during the First World War was doubtless also intended to offer her readers the strength to resist the forces of evil that were about to be unleashed once more under the Third Reich.

Beatrice Rohner died on 9 February 1947.

Sources and further reading

Sources

Pasha, Djemal [Cemal], *Memories of a Turkish Statesman, 1913–1919*, New York: George H. Doran, 1923. In 2008, his grandson Hasan Cemal, the well-known Turkish journalist and writer, bowed his head before the memorial to the Armenian genocide at Yerevan (Tsitsernakaberd) and asked for forgiveness from the Armenians. He dedicated his book *1915: Ermeni soykirimi* (1915: Armenian genocide) to the memory of Hrant Dink, assassinated in 2007 outside the Istanbul offices of his bilingual Armenian–Turkish newspaper *Agos* because of his position on the Armenian genocide and Armenian identity.

Studies

Kaiser, Hilmar, 'Beatrice Rohner and the Protestant Relief Effort at Aleppo in 1916', in *There Is Always an Option to say 'Yes' or 'No'*, pp. 171–213.

Kieser, Hans-Lukas, 'Beatrice Rohner's Work in the Death Camps of Armenians in 1916', in Andrieu, Gensburger and Sémelin, *Resisting Genocide*, pp. 367–82.

41

JAKOB KÜNZLER (1871–1949) AND ELIZABETH KÜNZLER-BENDER

'In the Land of Blood and Tears'

In 1921, a book entitled *Im Lande des Blutes und der Tränen* (In the land of blood and tears) was published in Switzerland. It was to prove of major importance for the study of the Armenian genocide. The author was the Swiss doctor and great humanist Jakob Künzler, and in its pages he described the events he had witnessed during his mission in Turkey. Künzler was an important eyewitness to the crimes committed in this period; his book contains numerous descriptions of the atrocities committed against the Armenians, whom he did everything in his power to help, and for this reason it occupies a special place in the study of the genocide.

Künzler was born into a large family in Hundwil, Switzerland, on 8 March 1871. He lost both his parents while still a child, and he was brought up by his godfather, who wanted him to become a carpenter like himself. After completing his apprenticeship as a carpenter, he decided to change direction, however, and went to Basel to train as a nurse.

After he qualified, he worked for six years at the hospital in Basel, where he proved to be as gifted in his skills as he was generous in his disposition. So obvious were his medical skills that he was often asked to take part in operations. At the hospital, he met Dr Hermann Christ, who was soon to leave for Urfa with the Deutsche Orient-Mission, run by the evangelical pastor Dr Johannes Lepsius.

In May 1899, Künzler was invited by Lepsius to go and work in the German mission hospital in Urfa. He accepted immediately and became assistant to Dr Christ. Before leaving for the field, he set about learning Turkish and English. Subsequently, he decided to add Armenian, Kurdish, Arabic and French to his languages and became fluent in all of them.

Künzler left for Urfa on 11 November 1899 and arrived there in December. A new life was opening up for him. As soon as he arrived, he began his work at the hospital, while at the same time continuing his medical studies in order to practise independently as a surgeon. In addition to his duties as a doctor, Künzler also became heavily involved in a range of voluntary activities, and so he embarked upon the rich career to which he was to devote the rest of his life.

A few years later, in 1905, he married Elizabeth Bender, the daughter of a German missionary and granddaughter of an Ethiopian princess, with whom he was to have five children. No account of Künzler's work is complete without paying due tribute to his wife's contribution. Elizabeth was a tremendous support to him, and she also played a major part herself in a number of initiatives to aid Armenian orphans. Künzler would always insist that without his wife he would never have been able to accomplish many of his projects.

The First World War years were a gruelling time for the Künzler family, as in addition to his work at the hospital they were both heavily committed to the herculean struggle to help the Armenians in Urfa. While Jakob worked long hours at the hospital, Elizabeth saved large numbers of Armenians from imminent death, as well as rescuing many Armenian orphans and giving them shelter in the family home. Armenian orphan girls who had managed to escape from Turkish harems also found a refuge with them. With money smuggled out to him from Europe, Jakob managed to buy bread and clothes for these Armenians in distress. When at the end of the war he counted up the numbers involved, he found that they had helped to save 2,700 Armenians. To this should be added those whom he saved by being the only person capable of offering medical assistance in and around Urfa, plus the fact that from May 1914 he and Elizabeth had sole responsibility for running the mission at Urfa.

The Künzler family also aided the Armenian resistance in Urfa, which was active from 29 September to 23 October 1915. This was the period during which the massacres across the Ottoman Empire reached their climax, resulting in the almost total annihilation of the Armenians in the region. As Jakob later wrote in *In the Land of Blood and Tears*: 'After what I had experienced, I had the impression of having been summoned down to Hell: the Lord showed me the way, leading me to a people who, despite all adversities and ordeals, were resolved to remain faithful to their Lord and God.'

Despite all the hardships and dangers they faced on a daily basis, Jakob and Elizabeth stayed in Urfa until 1919, when the British occupied the city. The Turks were ordered to free the women and children they had abducted, with the result that thousands of refugees and orphaned children ended up homeless and living on the streets, without any support or means of survival.

After the war, the Künzler family left for Switzerland for a brief period, during which Jakob wrote his book relating his memories of what he had witnessed in Urfa. Published in 1921, it also bore powerful witness to his response to these events and to his love for the Armenian people:

> Its villages razed to the ground, and victims by the tens of thousands. And yet this same people, with their resolute faith in God, continues to hope for better days, when they will be happier. God sent me to them so that I might tend their wounds, like a veritable brother. ... I therefore decided to serve them. Since then, I have become convinced that all the most barbarous plans to destroy the Armenian people are always doomed to failure.

Künzler's narrative is remarkable for several reasons. First and foremost, he came from a non-combatant nation and was therefore a neutral observer. It is noteworthy that although the Swiss Federal Council had no direct involvement in events at that time, a number of private initiatives were undertaken, and Swiss missions were opened in the region. Information concerning the situation in Urfa was passed on by members of the Armenian diaspora in Switzerland, as well as by representatives of diplomatic missions and individuals opposed to the Young Turk dictatorship.

Containing previously unseen photographs and a rich and fascinating bibliography, Künzler's book is also of particular historical importance because—in order to continue the mission's work in acceptable conditions—he was obliged to maintain cordial relations with the

Turkish authorities. Thus he became the reluctant witness to official discussions testifying to the fact that the widespread massacres of the Armenians were unambiguously the outcome of a premeditated and calculated policy of extermination. Künzler's report is all the more precious for being a record of events witnessed at first hand, with reliable information on the massacres and deportations supplied by missionaries who were present in the field. As a highly active individual in the humanitarian movement, Künzler submitted valuable reports to aid associations in Switzerland and Germany.

To put all this in context, when the great humanitarian figure Dr Johannes Lepsius composed the first comprehensive report on the genocide, he based it on the testimony he was able to gather from a large number of witnesses in Constantinople, since he was not himself authorized to visit the places where the tragedy had unfolded. By contrast, Künzler was an eyewitness to these events.

Jakob and Elizabeth were to devote the rest of their lives to the Armenians. Not long after they had arrived in Switzerland, the family set off back to Urfa to continue the work they had started. Their return was an event of major significance for the Armenian population of Urfa. As well as running a clinic, Jakob was to take on a huge responsibility for the future of thousands of Armenians. Initiatives undertaken by the Künzler family played a role of essential importance in the rebuilding of Armenian society in the post-war period.

The American Near East Relief organization now decided to transfer the Armenian orphans in Turkey to other countries, and they turned to Künzler for help. This immense undertaking, involving some 100,000 orphans, was to be the beginning of a long period of collaboration. When their clinic was shut down, Jakob and Elizabeth took charge of the transfer of 8,000 orphans to Syria and Lebanon, which involved shepherding them on foot to Jarabulus on the Syrian border, where they would catch the train onwards to Aleppo. The long march was extremely arduous for the children, and Jakob managed to get hold of two wagons for the weaker ones to ride on. Escorted in relays, in a series of journeys over four days, the children finally made it to Jarabulus, thanks to the kindly couple whom they called 'Papa and Mama Künzler'. When he was asked about this term of endearment, Künzler would reply without hesitation: 'They are my children and they will be for the rest of my life.'

JAKOB & ELIZABETH KÜNZLER

Another major commitment following their return was the running of the orphanage at Ghazir in Lebanon, which was home to over 1,000 Armenian girls, many of whom had been among the children whom Künzler had taken to Jarabulus. Over many years, the Künzler family was to accomplish remarkable feats in ensuring the smooth running of the orphanage.

In 1923, Jakob Künzler contracted an infection and had to have his right arm amputated at the shoulder, the only way then known of saving his life. No longer able to work as a surgeon, he now devoted all his energies to the orphan girls in his care, and with the help of Elizabeth, who took care of the day-to-day running of the establishment, he developed new plans.

Künzler's aim was always to find stable and lasting solutions for the girls' future lives. He was convinced that they should receive some training, so that they could use their skills to earn a living. With the help of his friend Hovhannes Tashjian, a weaver and dyer who had taught his trade in Urfa, Jakob and Elizabeth set up a carpet-weaving workshop in the orphanage, with the aim of teaching the girls skills and a trade that they could rely on, as soon they would grow up and have to manage by themselves. As they needed more funds, he launched an appeal in America. The response was slow initially, but with support from the press he was eventually able to raise the funds he needed to complete the project. Hundreds of girls were trained as carpet weavers in the workshop, which over two decades produced some 3,254 carpets and rugs. In 1929, Künzler was decorated by the Lebanese president for his contribution to the development of the country's textile industry.

In 1925, as a gesture of thanks to the American people for their aid to the Armenians and the setting up of the workshop, Near East Relief gifted President Calvin Coolidge with a magnificent rug that it had taken the girls ten months to weave. In a letter of appreciation, Coolidge wrote that the gift, later to become known as the Armenian Orphan Rug, 'has a place of honor in the White House where it will be a daily symbol of goodwill on earth'.

The Künzler family initiated so many projects that it is impossible to list them all here, even though each of these initiatives would merit a detailed study. One of them was the setting up of day nurseries for the children of Armenian widows, which—thanks to Elizabeth's efforts—made it possible for the mothers to work and so be financially independent. The Fédération Suisse des Amis des Arméniens agreed to fund the building of these nurseries, to plans designed by Künzler. He also took care of people with disabilities. Some of the money collected was used to buy land at Bourj Hammoud where, on Künzler's initiative, hundreds of houses were constructed.

But the project that Künzler considered his finest, after the evacuation of the 8,000 orphans from Urfa, was his idea of building a sanatorium in the mountains for Armenians who had lived through traumatic experiences. In order to make personal contact with the Armenians of the diaspora and appeal to them for funds, he himself undertook the journey to America. Thanks to the generous donations he elicited, the sanatorium building was opened at Azounieh in 1938.

In 1933, Künzler published another book in Basel, entitled *Dreissig Jahre Dienst am Orient* (Thirty years in the East), in which he gave further detailed descriptions of the events of 1915, the massacres at Urfa and the deportation of the Armenians under cover of the war.

On 19 May 1939, Jakob and Elizabeth Künzler were honoured at a ceremony organized by the Armenian community in Beirut.

Despite failing health, Künzler chose to stay in Lebanon. In 1947, he was awarded an honorary doctorate in medicine by the faculty of medicine at the University of Basel.

Jakob Künzler died at Ghazir on 15 January 1949. Embodying the highest humanitarian values, with the tireless support of his wife Elizabeth, he also established institutions that are still in existence today, all of which are run by Armenian organizations.

Sources and further reading

Sources

Künzler, Jakob and Hans-Lukas Kieser, *30 Jahre Dienst in Orient*, n.p.: BSA, 1931; Künzler and Kieser, *In the Land of Blood and Tears: Experiences in Mesopotamia during the World War 1914–1918*, n.p.: Armenian Cultural Foundation, 2007

Studies

'Jakob Künzler (March 8, 1871–January 15, 1949)', UACLA, http://www.uacla.com/jakob-kuumlnzler.html

Kieser, Hans-Lukas, 'Birader Yakup, ein Arzt ohne Grenzen, in Urfa, und seine Wahlverwandtschaft mit den Kurden (1899–1922)', *Kurdische Studien*, 1 (2001), pp. 91–120.

Künzler, Jakob, *Köbi, Vater des Armenier: Selbstbiographie des Dr.med.h.c. Jakob Künzler*, Kassel: Johannes-Stauda Verlag, 3. Auflage, 1967.

Zeigler, Felix, 'Jakob Künzler', https://artzakank-echo.ch/2015/03/24/jakob-kunzler/

42

ANNA HEDVIG BÜLL (1887–1981)

From Haapsalu to St Petersburg

On 30 December 2016, the Armenian Post issued a commemorative postage stamp in honour of Anna Hedvig Büll, the Baltic German-born Estonian missionary and supporter of the Armenians. The 50,000 stamps, to the value of 280 Armenian drams, featured a portrait of Anna Hedvig Büll against a background of written reports and eyewitness accounts of the genocide. These are the same reports and testimonies that give us an understanding of the part played by this courageous woman; of the scale of her contribution to the rescue of several thousand Armenian orphans; and of her unconditional love for the Armenian people, to whose protection and support she devoted her entire life. Her memoirs were written in Armenian, the language she had learned from her conversations with the Armenian orphans, who called her *Büll Mayrig* ('Mama Büll').

Anna Hedvig Büll was born on 4 February 1887, into a Lutheran family in Haapsalu, a spa and seaside resort in northern Estonia (annexed by Russia from 1910 to 1920) dubbed 'the Venice of the Baltic'. Famed for its mud spa, it was a favoured resort of the St Petersburg aristocracy: the composer Tchaikovsky and the painter Nicholas Roerich were among those who spent holidays there and visited the spa, built in 1898 by Anna's father Teodor Büll, a prominent local figure who also served as mayor of the town.

The sixth of eight siblings, Anna attended a state school in Estonia until she was fifteen, when her parents sent her to St Petersburg, where she spent three further years at a German Protestant school.

Later she would describe how during this time in St Petersburg, far from her family, she began to ponder her vocation and her mission in life: 'These were decisive years in my life, and the spiritual education I received there was to determine my future.'

During a visit to her family in Haapsalu in 1903, she was inspired by a talk given in her father's house by the celebrated evangelist Johann Kargel (1846–1933), a leading member of the Russian Baptist movement and later of the evangelical Christians. German on his father's side and Armenian on his mother's, he was celebrated in Russia for his humanist ideas. As she listened to him, Anna came to the realization that she wanted to devote her life to the service of God, and that this was her true vocation. After her return to St Petersburg, she found support among members of the Russian aristocracy, among whom evangelical spirituality was a strong influence at this time. The doors of the palace belonging to Prince von Lieven, for example, who hailed from a Livonian dynasty who had distinguished themselves in the service of the tsars, were always open to evangelical Christians. 'My conscience was caught up in an internal struggle,' she wrote in her memoirs, 'but I remained faithful to my chosen path, knowing that my choice was the right one.'

After obtaining her baccalaureate in 1903, she spent some time at the Missionshaus Malche at Bad Freienwalde in Brandenburg, where she learned about the activities of the Malche Protestant mission. During her studies there, she read a lot about the situation of the Armenians in Turkey, and she became increasingly determined to go out in the field in order to help the Armenian children.

Subsequently, she was invited to work at the mission in the Turkish city of Maraş, in eastern Cilicia. But before this, because she was still so young, she was sent to work with women and children in a German village and spent some months working among the poor in St Petersburg. In 1909, she tried again to leave for Turkey to work with the Armenians. That year, however, the massacres began again in and around Adana in Cilicia, leaving some 10,000 dead, and her departure was postponed once more. In the interim, she spent two years taking part in a new training for missionary teachers.

ANNA HEDVIG BÜLL (1887–1981)

An evangelical missionary in Cilicia

In 1911, she was finally given permission to leave and headed out to Maraş, where she was to work with the Swiss missionary Beatrice Rohner. 'Although I had to leave those who were dear to me,' she wrote, 'my heart was filled with joy: at last I could do what I had been longing to do for so long.' In her memoirs, she also described how it was the news of the terrible massacres at Adana that had made her decide to go out to this unknown country to help rescue Christian orphans, but also how hard it had been to obtain her parents' blessing for this mission. As the mayor and a member of the local aristocracy, her father in particular had difficulty in accepting that his daughter, still only twenty-four years old, wanted to devote her life to a humanitarian mission in such a far-off land. But her mind was made up.

Arriving in Cilicia in 1911, she became a teacher at the 'Bethel' (Beth-Ullah) orphanage founded by German evangelical missionaries to take care of the Armenian orphans in Maraş. Working with children who were sunk in depression and trauma, and who felt hopeless, lost and suspicious, presented enormous challenges for the missionaries. Earning the children's trust and motivating them to learn, since most of them could neither read nor write, was the first priority, and this was the task to which she devoted herself at the orphanage until 1916. These years were to map out her future: from this point on—helped enormously by her rapid mastery of both Armenian and Turkish—she was to devote her life entirely to working with Armenian children.

In 1915, Anna Hedvig Büll became a witness to the Armenian genocide in Cilicia. With other missionaries, she did everything in her power to save Armenian children during the massacres. Thanks to her efforts, some 2,000 women and children found places of safety, and Maraş became known as the 'City of Orphans'. In order to save their children, many Armenian women asked Anna to keep and protect them at the orphanage. As well as looking after the children, Anna was meticulous in preserving any information she could glean about their families, as she felt sure that later on the children would want to know where they came from.

THE RIGHTEOUS AND PEOPLE OF CONSCIENCE

Resistance to the slaughter

'It was a diabolical policy,' wrote Anna in her memoirs, composed in Armenian in 1957, 'and no words can describe the tortures and acts of barbarism committed by the Turks.' From 1916 to 1919, she was sent to work in an orphanage belonging to the same German mission in the village of Haruniye, south of Maraş. In 1918, by dint of extraordinary efforts, she managed to stop the deportation of the children. In her memoirs, she recalled with horror the day when a squad of Turkish soldiers arrived at the orphanage and announced that the children were to be taken away to a place of safety, in Syria: 'I knew straight away that this fictitious "place of safety" was in fact the desert of Der Zor.' To prevent the soldiers from taking the children, she insisted that this would be an infringement of international law:

> I threatened to write letters to the consuls and international missions of Germany, Britain, France and other countries. They replied in the same sarcastic tone that those countries were eternal friends of Turkey. I got some paper and started to write the letter in their presence; at that point they left, under pressure from me, in order to avoid more serious consequences.

From that day on, she wrote daily, in a range of languages, to European consulates, missions and numerous humanitarian organizations. A few days after this incident, three Turks came into the courtyard of the orphanage, surrounded her and threatened to take her to Der Zor if she refused to let them in: 'My whole being revolted. I told them that I had sent off many letters in all directions, and that if anything should happen to me, they would be obliged to provide an explanation to international bodies. They left, hurling insults at me. One small battle had been won.'

Geopolitical upheavals and shattered hopes

At the orphanage, Anna continued to teach the natural sciences and religion, mostly in German. When the First Republic of Armenia was declared on 28 May 1918, she was convinced that the Armenian orphans would go and live in the new republic, and that one day, when she left her parish in Cilicia, she too would move there to be with her 'adoptive children'. Realizing how important their maternal language was to the orphans, and how crucial it was for the preservation of their culture, she now began to teach the children in Armenian.

Her own gift for languages was remarkable. Already fluent in eight languages, she had gained an excellent command of Armenian during her years working with Armenian children. As well as speaking and reading the language fluently, she also had a flawless command of written Armenian, as may be seen from her reports, memoirs and letters in Armenian and her accomplished translations from German into Armenian. The richness of her vocabulary and her literary feel for Western Armenian and well-turned expressions bear ample testimony to her ability to formulate her thoughts in Armenian.

Unfortunately, the situation in Cilicia was now deteriorating yet further. In addition to the problems she faced in finding enough food, attacks by gangs of Turks now became a constant threat, while the Germans' precipitate departure from Turkey had left the Protestant mission without any protection. In 1919, Anna was forced to leave for Estonia. On the journey, she received warning that many members of her family had fallen victim to the revolutionary terror (like the other Baltic nations, Estonia was not to gain its independence until 1920, after a brief conflict with the Red Army). When she reached Constantinople, she learned that her mother was dead. Circumstances then forced her to stop at Graz in Austria to take care of her elderly aunt. After spending a year and a half there, she eventually arrived back in Estonia in 1921.

Return to Syria

After spending a few months at home, Anna set off once again for the Middle East, this time with a new mission called Action Chrétienne en Orient (ACO), set up by the Swiss pastor Paul Berron. Having lived in the Middle East from 1915 to 1918, Berron was a first-hand witness to the Armenian genocide and the ordeals of the survivors. ACO was a missionary organization set up principally to establish links with Protestant communities and churches in

THE RIGHTEOUS AND PEOPLE OF CONSCIENCE

Lebanon, Syria, Iran and Egypt. Still in existence today, it undertakes a wide variety of projects in these countries. The aim of this particular mission was to deliver aid to the Christian refugees in Aleppo. There were over 160,000 Armenian refugees in Syria at this time, living in extreme poverty and succumbing to epidemics of disease in their hundreds on a daily basis. Aleppo thus became Anna's new field of activity. Exploring every avenue to find ways to help the Armenian refugees, she managed—initially through her own repeated and persistent efforts but also by making use of her personal contacts—to convince the members of diplomatic missions to help her open a hospital in the city, to which she invited eminent Syrian doctors to come and work.

To supply the refugees' daily needs and offer them material support, friends from Maraş helped her to set up craft workshops that employed over 500 women and girls. The rugs and other items they made by hand in these workshops were sold in Europe, so enabling the women to earn enough money to meet their daily needs.

As well as obtaining bursaries for 250 Armenian children to attend various schools in Aleppo, Anna also pioneered an interesting and innovative adoption scheme for Armenian children, as she wrote in her memoirs:

> There were large numbers of orphans. I developed a unique adoption scheme, under which European benefactors would adopt one of the children in a refugee family in Aleppo and would send a gold coin to their adoptive family every month. Over 200 families were able to benefit from this initiative.

Concerned about the health of the children, who were weak and malnourished, Anna set up a rehabilitation centre in the village of Atek, in the *sanjak* of Alexandretta—the only centre of its kind, not just in Aleppo but in the whole of Syria. Over many years, large numbers of children were sent there for treatment, and the activities and conditions provided by the centre enabled them to feed and clothe themselves; some were also immunized against disease.

The other project that Anna managed to complete successfully, thanks to her dedication and commitment, was the building of living accommodation for the Armenian refugees. The conditions in which the refugees were living were inhumane and intolerable, with a lack of drinking water, food, clothes and the most basic of facilities, as she wrote:

> Winter started a few days ago. The weather is cold and rainy. The poverty in the refugee camp is appalling. The walls of the accommodation have been destroyed, the flimsy fencing does not keep the rain out of the rooms, and there is no floor. Everywhere, people are falling ill because of the cold and wet.

Making use of her connections with the French government (which had left Cilicia after its three-year mandate ended in 1921 but retained the *sanjak* of Alexandretta until 1939), Anna was able to obtain the necessary permissions and support for the construction of accommodation for the refugees. The old barracks were demolished, and work started on the building of a new residential quarter. Everyone, children included, lent a hand to bring to fruition a plan that would give them a chance of enjoying decent living conditions.

Attempt to 'repatriate' to Armenia

At the end of the Second World War, many of the Armenians in Syria, encouraged by Stalin's policy of open immigration by the Armenian diaspora to compensate for heavy war losses, emigrated to the Armenian Soviet Socialist Republic. When her children, friends and colleagues and all those she was close to and who had become her family left Aleppo, Anna was unable to conceive of life without them. She applied to go to Armenia too, but her application was refused. Now aged sixty-four and unable to return to Estonia, which had been annexed by the Soviet Union in 1940, she decided to leave Aleppo and move to Western Europe.

Anna Hedvig Büll spent the remainder of her life in a home for retired missionaries in Heidelberg, then in West Germany. She stayed in constant contact with the Armenian orphans, whose letters brought her great happiness. In 1965, when she was seventy-eight, she travelled to Aleppo and Beirut for the fiftieth anniversary of the Armenian genocide. At the end of her life, her native Estonian deserted her, along with her Russian, French, English, German and Turkish, and she spoke only Armenian. She died on 3 October 1981, at the age of ninety-four.

THE RIGHTEOUS AND PEOPLE OF CONSCIENCE

The memoirs that Anna Hedvig Büll wrote during her retirement give us an understanding of the fundamental role she played in the lives of thousands of Armenian orphans: a whole generation of children and teenagers had grown up with the values that she had handed down to them. On 29 April 1989, a commemorative plaque on the house where she was born on Kooli Street was unveiled in her memory by the Armenian–Estonian Cultural Association of Haapsalu. To this day, descendants of survivors of the genocide remember Anna Hedvig Büll as the 'mother of Armenians'.

Sources and further reading

Sources

Maroukhanyan, Vrej, *My Heart Is Armenian* [in Armenian], n.p.: n.p., n.d.

Studies

Grigoryan, Vardan, *Hedwig Büll, Estonian Friend of the Armenian People* [in Armenian], Yerevan: Naïri Editions, 2007.

'On the Occasion of the 125th Birth Anniversary of Hedvig Büll: "My heart is Armenian"', Armenian Genocide Museum Institute, http://www.genocide-museum.am/eng/04.03.2013.php

43

MARIA JACOBSEN (1882–1960)
KAREN MARIE PETERSEN (1881–?)

A charitable and effective partnership

At the outbreak of war in 1914, two young Danish missionaries, Maria Jacobsen and Karen Marie Petersen, were working in the 'twin towns' of Harput and Mezreh, a few kilometres apart from each other in the *vilayet* of Harput. Maria Jacobsen had been sent by the Women's Missionary Workers (Kvindelige Missions Arbejdere or KMA) to work as a nurse at the American hospital in Harput, and Karen Marie Petersen had been sent by the KMA to look after an Armenian orphanage belonging to them.

The two women were close friends, and at a time when missionaries, doctors and nurses from countries that were at war with Turkey were gradually being forced to leave the country and give up their humanitarian mission, this friendship must have been a great comfort to them.

Working virtually alone in the east of the Ottoman Empire, cut off from the outside world, the two women had to face up to the challenges of living through the Armenian genocide of 1915–16 and also of helping the increasing numbers of orphans left by the massacres to survive. In addition to these orphans, unknown to the Turkish authorities, Jacobsen and Petersen also took on the responsibility for elderly people who had escaped the massacres and young Armenian men who had fled conscription and certain death.

THE RIGHTEOUS AND PEOPLE OF CONSCIENCE

Maria Jacobsen: nurse and missionary

The two missionaries both left written accounts of the events they witnessed and what they accomplished during their time in Turkey. Maria Jacobsen left very detailed diaries, written in Danish and translated into Armenian in 1979 and English in 2001. Karen Marie Petersen left no diary that has yet been found, although her letters and postcards to members of the KMA contain reference to notes that she had made. We are able to follow her activities through Maria Jacobsen's frequent references to her in her diaries.

Born on 6 November 1882 in the small Danish village of Siim, near Ry, Maria spent her childhood in Horsens with her loving and devout family. In 1898, she attended a Congregationalist Christian meeting organized by Baroness Sigrid Kurck, who with other members of the Danish aristocracy was campaigning to make the world aware of the sufferings of the Armenians. Then aged just fifteen, Maria was deeply moved by what she learned about the massacres and persecutions of the Armenians, and from then on was determined to help them.

Later on, she was able to respond to this calling to alleviate the sufferings of the Armenian people as a member of the KMA, the Danish branch of which had been founded in 1900. In 1905, she went to Copenhagen to continue her studies, and very quickly found work as a student nurse in the paediatric department of the hospital at Sundby. In the autumn of that year, she joined the KMA mission school and was selected to become a member of its Armenia Committee. In 1906, she qualified as a nurse and travelled to London, to work in a general clinic and to learn English.

The Harput mission: early days

In November 1907, the young missionary began her work among the Armenians in Harput. American missionaries had already opened a mission station there, with a small temporary hospital staffed by doctors but without any nurses. The arrival of a Danish nurse was therefore a major event for the staff there. The day after she arrived, Maria—who had just turned twenty-four—began an intense work schedule with the American doctors, while devoting what little spare time she had to learning Armenian. Later on, when she was appointed to run the hospital, this helped her to communicate with the local people.

She also found time to keep a diary, which would later become a valuable testimony to the Armenian genocide. This voluminous diary of 600 pages, begun on 7 September 1907 and with the final entry on 6 August 1919, consists essentially of descriptions of the deportation and exile of the Armenians of Harput and the massacres perpetrated by the Turks from 1915 to 1919. Witnesses to the genocide as it unfolded, the missionaries were able to give aid to the survivors of the massacres while also gathering first-hand accounts from them.

Witness to genocide

In 1915, massacres of Armenians began to take place all around Maria Jacobsen and her colleague Karen Marie Petersen, as thousands upon thousands of Armenians suffered deaths of appalling cruelty. Writing in her diary on 22 November 1915, Maria Jacobsen showed she was clearly aware that the deportations were merely a pretext for a government-led campaign of extermination:

> How terrible it is to think that our friends will set out on this journey with the certainty that it will end in their death! It would be more merciful if they were killed on the spot instead of being made to walk for days in the cold and rain, with no food or clothes, given that everything they had with them was taken away from them when they left ... Those poor women now know very clearly that the aim of the Turks is simply to exterminate the Armenian nation by making it suffer as much as possible.

For six months, the missionaries were forbidden to leave Harput or Mezreh. They could do nothing except look on as this indescribable massacre unfolded. Maria Jacobsen related how they could smell from afar the stench of the dead, dying and sick deportees, and how 'those poor people no longer looked human; even animals would not be found in such a state, as people would take pity on them and put them out of their misery'.

On 29 July 1915, Maria described how 100 Armenians had been sent out of Harput on foot, and two hours later the soldiers had opened fire on them. A young boy of sixteen had been hit by seven bullets and had several bayonet wounds on his back but had managed to survive. He was able to reach the hospital, where his wounds were treated and he was given clean clothes. She gave no more details nor any explanations, as though nothing could equal the horror of the bald facts, presented without comment. Her diaries contain dozens of accounts of similar crimes, all described with equal economy and combining to create an impression of mounting horror.

Amid all these atrocities, Maria Jacobsen's diary entries also include some references that demonstrate that not all Turks supported the policy of extermination. On 20 December 1915, she wrote:

> Our chief of police is very affable and good and has done everything he can to help the Armenians. He has given more than one fatherly talk to the *kaymakam*, who when ordered by the *vali* to exterminate the Armenians responded, 'I am in poor health and cannot carry out this work. If you want it done, you will have to dismiss me and do it afterwards.'

In another incident, an elderly sheikh from Harput went to see the *vali*, threw himself at his feet and entreated him to stop the persecution of the Armenians, pleading: 'Enough is enough. Free the innocent. Our Koran forbids such cruelty.' The governor declared solemnly that the persecution must cease, but nothing changed.

Another Turk, who had hidden an Armenian in his house in Harput and was ordered by the government to hand him over, responded, 'I have known him from his earliest childhood and love him as though he were my son; I know that he is innocent, and I will not hand him over to you. If you want him, you will have to kill me first.' Maria Jacobsen also explained, however, that sadly cases of this kind were extremely rare, and that the seven Armenians who were officially allowed to remain in Harput because they practised essential trades were not treated well.

One little girl of seven who had been sold by the Turks to a Bedouin family managed to escape. She hid in a tree until, unable to cling on to the branches any longer, she fell to the ground. Just as a Turkish gendarme discovered the poor child, Maria Jacobsen happened to pass by and adopted the little girl on the spot. Hansa was the first child she adopted, later to be followed by Beatrice and Lilly.

Aid to the orphans

Over a few months in 1919, in the wake of the First World War, with the help of members of Near East Relief, Maria Jacobsen took care of over 3,600 Armenian orphans who had been found in various parts of the Ottoman Empire, most of them starving, skeletally thin and suffering from infectious diseases. Saving them was an extremely courageous enterprise in which she was aided by Karen Marie Petersen.

Later that year, after contracting typhus, Maria Jacobsen decided to return to Denmark for the sake of her health. When she got there, however, she received an invitation to go to America. There she embarked on a seven-month public lecture tour, describing the atrocities committed against the Armenians in the Ottoman Empire and raising funds for the Armenian orphans. In 1920–1, she attempted to return to Harput but was denied entry into the much-reduced Ottoman Empire. So she decided to go to Beirut and to continue her humanitarian work in Lebanon.

From 1919 to 1922, Turkey unleashed a fresh wave of persecution against the Armenians, especially Armenian orphans, and large numbers of children were evacuated from Turkish government orphanages. Near East Relief organized the evacuation of 110,000 Armenian orphans from the Ottoman Empire to Russia, Eastern Armenia, Lebanon, Syria and Greece. In January 1922, Maria Jacobsen and Karen Marie Petersen transferred a large group of orphans to Beirut.

In July 1922, Maria settled in Zouk Mikael, between the cities of Byblos (Jbeil) and Beirut, with 208 children from Cilicia, who were later transferred to Sayda (Sidon).

'Birds' Nest'

In 1928, the KMA bought the building of the Armenian orphanage in Jbeil from Near East Relief in order to set up the Danish 'Birds' Nest' orphanage. The establishment run by 'Mama Jacobsen', as the children called her, was a school as well as an orphanage, where the same syllabus was taught as in state schools in Lebanon.

Maria Jacobsen's humanitarian work was given recognition in her lifetime. In 1950, she became the first woman to receive the Gold Medal Award of the Kingdom of Denmark, and four years later she was awarded a gold medal of honour by the Lebanese government.

Maria Jacobsen died on 6 April 1960 and was buried according to her wishes in the courtyard at Birds' Nest. 'Mama Jacobsen' had given an education to thousands of Armenian orphans, who grew up to become doctors, teachers, scientists or simply citizens of their adopted country.

Having risked her life to bring her diaries back with her from the Ottoman Empire, she kept them secret for many years before they were eventually translated into Armenian and published posthumously in Beirut in 1979. During the First World War, she also wrote many letters to the KMA committee in which, escaping the censorship then in force with the help of the Germans, she was able to describe in Danish the horrific experiences of the survivors of the massacres at Mezreh and Harput.

In 2010, the Armenian Genocide Museum-Institute in Yerevan received a donation of personal documents relating to Maria Jacobsen, including previously unseen photographs, reports and postcards.

KAREN MARIE PETERSEN

Friend and colleague of Maria Jacobsen

Karen Marie Petersen was born in 1881 into a middle-class family in the provincial Danish town of Nykøbing Sjaelland. Her father was a customs inspector, and she received a good education, eventually speaking German, English, Armenian and Turkish as well as Danish.

We know the details of her humanitarian work as director of the Danish orphanage 'Emaus' at Mezreh during the First World War thanks to the diaries of her colleague Maria Jacobsen. Like Jacobsen, she also adopted an orphan, a girl whom she named Hope.

At the end of the First World War, the two missionaries handed over their work to the American Board of Commissioners for

MARIA JACOBSEN & KAREN M. PETERSEN

Foreign Missions, which had returned to Mezreh and Harput. After a period of recuperation in Denmark, they intended to return themselves, but as a consequence of the rise to power of Mustafa Kemal (Atatürk) and his nationalist movement, with its anti-missionary and anti-Armenian policies, they were denied permission to do so.

Wanting to continue her work with Armenian orphans, Karen Marie Petersen accompanied Maria Jacobsen to Syria and Lebanon, now independent nations following the break-up of the Ottoman Empire, to work with the KMA and in close partnership with the powerful American organization Near East Relief.

In Lebanon, the two women established the Birds' Nest orphanage, which expanded to provide a home for thousands of Armenians, and which accompanied the orphans into adulthood.

Testimonies

Petersen sent dozens of letters and postcards to KMA members, taking care to avoid being too explicit so as not to fall foul of the Ottoman censors. She also gathered testimonies from survivors of the massacres. From the outset, she had realized the importance of these eyewitness accounts and had recorded them with meticulous care. The detail she gives in these reports suggests that she intended to use them as the basis for a book or a diary.

The Danish historian Matthias Bjornlund has published an article entitled 'Recording Death and Survival: Karen Marie Petersen, Missionary Witness to Genocide', which contains English translations of three of these important Danish documents. Two of them are testimonies collected by Petersen, and the third is her own narrative of the tragic story of a young woman that seems to have affected her deeply.

The first testimony, to which she gave the title 'A Miserable Armenian Family', is the story of a woman survivor of the massacres. Her husband was killed, and she was forced to leave the large town of Bitlis, where they had lived, with her five sons and three daughters. During a death march to Mardin lasting five weeks, three of her sons and one daughter were taken by the Turks. On the gruelling journey from Mardin to Aleppo, on which she witnessed many horrors, three more of her children died from violence, typhus and starvation. The end of the war brought little relief to the survivors, as the Turks continued to attack them, while the British and French did little to come to their aid.

The second testimony is that of an Armenian girl around sixteen years of age whom Petersen calls Sevart Mikaelian. Sevart had survived a prolonged death march and its aftermath, during which she lost her aunt, who drowned herself after her four children had been killed, as well as her mother and a sister. Sevart was given to a Turkish official who was travelling to Mezreh and who treated her 'like his daughter'. Whether he released her or she escaped from him, she arrived at the orphanage in 1918.

The third testimony is the story of a woman called Digin Versjin. 'Digin' was an unusual term of respect when applied to an Armenian woman, meaning roughly 'Mistress' or 'Lady'. Born in Adana, Digin Versjin was a member of the local Armenian elite. Her husband, a man of some wealth, had lived in America and England (where they were married) for many years and had gained American citizenship. Just before the war, he had returned to Turkey with his wife and children and in order to reclaim some property had taken Turkish citizenship once again. Having lost his right of American protection, he was deported with his family, and on the orders of 'a powerful Kurd whose men were sent to do the killing', was brutally cut down in front of his family. The Kurd then turned his attention to Versjin, described by Petersen as 'a Madonna-like beauty', and asked her to marry him. She refused, but she was in his power; soon she became pregnant by him and gave birth to a daughter. Petersen took a special interest in this well-educated and devout Protestant woman, and after strenuous efforts managed to take her under her personal protection, at the risk of her own life. Despite Petersen's repeated efforts to rescue her from the Kurd, Versjin's story ends inconclusively. However, Bjørnlund adds a poignant coda to the story. In 1920, Petersen published a pamphlet entitled *Digin Virginie: The Sufferings of an Armenian Woman*, in which she added a conclusion to the tale. The baby died, and Versjin lost her sanity, until she recovered at the orphanage. In 1917, she was caught when attempting to escape to Dersim and spent a month in a brutal Turkish women's prison. In September 1919, she was due to leave Mezreh with Petersen and Maria Jacobsen, in an American car convoy bound for Denmark, when the car she was in suffered from engine trouble and was forced to turn back. Petersen concludes: 'It was the last car convoy of the year—the last chance to get out. I have not since heard if she managed to get out of the country.'

Sources and further reading

Sources

Jacobsen, *Diaries of a Danish Missionary*.

Studies

Bjørnlund, Matthias, 'Danish Missionaries in the Kharpert Province: A Brief Introduction', https://www.houshamadyan.org/mapottomanempire/vilayetofmamuratulazizharput/harputkaza/religion/missionaries.html; Bjørnlund, 'Recording Death and Survival: Karen Marie Petersen, Missionary Witness to Genocide', https://www.researchgate.net/publication/290996627_Recording_Death_and_Survival_Karen_Marie_Petersen_Missionary_Witness_to_Genocide

Dokozilian, Shoughik, 'Nid d'oiseaux: L'orphelinat arménien de Jbeil au Liban', D.E.A. thesis, Université Paul-Valéry Montpellier III, October 2001.

44

KAREN JEPPE (1876–1935)

The 'Danish Mother of the Armenians'

Thousands of Armenians who would otherwise have been condemned to die of starvation or other fatal consequences of the persecutions were saved thanks to Karen Jeppe, who championed the values of humanitarianism and solidarity throughout her life. Educated, open-minded and compassionate, she occupies a special place in the history of the Armenians after the genocide.

Karen Jeppe was born in Gylling, Denmark, on 1 July 1876, the daughter of a schoolteacher father who instilled her with humanist values and a love of nature. Modern in his thinking, he supported the idea of education for women and girls, and when Karen was thirteen, he sent her to live with his parents in Germany in order to learn the language. This she did with great alacrity, displaying a remarkable gift for languages that would enable her to learn six more in due course.

It was when she was teaching at a boarding school in Copenhagen, at the beginning of 1902, that she heard the head teacher H. C. Frederiksen, prompted by an article he had read, speak about the persecution of the Armenians in Turkey. The article, by the great writer and humanist Aage Meyer Benedictsen, described the massacres of Armenians perpetrated by the Turks in 1896.

Aage Meyer Benedictsen and Johannes Lepsius

Aage Meyer Benedictsen (1866–1927), born to a Danish Jewish father and Icelandic mother, was an outstanding figure, a champion of human rights and one of the first true world figures in Denmark. A philologist by training, he travelled throughout Eastern Europe and Asia and spoke Kurdish, Persian and Hindi, among other languages. He was deeply disturbed by the persecution of the Armenians. On one of his journeys, he met the German Protestant missionary Johannes Lepsius, an encounter that was to prove a turning point for him. In 1902, he founded a secular association called Danish Friends of Armenians.

In late February 1902, Jeppe attended a meeting at which Benedictsen spoke about the plight of the Armenians in the Ottoman Empire, which he had witnessed at first hand. So moving and persuasive was his description of these events that Jeppe began to seriously consider joining the Danish Friends of Armenians, whose leaders were determined to continue the struggle and promote the role of Denmark in bringing aid to the Armenians in the Middle East, and which was already working in the field.

Since it lacked the funds and contacts that were needed to operate autonomously in the region, the association set up a partnership with the more experienced Deutsche Orient-Mission, founded by Lepsius, which concentrated its activities around the city of Urfa in south-eastern Anatolia. At this time, the response to human tragedies was shouldered by private organizations and individuals rather than by government institutions and representatives. It was up to ordinary people, moved by the horror of the events that were unfolding, to contribute their efforts to the different initiatives set up to supply aid by various means to the Armenians in the Ottoman Empire. The work was carried out largely by Christian missionaries, whose motivation was primarily religious.

Teaching and professional training among the Armenians

When Jeppe learned that Lepsius was looking for a female teacher for his school in Urfa, she applied for the post and was accepted. So it was that on 1 October 1903, after a lengthy journey across Europe and Asia Minor, she arrived in Urfa, where hundreds of Armenians had gathered to greet her.

Jeppe was a dedicated and enthusiastic teacher. Using an audiovisual method designed for rapid language learning, she added to the languages she had learned as a girl and within a year was fluent in Armenian, Arabic and Turkish. Using the same method with her pupils, she was able to reduce the time needed to teach them one language and use it to teach them a second one. Her reputation as both a teacher and an administrator grew daily, and she became a prominent figure in the region. Driven by a determination to educate the children and strengthen the Armenian community, she used her teaching experience and intuitive methods to broaden ideas about teaching and improve the traditional curriculum in Armenian schools. Furthermore, other institutions became aware of the success of her methods and adopted them, and so these gradually became integrated into the educational system for the entire region. In parallel with her teaching activities, meanwhile, Jeppe took over as director of the German orphanage in Urfa.

It is worth stressing that Jeppe's activities were far from limited to the sphere of teaching. She was well known for her enlightened outlook and her practical approach, which drove her to find meaningful solutions to the problems facing the Armenian community. It was for this reason that she gave special attention to the development of professional training programmes, putting the emphasis on gaining specific skills. Convinced that Armenian children who were apprenticed to a trade would be able to earn their own living, she was confident that education and apprenticeships would together keep many young Armenians from a life on the streets.

Jeppe put forward ambitious plans for enlarging existing workshops and setting up new ones, and even raised the idea of buying a plot of land to raise livestock. With other Danes there, she was determined to foster a wide range of economic opportunities for the Armenians by publicizing the quality of their work and the products they made. However remarkable these efforts were, they were not sufficient, nonetheless, to ensure the survival of the Armenian community, which was still under threat and was also vulnerable to diseases, the treatment of which involved further expense. The funds that were made available to Jeppe were therefore of vital importance for the Armenians, who needed them for medical treatment and for food and clothes.

THE RIGHTEOUS AND PEOPLE OF CONSCIENCE

Massacres of 1909, genocide of 1915–16

Jeppe was a witness to the massacres that took place in Adana in 1909, which left many thousands of dead in the vilayet of Adana alone. But even in these extremely stressful conditions she carried on with her work: every day she would take survivors of the massacres into her home, securing food and other essential items for them and providing all kinds of support to the children who were left orphaned and homeless. It was at this time that she adopted an Armenian boy, Missak, and a girl whom she called Lucia. Later she would write a book about her time in Urfa, calling it *Missak* after her son.

After the outbreak of the First World War, a new wave of massacres was unleashed, and this time they were clearly organized by the Young Turk government. Once again, Jeppe organized aid for the survivors in Urfa. She also organized the distribution of food and water to the Armenians who were being deported from Urfa to Der Zor in the Syrian desert. Despite the extremely tense situation on the ground, she refused to leave her pupils. Though fully aware of the danger to her own life, she remained at her post and succeeded in saving thousands of Armenians. The enterprising methods she used included disguising some as Kurds or Arabs and hiding others in the cellars of her own house.

Jeppe did not adopt the attitude of a missionary, moreover, never laying the emphasis on the religious aspects of her activities, and always trying to find ways to re-establish cohesion between different ethnic groups by focusing on support, education, trades and Armenian culture. To gain the positive results she sought, she was ready to work not merely with Protestant missionary organizations and patriotic Armenian associations but also with Muslim leaders and the local population. According to her chief biographer, Ingeborg Maria Sick, Jeppe's attitude to the Armenians was 'scientific', or anthropological: in order to help the Armenians in as efficient a way as possible, she wanted to know everything about their language, religion, traditions and attitudes. She wanted to 'observe and be sensitive to the distinctive characteristics of the Armenian people, their faults and their virtues, to listen to the beating of their heart, just like when she and her father used to listen to the secrets of nature'.

KAREN JEPPE (1876–1935)

In 1918, suffering from physical and emotional exhaustion, Jeppe returned to Denmark. But not for long, as her heart belonged with the Armenians: 'My place is in Urfa', she would say. So she started to look for a way to go back.

In Syria with the League of Nations

In 1921, Jeppe arrived in Aleppo with a mandate from the League of Nations. As the Aleppo director of the Commission for the Protection of Women and Children in the Near East, her mission was to trace Armenian girls who had been forced into slavery during the period of the genocide.

Some 100,000 Armenians—most of them women, orphans or traumatized children, poor, sick or jobless—were scattered throughout the region. Between 20,000 and 30,000 women and children were living in captivity in Muslim households, the victims of abductions, forced marriages, rape and sex slavery, as attested by numerous first-hand accounts and diplomatic reports. Using funds that she raised in Europe, Jeppe managed to buy back large numbers of women and children from Arab slave owners.

In 1922, the situation deteriorated yet further, as fresh waves of Armenian refugees arrived in Aleppo, victims of the abandonment of Cilicia by the French government. In 1922 and 1923, Jeppe set up rehabilitation centres, medical services and food supplies for the refugees, as well as orphanages, clinics and schools. In all these ways, she strove to re-create the elements that go to make up a society, and to heal the wounds caused by the conflicts.

Agricultural colonies and craft centres in Syria

Jeppe also positioned herself as a champion of the cultural identity of the Armenians. Under the auspices of the League of Nations, she worked on a number of projects that in her view would help secure the future of the Armenians. The most ambitious of these was the planned settlement of Armenians in new agricultural colonies set up in rural areas throughout north-eastern Syria.

Far more than just a missionary, Jeppe always adopted a thoroughly practical approach, seeking to find effective and lasting solutions to improve the economic position of the Armenians. Thanks to her initiatives and her tireless efforts, their economic situation did indeed gradually get better, and they were able to set up more workshops and businesses. The establishment of a tannery, a weaving factory and a dye works not only created badly needed jobs but also generated income to support other important projects. Jeppe even launched a clothes-making venture, with models and designs brought from Denmark, while always taking care to incorporate traditional Armenian techniques. In another successful venture, she bought up Armenian handicrafts to sell them on the Danish market. The initiative she displayed in spotting local resources and building on them ensured that the Armenians were able to take an active part in the reconstruction of their own community.

Another project sprang from an agreement she managed to make with a wealthy Bedouin sheikh, Hajim Pasha, who owned a strip of land on the eastern side of the Euphrates. Jeppe resolved to meet him and make him an offer. After lengthy negotiations, she succeeded in persuading him to agree to rent part of the land to her at a very reasonable price, and an agreement was drawn up between them, based on mutual respect. Hajim was enthusiastic about the idea of supporting this courageous woman. By 1924, Jeppe had amassed enough farming land to feed around thirty families. Hajim Pasha went on to become an extremely good friend to Jeppe, helping her in her missions while also using his social standing and authority in the region to ensure the safety of the Armenian settlers. Jeppe explored every possible means of establishing good relations between the Bedouins and the Armenians, and she succeeded in founding six small Armenian farming villages outside Aleppo that continued to prosper in more recent times.

In 1933, after a visit to Denmark, Jeppe fell ill with malaria but made a partial recovery. In 1935, however, she suffered a more serious recurrence of the disease while staying at her 'White House' in the agricultural colony. She was taken from Tineh, one of the villages she had founded, to the French St Louis Hospital in Aleppo. There, on 7 July 1935, despite the efforts of the medical team, she succumbed to her prolonged struggles with illness and exhaustion, leaving behind a void in the Danish humanitarian presence in Syria that it would prove impossible to fill.

KAREN JEPPE (1876–1935)

A short but highly constructive life devoted to the Armenians

At her death, Karen Jeppe was only fifty-nine years of age, but although her life was short, her legacy remains immense. She devoted her life to the Armenian people, and she had no regrets. In a letter to her friend Ivara Nyholm, she explained that her life and the tasks she set herself were hard but not complicated, because her goal was always clear: to improve the living conditions of the Armenians. She had found her place, quite literally, and her only major anxieties were her fragile health and the constant pressure she put on herself through her conviction that she could never afford to lose a political battle. She was buried in the Armenian cemetery of Aleppo according to the rites of the Armenian Apostolic Church, as was her expressed wish.

Over three decades as a social worker with specialist understanding of Armenian affairs, including six years as the director of a League of Nations refugee agency, Jeppe displayed an unwavering spirit of innovation, humanity and compassion. She invariably stressed the importance of preserving the ethnic and cultural identity of refugees, while also balancing this with the need to resettle and reintegrate them into the wider community. Her ideas have undoubtedly contributed to the development of modern humanitarian aid programmes.

In 1946, the orphanage Jeppe founded in Aleppo became the first Armenian high school in the city, the Karen Jeppe Djemaran, later the Karen Jeppe Armenian College. The Yerevan International Film Festival (also known as the Golden Apricot Festival, after the fruit that according to legend is Armenian in origin), set up in 2004 under the presidency of the Canadian director Atom Egoyan, has honoured Karen Jeppe with the title 'Danish Mother of Armenians'.

Sources and further reading

Studies

Bjørnlund, Matthias, 'Before the Armenian Genocide: Danish Missionary and Rescue Operations in the Ottoman Empire, 1900–1914', *Haigazian Armenological Review*, 26 (Beirut, 2006), pp. 141–56; Bjørnlund, 'Karen Jeppe, Aage Meyer Benedictsen, and the Ottoman Armenians: National Survival in Imperial and Colonial Settings', *Haigazian Armenological Review*, 28 (2008), pp. 9–43.

Donikian, Denis, 'Carl Ellis Wandel (1871–1940), diplomate danois' and 'Lettre à son ministre de l'ambassadeur danois en poste à Constantinople datée du 4 septembre 1915', in *Petite encyclopédie du génocide Arménien*, p. 316; pp. 156, 158.

'Karen Jeppe: A Righteous Woman for the Armenians', Gariwo, https://en.gariwo.net/righteous/armenian-genocide/karen-jeppe-7530.html

Lous, Eva, 'Karen Jeppe (1876–1935) Jeppe Karen Vel', Dansk kvindebiografisk leksikon, 2003, https://www.kvinfo.dk/side/170/bio/825/

Shemmassian, Vahram L., 'The League of Nations and the Reclamation of Armenian Genocide Survivors', in Richard G. Hovannisian (ed.), *Looking Backward, Moving Forward: Confronting the Armenian Genocide*, New Brunswick, NJ: Transaction Publishers, 2003.

Storr, Katherine, *Excluded from the Record: Women, Refugees, and Relief, 1914–1929*, New York: Peter Lang, 2009.

45

BODIL KATHARINE BIØRN

Healthcare pioneer and witness in words and images

Bodil Katharine Biørn was born on 27 January 1871 at Kragerø in the Telemark region of Norway, some 200 kilometres from Oslo. The daughter of a wealthy shipowner, she received an unusually good education. Although her family's considerable fortune would have enabled to her to enjoy a life of luxury, she decided to devote her life to helping the victims of the Armenian genocide, with all the dangers and tragedies this would involve.

After her initial studies, Bodil decided to train as a nurse. She then worked as a nurse in Oslo, and for ten years in Germany. Out of curiosity, she began to go to talks given by German and Scandinavian missionaries in which they described the harsh lot of Armenians in Turkey, and as a result of what she heard she resolved to devote her life to humanitarian work.

Her future was now mapped out: in 1905, she was sent by the Women's Missionary Organization (WMO) to work as a nurse in the Ottoman Empire. On her arrival in Turkey, she worked in the large German mission hospital in Maraş. There German missionaries from Hülfsbund helped her in her work with widows and orphans. After this, she left to carry on her work in the city of Mezreh, in Harput province, where a new life awaited her.

As soon as she arrived, she applied herself to learning Armenian in order to be able to communicate with the local people. She spent the first year working in a German orphanage with German and Danish missionaries. Then, using funds granted by the WMO, she founded her own orphanage, where she took in the sick children and orphans whom she found in the poorest quarters of the city. In this work, she was assisted by two Armenian doctors and some Armenian women, a pioneering practice that mattered greatly to her, as she always wanted to place the emphasis on work done by the Armenians themselves. She was convinced that she could involve the Armenians in a variety of daily activities that would later help them find a trade.

After two years in Mezreh, she decided to leave in search of new horizons. Her next destination was the town of Muş, nearly 200 kilometres east of Mezreh, reached by an eight-hour journey on horseback. There she was to spend the following ten years. While there had been a number of foreign missions in Mezreh, Muş was a long way from any major centres and housed only two Protestant missions. In making her decision to work in Muş, Biørn was well aware of the many hardships she would face. The missionaries with whom she worked at Mezreh had tried to persuade her not to leave for this 'wild' spot, but she was determined to go to the place where she felt she could be of most use. When she arrived, she was struck by the poverty there: 'I have never seen so many poor and sick people as there are in Mush and the surrounding villages.'

Since there were only two doctors to serve the entire region, during her ten years there Biørn exercised her nursing skills in extremely difficult conditions. Because of the lack of specialists in the region, she would often have to take the place of a doctor, which in a world where women were excluded from the medical profession posed many practical problems. In order to be able to treat the people who came to her, including men, she taught the general principles of medicine to a young Armenian man, so that he would be able to help her in her work: an exemplary case of transnational training in healthcare, which was one of the major objectives of Biørn and other Danish missionaries. Biørn would regularly send Armenian girls to the hospital in Muş to train as nurses, in the conviction that they would then be able to help their people. She and other female missionaries were role models for Armenian women who wanted to work and pursue a career. The lack of medical personnel was soon resolved thanks to these training programmes in local institutions, with most of the women working on a voluntary basis, despite the major risks they ran.

Following all these efforts, Biørn was granted permission by the Turkish authorities to work as a midwife. Bringing infants into the world was a source of great joy for her, and a hope for the future. In addition to these important activities, Biørn was a true militant for the rights of Armenian women. Unable to comprehend the restrictions imposed on women in the Middle East, she constantly sought ways of integrating them into society and enhancing their status.

In 1915, Biørn was an eyewitness to the massacres perpetrated in Muş, and specifically to the persecution and extermination of orphans. While most of her colleagues confined themselves to the role of spectators during the massacres, in the face of these events Biørn found it impossible, and she saved the lives of hundreds of Armenian women and children who had been left homeless by giving them shelter and protection.

Biørn documented these terrible events in her diary. While the stories she had heard of the massacres when she was young had deeply moved her, she found the events that unfolded before her eyes both horrific and profoundly distressing. Despite the danger, faced with the silence of the international community she became relentless in gathering evidence of events during the genocide. In addition to collecting unpublished documents and survivor testimonies, she also took many photographs and collected them in an album, adding descriptions and commentaries on the back of each image. The courage that she displayed in amassing this considerable collection of testimonies, both written and visual, to events as they unfolded was extraordinary. She confronted all the ordeals and hardships of this period with indomitable bravery. But when the orphanage where she worked was destroyed by fire and she was forced to look on helplessly as the children perished in the flames, the scale of the tragedy was almost more than she could bear:

> When I lost my orphans, the psychological suffering was intense, but even this profound despair could not impel me to leave this place and go back to my own country. I spent five months in Harput, and I looked for an opportunity to go back to Mush and perhaps to find some of my orphans still alive, in order to soothe the torments of my heart.

When she did eventually return to Muş, she looked after the survivors, finding them food and shelter.

In 1917, Biørn took a two-year-old Armenian boy who had survived the genocide back to Norway and adopted him, changing his name from Raphael to Fridtjof in honour of the great humanist Fridtjof Nansen. She never married, and the boy was to remain her only child.

Back in the Middle East again, Biørn continued her work with orphans in Syria, Lebanon and Constantinople. In 1922, she left her son in a French school in Beirut to go to Soviet Armenia, where she founded an orphanage called Lusaghbyur ('source of light') in Alexandropol (now Gyumri). The thirty-three orphans there called her 'Mother Katarina'. But in 1924, the Soviet authorities in Armenia closed this little establishment because it was a Christian foundation and sent the children to the Amerkom (American Committee for Relief in the Near East) orphanage. Still devoted to her charity work, in 1926 Biørn settled in Syria with her son, in order to work with the estimated 120,000 Armenian refugees in the country. She remained there until 1935, founding a girls' orphanage and a women's evening institute in Aleppo.

Bodil Katharine Biørn died in 1960, at the age of ninety, and was buried in a modest plot in her hometown of Kragerø. On 22 July 2008, a glass urn filled with earth from her grave was sealed in the commemorative wall at the Armenian Genocide Museum-Institute.

Biørn's diary, believed to be lost, was discovered by chance by her grandson Jussi, who presented it to the Armenian Genocide Museum-Institute. The invaluable legacy consists of a handwritten journal to which Biørn had confided what she had seen and the testimonies of first-hand witnesses to the events, in which she had also included photographs of victims of the genocide and of children who had survived the massacres, and accounts of the fate of the survivors. On 3 December 2004, the Armenian community of Aleppo inaugurated a memorial in her honour. A second statue was erected outside the town hall in Kragerø. While Biørn is a figure of legendary proportions among the Armenian diaspora, the crucial role she played in spreading information about the genocide remains far less well known.

Sources and further reading

Studies

Naguib, Nefissa and Inger Marie Okkenhaug, *Interpreting Welfare and Relief in the Middle East*, Leiden: Brill, 2008.

Nielssen, Hilde, Inger Marie Okkenhaug and Karina Hestad-Skeie, *Protestant Missions and Local Encounters in the Nineteenth and Twentieth Centuries*, Studies in Christian Mission, Leiden: Brill, 2011.

46

JOHANNES LEPSIUS (1858–1926)

'Guardian angel of the Armenian people'

A pioneering missionary in the Near East

Born in Potsdam on 15 December 1858 into a distinguished family, the Protestant missionary, theologian and humanist Johannes Lepsius was the son of Professor Karl Richard Lepsius, the founder of Egyptology in Germany, and Elisabeth Klein, also from a family of intellectuals. It was on a trip to Egypt with his father that the young Johannes first came into contact with the Armenians. His first wife, Maggie Zeller, was the daughter of Reverend Johannes Zeller, from a well-known missionary family in Württemberg. The couple met in Jerusalem, then part of the Ottoman Empire, and had six children, before Maggie's early death in 1898. In 1900, Lepsius married Alice Breuning.

From 1884 to 1886, Lepsius was on the board of the Syrian orphanage in Jerusalem, founded after the massacre of the Christian population in 1860, and so became familiar with the problems affecting the community in Jerusalem. He became one of the founders of the Deutsche Orient-Mission and worked with Johannes Avetaranian (1861–1919), originally from Erzurum in Turkey, from a family reputed to be the descendants of the Prophet Muhammad.

The son of a Dervish, Avetaranian had been a mullah before converting to Christianity, changing his name from Mehmet Sükri to the Armenian Avetaranian, meaning 'son of the Evangelist', at his baptism in Tiflis in 1885. From 1892 to 1897, he worked with Swedish missionaries in the east of present-day Turkestan, and translated the New Testament into the Uyghur language, a close relative of Anatolian Turkish. From 1899, he worked for the Deutsche Orient-Mission and spent nine months travelling in the Middle East with Lepsius.

After training as an evangelical pastor, Lepsius began his missionary work in Turkey in the 1890s, when he became an eyewitness to crimes committed by the Turkish government at this time. At Urfa in 1895, with the American missionary and educator Corinna Shattuck, he witnessed what she described as the 'Holocaust', when Turkish troops set fire to the Armenian cathedral in the city, immolating the 3,000 Armenian Christians who had sought refuge within it. Shattuck had been sent to Turkey under the auspices of the American Board of Commissioners for Foreign Missions and lived and worked there from 1873 to 1910. She was particularly active in Urfa, where she founded orphanages and a school for the blind and set up a programme to produce braille editions of Armenian texts. During the First World War, the work Lepsius had begun in Urfa was carried on by the Danish missionary Karen Jeppe.

Work towards German–Armenian solidarity

Greatly distressed by the massacres suffered by the Armenians in 1894–6 under Sultan Abdul Hamid II, Lepsius devoted all his energies to the Deutsche Orient-Mission, of which he was the president. In 1914, he helped to found the Deutsch-Armenische Gesellschaft (German–Armenian Society), and in parallel with his humanitarian work he continued to study the political context and the causes behind the massacres of the Armenians.

In 1896, Lepsius published *Armenien und Europa* (Armenia and Europe), which he subtitled 'An indictment of the Christian Great Powers and an appeal to Christian Germany'. His first written account of the horrors committed by Abdul Hamid, an ally of Kaiser Wilhelm II (reigned 1888–1918), the work was translated into French and later into English, with extracts translated into Russian. To provide aid to the victims of these persecutions, he founded the Armenisches Hilfswerk, which funded support for Armenian refugees in Anatolia, Persia and Bulgaria. Between 1912 and 1914, he took part in conferences on the Armenian question in Constantinople, Paris, London and Bern.

JOHANNES LEPSIUS (1858–1926)

When he heard about the massacres and deportations in 1915, Lepsius travelled to Constantinople and carried out a lengthy investigation, gathering the materials that would form his celebrated report entitled *Bericht über die Lage des armenischen Volkes in der Turkeï* (Report on the situation of the Armenian people in Turkey), published in secret because of military censorship. This was followed by a second edition in which he included his interview with Enver Pasha in 1915, entitled *Der Todesgang des armenischen Volkes* (The death march of the Armenian people).

Lepsius versus the Turkish–German political and military alliance

On his return to Germany in February 1916, Lepsius gave talks in Berlin and Halle on the massacres of the Armenians, following which a ten-member delegation of churchmen was chosen to present the Christian church's concerns about the Armenian massacres to the Kaiser. Wilhelm II listened attentively and promised to intervene in support of the Armenians by writing to the sultan and to Enver Pasha, minister of war and one of the Young Turk triumvirate running the Ottoman Empire. Sadly, this initiative proved fruitless. In 1915, however, under pressure from Wilhelm II, Enver Pasha agreed to meet Lepsius in Constantinople. At this meeting, Lepsius deployed every possible argument to try to persuade Enver Pasha to halt the issuing of decrees aimed at the wholesale annihilation of Armenians in the Ottoman Empire. Enver Pasha's only response was a detailed exposition of his bloodthirsty ambitions and the nationalist ideology he had developed during his years as a student in Paris. An account of this interview is given by the Jewish writer Franz Werfel in his celebrated novel *The Forty Days of Musa Dagh*, first published in 1933, which centres on the epic resistance of a group of Armenians on Musa Dagh, the 'Mountain of Moses', and their eventual rescue by the French navy. Appalled by this interview, Lepsius returned to Germany, determined to alert public opinion to the atrocities being perpetrated against the Armenian Christians. Instead, however, he was accused of jeopardizing the wartime alliance between Germany and the Ottoman Empire. The German political classes, who were either enthusiastic supporters of this armed alliance (the liberals) or worried about disturbing the political truce that then held sway (the social democrats, with the exception of Karl Liebknecht, who opposed the war and who later founded the German Communist Party with Rosa Luxemburg), paid no heed to his warnings. His only support came from Matthias Erzberger, a politician of the Catholic Centre Party, who travelled to Turkey on his own initiative to hold talks with the Young Turk leaders. Later to be the German signatory to the Armistice signed with Marshal Foch at Réthondes on 11 November 1918, Erzberger was the only German politician to take a stand against his government's policy and to attempt to intervene in support of the Armenians, Greeks and Aramaeans. Eventually, the imposition of military censorship forced Lepsius to continue his activities outside Germany.

It was at the risk of his liberty and his life that Lepsius continued his work on his report on the situation of the Armenians in Turkey. After laying out the facts, he examined the question of who was responsible and discussed the economic repercussions and the issue of forced conversions to Islam. The report was a powerful indictment, systematically demolishing the Turkish claims one after another. It was censored by the German government, however, which forbade its publication. Nonetheless, Lepsius managed to send some 20,000 copies to ministers, missionaries and politicians throughout Germany before the censorship came into force and the original text was seized during a search of his home. In his preface to the report, Lepsius wrote:

> The most ancient people in Christendom is in danger of being annihilated, insofar as this is within the power of the Turks. Six-sevenths of the Armenian population have been stripped of their possessions, forced from their homes and—unless they convert to Islam—killed or deported into the desert. Just one-seventh have escaped deportation.

In 1919, Lepsius published one of his most important works, *Germany and Armenia 1914–1918: A Collection of Diplomatic Documents*. These documents by the German diplomatic staff and consuls in post in the Ottoman Empire formed a compendium of irrefutable evidence of the criminal intentions of the Young Turks, containing phrases such as: 'The manner in which the deportation is being carried out demonstrates that the government is actually pursuing the objective of exterminating the Armenian race in the Ottoman Empire.'

Lepsius's fame rests above all on this compendium of diplomatic reports, which—even if published under the constraints of censorship—forms a unique body of evidence demonstrating the Young Turk government's responsibility for the Armenian genocide of 1915–16.

Final testimony: the Talaat trial

In 1921, Lepsius appeared as an expert witness in the famous trial in Berlin of the young Armenian Soghomon Tehlirian, who had shot and killed Talaat Pasha, former minister of the interior and principal architect of the Armenian genocide, in a Berlin street. Using official documents, Lepsius was able to expose Talaat's intentions: only 10 per cent of the deportees were to survive the marches; the other 90 per cent were to be massacred along the way, except for the most attractive women, who would be carried off by Turks or Kurds. Lepsius based his evidence on documents he had consulted in the archives of the German embassy in Constantinople and the German Ministry of Foreign Affairs. Tehlirian was acquitted.

From 1908 to 1925, Lepsius lived and worked in the house that would become known as the Lepsiushaus in Potsdam, south-west of Berlin. Since 2011, the building has housed the Lepsius-Archiv, founded by the theologian Hermann Goltz. In addition to its library, the archive also hosts international meetings and research projects. The Deutsch-Armenische Akademie, planned by Lepsius in 1923, is now based there.

Lepsius died in 1926, aged sixty-eight, in the Italian spa resort of Merano, where he had gone for the sake of his health. He is buried in the Evangelical Cemetery there.

Sources and further reading

Sources

Chaliand and Ternon, *Armenians*, pp. 49–74.
Gust, Wolfgang (ed.), *The Armenian Genocide: Evidence from the Foreign Office Archives, 1915–1916*, New York: Berghahn Books, 2014.

THE RIGHTEOUS AND PEOPLE OF CONSCIENCE

Lepsius, Johannes, *Mikrofiche-Edition of the Documents and Periodicals of the Johannes Lepsius Archive*, ed. Hermann Goltz et al., Munich: K. G. Saur, 1999; Lepsius, *Le rapport secret du Dr Johannès Lepsius, Président de la Deutsche Orient-Mission et de la Société germano-arménienne* (preface by René Pinon), Paris: n.p., 1916.

Studies

Goltz, Herman (ed.), *Akten de Internationalen Dr Johannes-Lepsius-Symposiums 1986*, Halle-Saale: Der Martin-Luther Universität Halle-Wittenberg, 1987.

Kieser, Hans-Lukas, 'Témoins européens et américains', in Conseil scientifique international pour l'étude du génocide des Arméniens, *Le génocide des Arméniens*, pp. 61–8.

Zekiyan, Bedros Levon, 'Reflections on the Semantic Transposition of the Concept of the "Righteous" to the Context of the Armenian "Metz Yeghern"', in *There Is Always an Option to Say 'Yes' or 'No'*, pp. 215–44.

47

ALEXANDRA TOLSTOY (1884–1979)

Continuing the humanitarian legacy of Leo Tolstoy

Born on 18 June 1884 at Yasnaya Polyana, the Tolstoy family estate in the Tula region, Alexandra Lvovna Tolstaya was the twelfth of thirteen children born to the famous writer Count Leo Nikolaievich Tolstoy and his wife Sophia Andreievna, née Behrs. Well educated by governesses and close to her father, in 1901 she became his secretary, dealing with his correspondence and training as a shorthand-typist. From then on, she devoted the rest of her life to his ideals. After his death, she inherited the rights to the whole of his literary estate, which gave rise to tensions within the family.

Tolstoy's death, on 20 November 1910, turned Alexandra's life upside down: 'At his side, I did not have my own life or interests. Everything revolved around him. When he left us, he left behind him a great void that I was never able to fill.' She set to work to carry out his last wish, which was to have his unpublished works published. They were published in 1911.

When war broke out on 1 August 1914, she felt it was her duty to do something: 'Spending my time doing nothing, with my arms crossed, was intolerable,' she later recalled. 'One after another, my nephews and the workers left, taking with them my trotting horses. The estate was deserted, everything that filled our lives—organization and work in the cooperatives—was relegated to second place.'

When she read in the newspapers about the complicated relations between the military administration and the Russian Red Cross in their work caring for the wounded, this gave her the idea of becoming a nurse. Already equipped with some medical knowledge, she took nursing courses and passed her nursing examinations while working as a student nurse in the hospital at Zvenigorod, under the direction of Dr D.V. Nikitin, a family friend.

Nursing on the Caucasus and North Western Fronts

Once she had qualified as a nurse, Alexandra prepared to leave for the front, despite the disapproval of her family and friends, who thought she was betraying her father's pacifist ideals. Fate led her to the Caucasus, and in late 1914, with the 7th advance detachment of the All-Union Zemstvo Medical Service, set up to bring medical aid and provisions to the Turkish front, she set off on the gruelling journey from Tiflis to the foot of Mount Ararat, before reaching western Armenia.

In early 2015, military operations intensified as Russian troops advanced towards Erzurum along the whole of the Caucasus Front, causing serious anxiety to the Turks and considerably increasing the Russian nurses' work. Alexandra was then recalled to Iğdır to be given a new mission. The decision had been taken to send a small detachment to Van, where a massacre of Armenians had just been perpetrated. Around 1,000 survivors, mostly elderly people and children, had sought refuge with the American mission and needed to be cared for. Unable to deal with this problem on his own, the American doctor, Ernest Yarrow, had sent an appeal for help to the Russian detachment at Iğdır. Alexandra was put in charge of recruiting personnel, sourcing supplies of medication and other provisions and going out to help those who were in distress.

After working with the sick for just a week, her assistants fell ill with exanthematous typhus, and she had no choice but to take on all nursing duties singlehandedly, including caring for her assistants. When Yarrow, the only doctor, also fell ill, she nursed him too. In February 1915, she described the sufferings of the Armenians and her own feelings in an article entitled 'The Armenian Refugees', published in the Russian newspaper *Russkiye Vedomosti* and later in other newspapers, so alerting the Russian public to the situation in Iğdır and Van.

In August 1915, Alexandra obtained leave to return to Moscow. During the three months she spent there, she was repeatedly ill and confined to bed with fevers, headaches and toothache: worn out and utterly drained from overwork, her physical capacities were finally exhausted.

Barely had she recovered before she was sent out to the North Western Front as a representative of the Zemstvo Union, with responsibility for setting up orphanages. By 15 November 1915, she was already in Minsk. Alongside her nursing duties, for the rest of the war she did a great deal of charity and educational work with children, for which she was awarded the medal of St George.

From Soviet Russia to the United States

Arrested and briefly detained after the October Revolution, in 1920 Alexandra was arrested again, accused of anti-communist activities and imprisoned for two months in the notorious Lubyanka prison in Moscow while awaiting trial. Sentenced to three years in prison, she was transferred to the Novospassky Monastery, which had been converted into a prison camp, escaping the gulag only because of her training as a shorthand-typist. Released after a year, she returned to Yasnaya Polyana, where—wanting to be of use to her fellow citizens—she became director of the Tolstoy Museum and initiated many other educational projects on the estate. After many struggles with the Soviet authorities, in 1929 she obtained permission to travel to Japan, where she worked as a lecturer, principally on Tolstoy's life and works. In 1931, she decided to settle in the United States, where she taught, published Leo Tolstoy's memoirs and espoused the political ideals of her new home country. Obtaining American citizenship in 1941, she campaigned against communism and at a rally in Madison Square Gardens in 1956 denounced the repression of the Hungarian Revolution by Soviet troops.

In 1939, with her friend and fellow Russian exile Tatiana Schaufuss, she set up the Tolstoy Foundation, with a resettlement centre to provide assistance to large numbers of Russian émigrés and refugees from the Soviet regime (including Vladimir Nabokov among many others), as well as non-Russians from communist countries.

Sources and further reading

Sources

Persky, Serge M., *Tolstoï intime: Souvenirs, récits, propos familiers*, n.p.: Nabu Press, 2013 [original Russian published 1909].

THE RIGHTEOUS AND PEOPLE OF CONSCIENCE

Studies

Guardian Angels: The Steep Routes of Alexandra Tolstoy [in Russian], n.p.: Ria Dioum, 1996.

Isoyan, Albert, *The Black Book* [in Armenian], Yerevan: Hayakidak, 2011, pp. 583–5.

48

AARON AARONSOHN (1876–1919)
ALEXANDER AARONSOHN (1888–1948)
SARAH AARONSOHN (1890–1917)

A genuine empathy with the Armenians

Aaron Aaronsohn: from agronomy to espionage

It is largely thanks to the work of the Israeli historian Yair Auron, specialist in genocide studies, that the Aaronsohn siblings' work on behalf of the Armenians is now known. This account of their activities is based principally on the information he has assembled and texts that have been published for the first time as a result of his work.

Aaron Aaronsohn was born in Bacău in Romania, at a time when Romanian Jews were obliged to carry out military service but enjoyed no civil rights, and was taken to Palestine by his family in 1882, when he was six. The Aaronsohn family settled in a pioneering Jewish agricultural colony, Zichron Yaakov.

The young Aaron studied agronomy in France, with the encouragement and sponsorship of Baron Edmond de Rothschild (of the Parisian 'branch' of the family), who was more of a philanthropist than a banker; he was also a strong supporter of Zionism who bought land in Palestine and arranged work for Aaron at Metulla in Galilee. In all his agricultural work and research, Aaronsohn made it a point of honour to employ Arabs to work the land. Through his ground-breaking work on wild wheats, he was soon to establish a worldwide reputation as a botanist. His research work was carried out on his experimental farm at Atlit, near Haifa, and also in the field, when as a scientific consultant to a team fighting a plague of desert locusts in 1915, he was given permission to move around southern Syria and make detailed maps of the oases.

This work was to have major repercussions, both politically and strategically. Invited to go to America as the world's foremost agronomist, he seized the opportunity to make Jews in America more aware of the Zionist movement. And he was able to make his botanical maps of Palestine available to General Edmund Allenby, commander-in-chief of the British Egypt Expeditionary Force, who—armed with intelligence Aaronsohn was also able to provide on troop movements and the position of Ottoman encampments— was able to plan the capture of Beersheba as part of the Sinai and Palestine Campaign, before making his victorious entry into Jerusalem in December 1917.

As his work had taken him through the region from Palestine to Constantinople, Aaronsohn had observed with horror as the different phases of the genocide of the Armenians unfolded, each more terrifying than the last. Appalled by what he saw, he was afraid that the Jews would be next. This was what lay behind his militant support for the Armenians and his creation, with members of his family and his assistant Avshalom Feinberg, of the NILI intelligence-gathering network (NILI being an acronym for the Hebrew phrase meaning 'the Eternal One of Israel will not lie', from the Book of Samuel). Although most Jews then living in Palestine favoured an alliance with the Central Powers (the German, Austro-Hungarian and Ottoman Empires), in practice the Christian allies of the Ottoman Empire had done nothing to halt the genocide. In Aaron's view, moreover, even the most pro-Armenian of Germans, such as Johannes Lepsius (whose secretly published *Report on the Situation of the Armenian People* he suspected of being overseen by the German government), were too hidebound by their own natural subservience to discipline. In order to avoid a massacre of the Jews in Palestine, similar to that of the Armenians (and as with the Armenians, the Young Turks had begun to disarm the Jews, amid threats that their wives would be violated), Aaron judged that it was better to put the NILI group at the service of the Triple Entente (France, Britain and imperial Russia), as represented in this instance by Britain.

THE AARONSOHNS

Aaron Aaronsohn and Boghos Nubar Pasha

Aaronsohn had no qualms whatsoever about the ethics of becoming a spy, declaring that his only judge was his conscience. Although by virtue of his attachment to the War Office he carried a British passport, he was also fearless in serving as a courier to Boghos Nubar Pasha (1851–1930), head of the Armenian national delegation at the Versailles Peace Conference in 1919, so great was his wholehearted attachment to the Armenian cause (although he deplored the Armenians' lack of unity among themselves). Boghos Nubar was extremely well informed about the Arab world, as he was the son of Nubar Pasha, three times prime minister of Egypt between 1878 and 1895, lived in Egypt and spoke perfect Arabic. Aaronsohn gave him wise advice about adopting a moderate stand at the conference, urging him to ease back for the moment on any demands for an Armenian state combining Western Armenia and the Armenian Republic, declared in 1918, on the grounds that although this was a just and legitimate demand it was also diplomatically imprudent.

As early as 1914, Aaron Aaronsohn believed that the Ottoman government was planning a massacre of the Jews in Palestine. Horrified by what he saw of the massacre of the Armenians on his journeys between Palestine and Constantinople, he anticipated the sentiments expressed in a militant text on the Armenian genocide entitled *La suppression des Arméniens: Méthode allemande; Travail turc* and published in Paris in 1916 by the French publicist René Pinon. Aaron denounced the complicity between the Turks and the Germans, who had also profited hugely from the deportations, and the meticulous planning of the massacres by the Turkish authorities, 'odious acts' for which the Germans would also certainly have to pay. Convinced from the outset that the Young Turk government was planning to massacre the Jews, and aware of the new and destructive capabilities the Turks had gained from their relationship with the Germans, he shared his conviction that Turkey should be 'smashed to pieces'.

Aaron Aaronsohn and Mark Sykes: a convergence of views

In early 1916, through his contacts with the British Foreign Office, War Office and Secret Intelligence Service, Aaron Aaronsohn submitted a report to the War Office on the atrocities committed by the Turks, entitled 'Pro Armenia'. The report was both administrative and moral in tone, presenting facts that the head of British Military Intelligence described as harrowing. But the final version was edited to remove Aaronsohn's fears that the Jews would suffer the same fate as the Armenians, and his denunciation of German culpability. His political views on the future map of the Near East chimed with those of the War Office representative in the region, Lieutenant-Colonel Sir Mark Sykes, who had been appointed as head of the political mission to the commander-in-chief of the Egyptian Expeditionary Force. Informed of the terms of the Sykes–Picot Agreement (concluded in May 1916 with François Georges-Picot, the French high commissioner in the Near East, and not yet known to the Zionists), which gave prominence to the claims of the Armenians, Arabs and Jews at the expense of the Ottoman Empire, Aaronsohn joined forces with Sykes in April 1917 in order to alert public opinion to the deportation of Jews from Tel Aviv by the Turks.

Aaronsohn and Sykes concurred in their views on the future of the Near East. Both were enthusiastic supporters of an Arab–Jewish–Armenian alliance, to which the Hashemite dynasty appeared favourable. Sykes upheld the principles of nation states against the outmoded principles of imperialism, insofar as the envisaged alliance took British economic and political interests into account: this was to be the joint French and British policy in the face of the Turco-German alliance. It was Sykes' view 'that it is certainly our duty to get these people righted, and that it will be in our interest to get them righted on lines compatible with our economic and political interests'.

Aaronsohn supported these views, partly for ethical reasons that led him to support the Armenian cause, and partly for political reasons, as the existence of an Armenian state could hold the balance between a Jewish state and an Arab state.

Radical change in the policy of the Triple Entente

The British and French policy towards the Armenians—and towards the Arabs—was to undergo a radical change, however. Aaronsohn noted the lukewarm reaction of Britain, and likewise of France, to the declaration of Armenian independence on 28 May 1918. Forgetting that he had described Armenia as the Entente's 'valiant little ally', Georges Clemenceau, the French minister of war and the interior, was now reluctant to recognize Armenia as a belligerent. This reversal by the Entente meant that the Armenian national delegation could not play a direct part in the peace conference.

The French government, in the person of Clemenceau, had envisaged making the Armenian Legion (created out of the Légion d'Orient founded by Louis Romieu) the kernel of a national army and had viewed Cilicia as a potential state of Armenia, in the spirit of the Sykes–Picot Agreement. Now it wanted to impose a protectorate of unspecified duration over an Armenian territory stretching from the Mediterranean to the Black Sea, which in fact corresponded to the six *vilayets*, to which Trebizond had been added in 1867, and Cilicia. With no opposition from the British, the French government was in fact offering the Armenians, as Aaronsohn saw it, 'self-extermination' in place of self-determination. He denounced the Entente's political U-turn in the wake of the successes of Kemalism and its abandonment of the Armenians. This reversal in policy was disastrous for the Armenians, who were forced to renounce their claims to an Armenian state including Cilicia and the *vilayets* of Western Armenia. It was equally damaging for the Kurds, who had been promised a large Kurdish state to the south of Armenia. And on a much wider scale, it also had major repercussions for the Arabs, mobilized by Britain for the Arab Revolt of 1916–18, the leader of which, Hussein bin Ali, sharif of Mecca, with the encouragement of T. E. Lawrence as liaison officer, had gone as far as to proclaim himself king of the Hijaz in June 1916, and who was to retain the title until 1924. In 1917, the capture of Aqaba, the strategic Red Sea port, by Faisal bin Hussein, son of the sharif and future king of Iraq from 1921 to 1933, aided Allenby's Palestine campaign and enabled Faisal to demand that the British keep their promise to create a great Arab kingdom. But despite the decisive successes of the Arab Revolt, the British proved no better than the French at keeping their promises. The dream of a great and unified Arab state was brought to an end with the system of mandates set up by the League of Nations, under which Iraq, Palestine and Transjordan fell under the British mandate, while Lebanon and Syria came under the French. In 1917, under the Balfour Declaration, the League of Nations granted the British a mandate over Palestine, with a view to establishing 'a national home for the Jewish people'.

The plans that would have respected the national identities of Armenians and Arabs, among others, on which Aaronsohn and Sykes had agreed, had failed. Sir Mark Sykes died of Spanish flu, aged thirty-nine, on 16 February 1919, while in Paris for the peace conference. Aaron Aaronsohn was killed in an air crash in unexplained circumstances over the English Channel, on his way to Paris on 15 May 1919. He was forty-two.

Alexander Aaronsohn: a pro-Armenian campaigner in America

Alexander Aaronsohn, Aaron's younger brother and fellow member of the NILI spy ring, alongside their sisters Sarah and Rebecca, was sent to the United States from 1915 to 1917 to gain support among the American Zionist community for an alliance with the Triple Entente, and more generally to plead the Entente's cause with the American public. In his collection of articles, published in a single volume as *With the Turks in Palestine* in London in 1917 and translated into six languages for propaganda purposes, he described how he swayed audiences in favour of the Armenians, the Maronites (starved—possibly with genocidal intentions—by Cemal Pasha) and the Jews in Palestine, who were on the verge of extermination at the hands of the Turks.

In the wake of the Armenian genocide, Alexander Aaronsohn wrote a pamphlet entitled *Armenia* (of unknown date, first published by Yair Auron in *The Banality of Indifference: Zionism and the Armenian Genocide*), in which he expressed his wholehearted solidarity, founded on the shared destiny of the Jews and Armenians, and even on the proximity between their religions: 'Armenians, my brothers, a Jew is talking to you. A son of a race persecuted, outraged, wronged as your race is. You are suffering because you won't abandon the faith that Jesus has given the Christians, and we suffer because we have given Jesus to the nations that call themselves Christians.' He laid stress on the magnitude of the massacre, and the martyrdom of the victims: 'A million Armenians killed in less than a year! Unarmed, having committed no crime ... because they have the heroism of their convictions, because they cannot sell their soul for the sake of their body.' Referring to 'the martyrdom of a race', he implicitly identified the massacre of the Armenians with that of Jews persecuted for their faith and echoed the rhetoric of pro-Armenian figures in the West: '[F]or almost two thousand years the Armenians have been the bearers of the Christian banner among the barbarians. Because they have carried the ideals and aspirations of higher civilization, the Armenians have paid with their blood and soul.'

Sarah Aaronsohn: reliving the Armenian genocide

Sarah Aaronsohn, sister of Aaron and Alexander, is an iconic figure of female heroism and of the attitude of empathy displayed by certain members of the Jewish elite at the time of the Armenian genocide. Born at Zichron Yaakov in 1890, she worked as Aaron's assistant in his botanical research before going to Switzerland to continue her studies. In late 1915 and 1916, she made 'winter visits' to Zichron Yaakov to see her family and witnessed the horrors of the genocide on her return journeys between Constantinople and Aleppo. The accounts of these journeys that she promised to Aaron, as he noted in his diary, have not survived, but we have his testimony that '[i]n front of her very eyes, she saw the Armenians being tortured by the Turks. She saw hundreds of dead Armenians, lying on the ground, devoured by wild dogs.' He included the experiences indirectly in 'Pro Armenia' and testified to the psychological trauma she suffered as a result.

A highly active member of the NILI spy organization, Sarah became its de facto leader in Palestine when Aaron was away on foreign missions. In 1917, despite being warned of the dangers, she returned from British-controlled Egypt to Zichron Yaakov to continue her NILI activities. In September, the Turks intercepted one of her homing pigeons carrying a message for the British and decrypted the NILI code; in October, they surrounded Zichron Yaakov and made many arrests, including Sarah. Subjected to days of torture, she refused to give away any information. To avoid further torture, she managed to get hold of a revolver that she had concealed and shot herself.

THE RIGHTEOUS AND PEOPLE OF CONSCIENCE

In 1942, Alexander Aaronsohn wrote a tribute to his sister entitled *Sarah: The Flame of NILI*, published in Jerusalem the following year, in which he reported that she had made impassioned declarations on behalf of the Armenians and had called down curses on the Turks. The cries of the Armenians had pierced her ears, he wrote, her eyes had seen their sufferings and she had prayed to be made blind in order not to see any more. Furthermore, he went on, she had told her persecutors that they were lost, that she had saved her people and avenged the blood of the Armenians, and that her curse would pursue them to the end of their days.

A Jewish girl who had been allowed to go into the room where Sarah was being tortured later wrote her memoirs, in which she described Sarah's screams, groans and curses in terms that seem to substantiate—in substance at least—the words attributed to her by her brother.

On 9 October 1917, three days after she shot herself, Sarah Aaronsohn died. She was twenty-seven.

Sources and further reading

Sources

Aaronsohn, Aaron, 'Pro Armenia', n.p., 1916.

Aaronsohn, Alexander, *With the Turks in Palestine*, Boston: Houghton Mifflin Company, 1916; Aaronsohn, Alexander, *Sarah: The Flame of NILI*, n.p.: Karni, 1965.

Aaronsohn Diaries, Zichron Yaakov: Maison d'Aaronsohn, n.d.

Studies

Auron, Yaïr, *The Banality of Indifference: Zionism and the Armenian Genocide*, Abingdon: Routledge, 2001, pp. 157–8; Auron, 'Les Juifs du Yishouv et le génocide des Arméniens pendant la Première Guerre mondiale: Rapports officiels et récits de témoins', in 'Ailleurs, hier, autrement: Connaissance et reconnaissance du génocide des Arméniens', *Revue d'histoire de la Shoah*, 177–8 (2003), pp. 146–65.

Katz, Shmuel, *The Aaronsohn Saga*, Jerusalem: Gefen Publishing House, 2008

Kuciukian, *I disobbedienti*, pp. 203–9.

Neher-Bernheim, Renée, 'Le Nili', *L'Arche*, 56 (Paris, July 1978), pp. 48–55.

DIPLOMATS

49

FERNAND ROQUE-FERRIER (1859–1909)

Originator of the right of humanitarian intervention

Fernand Roque-Ferrier and Alphonse Cillière

Esprit-Fernand Roque-Ferrier, known as Fernand, was born in Montpellier on 20 February 1859, the son of Simon-Frédéric Roque-Ferrier, contractor to military convoys, and Thérèse-Françoise Michel. Simon-Frédéric was also a resident member of the local archaeological society and—until Louis-Napoléon Bonaparte's coup d'état in 1851—editor-in-chief of the republican newspaper *L'Indépendant*. Fernand's brother Louis-Alphonse was the founder of *Occitania* (1887–9) and *Le Félibrige Latin* (1890–1903) and author of numerous works in Occitan.

During this period, there were many Armenian students at the faculty of medicine and school of agriculture in Montpellier (as there were also in Nancy and Paris), and the city was also home to a branch of the Armenakan party, the first Armenian political party, founded in Van in 1855 by Mekertich Portukalian, a refugee in Marseille and publisher of the periodical *Pro Armenia*.

Fernand Roque-Ferrier's destiny was closely interwoven with that of the diplomat Alphonse Cillière (1861–1946), also a native of Montpellier. Close friends from childhood, they were students together at the École nationale des Langues orientales, where Roque-Ferrier graduated in Turkish and Persian. Cillière was French consul in Trebizond, then French consul general in Constantinople. An eyewitness to the massacres perpetrated at Trebizond in 1895 on the orders of Sultan Abdul Hamid II, he wrote a personal account of the atrocities under the title *Vêpres arméniennes: Les massacres de Trébizonde du 8 octobre 1895; Notes et impressions d'un témoin*. The typewritten manuscript was entrusted by his great-great-nephew to one of the present authors and published in 2010 under the title *1895, Massacres d'Arménians*.

In 1929, ten years after Fernand had sacrificed his life in the struggle for justice and human rights for the Armenians, Cillière began work on an important article devoted to his friend's life and memory, entitled 'Un agent français qui sacrifia sa vie à un haut devoir: Fernand Roque-Ferrier, Consul de France à Alep (1910)'. In writing this article, Cillière took over a project begun by Père Delarue, who had intended to devote a book to Roque-Ferrier, and consulted one of Delarue's fellow priests and Roque-Ferrier's former colleagues in Aleppo. Partly unfinished and unpublished, it has yielded most of the information presented here on the life of Fernand Roque-Ferrier, French consul and pioneer in the field of humanitarian intervention.

Prelude to the genocide of 1915

But first we need to go back to the massacres of 1894–6 in Erzurum, where Roque-Ferrier was consul, and in Cilicia in 1909, where he was also consul. In the face of Armenian demands for reform, street demonstrations in Constantinople and a scattering of revolts against taxes and Kurds in the region of Sassoun in south-western Armenia and the autonomous principality of Zeytun in Cilicia, both with large Armenian populations, Abdul Hamid II—the Red Sultan—had exacted brutal reprisals. The massacres he unleashed in 1894–6 left some 250,000 dead and around 100,000 refugees in Transcaucasia, in addition to countless rapes, abductions and forced conversions, along with the destruction of schools and churches. As this tragedy unfolded, the Western powers stood by and did nothing. Meanwhile, Armenian revolutionaries—and in particular the Dashnak party—directed their efforts towards the defence of the Armenian rural population in the face of the violence they were subject to both in the Ottoman Empire, in the form of attacks by the Kurds, and in the Russian Empire, in the form of anti-Armenian pogroms carried out by the Tatars (Azeris) of Baku. In contact with the Young Turk party—young officers from Salonika—who wanted to impose a constitutional regime, they applauded the constitutional revolution fomented by Turkish officers of the CUP in Salonika in July 1908. The revolution culminated in the re-adoption of the constitution of 1876 and the declaration of equal rights for all subjects of the Ottoman Empire, regardless of religion. Throughout the empire, people of all religions and creeds fraternized freely.

Some Muslims, however, took a dim view of Armenians—formerly *dhimmi* who were afforded legal protection under Sharia law and allowed to practise their faith but who remained of lower status—exploiting their newly proclaimed equality to the full, and demanding mixed commissions of inquiry and reparations for the violent attacks, murders and land confiscations carried out in the eastern provinces, and in so doing calling into question the part played in these events by Ottoman officials and officers and Kurdish *aghas*. In March and April 1909, massacres of Armenians were perpetrated in Adana and other towns in Cilicia. These massacres took place against the confused background of an attempted counter-revolution by Abdul Hamid—deposed by the Young Turks in late April 1909—which had united the anti-Armenian and anti-Christian sentiments of all the Turkish powers in the region, whether supporters of Abdul Hamid or the Young Turks. One of their particular grudges was the fact that the Armenians in Cilicia, a community of some 100,000, or a quarter of the population, were the dominant force in the local economy, across industry, trade and agriculture. Although responsibility for the massacres was generally attributed to the dying regime of Abdul Hamid, suspicions about the CUP were also aroused.

From Erzurum to Adana

In his article, Cillière set out to paint a portrait of his friend from every angle, physical, moral and psychological. Of athletic build and physically fit, he was an excellent horseman who liked to go off on long journeys on horseback, especially when he was working as a dragoman based at Tabriz, in Persian Azerbaijan. Cillière makes frequent reference to his magnanimity and his outstanding bravery: at times of danger, he would protect all those around him, and he was a man of action rather than a bureaucrat devoted to his dossiers.

THE RIGHTEOUS AND PEOPLE OF CONSCIENCE

In August 1895, Roque-Ferrier was posted to Erzurum as vice-consul. On his way there in October, he happened to be travelling through Trebizond when the massacre of the Armenian population was unleashed by the Turks, followed by an orgy of looting and pillaging. Cillière was French consul in Trebizond at this point, and together the two men toured the corpse-strewn streets of the city. Cillière confessed that it was reassuring to have at his side his 'old childhood friend, with his admirable sang-froid and his imposing height'. Also with them was Cillière's colleague and former fellow student Gaston Jousselin. Thus it was that in these harrowing conditions the three inseparable old friends from the École des Langues orientales in Paris all found themselves in Trebizond together.

The Hamidian massacres continued in Erzurum, starting three days after Roque-Ferrier's arrival on 30 October, followed by more looting and plunder. Keeping a cool head and demonstrating the breadth of his capabilities, he set up a field hospital where some 200 wounded were treated for their wounds, some of them extremely grave. Then, appointing himself as judge and witness, he took his Kodak camera and—just as the Danish missionary Bodil Katharine Biørn and the German army medic Armin T. Wegner were to do during the genocide in 1915—took photographs of mass graves and sent them to Cillière, for whom they were 'irrefutable evidence'.

Roque-Ferrier's tireless efforts to halt the clashes between different communities during his posting in Erzurum, from 1895 to 1901, were unanimously applauded, and he was praised in an official report to the French Ministry of Foreign Affairs by Paul Cambon, French ambassador to Constantinople: 'M. Roque-Ferrier has been extremely forceful in his dealings with the authorities and has shown no fear in fulfilling his duties at the risk of his life.' His courage was rewarded with the Légion d'Honneur in 1896.

After diplomatic postings to China and Brazil, Roque-Ferrier asked to return to the Near East and in 1906 was posted as consul to Aleppo, with an area of responsibility including not only the *vilayet* of Aleppo but also the *vilayets* of Adana, Diyarbekir and Mosul. Although he was unable to provide a detailed account of the tragic events of April–May 1909, he nonetheless confirmed, in his capacity as an official witness of unimpeachable standing, that 'they coincided with the end of Abdul Hamid's power and the beginning of the Young Turk regime'.

FERNAND ROQUE-FERRIER (1859–1909)

An epic journey on horseback

The massacres in the *vilayet* of Adana were followed by looting and burning. All the establishments run by the Jesuits were destroyed; the entire Armenian population of the city of Antioch was slaughtered; two French monasteries on Mount Amanus, in the Nur Mountains, were under siege; and the local Kurds had taken Armenian woman and children hostage. Informed of the critical nature of the situation, Roque-Ferrier lost no time in gathering a small group of men and leading them on an extraordinary, gruelling journey on horseback across the escarpments of Mount Amanus. The distance from Aleppo to Akbes, where the monastery that was most in danger lay, was 150 kilometres, with no proper roads. After searching for the Kurds' hostages for a month, Roque-Ferrier eventually found them and set them free. The local Armenian population—some 1,600 Armenian men, women and children—had taken refuge in the Trappist monastery at Akbes, which had been encircled by the Kurds. In May, with the aid of 200 Turkish soldiers, Roque-Ferrier finally succeeded in beating back the Kurds (as testified by a local preacher) and rescuing the Armenians. He then travelled on to the city of Adana, which now lay largely in ruins, where he fell seriously ill with dysentery. Making no allowances for his precarious state of health, he rode on to Antioch, where he set about locating and gathering up children of parents who had been massacred, entrusting them to the care of French nuns. Finally, he returned to Aleppo, where, weakened and exhausted by all he had endured, he was forced to take to his bed. He had contracted typhoid fever, and in July 1909 he died.

Roque-Ferrier was given an official funeral, attended by prominent figures from diplomatic and military circles, while a large crowd joined his funeral procession. In April 1910, his remains were transported on the steamship *Niger* to Marseille, where they were received by the official authorities and the local Armenian population. His body was then taken to the family vault in the cemetery of Saint-Lazare in Montpellier, where a large crowd of Armenians from the south of France gathered to pay their respects to this champion of human rights, who for the Armenians was already a founding figure in establishing the concept of humanitarian intervention.

THE RIGHTEOUS AND PEOPLE OF CONSCIENCE

Tribute by the Armenian community of the Midi

In May 1910, *La vie montpelliéraine et régionale* published a report on Roque-Ferrier's funeral ceremony in Montpellier, which was brought to the attention of the present authors by the Montpellier bibliophile Herman Girou. After a ceremony in the cathedral, where the coffin was flanked by tricolour flags, an emotional eulogy celebrating Roque-Ferrier's heroism was pronounced in the cemetery by a figure identified by the journalist as 'Monsieur H. Selian', who was probably in fact a French diplomat by the name of Srabian:

> Monsieur F. Roque-Ferrier was French Consul in Erzurum during the dreadful massacres that soaked that region in blood in 1895–6. At that time, he demonstrated a selflessness and an unfailing sense of duty in his determination to protect the unfortunate Armenians who were destined for certain death, so saving the lives of hundreds of people thanks to his sang-froid and his heroism.
>
> But there was a point at which this selflessness and sense of duty assumed herculean proportions, and that was during the horrific and terrible massacres last year at Adana. Monsieur Roque-Ferrier was Consul General in Aleppo. I do not know whether Adana fell within his competence; I do not know whether he was obliged by his professional duty; I do not know whether his government had instructed him to risk his life. I do not think so. This man, casting aside the obligations of official protocol, apparently ignoring any instructions he might have received, and above all paying no heed to the inept notion of non-intervention while people are being massacred; this man, I repeat, heeding only the voice of his generous heart, flew to the aid of those unfortunate people as soon as he heard the news, travelling from city to city, from town to town and from village to village, everywhere where his presence was needed, using his person, his official status and his national flag as a bulwark between the slaughtered and the slaughterers, and so succeeding in saving hundreds and thousands of human lives, in so doing adding lustre to the prestige of the tricolour flag, and heaping further glory on the name of the French people. Following these heroic actions, what is more, he fell on the field of battle. In those places of carnage he became infected with the pitiless malady that has taken him for ever, stealing

FERNAND ROQUE-FERRIER (1859–1909)

him from the affections of those around him and from the admiration of the world.

Following the massacres in Cilicia, the rift between the CUP and the Armenians, including those who had applauded the Young Turk revolution, deepened further with the defeats of the Ottoman army in Tripolitania in 1911 and the Balkans in 1912–13. These defeats exacerbated an exclusively Turkish nationalism at the expense of an Ottomanism that acknowledged equality between different communities. The revival of the Armenian question and the installation in April 1914 of two foreign general inspectors (one Dutch and the other Norwegian) in the six eastern provinces (with large Armenian populations) and Trebizond, with a view to applying the reforms laid out in the 1878 Treaty of Berlin that sought to put an end to the insecurity of people and their possessions, could hardly fail—against this background—to be perceived in a deeply negative manner by the CUP, which since 1909 had steadily established a monopoly on power. With the outbreak of the First World War, the way was wide open for the Young Turks to put into action the genocide of the Armenians.

Sources and further reading

Sources

Cillière, Alphonse, *1895, Massacres d'Arméniens*, ed. Gérard Dédéyan, Claire Mouradian and Yves Ternon, Toulouse: Privat, 2010; Cillière, 'Un agent français qui sacrifia sa vie à un haut devoir' [unpublished MS].

Poghosyan, Varoujean, *The Massacres of the Armenians of Cilicia in 1909: The Judgement of French Historiography* [in Armenian], Yerevan: n.p., 2009; Poghosyan, *Les massacres hamidiens*; Poghosyan, *Les Turcs ont passé là … Les massacres d'Adana en 1909*, ed. Georges Brézol, new edn, Yerevan: Armenian Genocide Museum-Institute, Yerevan, 2009 [Paris, 1911].

Studies

Dédéyan, Gérard, 'Fernand Roque-Ferrier (1859–1909): Un initiateur du "droit d'ingérence"', in Danielle Delmaire, Lucian Zeev-Herscovici and Felicia Waldman (eds), *Roumanie, Israël, France: Parcours juifs; Hommage au professeur Carol Iancu*, Paris: Champion, 2014, pp. 299–308.

Kévorkian, Raymond H. 'The Cilician Massacres, April 1909', in Richard

Hovannissian and Simon Payaslian (eds), *Armenian Cilicia*, Costa Mesa, CA: Mazda, 2008, pp. 339–69; Kévorkian, *Des massacres d'Adana au mandat français*, vol. 3, *La Cilicie (1909–1921)*, published in *Revue d'Histoire arménienne moderne et contemporaine* (Paris, 1999).

Moreau, Odile, *L'Empire ottoman*, Malakoff: Armand Colin, 2020, pp. 212–16.

Mutafian, Claude, 'Les Arméniens de Cilicie et des environs: Regards de voyageurs (1375–1936)', *Revue annuelle d'arménologie Hasq* (Antelias, Lebanon, n.d.), pp. 28–48.

Ternon, Yves, *Les Arméniens, histoire d'un génocide*, Paris: Le Seuil, 1996, pp. 174–81.

50

GIACOMO GORRINI (1859–1950)

A diplomatic mission to support the Armenians

Giacomo Gorrini was an Italian diplomat, born on 12 November 1859 in Molino dei Torti in the province of Alessandria in the Piedmont region. An outstanding student, he went on to become director of the archives of the Italian Ministry of Foreign Affairs, where he adopted an intelligent and innovative approach that ensured the preservation of the history of the Italian diplomatic service. Nominated as a member of the Société d'Histoire Diplomatique in Paris, he was subsequently elected to the Società Geografica Italiana and the Philologikos Syllogos Parnassos in Athens.

Gorrini displayed an interest in Armenia even before he was posted to Trebizond as Italian consul general. For the next four years—with a hiatus in 1911–12 when he was forced to leave because of the Italo-Turkish Tripolitanian War—his duties covered the *vilayets* of Erzurum, Van, Bitlis and Samsun, all with large Armenian populations. He took a great interest in the economies of these regions, as well as that of the Caucasus.

Gorrini was a deeply committed champion of the Armenian people. With the aid of Monsignor Angelo Dolci, the apostolic vicar of Constantinople, and Henry Morgenthau, the American ambassador to the Ottoman Empire, with whom he was in regular contact, he managed to save as many as 50,000 Armenians. He also kept up a relentless campaign of denunciation of the massacres committed by the Young Turks—which he witnessed at first hand—in the international press. He remained in post until July 1915, when Italy's entry into the war on the side of the Allies forced him to leave the Ottoman Empire once more.

THE RIGHTEOUS AND PEOPLE OF CONSCIENCE

Powerless to intervene, Gorrini had looked on as thousands of Armenians were loaded on to boats, taken out into the Black Sea and drowned. The interview that he gave to *Il Messaggero* on his return to Italy, printed on 25 August 1915 under the headline 'Horrific Episodes of Muslim Savagery against Armenians', is an eyewitness account that holds a place of critical importance in the historiography of the Armenian genocide. Among other atrocities, Gorrini described how children were

> torn from their families and from Christian schools and placed by force with Muslim families, or else loaded by the hundred on to boats, dressed only in their undergarments, then capsized and drowned in the Black Sea or the Degirmendere River—these are my last, indelible memories of Trebizond, memories that still, a month later, torture my soul and drive me to madness.

In the same interview, he explicitly denounced the complicity between Turkey and Germany within the framework of the Triple Alliance:

> In an attempt to prolong its agony, the Germans are administering oxygen to an Empire in its death throes, but they cannot achieve the miracle of breathing life back into a corpse. With the exception of a handful of madmen, everyone prays for a rapid peace, even if this entails the foreign occupation of Ottoman territory. There is no stomach for an uprising. The Germans and the Committee of 'Union and Progress' are universally detested and loathed, but only in the depths of people's hearts and their private conversations, since the Germans and the Committee are the only real and solid organization currently in existence in Turkey—an effective and exceedingly ruthless organization that has no hesitation in making use of any weapon, an organization of audaciousness, terror and mysterious and ferocious vengeance.

Gorrini became the first Western ambassador to the short-lived Republic of Armenia (1918–20), a posting that gave him the opportunity to indulge his deep interest in Armenia and to compensate for his premature departure from Trebizond in 1915. In a memorandum appended to the Treaty of Sèvres in 1920, he argued that Italy should support Armenian independence. Between 1920 and

GIACOMO GORRINI (1859–1950)

1940, he helped numerous Armenians to leave Turkey for Italy. He also personally saved an Armenian girl, who was to remain with him until his death in Rome on 31 October 1950, at the venerable age of ninety-one.

In 1940, Gorrini published a book, *Testimonianze*, in which he declared that no time should be lost in restoring to the Armenian people the lands they had lost. It should also be noted that Monsignor Dolci, the Vatican's envoy to Constantinople, played a diplomatic role of crucial importance, lodging protests with the Ottoman rulers, setting up an orphanage in the name of Pope Benedict XV and rescuing 300 orphans from pasha households.

A commemorative plaque in honour of Giacomo Gorrini has been erected at the Armenian Genocide Memorial complex at Tsitsernakaberd in Armenia.

Sources and further reading

Sources

Gorrini, Giacomo, *Testimonianze*, Rome: Edizioni HIM, 1940.
Kévorkian and Ternon, *Mémorial du génocide des Arméniens*, pp. 316–17.

Studies

Kiuciukian, *Voci nel deserto*, pp. 79–101.

51

HENRY MORGENTHAU (1856–1946)

Denouncer of Turkey's 'crimes against humanity and civilization'

A model citizen, rooted in his Jewish faith

As US ambassador to the Ottoman Empire from 1913 to 1916, Morgenthau was a staunch opponent of Talaat Pasha and his policy towards the Armenians.

Morgenthau arrived in America with his family in 1868. His parents, Lazarus and Babette, were Ashkenazi Jews from a solid middle-class background in Mannheim, Germany, and he was one of thirteen children. From an early age, he displayed great intelligence and a highly developed ethical awareness, influenced by his family's Jewish faith and also by the Quaker movement.

In New York, Morgenthau forged a successful career as a lawyer and, at the suggestion of Rabbi Stephen Wise, became president of the Free Synagogue, a position that—combined with the affection in which he was held by Wise—enabled him to develop a large network of contacts within the American Jewish community. In 1911, Woodrow Wilson was invited to a dinner at the Free Synagogue, and he and Morgenthau got on well together. The following year, Morgenthau was a generous supporter of Wilson's successful presidential election campaign, and he was included on the exclusive guest list to Wilson's post-election dinner.

After his election in 1912, Wilson offered Morgenthau the post of ambassador to the Ottoman Empire, in order to look after the interests of the Jewish community there. Morgenthau initially turned the job down, believing—along with other members of the

Jewish community—that this was the only post of importance that the United States would consider offering to a Jew, and that this was an affront to the Jewish community. But on a trip to Paris he met the American ambassador there, who talked through the significance of the posting with him. This was underscored by Rabbi Wise, who emphasized the necessity of watching over the Jews in Palestine.

From the defence of the Jews to the defence of the Armenians

Morgenthau finally accepted the posting in 1913. In August 1914, he launched an appeal to American Jewish associations for aid for the Jews in Palestine, on whom the Ottoman Empire was imposing very heavy requisitions, and who, following an imperial decree, were being forced to accept Ottoman citizenship or leave Palestine. Morgenthau intervened to ensure that their possessions were protected from being plundered.

While he was fully aware that there were problems in Constantinople associated with the activities of American missionaries, and others associated with Ottoman antisemitism in Palestine, Morgenthau viewed the Armenian question as the most pressing problem, and he made it his priority. From the outset, he had no confidence in the Three Pashas—Talaat, Enver and Cemal—and viewed them as sinister operators. With the entry of the Ottoman Empire into the First World War and the accompanying declaration of jihad, he began to worry for the safety of Christians in the empire. When the genocide of the Armenians was unleashed, he received and centralized the many reports sent by consuls from their posts throughout the Ottoman Empire, including Leslie A. Davis, Jesse B. Jackson, Oscar S. Heizer, Edward I. Nathan and George Horton. Through these, Morgenthau became aware of the scale and extent of the massacres, of the frenzy of looting and pillaging, and of the drownings of large numbers of Armenians in the Black Sea. Streaming in from all corners of the empire, the reports of American consuls and missionaries offered a panoramic vision of the atrocities that were unfolding.

When Morgenthau challenged Talaat Pasha directly, he responded that as a Jew the ambassador had no business taking an interest in the fate of Christians. When Morgenthau reminded him that he was ambassador for the United States, and that the American people were outraged by the treatment being inflicted on the Armenians, Talaat admitted quite cynically that he wanted to get rid of all the surviving Armenians to prevent them from seeking vengeance, as Morgenthau recalled in his personal account of the genocide, published in 1918 under the title *Ambassador Morgenthau's Story*:

> 'It is no use for you to argue,' Talaat answered, 'we have already disposed of three-quarters of the Armenians; there are none left at all in Bitlis, Van, and Erzurum. The hatred between the Turks and the Armenians is now so intense that we have got to finish with them. If we don't, they will plan their revenge.'
>
> 'If you are not influenced by humane considerations,' I replied, 'think of the material loss. These people are your businessmen. They control many of your industries. They are very large taxpayers. What would become of you commercially without them?'
>
> 'We care nothing about the commercial loss,' replied Talaat. 'We have figured all that out and we know that it will not exceed five million pounds. We don't worry about that. I have asked you to come here so as to let you know that our Armenian policy is absolutely fixed and that nothing can change it. We will not have the Armenians anywhere in Anatolia. They can live in the desert but nowhere else.'
>
> 'You are making a terrible mistake,' I said, and I repeated the statement three times.
>
> 'Yes, we may make mistakes,' he replied, 'but'—and he firmly closed his lips and shook his head—'we never regret.'

It was an exchange that clearly demonstrated the Young Turks' determination to exterminate the Armenians. Having failed to convince Talaat, Morgenthau tried to sway Enver Pasha, but with no greater success, except that on the feast day marking the end of Ramadan he managed to obtain pardons for seven Armenians who had been condemned to death. Meanwhile, Mrs Morgenthau, unable to endure the treatment of the Armenians any longer, left to return to America. Her journey took her through Bulgaria, then poised to enter the war. As Turkey was prepared to make concessions in order to gain Bulgaria as an ally, this seemed a propitious moment to raise the tragic lot of the Armenians with Queen Eleanor, 'a high-minded woman ... who was spending most of her time attempting to improve the condition of the poor in Bulgaria'. As Morgenthau reported, 'Queen Eleanor was greatly moved.'

Beyond US official neutrality

During the summer of 1915, and despite America's neutrality, Morgenthau persisted in urging Wilson to demand a halt to the extermination of the Armenians and in pressing for humanitarian aid from America. As a result of his appeals, the organization that became known as Near East Relief came into being to offer essential aid to Armenian survivors.

Morgenthau's condemnations of the Young Turk programme were regularly reported in the American press. He advocated that America should take in 500,000 Armenians in order to save them from Turkish barbarity, arguing that these honest and hardworking people should be settled in the thinly populated regions of the American West. His calls for a halt to the extermination (which by September 1915, according to American newspaper reports, had already claimed between 800,000 and a million victims) aroused the ire of the Young Turks, who responded to his call to reason by hanging twenty prominent members of the Armenian community in Constantinople. Morgenthau was relentless in his denunciations of the massacres, which were reported throughout the world. Today, these reports form a body of evidence of paramount importance in the history of the Armenian genocide.

In his published account, Morgenthau was unequivocal not only in laying bare the premeditated and planned determination of the Young Turks in carrying out their policy of extermination but also in pointing an accusing finger at German complicity. In 1916, he left Turkey, which for him had become 'a place of horror', where he could no longer tolerate 'my further daily association with men who, however gracious and accommodating and good-natured they might have been to the American Ambassador, were still reeking with the blood of nearly half a million human beings'. He felt his place was now in the United States, where he would work for the re-election—imperative, in his view—of Woodrow Wilson. Though

HENRY MORGENTHAU (1856–1946)

he ceased to be ambassador from January 1916, he continued to devote his energies to watching over the lot of minorities in the Ottoman Empire and to fundraising on behalf of Armenian survivors. In 1918, he alerted public opinion to the fact that the Greeks and Assyrians in the empire were now being subjected to the same 'wholesale massacres' as the Armenians. From 1919, he headed a fact-finding mission into the Jewish pogroms in Poland, set up by President Wilson, while still continuing to support Armenian survivors. He campaigned actively for the creation of 'Wilsonian Armenia', under a US mandate, which in the end was never ratified. He continued his philanthropic activities and represented the United States at the Geneva Conference in 1946. He died in 1946.

Sources and further reading

Sources

Morgenthau, Henry, *Ambassador Morgenthau's Story: A Personal Account of the Armenian Genocide*, n.p.: Adansonia Press, 2018 [1918].

Sarafian, Ara (ed.), *United States Official Records on the Armenian Genocide 1915–1919*, Princeton: Gomidas Institute, 2004.

Studies

Adalian, Paul, 'L'Ambassadeur Morgenthau et l'élaboration de la politique américaine de protestation et d'intervention contre le génocide (1914–1915)', *Revue d'histoire de la Shoah*, 177–8 (January–August 2003), pp. 425–35.

Balakian, *Burning Tigris, passim*.

Kiuciukian, *Voci nel deserto*, pp. 18–41.

Payaslian, Simon, 'The United States' Response to the Armenian Genocide', in Hovannissian, *Confronting the Armenian Genocide*, pp. 51–80.

Ternon, Yves, *La cause arménienne*, Paris: Éditions du Seuil, 1983, pp. 56–9, 81–2.

52

LESLIE A. DAVIS (1876–1960)

American consul moved by compassion to overcome his preconceptions

Among the non-Turks from neutral countries who remained in the interior of Turkey when war was declared in 1914, a small number committed to paper the atrocities committed against the Armenians and Christians to which they were eyewitnesses. These independent observers were in agreement with the American consul in Harput, Leslie A. Davis, that 'everything had been planned months ago' by the Ottoman authorities and was being put into action by their agents. Though not by his own admission a great admirer of the Armenians, Davis had a keen sense of justice and could not remain indifferent to the atrocities he witnessed. 'It is not that I am in any way a champion of the Armenian race,' he wrote in one of his diplomatic dispatches, but 'the punishment inflicted upon these people is so severe, the tragedy is so terrible, that one cannot contemplate it and certainly cannot live in the midst of it without being stirred to the depths of one's nature.'

He was one of the first to denounce the crimes perpetrated against the Armenians by the Turkish government, providing first-hand testimony that was both detailed and unique, as well as going above and beyond his diplomatic duties to personally save as many Armenians as he was able to.

From May 1914 to April 1917, when he was forced to leave Turkey after America's entry into the war on the Allied side, Davis was the only foreign diplomat in central Anatolia. Lying several days' journey from the nearest port or railway, Harput was virtually inaccessible—Davis described the consulate there as 'one of the

THE RIGHTEOUS AND PEOPLE OF CONSCIENCE

most remote and inaccessible in the world'—and it was in this wild and remote region that large numbers of Armenians were slaughtered. The campaign to eliminate the Armenians had been planned by the Turkish government at a time when Europe was plunged into a murderous war and all communications from Anatolia were censored and often destroyed. The diplomatic dispatches that Davis used to communicate with Henry Morgenthau, his ambassador in Constantinople, hundreds of miles from Harput, were frequently delayed or lost altogether, according to the whim of the censors.

After the war, Davis wrote a report of 130 pages on his activities in Harput, dated 9 February 1918. Together with some of his dispatches from 1915, the report was classified. It lay unread in the State Department archives until it was declassified in 1961, and it was only in the 1980s that the researcher Susan Blair stumbled upon them. They were published in 1989 under the title *The Slaughterhouse Province*.

Davis had studied law and worked in New York City as a lawyer before embarking on a diplomatic career. His first posting was to Batumi in Georgia, and it was in 1914 that he was posted to Harput. There he was to become an eyewitness to massacres and other persecutions to which this man of integrity and honesty was unable to remain indifferent. From the outset, he denounced these atrocities forcibly and unambiguously in his dispatches to Morgenthau. On 30 June 1915, as on previous days, he drew the ambassador's attention to the critical situation in Harput and the fears of the Armenian population that a massacre and deportations were being planned:

> Last week there were well founded rumors of a threatened massacre. I think there is very little doubt that one is planned. ... Another method was found, to destroy the Armenian race. This is no less than the deportation of the entire Armenian population, not only from this Vilayet, but, I understand, from all six Vilayets comprising Armenia. There are said to be about sixty thousand Armenians in this Vilayet and about a million in the six Vilayets. All of these are to be sent into exile; an undertaking greater, probably, than anything of the kind in all history.

In a worrying sign, the *vali* would not allow American missionaries or medics to go with the convoys sent from Harput: 'Another bad omen is that the Vali has refused permission for any Americans to accompany the parties leaving here.'

But whatever happened, it was clear that any Armenians who survived were going to need a great deal of relief: 'In any case, there is going to be terrible suffering and great need to help among those who survive the journey. Those who were formerly rich and the poor will alike be destitute.'

Davis described how the local Turks were profiteering from the Armenians' plight:

> The Turks are, of course, taking advantage of the situation to get things at practically nothing. Robbery and looting were never undertaken in a more wholesale manner. Turkish men and Turkish women are entering the houses of all the Armenians and taking things at almost any price. ... The scene reminds one of a lot of hungry vultures hovering over the remains of those who have fallen by the way.

Knowing that they were being sent to their deaths, many Armenians entrusted the consul and American missionaries with their life savings, begging them to send the money to their relatives in America:

> I have never seen a more pathetic or tragic scene. All feel that they are going to certain death ... They hand over the savings of a lifetime with the simple request that if they are not heard from after a few months to send their money if possible to their relatives.

As for their houses and lands, they knew that they would be confiscated: 'All the real estate belonging to the Armenians will be confiscated by the Government. Many people will be unable to dispose of their personal property and will probably walk out leaving their houses and stores with all their contents. Those who have made fortunes will lose everything.'

By 11 July, Davis was no longer in the slightest doubt as to the criminal intentions of the Turkish authorities, as he wrote to Morgenthau:

> If it were simply a matter of being obliged to leave here and go somewhere else it would not be so bad, but everyone knows it is a

case of going to one's death. If there was any doubt about it, it has been removed by the arrival of a number of parties, aggregating several thousand people, from Erzurum and Erzincan. The first ones arrived a day or two after my last report was written. I have visited their encampment a number of times and talked with some of the people. A more pitiable sight cannot be imagined. They were almost without exception ragged, filthy, hungry and sick. This is not surprising in view of the fact that they have been on the road for nearly two months with no change of clothing, no chance to wash, no shelter and little to eat.

The condition of these people indicated clearly the fate of those who have left and are about to leave from here. I believe nothing has been heard from any of them as yet and probably very little will be heard. The system that is being followed seems to be to have bands of Kurds awaiting them on the roads to kill the men especially and incidentally some of the others. The entire movement seems to be the most thoroughly organized and effective massacre this country has ever seen.

In his dispatch of 24 July, this seasoned and level-headed lawyer expressed his conviction, based on first-hand accounts that he had gathered, that the Turkish government was bent on the total destruction of 'the Armenian race':

> It has been no secret that the plan was to destroy the Armenian race as a race, but the methods have been more cold-blooded and barbarous, if not more effective, than I had first supposed. ... I do not believe there has ever been a massacre in the history of the world so general and thorough as that which is now being perpetrated in this region or that a more fiendish, diabolical scheme has ever been conceived by the mind of man.

In addition, very little resistance had been possible, a fact that was 'due very largely also to the clever way in which the scheme had been carried out':

> when practically all the Armenian men had been gotten out of the way and every weapon surrendered or found by the police, it was announced that all Armenians must be deported. Effective resistance to such an order was impossible.

LESLIE A. DAVIS (1876–1960)

He gave a detailed description of the circumstances surrounding the death of the archbishop of the local Armenian Catholic church, Monsignor Israelian, with some forty others, even though all of them had been granted safe conduct by the *vali*. Among the dead was a Frenchwoman who was known to Davis, Mlle Marguerite Gamat. Three young women were saved and taken away to marry Muslims. 'One succeeded in getting free,' added Davis, always scrupulous in giving his sources, 'It was from her that I obtained the above information.'

Another witness to an atrocity was a local gendarme:

> Another incident that was reported to me the other day was that some of the people who were sent from here were actually burned alive in a cave between here and Diarbakir. This was told me by a gendarme who was with them and who expressed himself as being very strongly opposed to the barbarous treatment the Armenians were receiving.

Davis himself witnessed the conditions in which those who were too weak to go any further were left behind in Harput to perish: 'After the departure of the parties that arrived here from Erzurum and Erzincan a few hundred of those who were too sick or feeble to continue with the others were left here to die. Their camp is a scene from the Inferno. Greater misery could not be imagined.' His descriptions of the dead and dying, mostly women and children, are harrowing.

In his dispatch of 7 September 1915, Davis confirmed that all the Armenians in Harput and Mamuret ul-Aziz had been massacred, along with thousands more from the outlying villages, with only a small number of women and children remaining. A few days later, he added, the women and children had been rounded up and massacred as well: 'During the last week of July and the first part of August large numbers of women and children were rounded up both here and in the villages. They were sent away under guard and there have been persistent reports that they were killed as the men had been.'

He was now under no illusion about the possibility of re-opening the American schools in the autumn:

> The situation in regard to the American schools is well summarized in Mr. Riggs' letter of July 19th to Mr. Peet, copy of which was

sent to the Embassy. He calls attention to the fact that two-thirds of the girl pupils and six-sevenths of the boys have been taken away to death, exile or Moslem homes; that four of the seven professors have been murdered on the road in general massacres.

After recounting a litany of atrocities, he concludes: 'This may well be called the "Slaughterhouse Vilayet" of Turkey, for it appears that exiles from all directions have come this far safely only to be massacred in some part of this Vilayet.'

In his dispatch of 30 December, Davis described the fear and anguish of the remaining Armenians in the province, not knowing when they would be arrested, deported and massacred, and the duplicity of the Turkish authorities in their stratagems for luring those who were in hiding out into the open. Even converting to Islam proved no guarantee of safety:

> The last four months have been full of uncertainty and anxiety for every one. There has been no security for any of the few Armenians who were left here after the deportations of July and August ... On Sunday, September 26th, the Vali had an announcement made that no more Armenians would be deported. For several weeks afterwards everything appeared to be quiet and many Armenians who had been in hiding up to that time ventured to come out. Some became Moslems thinking they would be in no further danger. Suddenly in the middle of the afternoon on Thursday, November 4th, the day being a fair one when many people were in the streets and market-place, the police began to arrest all the Armenians and Syrians they could find.

The lengthy report that Davis wrote for the State Department on 9 February 1918 makes it clear that in the face of the persecution and annihilation of the Armenians, his integrity and sense of justice impelled him to do all he could to save desperate people who would otherwise face a certain death, and that he managed to save many of them through his personal intervention. Extending the protection of the consulate not only to American passport holders but also to those who had given up their American nationality, he prioritized anyone 'who had documents of any kind'.

Taking full advantage of his good relationship with the *vali* and local officials, he went far beyond his consular duties, which required him to protect American citizens and institutions, and took huge risks in allowing dozens of Armenians to seek sanctuary within the substantial walls of the consulate and its extensive grounds. When he ran out of space, he found other accommodation close by:

> I have, as a matter of fact, been keeping about thirty or forty people at the Consulate ... As the garden of the Consulate is very large it has not been so very difficult to keep people here in summer. I have recently found two or three houses in the neighborhood in which I have placed some of them.

Throughout the summer of 1915, Davis had done everything in his power to help the Armenians. When it became clear that despite his efforts the deportations were going to take place, he tried unsuccessfully to persuade the *vali* to allow missionaries to accompany the deportees in order to care for the sick and help with the children. When some of those who were forced to leave asked him to look after their money and precious documents, he agreed to do so and to follow their instructions if they did not return. When he became aware of the scale of the looming catastrophe, he informed his ambassador and asked for large sums of money to aid the survivors.

With this money, he was able to help the Armenians who arrived from Erzurum in a pitiful state and convinced the local police chief to let them stay in Mamuret ul-Aziz. When Erzurum was captured by the Russians, he helped the refugees to get away and return to their towns and villages. Often, to allay suspicion, he would go to the market himself to buy provisions to feed the Armenians to whom he gave refuge in the consulate for two years. Meanwhile, he helped others to escape to the Dersim region, guided by Kurds whom he paid, in some cases taking them to the Kurds and handing them over himself.

The few thousand Armenians who remained in Harput and the surrounding region were dependent on what Davis was able to give them. In addition to this, he gave monthly sums to foreigners— French, British and Russian—from nations with whom Turkey was at war.

Above and beyond the humanitarian aid he provided, Davis was also a conscientious witness, setting out to verify accounts of massacres and so becoming an eyewitness to the aftermath, describing the corpses and skeletal remains of slaughtered Armenians. On one journey to Lake Geoljuk (now Lake Hazar), he estimated that he had seen the remains of 10,000 Armenians. His determination to keep his ambassador informed of what he had seen and of what he had heard directly from survivors of the massacres, and even from some gendarmes, made him an invaluable and arguably unique witness to the tragedy that was unfolding in the 'slaughterhouse province'. He was also quick to detect and denounce the duplicitous stratagems by which the Turkish authorities issued false reassurances and guarantees to the Armenians in order to capture and arrest them without resistance.

While his duties as consul required him to offer assistance to American citizens and safeguard American possessions, Davis was unable to stand by in the face of the tragic events to which he was witness. His dispatches and the report he composed reveal a man of uncompromising integrity, independence and courage, who in his determination to do everything in his power to—as he put it to Morgenthau—'keep people alive for the present', fully deserves his place among the Righteous.

Sources and further reading

Sources

Davis, Leslie A., *The Slaughterhouse Province*, New Rochelle, NY: Aristide D. Caratzas, 1989.

Studies

Isoyan, *Black Book* [in Armenian], pp. 537–48.
Kévorkian, *Armenian Genocide*, *passim*.
Ternon, *Armenians*, pp. 273–6.

53

OSCAR S. HEIZER (1869–1956)

American consul general and witness to savagery and greed

Born into a Protestant family, Oscar S. Heizer, an American diplomat who occupied a variety of consular posts in the Ottoman Empire, was one of the first witnesses to speak openly about the massacres of the Armenians, appealing to the international community to intervene to guarantee their protection. As consul general in Trebizond during the First World War, he became an eyewitness to the massacres, and he frequently risked his own life to save those of the Armenians and to attempt to prevent the Young Turk leaders from carrying out their policy of extermination.

Trebizond's economic and strategic importance

Wedged between the Black Sea and the Pontic Mountains, the *vilayet* of Trebizond had one of the largest populations in the Ottoman Empire before the First World War, with 1.1 million inhabitants in an area of 32,400 square kilometres. Made up mostly of Greeks, Turks, Lazi, Adjars and Abkhazians, the population also included a flourishing Armenian minority of some 73,300, settled in eighteen localities, with 106 churches, three monasteries and 190 schools, attended by some 10,000 pupils, plus a few Catholic and Protestant schools.

A major transit port, Trebizond boasted consulates representing all the world's great powers, shipping offices and the private mansions of wealthy Greek and Armenian merchants. Over time, the Armenian community began to make an impact in every sphere of life in the province. Combined with the ever-increasing involvement of Armenians in Trebizond's economy, this gave rise to concern among the Turkish administration, which set out to curtail the rights and business activities of the Armenians by every possible means. And, as Raymond Kévorkian points out in a reference to Hovagim Hovagimian's *History of Pontic Armenia*, published in Armenian in Beirut in 1967, 'It also seems that instructions were sent from central government to organize, as elsewhere, a boycott of the Greek and Armenian merchants in Trebizond.'

With Russia's entry into the war on the side of the Entente powers, the situation only deteriorated further, since Trebizond was a port of major strategic importance.

The decree of 26 June 1915

The Young Turks' plan to exterminate the Armenians was put into action in Trebizond from 2 May 1915, when gendarmes searched every Armenian household for possible deserters, weapons and 'Russian spies'. In early June, some 250 leading members of the community were arrested. The persecutions of the Armenians were put on a legal standing by a decree of 26 June, by which they were ordered to go into exile:

> The Armenians must be sent to destinations that have been prepared to this effect in the interior of the provinces; and all Ottomans are commanded strictly and absolutely to obey the following orders: 1. All Armenians, with the exception of the sick, will be forced to leave within five days of the date of the present proclamation, by villages and neighbourhoods, escorted by the gendarmerie. 2. While they will be permitted if they so wish to take some of their belongings that they can carry with them for the journey, they are forbidden to sell their properties and other goods, or to entrust these to other persons, as their exile is merely temporary.

Under the terms of the decree, the Armenians were forbidden from acquiring any form of transport before they were deported, and they were forced to hand over to the state any possessions that they were unable to carry, ostensibly to be returned to them after the war. American and European sources testified to the fact that their possessions were plundered and either sold at derisory prices or given to Kurds as an inducement to take part in the massacres.

Oscar Heizer was in post as consul general in Trebizond when the persecutions and massacres began. Having no legal powers to make any official interventions but deeply distressed by the events that he had personally witnessed, he tried to find ways to save the Armenians of Trebizond, and especially the children and young women, who were the most vulnerable and also subject to ruthless humiliation by the forces representing the CUP. The *vali* of Trebizond, Cemal Azmi Bey, the CUP delegate, Nail Bey, and the head of the local *çetes* (gangs of armed criminals operating under the Special Organization), a retired major by the name of Riza, applied themselves zealously to eliminating the city's Armenians, including the women and children.

As these events began to unfold, Heizer took measures to draw the attention of the Turkish authorities to the fate of the Armenians, sending a number of appeals and requests both to the local authorities and to central government.

Heizer's reports to Henry Morgenthau

Since none of his attempts to negotiate with the local authorities met with success, Heizer concluded that the only way forward was for the Great Powers to respond to the tragic events taking place in the *vilayet* of Trebizond. Throughout his posting there, and even after his departure for his next posting in Baghdad, he sent numerous reports to Henry Morgenthau containing detailed and comprehensive accounts of local events. These accounts provide irrefutable proof of the atrocities committed by the Turks, and they are an important source for tracing the sequence of events.

In one of his first reports, Heizer gave a detailed account of the events of the first few days. On Saturday, 26 June, the order concerning the deportation of the Armenians was proclaimed in the streets. On Thursday, 1 July, every street was occupied by gendarmes with fixed bayonets, and the task of evicting the Armenians from their houses began. Groups of men, women and children with bundles and modest parcels on their backs were rounded up on a narrow path near the American consulate. As soon as they reached

100 or so in number, each group of Armenians was pushed in front of the consulate by the gendarmes, in the heat and dust, along the road to Erzurum. Outside the town, they were formed into groups of 2,000 or so to be sent onwards. Three such convoys were deported over the first three days, making 6,000 or so altogether. Other smaller groups from Trebizond and the surrounding area were deported later, making a further 4,000 or so. Between 1 and 18 July 1915, five convoys left Trebizond, and according to Heizer the deportees were killed as soon as they left the city. In July, he reported on the fate of these people's houses and belongings:

> The 1,000 Armenian houses are being emptied of furniture by the police one after the other. The furniture, bedding and everything of value is being stored in large buildings about the city. ... The goods are piled in without any attempt at labeling or systematic storage. A crowd of Turkish women and children follow the police about like vultures and seize anything they can lay their hands on and when the more valuable things are carried out of the house by the police they rush in and take the balance. ... I suppose it will take several weeks to empty all the houses and then the Armenians' shops and stores will be cleared out. The commission that has the matter in hand is now talking of selling the great collection of household goods and property in order to pay the debts of the Armenians.

The responsibility of Nail Bey

The official who was chiefly responsible for the mass violence inflicted on the Armenians of Trebizond was Nail Bey, the local CUP leader. There can be no doubt that the Special Organization and the local representatives of the CUP, under the leadership of Nail Bey, played a role of fundamental importance in the persecution of the Armenians. Heizer uncovered the direct link between central government in Constantinople and a local committee, as he wrote to Morgenthau on 12 July: 'The real authority here seems to be in the hands of a committee of which Nail Bey is the head and he apparently receives his orders from Constantinople and not from the vali.'

In his reports, Heizer described in detail the atrocities committed against women and children on the orders of Nail Bey. This 'monster', as Heizer called him, had insisted that the Armenian children should be deported rather than being taken into the care of the authorities. Later on, when the perpetrators of the atrocities in Trebizond were put on trial, members of the CUP central committee declared that the decision to deport the Armenians had not been adopted by the party's central committee, but that the government had taken the decision and authorized Nail Bey to organize the deportation.

On 13 August 1915, Heizer wrote that Nail Bey had declared that any Muslim who wanted to take any Armenian girls or boys should go to certain houses, and that very many children were taken in this way. He went on: 'The best looking of the older girls are kept in the houses for the pleasure of members of the gang which seems to rule affairs here. I heard on good authority that a member of the Committee of Union and Progress here has ten of the handsomest girls in a house in the central part of the city for the use of himself and friends.' In a report addressed to the US secretary of state in 1919, by which time he had been posted to Baghdad, he wrote of the fate of 'nearly 3000 children ... many of [them] were loaded into boats and taken out to sea and thrown overboard. I myself saw where 16 bodies were washed ashore and buried by a Greek woman near the Italian Monastery.' It was also on Nail Bey's orders that young women and children from the wealthiest Armenian families were distributed to Muslim families, while Greek families were forbidden from taking them in.

Heizer expressed the wish that those who were responsible for the massacres should be put on trial, and his sincere hope that Nail Bey, 'this monster', would not escape justice. On 22 May 1919, Nail Bey and the former *vali* Cemal Azmi Bey were sentenced to death in absentia.

The fate of children and girls

With no power to take direct action, Heizer nevertheless sought ways to save and protect Armenian children, including a plan to set up an orphanage, which he was forced to abandon. As he explained in one of his reports, the girls had been split up and put into Muslim households. The closure of the orphanages and the distribution of the children among Muslim households, many of them outside the city in rural areas, dismayed the Greek archbishop, who had fought tirelessly on their behalf and had been assured of the support of the *vali*. But Nail Bey did not approve. The oldest of the children had been sent to a Turkish school and the youngest had been entrusted to Heizer, while the rest were sent off on the deportation marches with the women. Nail Bey would not allow the oldest children to stay at school, however, and a few days later the children who had been entrusted to Heizer were taken away from him on the pretext of being sent to an orphanage in Sivas. Heizer later learned of their fate, as testified by a Muslim officer in the Ottoman army, Lieutenant Said Ahmed Muhtar: 'They were taken out to sea in little boats. At some distance out they were stabbed to death, put in sacks and thrown in the sea. A few days later some of their little bodies were washed up on the shore of Trebizond.' Meanwhile, as detailed earlier, the most attractive of the older girls were placed in houses in the city centre where they were kept for the enjoyment of Nail Bey and his CUP cronies. Some former pupils of the American mission were placed in Muslim households near the mission, but naturally—as Heizer pointed out—most were not so fortunate.

A year later, in April 1916, when Trebizond was captured by the Russians, Heizer described how Armenian children had been driven into the sea like little dogs. After living among the Turks for ten years, he declared he would never have believed them capable of such atrocities. Such was the horror of the spectacle in Trebizond that Turkish women wrung their hands and declared that if Allah had abandoned the Ottomans it was because of their cruelty to the Armenians.

In May 1923, Heizer was appointed American consul in Jerusalem, before returning to the United States and being put in charge of a government fund to support refugees from the catastrophic burning of the Armenian and Greek quarters of Smyrna in September 1922, for which, largely through contacts in Greece, he raised $200,000.

Oscar Heizer was clearly a remarkable individual who showed no hesitation in speaking openly about events in Trebizond and—even though he was in the eye of the storm—no fear of being persecuted himself. Even after the end of his mission there, he continued to raise the subject of the violence of which the Armenians in Trebizond had been the victims, as testified by the many reports that he sent while in post in Baghdad. As a conscientious witness to the genocide of the Armenians in the *vilayet* of Trebizond, and at the risk of his own safety, he revealed the true objective of the transfer of populations as being the extermination of the Armenians, and he documented the accompanying confiscation of their possessions in a planned and premeditated fashion and as a contributory factor to the genocide. In his reports, he became a staunch defender of the Armenian women, while denouncing the bestiality of the Young Turk leaders and their henchmen, and he was equally vehement in condemning the forced conversion of children to Islam.

Sources and further reading

Sources

Kévorkian and Ternon, *Mémorial du génocide des Arméniens*, pp. 308–15.

Studies

Dadrian, Vahakn, 'Children as Victims of Genocide: The Armenian Case', *Journal of Genocide Research*, 5, 3 (2003), pp. 421–37.
Kévorkian, *Armenian Genocide*, pp. 598–603.
Matosyan, Bedros Der, 'The Taboo within the Taboo: The Fate of "Armenian Capital" at the End of the Ottoman Empire', *European Journal of Turkish Studies* (2011), https://journals.openedition.org/ejts/4411
Sarafian, Ara, 'The Absorption of Armenian Women and Children into Muslim Households as a Structural Component of the Armenian Genocide', in Omer Bartov and Phyllis Mack (eds), *In God's Name: Genocide and Religion in the Twentieth Century*, New York: Berghahn Books, 2001.

54

GERMANY

A SPECIAL CASE

Germany and the Armenian genocide

Two successive events signalled the Ottoman Empire's entry into the First World War at Germany's side. The first came on 29 October 1914, when two German warships, bought by Turkey and soon to be renamed, bombarded the Russian coasts of the Black Sea, at the sole command of the Three Pashas (Talaat, Enver and Cemal), leaders of the Young Turks. The second was on 24 November, when Mehmet V, who like his predecessors was both sultan and caliph, proclaimed jihad against the Entente powers. Entering the war without any provocation whatsoever, Turkey was armed with absolute confidence in German military superiority, even though Paris and London had pressed the case for it to retain its neutral status.

German intervention in support of the Ottoman Empire was partly the result of Germany being a latecomer to the history of imperialism and colonialism. Following initial overtures by German chancellor Otto von Bismarck (in office 1871–90), solid relations had developed during the reigns of Kaiser Wilhelm II (1888–1918) and Sultan Abdul Hamid II (1876–1909). German banks and Krupp armament factories now began to operate in the Ottoman Empire. Abdul Hamid's request for German officers as early as 1880 did not see actual results of any significance until after the Young Turk revolution of 1908, when General Colmar von der Goltz played a prominent part in modernizing the Ottoman army. In December

THE RIGHTEOUS AND PEOPLE OF CONSCIENCE

1913, after suffering defeat at the hands of the Greeks in the first of the Balkan Wars of 1912–13, Germany sent fifty-two army officers to the Ottoman Empire under the command of General Otto Liman von Sanders (which was not as surprising as it might at first seem, given that the British obtained a naval mission and France was overseeing the training of the Ottoman gendarmerie). With the backing of Grand Vizier Said Halim, the German general was to become a senior commander in the Ottoman army during the First World War. The chief of staff of the Ottoman army was Major General Friedrich (Fritz) Bronsart von Schellendorff, and there were numerous German army officers shadowing their Turkish counterparts. At least three were directly implicated in the massacres.

Germany had hitherto supported the programme of reforms in the Ottoman Empire, and particularly in the Armenian provinces. The German–Ottoman alliance would now enable it not only to hinder the advance of the Russian army but also to protect German interests in a project that was ultimately to become the Berlin–Baghdad Railway, a strategically important railway line then under construction from Konya to Baghdad, which would provide greater unity for the Ottoman Empire and offer new economic outlets.

Germany had pushed Turkey towards joining the war as a means of opening up an economic space for itself in Mesopotamia, while also spelling the end of British supremacy in the Persian Gulf. As Vahakn Dadrian points out, Schellendorff vilified the Armenians, comparing them to Jews in deeply derogatory terms; in a diary entry from May 1916, after denouncing them as 'agitators' and 'parasites', he claimed that the Armenians were 'hated even more in all of Turkey, and rightly so, than the worst Jews'. Admiral Wilhelm Souchon, meanwhile, viewed the extermination of the Armenians as the elimination of public enemies and 'bloodsuckers'. The German ambassador to Constantinople, Baron Hans von Wangenheim, noted in a report to Reich Chancellor Theobald von Bethmann Hollweg that 'the measures and conditions under which the deportation is being carried out make it clear that the [Young Turk] government is most certainly pursuing the eradication of the Armenian race within the Ottoman Empire'.

The only representative of the Reich to make any real protest against the genocide of the Armenians, however, was the previous ambassador, Paul Wolff Metternich, whose denunciation of this crime had cost him the posting in 1916—but not before he had reported to the chancellor that 'in its destruction of the Armenian race, the Turkish government is not stopped either by our representatives or by public opinion in the West'. But in December 1915, concerned above all with the outcome of the war, the chancellor wrote to the minister for foreign affairs: 'Our sole objective is to keep Turkey on our side until the end of the war, irrespective of whether Armenians are killed in the process or not.'

This alliance between Germany and Turkey accounts for the fact that, after the victory of the Entente powers and during the Istanbul Trials of 1919–20, Germany (then moving from Reich to Weimar Republic) helped the Young Turk leaders to flee, and in some cases—including Talaat Pasha, the most active of the Three Pashas—offered them sanctuary.

During an ecumenical service of remembrance in Berlin Cathedral on 23 April 2015, German president Joachim Gauck made a speech publicly recognizing the Armenian genocide, in so doing choosing to ignore the electoral implications of the fact that 3 million Turks were living in Germany. A worthy heir to the values championed by Pastor Johannes Lepsius and himself a pastor, Gauck did not shrink from declaring that in coming to terms with the past, 'we Germans as a whole must also take part in this process insofar as we share responsibility, perhaps even guilt, in the genocide committed against the Armenians'. And he stressed the involvement of some German military officers in planning, and to some extent carrying out, the deportations.

On 25 April, Norbert Lammert, president of the Bundestag, described the events of 1915 as 'genocide'. On 2 June 2016, the Bundestag voted almost unanimously—after a debate in which the Turkish-born Green deputy Cem Özdemir played a decisive part—to recognize the Armenian genocide, attributing a share of the responsibility to the German Reich as principal ally of the Ottoman Empire. In 2014, the Turkish-born German film director Fatih Akin had directed *The Cut*, the first major international production to deal with the Armenian genocide. And on 22 April 2015, the Austrian parliament had voted to recognize the Armenian genocide with a resolution stating: 'It is our duty to acknowledge and condemn these terrible events as genocide because of our historical responsibility—

the Austro-Hungarian monarchy was an ally of the Ottoman Empire in the first world war.'

The Turkish Republic's denial of the genocide, from its creation in 1923 by Mustafa Kemal Atatürk, and its impunity in its aftermath were to lend encouragement to the programme to exterminate the Jews that would later be pursued by the Third Reich. Between 1921 and 1923, articles in the German press made frequent reference to the 'reconstruction' of the Turkish state under Mustafa Kemal, and in 1921 the *Völkischer Beobachter*, official organ of the Nazi Party, impressed upon the German people the unavoidable necessity of 'having recourse in their turn to Turkish methods'. Obsessed with the notion of ethnic cleansing and a great admirer of the mass slaughters perpetrated by Genghis Khan in the early thirteenth century, Adolf Hitler described his own plans for 'a major policy of depopulation' to a German journalist in 1931, adding, 'And remember the extermination of the Armenians.' This foreshadowed the remark that he is supposed to have made to his generals—though not reliably authenticated—in August 1939: 'Who, after all, speaks today of the annihilation of the Armenians?' In 1943, Hitler presented the ashes of Talaat Pasha, who had been assassinated by an Armenian in Berlin, to a neutral Turkey, which he hoped to persuade to enter the war on the Axis side. The ashes are now interred in the 'Monument to Liberty' in Istanbul.

Many German officers who had been posted to the Ottoman Empire during the First World War were in fact able to give Hitler detailed accounts of the liquidation of the Armenians. Max Erwin von Scheubner-Richter, who as vice-consul in Erzurum had been an outspoken defender of the Armenians, was Hitler's closest associate until he was killed in the Beer Hall Putsch in 1923. The generals who surrounded Hitler included Fritz Bronsart von Schellendorff, who signed deportation orders for the Armenians, while retired general Kress von Kressenstein had written numerous reports on the extermination of the Armenians. Other prominent figures who had served in Turkey as soldiers or diplomats occupied high positions in the Nazi Office of Foreign Affairs. The trajectory of Rudolf Höss is particularly instructive: after starting his military career with the German forces in Turkey in 1916, he ended it as commandant of Auschwitz-Birkenau from 1939 to 1943 and of Ravensbrück in 1944.

GERMANY: A SPECIAL CASE

The argument surrounding Germany's responsibility is far from over, although in fact it focuses chiefly on the degree of Germany's responsibility rather than the question of its guilt or innocence. But if an individual who refuses to help another who is in grave danger despite having the opportunity to do so can be held to account, how much more powerfully is this the case when a nation is destroyed?

Individual Germans, meanwhile, have risen above their country's official complacency, if not complicity: Yves Ternon mentions a number of prominent Germans and Austrians, and Hilmar Kaiser names the Germans living in Turkey who endeavoured to protect orphans left abandoned by the massacre of their families.

Some Germans are of special interest to us in this context, as they went further than expressing their pity for suffering children and denounced the slaughter of a nation while bringing aid to the victims. Some who were prevented from taking action by the conditions of war left written testimonies, often at considerable personal cost. Among them are the journalist Harry Stuermer, the diplomat Walter Rössler and the army medic, essayist, poet and photographer Armin T. Wegner.

Sources and further reading

Sources

Gust, *Armenian Genocide*.

Studies

Amaël, François, 'Le rôle méconnu de l'Allemagne dans le génocide arménien', https://www.nouvelobs.com/monde/20150424.OBS7909/le-role-meconnu-de-l-allemagne-dans-le-genocide-armenien.html

Dadrian, *History of the Armenian Genocide*, pp. 399–477, 617–58.

Gottschlich, Jürgen, *Beihilfe zum Völkermord. Deutschlands Rolle bei der Vernichtung der Armenier*, Berlin: Links, 2015.

Moreau, *L'Empire ottoman*, pp. 233–45.

Schmutz, Thomas, 'La question arménienne et l'alliance turco-allemande', 12 March 2015, http://orientxxi.info/auteur/thomas-schmutz

Ternon, Yves, *Guerres et génocides au XXe siècle*, Paris: Odile Jacob, 2007, pp. 170–7.

55

HARRY STUERMER

Putting ethics before patriotism

The slim volume that the German journalist Harry Stuermer published in 1917, in which he denounced the persecution of the Armenians and the complicity of the German government, is like no other work on this subject. In *Zwei Kriegsjahre in Konstantinopel 1915–16: Skizzen deutsch-jungtürkischer Moral und Politik*, published in English in the same year as *Two War Years in Constantinople: Sketches of German and Young Turkish Ethics and Politics*, Stuermer bared his soul, allowing readers to follow the evolution of his feelings and opinions with regard to the Turks and Armenians.

As early as August 1914, he had shared with his father his disgust at the jingoism and militarism he encountered in the German army, adding that he had no doubt it would win the war. After being invalided out of the army, Stuermer became Constantinople correspondent for the Cologne-based *Kölnische Zeitung*, reporting from the Dardanelles and Gallipoli. While acknowledging the courage of the Turkish troops, he offered not a single word in support of the war. He was also initially favourable towards the Young Turk government, believing in their promises of reforms.

Upon his arrival in Constantinople, Stuermer witnessed the systematic persecution of the Armenians, although he did not at first feel any particular sympathy for them. Gradually, however, he lost all respect for the Turkish government, and he accused the German government of cowardice for standing by and accepting the crimes committed against the Armenians:

My first experience when I returned to the capital was the beginning of the Armenian persecutions. And here I may as well say at once that my love for present-day Turkey perished absolutely with this unique example in the history of modern human civilisation of the most appalling bestiality and misguided jingoism. This, more than everything else I saw on the German–Turkish side throughout the war, persuaded me to take up arms against my own people and to adopt the position I now hold. I say 'German–Turkish', for I must hold the German Government as equally responsible with the Turks.

But it was a personal incident that led to his breaking all ties with Germany. 'One day in the summer of 1916,' he explained,

> [m]y wife went out alone about midday to buy something in the 'Grand Rue de Péra'. She returned to the house trembling all over, for as she passed in front of the police station, she had heard through the open hall door the agonising groans of a tortured being, a dull wailing like the sound of an animal being tormented to death. 'An Armenian', she was informed by the people standing at the door.

His wife, who was Czech, 'let loose all her pent-up passion', crying, 'You are brutes, you Germans, miserable brutes, that you tolerate this from the Turks when you still have the country absolutely in your hands. You are cowardly brutes, and I will never set foot in your horrible country again. God, how I hate Germany!'

Stuermer could no longer avoid the terrible reality of the torture and massacre of the Armenians, nor his own compassion for the victims: 'It was when my own wife ... flung this denunciation of my country in my teeth that I finally and absolutely broke with Germany.' He explained his reasons for this break with his country:

> [O]ne only requires to have a slight feeling of one's dignity as a German to refuse to condone the pitiful cowardice of our Government over the Armenian question.

> The mixture of cowardice, lack of conscience, and lack of foresight of which our Government has been guilty in Armenian affairs is quite enough to undermine completely the political loyalty of any thinking man who has any regard for humanity and civilisation. Every German cannot be expected to bear as light-heartedly as the

diplomats of Pera the shame of having history point to the fact that the annihilation, with every refinement of cruelty, of a people of high social development, numbering over one and a half million, was contemporaneous with Germany's greatest power in Turkey.

As a record of the events and scenes Stuermer personally witnessed and an impartial analysis of the political situation in the region, *Two War Years in Constantinople* is the testimony of a journalist with a strong sense of mission, who placed objectivity, impartiality and truth above any misplaced feelings of patriotism. The exceptional value of his memoir, even though it ends in late 1916, lies in its shrewd analysis of events and its astute judgement of the individuals involved, and especially the Young Turks in power. In the appendix to the main text, he explains how the torture of the Armenian in Pera and his decision to defend the Armenians and denounce the Young Turks and the Germans led to his being held in suspicion and even denounced by his own newspaper, the press corps in Constantinople (who branded him a 'dangerous character who must be got rid of') and the authorities in general:

> That dramatic event which finally alienated me from the German cause took place just after the end of a severe crisis in my relationship with German–Turkish Headquarters. Some slight hints I had given of Turkish mismanagement, cynicism, and jingoism in a series of articles appearing from February 15th, 1916, onwards, under the title 'Turkish Economic Problems', so far as they were possible under existing censorship conditions, was the occasion of the trouble. One can imagine that Headquarters would certainly be furious with a journalist whose articles appeared one fine day, literally translated, in the *Matin* under the title: 'Situation insupportable en Turquie, décrite par un journaliste allemand' [Insufferable situation in Turkey, described by a German journalist], and cropped up once more on June 1st, in the *Journal des Balcans*.

Having resigned from his job with the newspaper and after spending three more months in Constantinople as a silent observer, Stuermer resolved in 1917 to leave Turkey for Switzerland, where he would be able to speak freely of the events he had witnessed.

Harry Stuermer deserves to be recognized as one of the Righteous for his denunciation of German complicity, for his rejection—

morally at least—of his German nationality, for his condemnation of the German government, for his break with the German press and for his voluntary exile, all of which posed serious risks to both his position in public life and his professional activity. He would accept no compromise in his quest for the truth.

On the day before he was eventually allowed to leave Turkey, he had no choice but to burn all his notes, 'which would have produced a much more effective indictment against the moral sordidness of the German–Young Turkish system than these very general sketches. But,' he concluded, 'the strictest frontier regulations could not prevent me from taking with me, free of all censorship, the impressions I had received in Turkey, and the opinions I had arrived at after a painful battle for loyalty to myself as a German and to the duties I had undertaken.'

Stuermer published his book in German in 1917, followed swiftly the same year by editions in French and English, despite the efforts of the German Foreign Office to prevent the publication of any translations by buying the foreign rights.

Stuermer was no saint, but rather a man of his time who was not immune to the prevailing prejudices of his era. In his writings, he used strongly racist language in his descriptions of African peoples and the peasants of Asia Minor; he was extravagant in his praise of colonial regimes, especially the British and French; and he accused the Jews and the Greeks of profiting from the annihilation of the Armenians. But his great merit lay in his ability to see through the hypocrisy and lies of the Ottoman leaders, and to reveal the truth of their policies: that what they sought was nothing less than the eradication of the Armenian people, and that this policy was pursued with the tacit support of the German government.

Sources and further reading

Sources

Stuermer, Harry, *Deux ans de guerre à Constantinople*, Paris: Le Cercle d'écrits caucasiens, 2005 [Paris: Payot, 1917]; Stuermer, *Two War Years in Constantinople*, Memphis: General Books, 2012 [New York: George H. Doran Company, 1917]; Stuermer, *Zwei Kriegsjahre in Konstantinopel 1915–1916: Skizzen deutsch-jungtürkischer Moral und Politik*, critical edition by Hilmar Kaiser, Bremen: Donat Verlag, 2015.

56

WALTER RÖSSLER (1871–1929)

German consul who went above and beyond the call of duty

Born in Berlin, the son of a university professor, Walter Rössler entered the German diplomatic service and was given postings in Africa, the Near East (in Jaffa) and China, before being appointed consul in Aleppo from 1910 to 1918.

Cooperation with the vali and reports to the German authorities

Aleppo formed the meeting point between the French railway network in Syria and the German–Baghdad Railway network. During the deportations, the vast majority of Armenian deportees were sent to Aleppo, either by rail or on foot. There they were forced to live in makeshift camps outside the city, deprived of any means of subsistence, while they waited to be sent on into the desert. Countless numbers died in the camps or on the marches, while those who were able to find refuge in the city itself, thanks to their own money or to wealthy relatives, died from typhus or dysentery at the rate of over 100 a day.

Rössler and the other foreigners who were still in Aleppo became witnesses to this tragedy. As early as 10 May 1915, Rössler wrote to the German ambassador in Constantinople, Hans von Wangenheim, and the Reich chancellor, Theobald von Bethmann Hollweg, to inform them of the Young Turk government's intention to remove Armenians from all positions of responsibility. When the deportations got under way, Rössler and his American colleague Jesse B. Jackson set out to do all they could to relieve the sufferings of the deportees with the means at their disposal. Rössler was also able to combine forces with the *vali* of Aleppo, Celal Bey, and the chief of police, both of whom refused to give assistance to the official sent from Constantinople to organize the 'settlement' of the deportees in the desert and their supplies, but whose true objective was the extermination of the Armenians. After a brief period of respite, however, during which it was possible to delay sending the deportees to their deaths, the governor was replaced by a hard-line supporter of the Young Turk leaders and their anti-Armenian policies.

Rössler now turned to his superiors, urging them to intervene to stop the deportations. He pointed out to them that Aleppo was not on the coast, which gave the lie to the Turks' claim that they needed to displace the Armenians to prevent them from giving aid to a potential seaborne invasion by the Entente powers. And he informed them that Celal Bey had been dismissed as governor because of his resistance to the deportations. Having lost all confidence in the good faith of the Ottoman government, he implored his ambassador in Constantinople and the German minister for foreign affairs to do everything in their power to stop the deportations, or at the very least to ensure that they took place under conditions that were more acceptable. He appended to his request a long list of recent massacres for which he declared the Turkish authorities responsible.

A career diplomat, he could have felt that sending these reports was enough and left it at that. But his conscience and his compassion for those who were being sent to their deaths would not allow him to do so. Now he turned to the American and German missionaries in Aleppo, seeking their help to feed the Armenians who remained there, estimated at some 6,000 people without any means of support. At the same time, he alerted the German community in the city, so that they could provide aid to the Armenian orphans. And in addition to all this, he also managed not only to secure exemption from deportation for the Armenians in the employ of the German consulate but also a temporary halt to the deportation of Armenians of the Protestant faith. He also undertook the risky business of conveying American and German funds to the missionaries, who would then ensure they reached the deportees who were perishing on the outskirts of the city.

Rössler fought this battle on several fronts: as well as appealing for a compassionate approach, he also underlined the strategic importance of protecting army supply lines. Menaced as they were by the same diseases as were running rampant among the deportees, they represented a looming catastrophe that could only be avoided by providing aid to the Armenians.

Reports to the Reich chancellor

The telegrams and reports that Rössler sent to his superiors are remarkable both for their courage and for their lucid accounts of events. On 27 July 1915, he addressed the following report to Reich Chancellor von Bethmann Hollweg from the consulate in Aleppo:

> [T]he Turkish government has driven thousands upon thousands of innocent Armenians into the desert, naturally under the pretext that they must be removed from the combat zone, making no exception for the sick, pregnant women or the families of soldiers on active service; they have left them without adequate water or food, with any supplies being meagre and irregular; they have done nothing to combat the epidemics to which they have been prey; they have pushed women to such a pitch of distress and despair that they have abandoned their infants and new-born babies along the road, sold their daughters approaching the age of puberty, and thrown themselves into the river with their young children; they have left them at the mercy of their escort, abandoning them to their violations—one escort took the girls away and sold them, throwing them into the hands of Bedouins who stripped them of their belongings and carried them off; they have had the men taken away to remote spots and shot, in contravention of every law, and have left their corpses to be scavenged by dogs and birds of prey; they have murdered parliamentary deputies who were supposedly being sent into exile; they have freed convicts, given them army uniforms and sent them out into the regions through which the deportees must travel; and they have recruited Circassian volunteers to unleash them against the Armenians. And what do they say in their semi-official declaration? 'The Ottoman government ... extends its benevolent protection to all loyal and peaceful Christians living in Turkey.'
>
> When I saw this declaration I truly could not believe my eyes, and there are no words that I can find to describe this chasm of lies. For

the Turkish government cannot evade the responsibility for what has happened: even if, to a certain extent, it is all the result of a lack of foresight and organization, of the corruption of those carrying out orders and the virtually anarchic conditions in the Eastern provinces, it nonetheless remains true that it was the government that sent the exiles out into this chaotic situation, and that did so in premeditated fashion. Even if they have lost control of the forces they have recruited, as may well be the case in the province of Diyarbekir especially, the major responsibility lies with them. Since there is a tendency in this region to view Germany as the instigator of the extermination of the Armenians, the Turkish government is attempting to take cover behind our authority in the eyes of European opinion.

I beg Your Excellency most respectfully to examine the problem and to judge whether it is advisable for other declarations on the Armenian question made by Turkey to be published in the German press, and whether we are not exposing ourselves to being compromised by our own allies.

Testimonies by Consuls Rössler and Hoffmann

In October 1915, the interim consul in Aleppo, Hermann Hoffmann, reported on the methods used by the authorities to destroy the deportation convoys, basing his information on the testimony of a senior Turkish official:

> 300,000 people have to head south (to the western Hauran, Raqqa, Der Zor) to be 'settled' there. Once they arrive at their destination there will be no alternative, according to the official in question, but to abandon them to their fate, and 'they will all die'. ... Whatever the case, all essential supplies are lacking. The concentration camps have not been provided with enough tents, flour or fuel. The authorities have themselves taken away the picks and shovels of the deported peasants. Everyone is convinced that all the deportees are facing certain death. Germany's complicity with those responsible for this massacre is acknowledged, moreover, not only by the whole Christian population but also by part of the Muslim population, with the approval of some, in the latter case, but also the disapproval of others.

WALTER RÖSSLER (1871–1929)

On 29 July 1916, a year after his devastating dispatch of 27 July 1915, Rössler reported from Aleppo on the 'demographic engineering' being carried out by the Young Turk leadership in the Der Zor region, and on the fate of Armenian women:

> A senior official of the German imperial government informed me on 18 July that the Sabcha–Haman–Meskene road was littered with shreds and tatters of clothing: it looked as though a retreating army had passed through. A Turkish army pharmacist, in post at Meskene for the past six months, told him that 55,000 Armenians were buried in that town alone. Moreover this same figure had been quoted to him by a Turkish officer who was second in command.
>
> We received a despatch from Der Zor of 16 July [1916] informing us that the Armenians had been ordered to leave the city. On the 17th, all the religious leaders and dignitaries were thrown into jail. The Armenians were given until 22 July to set off on the road once more. Central government had already issued initial orders that only a number of Armenians equal to ten per cent of the city's population would be allowed to remain in Der Zor; now those who remained were to be exterminated in their turn. It is very likely that this measure has a direct connection with the arrival of a new and ruthless *mutesarif*, appointed to replace the much more humane Suad Bey, who has been transferred to Baghdad.
>
> The gendarmes beat exhausted and defenceless women and children with whips and sticks. This scene, of a type that has been witnessed on numerous occasions, has just been confirmed to me by a German officer who has returned from down there and saw it with his own eyes.
>
> A German officer who arrived from Diyarbekir via Urfa informed me on 24 July that some time before this a further 2000 Armenian women had been brought to Urfa from the eastern and northern provinces. This appears to be a second round-up aimed at women who had managed to go into hiding during the first deportation, or who had been placed in Muslim families who now wanted to get rid of them.

Walter Rössler and Beatrice Rohner

Rössler was amply qualified by his own courage and dedication to appreciate the unstinting commitment and benevolence of others.

THE RIGHTEOUS AND PEOPLE OF CONSCIENCE

On 16 March 1917, he reported on the work of the Swiss missionary Beatrice Rohner, assisted by Sister Anna Jensen, at a juncture when the Turkish government was carrying out its plan to close the orphanages she ran, where she had also given protection to hundreds of Armenian children. He described the way Rohner worked with the Turkish colonel Kemal Bey, who wanted to help the Armenian women in the weaving and spinning workshops and to open two orphanages (which he was unable to do):

> Meanwhile, the American consul and the Turkish services behind the lines asked Sister Rohner to reorganize the emergency centres in Aleppo. The American consul believed that the conditions under which this work had been carried out were not good enough. As for the Turkish colonel Kemal Bey, he is responsible for the weaving and spinning workshops, in which production and pay are so low that the women who work there cannot earn enough to meet their needs or their children's. As far as his superiors are concerned, he is quite welcome to abandon those who do not resist to their fate, but he has a heart and wants to help them. With the support of Sister Rohner, he hopes also to use the available funds to help the women and children. He plans to open two orphanages, either residential or as schools with canteens. The nun has agreed. She has started by reorganizing the distribution of the funds intended for the 20,000 needy Armenians in Aleppo. On 19 March, she will leave for Marash for a month's respite, then she will make herself available to the services behind the lines to take care of the 1200 abandoned children. She has refused to open a new establishment in her own name, but by contrast she has let Colonel Kemal Bey know that she is perfectly ready to help him. In addition to the 1200 children in question, there are another 450 in the Gregorian church, who are being looked after by Armenians, and 400 in the Armenian orphanage I mentioned above, which is now full again.

The Naim–Andonian documents

By virtue of his time as consul in Aleppo, Rössler was subsequently asked to give an expert opinion on documents in the possession of Aram Andonian, an Armenian journalist and essayist and survivor of the genocide, who had been given them (or those that were still

WALTER RÖSSLER (1871–1929)

in his possession) by a high-ranking Ottoman official, Naim Bey. In April 1921, Andonian took these documents (reproduced in his book *Documents officiels concernant les massacres arméniens*, published in Paris in 1920) to Berlin for the trial of Soghomon Tehlirian, who had assassinated Talaat Pasha, former minister of the interior and the principal architect of the genocide. In his report on the documents, which he addressed to Pastor Johannes Lepsius, Rössler cast no doubt on their authenticity (they were later found to contain major errors).

Rössler died in Berlin on 4 April 1929, aged fifty-eight.

Sources and further reading

Sources

Gust, Wolfgang, *Der Völkermord an den Armeniern 1915–1916*, Munich: Carl Hanser, 1993; Gust, *Armenian Genocide*.

Studies

Kaiser, 'Beatrice Rohner and the Protestant Relief Effort at Aleppo in 1916', in *There Is Always an Option to Say 'Yes' or 'No'*, pp. 171–213.
Kieser, 'Beatrice Rohner's Work in the Death Camps of Armenians in 1916', in Andrieu, Gensburger and Sémelin, *Resisting Genocide*, pp. 383–98.
Ternon, *Enquête sur la négation d'un génocide*, pp. 51–2, 171–9, 182–4, 194–6.

57

ARMIN T. WEGNER (1886–1978)

Righteous on behalf of the Armenians and the Jews

A founding figure of Expressionism

Nothing in Armin T. Wegner's earlier career could have suggested that he would come to be a witness to the Armenian genocide. Born on 16 October 1886 in Elberfeld, Westphalia, he trained as an agronomist before studying political science and law. He then travelled around Europe, writing about his travels, composing poetry and doing a picaresque variety of jobs, including (in his own words) 'farmer, docker, drama student, private tutor, editor, public speaker, lover and idler'. In 1913, he published a collection of pre-Expressionist poetry and in the 1920s became celebrated as one of the founding figures of German Expressionism. When war broke out in 1914, he volunteered as an army medic, and in the autumn of 1915 he was sent to the Ottoman Empire in a division that was posted along the Baghdad Railway in Syria and Mesopotamia. He was thus very close to the camps where deported Armenians were being held. Deliberately disobeying orders, he began to photograph the tragic events of the unfolding genocide, notably at Der Zor. He expressed his horror at his experiences in the Ottoman Empire in his letters to his mother and in his private diary. To his mother he wrote:

> I have taken numerous photographs ... on penalty of death. I do not doubt for a moment that I am committing a treasonable act. And yet I am inspired by the knowledge that I have helped these poor people in some small way. ... Hunger, death, disease, despair shout at me

from all sides. Wretched me, for I carried neither bandages nor medications ... I was overcome by dizziness, as if the earth were collapsing on both sides of me into an abyss ...

'Images that horrify and indict'

The hundreds of photographs that Wegner took of the concentration camps in which the deported Armenians were held could scarcely be more explicit, capturing in searing images the populations abandoned in the desert and deliberately left to perish for lack of food and water. When he went into the concentration camps around Meskene and Aleppo, Wegner took the additional risk of accepting notes written by the deportees begging for help and addressed to family members living abroad. These he successfully passed on to the American embassy in Constantinople. When the Turkish military command learned of his activities, they demanded that the Germans put a stop to them: Wegner was transferred to the service treating cholera victims, where he fell seriously ill.

Nothing would deter Wegner from taking more photographs, however. On 19 October 1916, he wrote in his diary:

> I have taken numerous photographs. They tell me that Jamal Pasha, the hangman of Syria, has forbidden the photographing of the refugee camps on pain of death. I carry these images that horrify and indict under my cummerbund ... I do not doubt for a moment that I am committing an act of high treason and yet the knowledge of having helped those most wretched people at least in a slight respect fills me with a feeling of greater fortune than could any other deed.

It was on his return journey from Baghdad to Constantinople in November 1916 that he took most of his photographs of concentration camps, in the camps at Raqqa, Meskene, Der Zor and Ras al-Ayn, concealing photographic negatives and notes appealing for help in his uniform belt. He was recalled to Germany the following month.

Against the express orders of the German and Turkish authorities, Wegner managed to smuggle the photographs he had taken from his arrival in the Ottoman Empire in April 1915 into Germany. With the help of foreign embassies, he had also sent his images of the concentration camps to Germany and the United States. Today, his

ARMIN T. WEGNER (1886–1978)

photographs and notes form perhaps the most tangible proof of the horrific crimes committed by the Turkish authorities at this time.

Photographic evidence temporarily withheld

In a detailed study based on research in the Wegner archives in Marbach, the Armenian historian Tigran Sarukhanyan has explored the reasons why, despite all the risks he had taken, Wegner never published his diary—in which he describes the atrocities he had witnessed in the concentration camps—and did not show his photographs or reveal his role as witness until he took part in a conference in Berlin in 1919.

In 1917, after he returned to Germany and was relieved of his military duties, Wegner had in fact worked for the propaganda department of the German 6th Army in Breslau, and in 1918 he joined the editorial committee of the German Oriental Institute's *Der Neue Orient*, of which he subsequently became joint editor-in-chief. For this journal, he wrote a series of articles in which he defended the alliance between Germany and Turkey. He also gave several talks to the Deutsche-türkische Vereinigung (German-Turkish Association), which included the Three Pashas among its members of honour, in which he made derogatory references to the Armenians (often described as 'refugees' without reference to their ethnic group) as treacherous troublemakers and spreaders of disease among the Turkish and German troops.

It was only after the war was over, with the abdication of Kaiser Wilhelm II on 9 November 1918 and the beginning of the Weimar Republic and its anti-militarist and pacifist sympathies, that Wegner denounced the Young Turk leaders' crimes and German complicity. Sarukhanyan describes this U-turn as opportunistic, as illustrated by an open letter Wegner wrote to President Woodrow Wilson in February 1919.

Wegner performs a 'volte-face'

From 1919, Wegner became an active member of a pacifist and anti-militarist organization, and it was in this context that he denounced his country's complicity and involvement in the

Armenian genocide. In January of that year, he published *Der Weg ohne Heimkehr* (Road of no return), submitted to President Wilson at the peace conference of 1919, in which he wrote:

> From their places of origin, where the Armenians had lived for over two millennia, and from all corners of the empire, they were expelled into uninhabited deserts. No logical explanation could be given to justify the need for these new places of residence. The men were slaughtered en masse, and groups of people were chained or roped together and pushed into rivers or down rock faces. The women and children were sold at auction, the old people and adolescents were set to forced labour. But this was not enough: people were thrown out of their houses, half-naked, their houses were plundered, their villages set on fire, churches destroyed or converted into mosques, innocent young girls raped ...

On 23 February 1919, the *Berliner Tageblatt* published an open letter from Wegner to President Wilson. Writing as 'one of the few Europeans who have been eyewitnesses of the dreadful destruction of the Armenian people', the picture of whose misery and terror would never be obliterated from his mind, he recalled their 'unimaginable sufferings' and appealed to the American president's conscience to create an independent Armenia. It is this letter and Wegner's subsequent actions in support of the Armenian cause that the Armenians remember today.

In 1920, Wegner married Lola Landau (1892–1990), a Jewish writer with whom he had a daughter, Sibylle-Anouch, in 1923 ('Anouch' was a popular Armenian girls' name, meaning 'sweet'). In 1939, in the face of the growing threat of Nazism and Lola's departure for Palestine, the couple divorced by mutual consent. But the marriage had confirmed Wegner in his commitment to the Armenian cause and made him increasingly aware—to his own peril—of antisemitic persecution. His second wife, whom he married in 1945, was also Jewish.

At the beginning of his marriage, in 1921, Wegner gave written evidence at the trial of Soghomon Tehlirian for the murder of Talaat Pasha in Berlin, so helping to secure his acquittal. In 1922, following on from his open letter to Woodrow Wilson, he published *Der Schrei von Ararat* (The cry from Ararat) in support of the Armenian survivors. In 1927–8, by which time he was at the peak of his popularity as a writer and celebrated as a leader of German Expressionism, he went with his wife, at Moscow's invitation, to visit Soviet Armenia for the first time. Although the highly successful book that he subsequently published recounting his travels in the Caucasus and Persia was measured in tone, he was nonetheless accused by German nationalists of being a Bolshevik sympathizer.

Prophet of the Holocaust

On 11 April 1933, Wegner sent an open letter (which no newspaper would publish) to Hitler, whose coming to power as chancellor had sounded the death knell of the Weimar Republic, to protest against the treatment of the Jews, stressing the honour that numerous German Jews had brought to their country and outlining in prophetic fashion the catastrophic events that lay in store for them.

Hitler's response came a few days later, when he was arrested and brutally tortured by the Gestapo, before being incarcerated in seven Nazi prisons and concentration camps. At the end of 1933, he and Lola managed to emigrate from Germany, and after spending time in Britain and Palestine settled in Positano on Italy's Amalfi Coast. In 1938, all his books were banned in the Reich. In 1945, Wegner married Irene Kowaliska, the Jewish artist with whom he had been living since 1940 and had had a son in 1941.

For the rest of his life, Wegner felt like an exile, which caused him great pain. When his photographs were rediscovered, he was viewed as one of the Righteous Among the Nations by the Armenians as well as the Jews. In 1967, this honour was bestowed upon him by the World Holocaust Remembrance Center at Yad Vashem. In 1968, he was invited to Etchmiadzin in Armenia, where he was invested with the Order of St Gregory the Illuminator by the Catholicos of all Armenians.

Armin Wegner died in Rome, 'virtually forgotten by his own people' according to Yad Vashem, on 17 May 1978, aged ninety-one. His ashes are interred in the Armenian Genocide Memorial in Yerevan.

The position that Wegner adopted in 1917–18 in the context of his professional relationship with the German Ministry of Foreign

Affairs may perhaps be explained as an excess of patriotic fervour aimed at warding off the consequences of the dereliction of his military duties during his time spent in the Ottoman Empire. Though it may also be argued that there was an element of opportunism in the pro-Armenian position he adopted repeatedly from 1919, when he was still a relatively young man of thirty-three, he also manifested a growing awareness of the failure of German warmongering and pan-Germanism. But the spirit of sacrifice that Wegner had shown in documenting the Armenian genocide and that was to come to the fore again in the face of Nazism, finding expression in his fearless public defence of his Jewish fellow citizens—which resulted in his being tortured and incarcerated in concentration camps, recalling the sufferings of the Armenians—go a long way towards validating the tardiness of his public defence of the Armenian cause, which in the eyes of the Armenians, following the example of the Jews, justifies his place among the Righteous Among the Nations.

Sources and further reading

Sources

The Armin T. Wegner Archives are held at Marbach am Neckar in Baden-Württemberg.

Wegner, Armin T. *Brief an Hitler*, Wuppertal: Peter Hammer Verlag, 2002.

Studies

'The Armenian Genocide and the Holocaust: One Man Takes a Stand', VHEC,

http://vhec.org/wp-content/uploads/armenian-teachers-guide.pdf

'Chronology of the Armenian Genocide—1914', https://www.armenian-genocide.org/1914.html

Donikian, Denis, 'Lettre ouverte au président Wilson d'Armin T. Wegner'; 'Armin Theophil Wegner (1886–1978)'; and 'Armin T. Wegner et le Der neue Orient', in *Petite encyclopédie du génocide Arménien*, p. 416; p. 423; p. 515; and p. 517.

Kiuciukian, Pietro, 'Armin Wegner', in *Voci nel deserto*, pp. 159–81.

Rooney, Martin, 'A Forgotten Humanist: Armin T. Wegner', *Journal of Genocide Research*, 2, 1 (2000), pp. 117–19; Rooney, *Leben und Werk*

ARMIN T. WEGNER (1886–1978)

Armin T. Wegners (1886–1978) im Kontext der soziopolitischen und kulturellen Entwicklungen in Deutschland, Frankfurt am Main: Haag und Herchen, 1984.

Sarukhanyan, Tigran, 'Armin T. Wegner's (1886–1978) WWI Media Testimonies and the Armenian Genocide', in Martin Tamcke (ed.), *Orientalische Christen und Europa: Kultur-begegnung zwischen: Interferenz, Partizipation und Antizipation*, Wiesbaden: Harrassowitz Verlag, 2012, pp. 267–79.

Wernicke-Rothmayer, Johanna, *Armin T. Wegner: Schrifsteller, Reisender, Menschenrechtsaktivist*, Göttingen: Wallstein, 2011.

THE MILITARY

58

REAR ADMIRAL LOUIS-JOSEPH PIVET (1855–1924) AND VICE ADMIRAL LOUIS DARTIGE DU FOURNET (1856–1940)

Two men of conscience

Under the command of officers who were remarkable not only for their military skills but also for their ethical principles, the French navy intervened to aid Armenians in Cilicia on two occasions, first during the Adana massacres in 1909, and secondly during the Armenian genocide in 1915. A major study of these two interventions has been carried out by the French naval engineer and submarine specialist Georges Kévorkian, who published his findings in *La flotte française au secours des Arméniens en 1909 et 1915*, on which these portraits of two men of conscience is largely based.

The Adana massacres (1909)

The Young Turk revolution of 1908 deposed Sultan Abdul Hamid II in favour of his brother Mehmet V and reintroduced the Ottoman constitution of 1876, thus in principle establishing equality for all—Muslims, Christians and Jews—before the law. However, the revolution's effects did not always penetrate the provinces, where Ottoman local governors and Kurdish *aghas* largely continued to discriminate against minorities who had formerly been classified as *dhimmis*, or 'protected', while in Constantinople an Islamic counter-revolution had given temporary power to conservative supporters of the restoration of Abdul Hamid II. In Cilicia, where the Armenian population had made a major contribution to the growth of the local economy, this reactionary movement was supported by the Turkish local authorities, who armed the Muslim population. The massacres in Cilicia—triggered by an act of self-defence by a young Armenian—were perpetrated in two stages in April and May 1909. Claiming some 10,000 victims, most of them Armenians (out of a population in the region of 100,000) and destroying around 200 villages, they brought economic ruin to one of the wealthiest provinces in the Ottoman Empire. Orders from the Young Turks who had now seized power in Constantinople to regain control of the Muslim population were barely enforced by the Turkish soldiers sent out to the province, who were caught up in the spiral of violence unleashed by local people. Thanks to the efforts of the nationalist wing of the party, a veil was drawn over the findings of the inquiries that were immediately launched by the Young Turks. The blind loyalty of some of the Armenian leaders to their Young Turk colleagues, in whom they continued to place some hope, and the desire of the European powers to close the incident, the better to protect their economic interests in an Ottoman Empire that was modernizing under new leadership, combined to ensure that the Cilician massacres were effectively disregarded.

Some Western powers did intervene, however, by dispatching a naval force to the Eastern Mediterranean. The intervention was initially intended to ensure the safety of these countries' own citizens, consular staff and missions in the region, but it was expanded in the face of the dramatic situation facing the local Christian population, largely to the benefit of the Armenians. The French government ordered the navy to intervene.

Intervention by the commander-in-chief of the French navy

On 22 April 1909, the chief of the French navy, at the request of the Ministry of Foreign Affairs, sent a despatch to Rear Admiral Louis Pivet, commander-in-chief of the Mediterranean Flying Squadron, who was then on board the armoured cruiser *Jules Ferry*, and the commanding officers of two other armoured cruisers. They were ordered to take on board French citizens, foreigners and local Christians whose lives were in danger, but to do so only in a joint operation with commanding officers from other countries.

On 24 April, representatives from the French, British and German navies and the German and American consulates visited Armenian refugees in French institutions and German missions in Adana. They then made strongly worded objections to the Turkish authorities about the massacres, looting and the risk of epidemics, but to no effect. On 26 April, the Messageries Maritimes ocean liner *Niger* took on board 2,200 Christians who had taken refuge on the shores of the Bay of Bazit, near Latakia. Following this, 1,450 more refugees, two-thirds of them women and children, were taken on board the *Jules Ferry*.

The engagement of Louis Pivet: measured but true

The refugees were eventually brought back to land, before the restoration of order by central government and before the establishment of Ottoman courts martial to try those responsible for the massacres and looting committed in Cilicia could demonstrate its impartiality.

Nonetheless, Rear Admiral Louis Pivet had sent reports to the French Ministry for the Navy, issued warnings to the Ottoman officials in the *vilayet* of Adana, given financial help to some of the Armenians and afforded protection to the vessels involved. It did not cost him his life, but in other respects his engagement may be likened to that of Fernand Roque-Ferrier, French consul in Aleppo in 1909, who gave French protection to the Armenians of that city and died there following his heroic expedition to the Amanus Mountains in the wake of the Adana massacres.

Resistance on Musa Dagh (1915)

In 1915, it was Breton sailors—of all ranks, up to and including Vice Admiral Louis Dartige du Fournet and his successor, Rear Admiral Gabriel Darrieus—who acted as men of conscience, and even as Righteous people, in the perilous evacuation of some 4,000 Armenians.

Seven hundred of these were resistance fighters who had withdrawn to the heights of Musa Dagh—the Mountain of Moses—near Antioch, and who for fifty-three days had held out against Turkish forces (reinforced to 15,000 men after a daring and successful night raid carried out by the Armenians) who were vastly superior in numbers and arms.

Rather than face a terrifying deportation march into the Syrian desert, the Armenians in the plain of Antioch—and notably in the town of Yoghonolook—decided to resist. Given the crushing superiority of the Turks in both men and logistics, the Armenians' lack of munitions, the scarcity of their food supplies and the absence of any prospect of help arriving from any quarter, it was a decision that seemed as desperate as it was hopeless.

The dramatic events that ensued were related afterwards by one of their main protagonists, the pastor of the Armenian Protestant church of Zeytun, Dikran Andreassian, who had escaped the massacre and deportation of the 7,000 Armenians of Zeytun. On 20 December 1915, his story was published in the *Nottingham Evening Post*:

> Knowing that it would be impossible to defend our villages in the foothills, it was resolved to withdraw to the heights of Mousa Dagh, taking with us as large a supply of food and implements as it was possible to carry. All the flocks of sheep and goats were also driven up the mountain side, and every available weapon of defence was brought out and furbished up. We found that we had 120 modern rifles and shot-guns, with perhaps three times that number of old flint-locks and horse-pistols. That still left more than half our men without weapons. It was very hard to leave our homes. My mother wept as if her heart would break. By nightfall the first day we had reached the upper crags of the mountain.
>
> At dawn the next morning all hands went to work digging trenches at the most strategic points in the ascent of the mountain. Where there was no earth for trench-digging, rocks were rolled together, making strong barricades behind which groups of our sharpshooters were stationed. We were hard at it all day strengthening our position against the attack which we knew was certain to come.

A heroic evacuation

Strong swimmers were selected to stand on watch for any passing ship in the Gulf of Alexandretta—French, Italian, British, American or Russian—to which they were ready to swim out with a message appealing for help. When no ships were spotted, Pastor Andreassian laid out two immense white flags made by the Armenian women, one bearing a red cross and the other an inscription in English, written in large, clear letters by the pastor: 'Christians in distress; Rescue.' Miraculously, on the fifty-third day of the siege, the French battleship *Guichen* spotted the red cross flag. Soon it was joined by the flagship *Ste Jeanne d'Arc*, with Vice Admiral Louis Dartige du Fournet, commander of French naval forces in the Mediterranean, on board, as well as the *Destrées*, the *Desaix*, the *Amiral Charner* and the *Foudre*.

All these battleships were also to take part in the evacuation of the Armenians, under the command of Rear Admiral Darrieus, whose mission was to blockade the coasts of the Near East. Reassured by a discussion with one of the leaders of the Armenians, Pierre Demlakian, who like all members of the Armenian elite in the Ottoman Empire spoke their language perfectly, the French first shelled the Turkish positions in order to deter any opposition and then worked out a daring plan for bringing the Armenians on board their battleships. In the tumultuous seas, it proved almost impossible to bring the rafts they had constructed to shore, so the Armenians were brought out to launches lowered from the cruisers. Eventually, the women, children and older men were brought safely on board, while the younger men stayed on land to mount one last attack on the Turkish positions. The following day, they too boarded the ships.

The bravery and sense of duty of the sailors who saved these desperate people, in heavy seas and under enemy fire, were widely recognized. Lieutenant Christian Le Mintier de la Motte Basse, for instance, who with his fellow crewman Maraudon captained the whaling boat of the *Guichen*, was mentioned in despatches on 17 November 1915: 'In command of his ship's embarkation vessels, in difficult circumstances displayed great qualities of dynamism, initiative and devotion to duty.'

The episode of Musa Dagh represents one of the earliest examples of 'humanitarian intervention', as Georges Kévorkian notes, since the rescuers set aside the fact that the Armenians there were citizens of an enemy empire with whom they were then at war and were motivated solely by the overriding necessity of saving them from the Young Turk government and its crimes.

The first memorial

In September 1932, a memorial to the Armenian resistance on Musa Dagh and their rescue by the French navy was inaugurated on the mountaintop. Present at the ceremony as the official representative of France, under whose mandate Syria and the mountain then lay, was Rear Admiral Henri Jobert, commander of the Levant naval division, who had helped to save thousands of Armenians during the Greco-Turkish War of 1919–22. Among the many Armenian guests was Movses Der Kalousdian, a leader of the resistance on Musa Dagh and hero of the Armenian Legion. The inscription on the monument referred by name to the man who had initiated the rescue mission:

> To the French Navy from the Armenians of Musa Dagh threatened with extermination, rescued after a heroic struggle by the Syrian squadron under the command of Vice Admiral Dartige du Fournet on 12, 13 and 14 September 1915, in gratitude and remembrance. On these heights your memory will live forever.

The following day, the president of the 'Monument Committee', Sarkis Tossounian, a retired officer of the Armenian Legion, wrote to Dartige du Fournet, now retired and living in Périgueux:

Monsieur l'Amiral

> Perhaps for a moment you thought the memory of the noble action through which you saved the people of Djebel Musa had been extinguished, and that no one still felt the slightest gratitude towards you. ... Rest assured that your name is inscribed not merely on the marble of the memorial but also in the hearts of all the Armenians of Djebel Musa.

The Monument Committee also produced a sort of wall calendar illustrated with photographs of the principal heroes of Musa Dagh. This 'image of devotion' was to be distributed to the families of the rescued so that they could pray in front of it. Prominent among those honoured were Dartige du Fournet and the French navy interpreter Diran Tekeian (who later retired to Provence and became a historian of Armenian immigration to that region).

Commemorative events

On 21 December 1935, Armenian veterans in Paris organized an evening event to commemorate the 'heroism of Musa Dagh', under the high patronage of General Brémond, former administrator of Cilicia. They could not then have known that in 1939—in a major affront to the French and Armenian heroes of 1915—the French government would include Antioch and Musa Dagh in the *sanjak* of Alexandretta when they ceded it to the Turkish republic created by Mustafa Kemal in 1923. A monument bearing the French and Armenian flags with the red cross flag spotted by the *Guichen* on 5 September 1915 and a museum commemorating the rescue of the inhabitants of Musa Dagh and of their local traditions now stand in the Armenian village of Musaler near Yerevan.

At an event in Paris in November 2015 to mark the centenary of the Armenian genocide, the heroic French–Armenian spirit of Musa Dagh was invoked by Pierre Brunet de Coursou, speaking on behalf of officers trained at the École navale, the elite French naval college:

> The magnificent history that unites the Armenians, and particularly those of Musa Dagh, with the admirals, commanders, officers and crews of the French navy, perfectly illustrates the three essential features that enabled on the one side an unprecedented act of resistance, and on the other an audacious rescue operation: a fine nobility of spirit, an unwavering trust in destiny, and feelings of compassion towards those in distress.

The 4,058 Armenian survivors from Musa Dagh were sent to a refugee camp in Port Said, Egypt, a British protectorate since 1914 that served as a support base for Allied operations in the Middle East during the First World War. It was from among the refugees from Musa Dagh that the first volunteers for the Légion d'Orient were recruited, with French support and instructors from the French navy. In 1916, the first Armenian battalion of the Légion d'Orient, formed in Cyprus, was integrated with the French detachment in

Palestine, where it fought heroically against the Germans and Turks at the Battle of Arara. The founder of the Legion, Louis Romieu, would remain faithful to the Armenians until the end of his command in Cilicia in 1918–20.

The heroic episode of Musa Dagh was famously to inspire the Austrian Jewish writer Franz Werfel to compose his epic novel *The Forty Days of Musa Dagh* (though in fact the resistance endured for fifty-three days), published in 1933. Banned by the Nazi regime, the novel would in turn provide inspiration and encouragement to Jews in the ghettos of Central Europe during the Holocaust.

Sources and further reading

Sources

Andréassian, Dikran, *Comment un drapeau sauva quatre mille Arméniens*, Paris: Librairie Fischer, 1916, extract quoted in Annick Asso, *Le Cantique des larmes: Arménie 1915*, Paris: La Table ronde, 2005, pp. 228–33.

Fournet, Louis Dartige du, *Souvenirs de guerre d'un amiral 1914–1916*, Paris: Librairie Plon, 1920.

Studies

Dédéyan, Charles, *Une guerre dans le mal des hommes*, Paris: Éditions Buchet-Chastel, 1971, *passim*.

Dédéyan, Gérard, 'Le colonel Louis Romieu (1872–1943), une carrière sacrifiée pour l'honneur et pour la fidélité aux Arméniens', in Hilda Tchoboian (ed.), *Cent ans après le front de l'est, L'Arménie et le Levant entre guerres et paix, Actes du Colloque de l'Adcarly, du Centre Covcas et de la Fondation Bullukian, Lyon, 9 et 10 novembre 2018*, Marseille: Éditions Thaddée, 2021.

Kévorkian, Georges, *La flotte française au secours des Arméniens en 1909 et 1915* (preface by Vice-Admiral Henri Darrieus), Rennes: Marines éditions, 2008; Kévorkian, *La France chassée de l'Empire ottoman: Une guerre oubliée; 1918–1923* (preface by J.-Fr. Cordet), Paris: L'Harmattan, 2013.

Kévorkian, Raymond H. and Paul B. Paboudjian, *Les Arméniens dans l'Empire ottoman à la veille du génocide*, Paris: Les éditions d'Art et d'Histoire ARHIS, 1992, pp. 341–52.

Lafon, Jean-Marc, 'Roman, histoire et mémoire: Un épisode méconnu du génocide arménien; La résistance du Musa Dagh', *Guerres mondiales et conflits contemporains*, 202–3, no. 2 (Paris, 2001), pp. 137–53.

Nersissian, Achot, *Movsês Dêr Kalousdian* [in Armenian], Yerevan: n.p., 2011.

Ternon, *Empire ottoman*, pp. 484–7.

Vartanian, Raphaël, 'Les Volontaires arméniens au service de la France pendant la Première Guerre mondiale, du Musa Dagh à la Légion d'Orient', MA thesis, Université Paris IV Sorbonne, 2017.

Waldman, Felicia, 'Quelques ressemblances entre la déportation des Arméniens et celle des Juifs', in Gérard Dédéyan and Carol Iancu (eds), *Du génocide des Arméniens à la Shoah*, Toulouse: Privat, 2015, pp. 47–72.

59

ABBÉ JULES CHAPERON (1877–1951)

Army chaplain and pioneering humanitarian

Born in the Isère department in south-eastern France in 1877, Jules Chaperon trained at the Major Seminary of Carthage in Tunis before becoming a parish priest at La Martre in the Var. There he founded one of the first summer camps for children in France, a farming association, a home for the elderly, and above all his famous Notre-Dame de la Montagne orphanage, which from 1922 took in Armenian orphans.

The pro-Armenian movement included some remarkable clerics, including Monsignor Félix Charmetant (1844–1921), director of the Oeuvre des Écoles d'Orient who published a collection of documents in his *Martyrologe arménien,* and Abbé Pisani, who in 1896 at the Institut Catholique in Paris gave an important talk on the Armenian massacres. But Abbé Chaperon was also a man of action, who attempted to sign up as an auxiliary during the First World War but was rejected on health grounds. Not content with setting up a military hospital at La Martre, he finally succeeded in joining up in 1916 and was sent to the German and Italian fronts, and eventually to the Middle Eastern theatre.

From March to October 1920, Chaperon was chaplain to the 2nd Division of the Army of the Levant, then occupying Cilicia in the face of attacks from Turkish nationalist forces under Mustafa Kemal. From November 1921 to September 1923, he was stationed in Constantinople as chaplain to the French occupation forces. When the French troops evacuated the capital of the defunct Ottoman Empire in 1923, he went with them, taking with him a group of

Armenian orphans—including children from the Saint Joseph orphanage he had founded in the city—and refugees, whom he embarked on the ocean liner *Tourville*. From then until his death in 1951, he devoted himself to his parishes in the Var and the orphanages he had founded in La Martre and Grasse, where he continued to take in Armenian orphans and refugees who found him via a variety of routes. From 1924 to 1926, he made trips to the United States, where he gave talks and published articles in the press that helped to raise the funds he needed to continue his work.

On the battlefield, Chaperon acted with all the courage of a soldier and was mentioned in despatches five times and awarded numerous medals for rescuing the wounded under heavy fire. On his death in 1951, he was buried with full military honours. He left a collection of notebooks containing his copious diaries, later discovered by his great-nephew Claude Olchowik, from which the eminent medieval historian Abbé Raymond Boyer extracted and published the diaries covering his Armenian period.

'Cilicia 1920'

Whether the events he described were those endured by Armenian and French troops in Cilicia in 1920 or the struggles of the survivors of the genocide of 1915, Abbé Chaperon was a candid and uncompromising witness. The diaries he kept in Cilicia cover the events surrounding two developments with major ramifications for the Armenians. The first was the Treaty of Sèvres of 10 August 1920, to which Turkey was a signatory, which recognized the de jure existence of a free and independent Armenian state, including Caucasian Armenia and the provinces of Eastern Anatolia, with frontiers laid down by US President Woodrow Wilson. Never ratified, it was responsible for inciting the attacks by Turkish nationalist forces on the Republic of Armenia in 1918–20. The second development was the Treaty of Ankara concluded between France and Kemalist Turkey on 20 October 1921, by which France renounced its costly occupation of Cilicia (which had been made a zone of French interest in the division of the Ottoman Empire contained in the secret Sykes–Picot Agreement of 1916).

Under the terms of the Armistice of Mudros, signed by Britain and Turkey on 30 October 1918, the Allies were entitled to occupy strategic points of their choosing. Plans to establish an Armenian national homeland under French protection could therefore be put into effect, and some 150,000 Armenians were repatriated to Cilicia under the administration of Turkish officials (working for the government in Constantinople, which was under Allied control), overseen by the French authorities. The French army in the region consisted largely of colonial troops from North Africa and Senegal and the Armenian Legion (formed from the Armenian and Syrian Légion d'Orient), under French officers. But in November 1919, François Georges-Picot, French high commissioner in Syria and Armenia, made contact with General Mustafa Kemal, who after the Armistice of Mudros had immediately taken command of the Turkish troops who had withdrawn to Anatolia and galvanized them into action with the aim of reconquering the region.

The year 1920 was marked by withdrawals and abandonments, as the French troops in Cilicia—consisting largely of the Armenian Legion—were no longer receiving any real support from their leaders in Paris. On 10 February, the city of Maraş was evacuated by French troops, just when the Turks were ready to surrender, leaving the way open for a massacre of the Armenians who were still there; in April, Urfa surrendered, after a siege lasting nearly two months; in October, Hadjin followed suit, after a seven-month resistance led by the lawyer Tchalian (great-uncle of the French geopolitical strategist Gérard Chaliand); and Ayntab (Gaziantep), where the local Armenians combined with French forces resisted a year-long siege to emerge victorious (in what became known to the Turks as the 'Anatolian Verdun'), was surrendered back to the Turks a month after their capitulation, in March 1921.

From April to August 1920, Chaperon was stationed at Katma, a small town on the Adana–Aleppo railway line that formed a communications hub between the Syrian anti-French forces under Emir Faisal and the Turks and was therefore a scene of constant attacks that became a battle for the railway. On 1 May 1920, Chaperon described the remarkable organization of the Armenians in the town, the administration of which was in the hands of Lieutenant-Colonel Flye Sainte Marie, commander of the Armenian Legion:

> Straight away, the Armenians organized the defence of their neighbourhood. They dug trenches and blocked up windows with stones.

THE RIGHTEOUS AND PEOPLE OF CONSCIENCE

> In a single night, the women and children had dug a trench to separate the Turkish quarter from the Armenian quarter. The Turks had captured the lieutenant and second-in-command to Colonel Flye Sainte Marie, governor of the town, and M. Lecoq, director of the Ottoman Bank, and were holding them prisoner. They eventually released them after a few days. With 400 rifles and a few VB grenades, the Armenians mounted a brilliant resistance, then gained ground. They flew the French flag on six mosques that they captured. ... Their foundry workers succeeded in casting two bronze cannon that were antediluvian in design but useful all the same. Since there were not enough rifles, they forged spears, being implacably determined to fight by all possible means. The power wielded by their committee is as intelligent as it is unyielding ... The small French garrison is but a puny partner in the defence, since the orders it receives are ambiguous, absurd, contradictory. The general directive is not to rile the Turks.

It was after his transfer to Ayntab that Chaperon learned details of the genocide of 1915 in the region, in a meeting with an Armenian priest called Der Nerses, as he wrote on 31 October 1920:

> I expressed my sympathetic feelings towards the ancient Christian traditions he represents and assured him of my wish to work with him for the wellbeing of the people of Ayntab. The priest told me the story of their deportation. They were sent with their families first to Homs, then to Hama. From there, after a while, when they refused to recant, they were sent to the shore of the Red Sea. Their wives and daughters fell victim to the lustful urges of the Turkish gendarmes. Der Karekin saw his twenty-year-old son slain in front of him.

'Constantinople 1922–3'

It was in the Ottoman capital that Abbé Chaperon's humanitarian work began in earnest, with all the physical risks entailed in evacuating the war-wounded from Cilicia. In 1922–3, he was stationed at Makriköy (now Bakırköy), some four kilometres southeast of Constantinople, where he gathered further valuable testimonies from survivors of the genocide. This period was marked by two events that were to have tragic repercussions for the Armenians in the Ottoman Empire. In 1922, the war between Turkey and Greece—to whom the Treaty of Sèvres of August 1920 had entrusted the administration of the region of Smyrna—ended with a Turkish victory, marked by the capture and sacking of Smyrna in September. Greece was abandoned by its allies, and the Greeks and Armenians of Smyrna were massacred. On 24 July 1923, the Treaty of Sèvres was annulled by the signing of the Treaty of Lausanne, which made no specific reference to the Armenians or the question of a homeland or reparations but merely cited the 'protection of minorities', who had virtually disappeared with the massacre or expulsion of the Armenians and Greeks of Asia Minor.

At Makriköy, Chaperon found a kindred spirit for his humanitarian work in an Armenian priest named Papazian, who 'has recently opened, on his own and without any staff whatsoever, an orphanage for 30 young Armenian boys where he is the cook, laundryman, tailor and teacher, all at once'.

On a visit to the orphanage run by the Armenian Catholic Sisters of the Immaculate Conception, he was witness to a touching reunion, as he described on 11 October 1922:

> I was with the nuns [of the girls' orphanage] this evening when a fine Armenian peasant woman from Anatolia came in and asked for her daughters. They were found among the orphans recently brought in; one of them was only three years old. Deep joy, tears of happiness for this good woman who, amid the terrifying scenes of a massacre, had become separated from her children ... We gave her back her little girls. She took them away with her, with infinite joy.

Chaperon also quoted praise in the Constantinople press for his Saint Joseph orphanage, the running of which he had entrusted to an Armenian nun from the Sisters of the Immaculate Conception. And he referred to events in Ionia, on the west coast of central Asia Minor. Following the massacre in Smyrna in September 1922, the orphanage also took in Greek children: 'In the afternoon, I had photographs of the orphanage taken by Papadopoulos. When he saw the care with which we surround little Marika, found in Smyrna after the massacre, that good Greek wept.'

On the same day, Chaperon also met Monsignor Gregory Bahabanian, formerly Armenian Catholic bishop of Angora (Ankara after 1923), who had been deported in 1915 and who was worried about his nephew, imprisoned at Brousse, 'a young twenty-seven-year-old priest accused of being pro-Greek'. On 9 November, he added: 'I avoided speaking to Monsignor [Bahabanian] about his nephew, but I know that he has been told of the death of that poor martyr, beheaded by the Kemalists at Brousse the other day.'

The Armenian servant to the French consul in Brousse testified that Turkish reprisals had not spared foreigners, as Chaperon wrote on 21 November: 'This woman relates that 5 French Sisters of St Vincent de Paul were raped by Kemalist officers, then burned by the soldiers at Ismid. In "Stamboul", the French embassy denies that anything happened at Brousse, but says nothing about Ismid or Smyrna.'

Chaperon also devoted a good deal of space to the tragic fate of the Armenian population of Angora, the majority of whom were Catholics. On 13 November, he noted: 'The [Armenian] Catholic priest of Angora has been hanged by the Turks ... The Christian population has been expelled from this city, as it has from the whole of Anatolia.' On 23 November, he described the arrival in Constantinople of caravans of refugees from Angora.

Abbé Chaperon's diaries also contain lists of names of Armenian families who received help, and of children and nuns taken to France and for whom he obtained passports.

Today, ceremonies held occasionally at La Martre keep alive the memory of Abbé Jules Chaperon, a memory that has been perpetuated by his late colleague Abbé Raymond Boyer, among others. As a denouncer of genocide and champion of humanitarian action, he richly deserves to be included as one of the Righteous.

Sources and further reading

Sources

Boyer, Abbé Raymond, *Un aumônier militaire français témoin du drame arménien. Journal de l'abbé Chaperon (Cilicie 1920–Constantinople 1923)* (introduction by Yves Ternon), Marseille: Institut euroméditerranéen pour l'Arménie, 1998.

Chaliand, Gérard, *Mémoire de ma mémoire: Récit*, Paris: Éditions Julliard, 2003.

Mouradyan, S. and S. Sahakyan, trans. *Journal de l'abbé Chaperon* [in Armenian], Yerevan: Armenian Academy of Sciences, 2002.

ABBÉ JULES CHAPERON (1877–1951)

Poghosyan, Varoujean, *Les massacres des Arméniens de Marache en 1920, recueils de documents*, Yerevan: n.p., 2010.

Véou, Paul Du, *La passion de la Cilicie, 1919–1922*, Paris: Le Cercle d'écrits caucasiens, 2004 [Paris, Geuthner, 1954].

Studies

Bruna, Aurore, *L'accord d'Angora de 1921, théâtre des relations franco-kémalistes et du destin de la Cilicie*, Paris: Collection Cerf Patrimoines, 2018.

Dédéyan, Gérard, 'Le Témoignage de l'aumônier militaire Jules Chaperon', in Dédéyan and Iancu, *Du génocide des Arméniens à la Shoah*, pp. 123–32.

Franck, Roger, *La vie mouvementée du curé Jules Chaperon: Biographie d'un prêtre social dans la haute vallée de l'Artuby (Var) (1877–1951)*, Paris: L'Harmattan, 2000.

Mavian, Isabelle [Seda], 'La communauté arménienne de la région de Kessab à l'époque du mandat français sur la Syrie (1918–1940)', MA thesis, Paris-Sorbonne, 1993–94.

Mutafian, Claude, 'La France en Cilicie: Histoire d'un échec (1919–1939)', *Les Temps modernes*, 504–6 (1988), pp. 90–108.

Nakache, Karen, 'La France et le Levant de 1918 à 1923: Le sort de la Cilicie et de ses confins militaires', PhD thesis, 4 vols, University of Nice Sophia Antipolis, 1999, *passim*.

Poghosyan, Varoujean, 'Le génocide des Arméniens et les religieux français', in Dédéyan and Iancu, *Du génocide des Arméniens à la Shoah*, pp. 273–84.

Sahakian, Rouben, *Franco-Turkish Relations in Cilicia (1919–1921)* [in Armenian], Yerevan: Academy of Sciences, 1970.

Tachjian, Vahé, *La France en Cilicie et en Haute-Mésopotamie: Aux confins de la Turquie, de la Syrie et de l'Irak (1919–1933)*, Paris: Karthala, 2004.

JURISTS OF COMMITMENT

In the face of crimes of mass murder, it was not just committed humanitarians, diplomats and military personnel who became involved but also jurists. The Armenian question had aroused the interest of lawyers since the Treaties of Paris (1856) and Berlin (1878). At the time of the Hamidian massacres, international jurists had striven to find legal solutions that would put an end to the fears and insecurities that ruled the daily lives of Christian minorities within the Ottoman Empire.

It was the genocide of 1915 that was to lend added urgency to the deliberations of jurists. Prominent among them were André Mandelstam and Raphael Lemkin: by defining genocide and making it a crime liable to criminal sanctions, they made it possible to conceive of the inconceivable.

60

ANDRÉ MANDELSTAM (1869–1949)

Russian Jewish lawyer who championed protection of the Armenians

From university to diplomacy

The work of André Mandelstam, champion of the Armenian people, has been studied in depth by the historian Dzovinar Kévonian, to whom we are indebted for much of what follows. Born into a family in the large Jewish population of Mogilev in present-day Belarus, Andrei Nikolaievich Mandelstam studied law and oriental languages before spending a year at the École Libre des Sciences Politiques in Paris. There he studied under Albert Sorel, one of the founders of the concept of diplomatic history, and the celebrated Russian jurist and Baltic baron Boris Nolde, soon to occupy the chair of international law at the St Petersburg Polytechnic University.

When Mandelstam returned to St Petersburg (then Petrograd), he taught under the great jurist and professor of international law Friedrich Fromhold von Martens (known as the architect of the negotiations at the Hague Peace Conferences of 1899 and 1907). He gained his doctorate in international law with a thesis entitled 'The Hague Conference for the Codification of International Law', which he defended at the University of St Petersburg in 1900.

In 1893, he had embarked on a diplomatic career as first dragoman at the Russian embassy in Constantinople. A contemporary of Abdul Hamid II, and later of the Young Turk regime, he became an expert on the Ottoman Empire and frequently acted as an advisor to the Russian Foreign Ministry.

In Constantinople, he greeted the coming to power of the Young Turks in 1908 and the fall of Abdul Hamid II in 1909 as positive developments. After the Hamidian massacres of 1895–6, he viewed these events as offering the hope of a liberal power:

> Arriving in Constantinople after the Armenian massacres of 1895–1896, and seeing Turkish liberals suffering no less than the Christians, perhaps, in the bloody clutches of Abdul Hamid, we had no difficulty in believing what our Turkish colleagues at the École des Sciences Politiques in Paris had told us: that the Turkish people were fundamentally good and noble, and that only their government dishonoured them by committing in their name crimes of a horror that made their Turkish subjects shudder no less than Europe. It was therefore with sincere happiness that we Russian liberals welcomed the rising sun of the Young Turk revolution of 1908, the early rays of which promised better times for all the populations living in the vast territory of the Ottoman Empire.

To Mandelstam, the Ottomanist doctrine seemed to offer a solution to the question of national identities with the advent of a regime based on the rule of law and legal precepts.

From drafting reforms to denouncing massacres

It was not long, however, before Mandelstam became disenchanted with the dictatorial and ultra-nationalist tendencies of the Young Turkish triumvirate, of which he issued fierce denunciations.

With his legal training, Mandelstam studied how the Ottoman judicial system could be reformed. In a series of articles published in the *Revue générale de droit international*, he criticized the policies of the Young Turks, and above all the relationship between the central power and provincial administrations and the minority nationalities.

In addition, Mandelstam was actively involved in the question of Armenian reforms, given fresh impetus by Russia in 1912–14, and assisted the Russian ambassador Nikolay de Girs in his negotiations with the Ottoman government and the other powers represented in Constantinople. It was Mandelstam who presented the plan for reforms in the Armenian provinces to the Russian government, and who held meetings on this issue with Krikor Zohrab, a member of the Ottoman parliament. His ideas were contained in the preliminary draft presented by the Russian diplomatic legation, which was adopted in June 1913. The plan recommended combining the eastern *vilayets* into a single province under the leadership of a Christian governor-general, either Ottoman or European, in whose hands all executive powers would be concentrated, supported by a provincial assembly that would also represent Christians and Muslims alike. On declaration of war, Mandelstam left Constantinople.

In 1916, while on an official mission in Switzerland, he wrote a seminal work entitled *Le sort de l'Empire ottoman* (published in French in 1917), co-authored with Alexander M. Michelson, professor of public finance at the University of Moscow, based on the meticulous study of a great number of official documents and especially Turkish sources and supported by his own observations and testimonies. In its pages, he described the massacres and deportations of the Armenians in the Ottoman Empire, crimes that unmasked the Young Turks to reveal them in their true light. The first part of the book, which dealt with the policies of the Young Turks up to the First World War and the massacres perpetrated during the war, was translated into Armenian and published in Constantinople in 1919. Mandelstam's professional skills and expertise naturally enabled him to weigh up the legal arguments and base his reasoning on sound professional expertise, so producing an in-depth analysis of the state of Turkey.

In a section devoted exclusively to the deportation and massacres of Armenians in Turkey, he offered evidence and documentary material that laid bare the criminal intent of the Turkish leadership. According to Mandelstam's account, the Young Turk government had taken the decision—unapologetically, with premeditation and in plain sight—to obliterate the Armenian people.

Exile: Armenia's cause was that of all humanity

The October Revolution forced Mandelstam into exile. He settled in Paris, where he became part of a group of distinguished Russian jurists including Boris Nolde, many of whom were Jewish, such as Maxim Vinaver and Boris Mirkin-Getzevich. For Mandelstam, the three decades of exile that followed were to prove a productive period of reflection on matters of law in which he produced a succession of seminal works in flawless French, including *La société des nations et les puissances devant le problème arménien* (Paris: Pédone, 1926) and *Confiscation des biens des réfugiés arméniens par le gouvernement turc* (Paris: Massis, 1929). The Constantinople-born publicist Lévon Pachalian (1868–1943), who had settled in Paris in 1920 and with Arshag Chobanian ran the 'Central Committee for Armenian Refugees', wrote in the preface to the latter:

> Beneath the indifferent gaze of the signatory Powers to the Treaty of Lausanne and of the League of Nations, a great injustice has been committed and continues to be committed against Armenians of Turkish origin who are outside their country, who find themselves deprived of the right to return to the land where their ancestors lived long before the arrival of the Turks, and where all their property has been confiscated and sold to profit the Turkish state. After suffering unimaginable calamities during and after the war, after losing a million of their own through mass deportations and massacres, the Armenians, the only participants in the Great War not to be granted any justice or reparations, despite the solemn promises made to them by the Allies and the unanimous resolutions passed in their favour by the League of Nations, hoped that at least the amnesty proclaimed under the Treaty of Lausanne and Turkish recognition of minority rights under the protection of the League of Nations would enable them to reclaim their last remaining possessions.

In the view of the Turkish leadership, however, this project was an attack on the sovereignty of the Ottoman state and an interference by the European powers, a prelude to the carving up of an empire that was already profoundly weakened.

The question of Armenian reforms, and—more importantly—the position of the Armenians in the Ottoman Empire between the Treaty of Berlin of 1878 and the genocide of 1915–16, were to underpin Mandelstam's thinking on the theory of humanitarian intervention, to which he devoted the war years.

In his book *La société des nations et les puissances devant le problème arménien*, Mandelstam concluded that in the aftermath of the Treaty of Lausanne of 24 July 1923 the situation of the Armenian people was 'infinitely worse' than it had been on the eve of the First World War, as a result of the genocide—'the extermination of the nation'—and of the failure of the Entente powers to commit to the creation of an Armenian state. With some anxiety, he questioned 'the new direction of international law'. It was in a loftier spirit that, when informed of the Nansen project to settle Armenian refugees in Soviet Armenia, Baron de Brouckère, the Belgian delegate to the Fifth Assembly of the League of Nations in September 1924, declared: 'This problem is not a matter of providing relief for the Armenian refugees, it is a matter of the resettlement on its own soil, with full rights and full security, of the Armenian nation, which has a right to national existence.'

The Treaty of Lausanne annulled the Treaty of Sèvres of 10 August 1920, the international agreement signed by Turkey that de jure recognized an Armenian state including the *vilayets* of Eastern Anatolia and envisaged reparations. In the Treaty of Lausanne, however, there was no reference to a 'national home' for the Armenians but only a vague allusion to the need for the 'protection of minorities': minorities who—after the Armenian genocide, the massacre of the Pontic Greeks and the exchange of populations with Greece—had been reduced to virtually nothing. In Mandelstam's view, the conference had given 'implicit recognition of a general right of populations to strengthen and consolidate their existence by the destruction or violent assimilation of other nations'.

By virtue of his wholehearted dedication to the Armenian cause, which for him was humanity's cause; of his denunciation of the destruction of a people by the barbarism of their government and of the international failure to comply with a commitment to the creation of an independent Armenian state; and of his personal involvement in the process of recovering Armenian property confiscated during the genocide, this great jurist of international distinction, whose response to the Armenian tragedy was influenced by his own origins and Russian culture, truly deserves to be considered as one of the Righteous.

Sources and further reading

Sources

Mandelstam, André, *La confiscation des biens des réfugiés arméniens par le gouvernement turc*, Paris: Massis, 1929; Mandelstam, *La Société des Nations et les Puissances devant le problème arménien*, Marseille: Imprimerie

Hamaskaïne, 1970 [Paris: Pédone, 1926]; Mandelstam, *Le sort de l'Empire ottoman*, Paris: Payot, 1917, preface and pp. 206–45.

Studies

Annuaire de l'Institut de Droit International, 1921, pp. 273–4 [biographical notice].

Aust, Helmut Philipp, 'From Diplomat to Academic Activist: André Mandelstam and the History of Human Rights', *The European Journal of International Law*, 25, no. 4 (2015), pp. 1105–21.

Jilek, Lubor, 'Violences de masse et droits de l'homme: Andrei Mandelstam entre Constantinople et Bruxelles', *Cahiers de la Faculté des Lettres de Genève* (2000), pp. 64–71.

Kévonian, Dzovinar, 'André Mandelstam and the Internationalization of Human Rights (1869–1949)', in Miia Halme Toumisaari and Pamela Slote (eds), *Revisiting the Origins of Human Rights: Genealogy of a European Idea*, Cambridge: Cambridge University Press, 2015, pp. 239–66; Kévonian, 'Exilés politiques et avènement du "droit humain": La pensée juridique d'André Mandelstam (1869–1949)', *Revue d'Histoire de la Shoah*, 177, no. 8 (January–August 2003), pp. 245–73; Kévonian, 'Les juristes juifs russes en France et l'action internationale dans les années vingt', *Archives juives*, 34, no. 2 (2001), pp. 72–94.

Louvier, Patrick, 'Un engagement savant humanitaire et pacifiste: Les juristes internationalistes et la "question arménienne" des grands massacres de 1894–1896 à la fin de l'ère hamidienne (1894–1908)', in Asso, Demirdjian and Louvier, *Exprimer le génocide des Arméniens*, pp. 51–64.

61

RAPHAEL LEMKIN (1900–59)

Jewish jurist who coined the concept of genocide

The fate of Jewish populations viewed through a multidisciplinary prism

The name of the jurist Raphael Lemkin is indelibly linked with the origins of the term 'genocide'. This distinguished jurist and polymath revolutionized the world of international law when he drew up a definition of a crime that had existed for centuries but had never been given a name. In coining the term 'genocide', Lemkin formulated a definition that was not merely sociological and ideological but also legal, and that laid the foundations of the academic discipline of genocide studies. Forming the word 'genocide' from the Greek *genos* (meaning clan, family, people) and the Latin *caedere* (to kill or massacre), Lemkin created a specific legal definition for a crime that included intentional and planned mass murder, a new category into which would fall the Armenian genocide, the Holocaust, and the genocide of the Tutsis in Rwanda, among others.

Lemkin was born into a traditional middle-class Polish Jewish family on 24 June 1900, in a village near the town of Volkovysk in present-day Belarus. He was educated by his mother, an intellectual, painter, linguist and philosopher with a large library of literature and history books, who believed that the best education for young children should focus primarily on fostering feelings and sensibility. Under her influence, by the age of fourteen the young Raphael had mastered no fewer than ten foreign languages, including Russian, Ukrainian, Yiddish, Hebrew and Polish—the language of his native country—and later English, French, German and Swedish.

THE RIGHTEOUS AND PEOPLE OF CONSCIENCE

Having displayed an early aptitude and passion for the law, Lemkin studied the subject at the universities of Lwów (then in Poland, now Lviv, Ukraine) and Heidelberg. His career in the law was clearly shaped by his humanist upbringing and his Jewish family background: he had been fascinated and appalled from an early age by tales of the cruelties suffered by the Jews and how they had been treated as being virtually 'outside humanity' throughout their history. But the deciding factor in his decision to study law was the Young Turk government's massacre of Armenians in the Ottoman Empire in 1915–16.

While Lemkin's thinking was influenced principally by the experience of two populations who were destroyed in his lifetime, the Armenians and the Jews, it is nevertheless surprising—as the French historian Annette Becker has pointed out—that historiography has only very recently taken into account the conclusions that he drew on the links between the two world wars.

According to Lemkin's own account, he was about eighteen when he began to ponder the meaning of the destruction of human populations. Even before this, when he was fourteen or fifteen, his attention had been gripped by press reports of the massacre of the Armenians in the summer of 1915, when 'more than 1.2 million Armenians were killed', as he wrote, 'for no other reason than they were Christians'. In his memoir, published much later under the title *Totally Unofficial*, he explains how shocked he was by the British government's decision to release 150 Turks who were responsible for the extermination of Armenians and had been interned on Malta in 1919. 'A nation was killed and the guilty persons set free,' he wrote. 'Why is the killing of a million a lesser crime than the killing of an individual?'

Lemkin's thoughts on the matter were initially prompted by the trial of Soghomon Tehlirian, the young Armenian who in 1921 killed Talaat Pasha, one of the Young Turk triumvirate and the main instigator of the genocide, in a street in Berlin where he had taken refuge. In the absence of any judicial sanction for state criminals, Lemkin was driven to the conclusion that Tehlirian had acted as an agent of justice. Lemkin's attention was also caught by the trial of Samuel 'Sholem' Schwarzbard (a French Yiddish poet who in Paris in 1926 killed Symon Petliura, the Ukrainian nationalist leader of Jewish pogroms committed by bands of Cossacks). As Becker has pointed out, the defendants were an Armenian and a Jew whose

RAPHAEL LEMKIN (1900–59)

families had been victims of collective crimes between 1915 and 1920, and who had taken justice into their own hands in the form of personal revenge in Germany and France, the countries where they had sought refuge. The German and French social systems under which they were held to account could neither condemn nor acquit them; in both cases, accordingly, the defendants were held not to have been responsible for their actions.

Lemkin later recalled how he had asked one of his law professors why the Germans, knowing that Talaat Pasha was living in Berlin, had not arrested him, although they put his assassin on trial. The professor replied: 'When you interfere with the internal affairs of a country, you infringe upon that country's sovereignty.' In *Totally Unofficial*, Lemkin wrote:

> The court in Berlin acquitted Tehlirian. It had decided that he had acted under 'psychological compulsion'. Tehlirian, *who upheld the moral order of mankind*, was classified as insane, incapable of discerning the moral nature of his act. He had acted as the self-appointed legal officer for the conscience of mankind. But can a man appoint himself to mete out justice? Will not passion sway such a form of justice and make a travesty of it? At that moment, my worries about the murder of the innocent became more meaningful to me. I didn't know all the answers, but I felt that a law against this type of racial or religious murder must be adopted by the world.

Later, in a television interview, Lemkin concluded: 'I believed that crime should not be punished by victims but should be punished by law.' You could not allow individuals to mete out their own justice, there had to be an international law.

Lemkin would spend the rest of his life pondering this question and fighting for these crimes to be recognized and judged for what they were. It was essential, he maintained, that an international law—and not victims acting on their own account, such as Tehlirian—should mete out justice for such crimes.

From the crime of barbarism to the crime of genocide: a legal argument of international reach

After finishing his studies, Lemkin pursued a successful career in law. Starting as a young assistant prosecutor in Warsaw, he later served as secretary of the Committee on Codification of the Laws of the Republic of Poland, and he taught and practised law until the outbreak of the Second World War.

According to Ryszard Szawłowski, Lemkin's first great moment came in 1931, when he attended the 4th International Conference on the Unification of Criminal Law in Paris and presented a report in support of the efforts of the Polish Jewish lawyer and jurist Emil Rappaport to create a collective protection against acts of violence. Two years later, he wrote a pamphlet in which he introduced the idea of a new international framework to outlaw 'barbarity' and 'vandalism', arguing for these crimes to be added to the list of legal protections to both individuals and groups drawn up by Rappaport in 1927. He cited as precedent the argument that the protection of groups from harm went hand in hand with the inclusion of the crime of 'aggressive war propaganda', to protect normal relations between groups and communities.

In the same year, 1933, while serving as public prosecutor in Warsaw (an office he held from 1929 to 1934), Lemkin attended the 5th Conference for the Unification of Criminal Law, held in Madrid under the auspices of the League of Nations. There he presented an essay on the crime of barbarism, basing his argument on the unpunished crime of the Armenian genocide, so developing a concept that was eventually to culminate in the formulation of the crime of genocide.

Narrowly escaping capture by the Germans after the outbreak of the Second World War, Lemkin went into hiding, joined the Polish resistance and fled to Sweden. In 1941, he gained permission through his legal contacts to enter the United States, where he joined the faculty of Duke University in North Carolina. His numerous prestigious appointments and publications on legal aspects of the conduct of the war led to his being appointed advisor in 1945–6 to Supreme Court Justice Robert H. Jackson in his work as chief counsel at the International Military Tribunal at Nuremberg.

In 1944, with the support of the Carnegie Endowment for International Peace, Lemkin published his seminal work *Axis Rule in Occupied Europe*, in which he first introduced the term 'genocide'. An entire chapter was devoted to the necessity of finding a new term to describe planned and deliberate mass murder.

RAPHAEL LEMKIN (1900–59)

In *Axis Rule*, Lemkin considered the concept of 'genocide' as a development from his definition of barbarism and vandalism of 1933. This represented a significant development in his thinking, even if the earlier definition was in some respects clearer, since it covered a wider range of victim groups (ethnic, religious or social) and also specified the nature of the actions involved (pogroms, massacres, economic destruction). In his memoir, Lemkin refers to a number of genocides spread over a long period. Two massacres seem to have had a direct effect on him, however: the Kishinev pogrom of 1903 and the Armenian genocide of 1915, both because of his memories of contemporary reports and the later circumstances of the assassination of Talaat Pasha. Indeed, as the American historian Anson Rabinbach has noted, in virtually everything he wrote about development of the concept of genocide and his decision to devote his life to it, Lemkin stressed the fact that although he coined the concept in 1933, it was not until a decade later, when he wrote *Axis Rule*, that he coined the word. Becker, meanwhile, contends that the invention of the word was linked to the atrocities carried out by the Nazis, the massacre of Armenians in 1915–16, and the German occupation of Belgium and northern France during the First World War. If 'the practice was old, the word was new'.

In 1945, in an article entitled 'Genocide: A Modern Crime', Lemkin suggested a broader definition that he apparently intended to propose as the basis for work on the UN Convention on the Prevention and Punishment of the Crime of Genocide. The techniques of the crime of genocide, Lemkin wrote, could be divided under eight headings: political, social, cultural, religious, moral, economic, biological and physical.

Towards the UN Genocide Convention (1948)

Lemkin's proposals gave rise to much discussion, as well as some criticism. Some scholars wanted to widen the definition to include more victim groups, whether political affiliations, social classes or simply innocent citizens. They suggested that the concept of criminality should be extended not only to states, as Lemkin proposed, but also to representatives of nation-states (soldiers, colonists and missionaries). They also attempted to redefine the scope of genocide by including events such as mass bombings, depopulation, starvation, disease, destruction of the environment and acts of criminal negligence, thereby removing or ignoring the notion of intent.

The United Nations Convention on the Prevention and Punishment of the Crime of Genocide, for which Lemkin had so long campaigned, was adopted on 9 December 1948. It became a legally binding treaty on 12 January 1951 and is still in force today. The road to the adoption of the convention was long and painful, and it was only through Lemkin's perseverance that it finally entered international law. There is no question that Lemkin's coining of the neologism 'genocide' was prompted by his shock at the lack of any legal framework to define the deliberate extermination of the Ottoman Armenians by the Young Turks in 1915–16.

One of a distinguished group of Central European intellectuals who believed that barbarism could be fought with new laws, Lemkin referred back to the mass slaughter of the Armenians on 22 January 1949. He observed that when, during the First World War, the Armenians were deported, 1,400,000 were marched in convoys towards Aleppo. Only a tenth of these men and women reached their destination: 90 per cent of their number succumbed along the way to exhaustion, hunger, disease or ill treatment. There could be no doubt that this was the crime of genocide before the name: between brutal killings and gradual deaths from harsh treatment, there was no essential difference.

Lemkin continued to research the history of the Armenian genocide, determined to validate the concept of genocide and to demonstrate the importance of ratifying the Genocide Convention. In support of his thesis, he collected testimonies from a number of survivors of the genocide, such as Monsignor Jean Naslian. The Catholic Armenian bishop of Trebizond had written about the experiences he had shared with his congregation during the 1915 genocide in his book *Les mémoires de Monseigneur Jean Naslian*, about which Lemkin published an article in *Haïrenik Weekly* on 1 January 1959. In the article, he also described his meeting with Aram Andonian, another survivor of the genocide with valuable documentary evidence, and recalled the interventions made by Pope Benedict XV, by the American ambassador to Constantinople Henry Morgenthau and by the German pastor Johannes Lepsius. Basing his arguments on the testimonies of Morgenthau and Lepsius, he demonstrated that Turkey's accusation that the Armenians had fomented an uprising was unfounded.

By this time, Lemkin was living in destitution in New York. In August of that year, he died of a heart attack, aged fifty-nine, alone and largely forgotten. He was buried in Mount Hebron Cemetery.

In 2005, Anson Rabinbach, Emeritus Professor of History at Princeton University, began an article entitled 'The Challenge of the Unprecedented: Raphael Lemkin and the Concept of Genocide', with the observation that over the previous decade, Lemkin, the man who had invented the concept of genocide, had emerged from obscurity. Although no biography had yet been devoted to him, his great achievement and contribution had been recognized by the tribute paid to him by the United Nations in 2001 to mark the centenary of his birth—probably, as Rabinbach noted, a year too late.

Through the breadth and depth of his research and analyses, the unstinting and tenacious generosity of his personal engagement and the brilliant scholarship of his writings, this outstanding jurist laid the foundations for all studies of the crime of genocide by contemporary international lawyers. Following decades of obscurity, he is now recognized internationally as—in the words of the inscription on his tombstone—the 'Father of the Genocide Convention'.

Sources and further reading

Sources

Becker, Annette (ed.), 'L'extermination des Arméniens pensée de la Grande Guerre aux années cinquante: Raphaël Lemkin et Varian Fry', *Revue d'Histoire de la Shoah: Se souvenir des Arméniens 1915–2015, Centenaire d'un genocide*, 1, no. 202 (2015), pp. 551–79.

Lemkin, Raphael, *Axis Rule in Occupied Europe: Laws of Occupation—Analysis of Government—Proposals for Redress*, Washington, DC: Carnegie Foundation for International Peace, 1944; Lemkin, 'Genocide: A Modern Crime', *Free World: A Non-Partisan Magazine Devoted to the United Nations and Democracy*, 4 (April 1945), pp. 39–43; Lemkin, *Totally Unofficial: The Autobiography of Raphael Lemkin*, ed. Donna-Lee Frieze, New Haven: Yale University Press, 2013.

THE RIGHTEOUS AND PEOPLE OF CONSCIENCE

Studies

Beauvallet, Olivier, 'Lemkin et le génocide arménien sous l'angle juridique', in Asso, Demirdjian and Louvier, *Exprimer le génocide des Arméniens*, pp. 203–12.

Becker, Annette, 'Raphaël Lemkin, l'extermination des Arméniens et l'invention du mot génocide', in Asso, Demirdjian and Louvier, *Exprimer le génocide des Arméniens*, pp. 192–202; Becker, 'Des violences extrêmes contre les civils des années 1917–1923 à l'invention du concept de génocide', in François Lagrange, Christophe Bertrand, Carine Lachèvre and Emmanuel Ranvoisy (eds), *À l'Est la guerre sans fin, 1913–1923*, Paris: Gallimard, Musée de l'Armée, 2018, pp. 77–88.

Donikian, Denis, 'Figures d'une justice post-génocidaire', in *Petite encyclopédie du génocide Arménien*, p. 418.

Gasparyan, S., S. Paronyan, A. Chubaryan and G. Muradyan, *Raphael Lemkin's Draft Convention on Genocide and the 1948 UN Convention: A Comparative Discourse Study*, Yerevan: Yerevan State University Press, 2016.

Jacobs, Steven Leonard, 'The Complicated Cases of Soghomon Tehlirian and Sholem Schwartzbard and Their Influences on Raphael Lemkin's Thinking about Genocide', *Genocide Studies and Prevention: An International Journal*, 13, no. 1, *Revisiting the Life and Work of Raphael Lemkin* (2019); Jacobs, 'Raphael Lemkin and the Armenian Genocide', in. Hovannisian, *Confronting the Armenian Genocide*, pp. 125–35.

Rabinbach, Anson, 'The Challenge of the Unprecedented: Raphael Lemkin and the Concept of Genocide', Simon Dubnow Institute Yearbook 4, 2005, pp. 401, 411–16.

Robertson, Geoffrey, QC, *An Inconvenient Genocide: Who Now Remembers the Armenians?*, London: Biteback, 2015.

Sands, Philippe, *East West Street: On the Origins of Genocide and Crimes Against Humanity*, London: Weidenfeld & Nicolson, 2016.

Ternon, Yves, *The Criminal State*, n.p.: Threshold, 1995, pp. 17–57; Ternon, *Genèse du droit international*, Paris: Karthala, 2016, pp. 447–58.

THE RIGHTEOUS AT A DISTANCE OF PLACE OR TIME

The efforts of the men and women who took action on the spot while the Armenian tragedy was unfolding were also supported by the energies of people of conscience in other countries. In addition to all those who launched fundraising aimed at alleviating the suffering of the Armenians, there were also intellectuals who worked to find a solution to the refugee problem, or who spoke out powerfully against the fate of the Armenians in the Ottoman Empire and demanded justice for the Armenian people.

While verdicts were passed against numerous members of the Young Turks at the Constantinople war crimes trials in 1918, in many cases their sentences were never carried out as the criminals had made their escape. This prompted the genesis of 'Operation Nemesis', as Armenians sought to take justice into their own hands; in so doing, they shone a spotlight on the genocide and laid controversial ethical and legal dilemmas before the international public.

62

LEADING FIGURES IN NEAR EAST RELIEF

Although the United States was a neutral power, Henry Morgenthau, American ambassador to the Ottoman Empire, was appalled by the treatment to which the Armenians were being subjected, and he issued a number of alarm calls on their behalf. On 3 September 1915, he denounced the extermination of the Armenians and urged Americans to set up a humanitarian organization to come to their aid. The organization that came into being as a result was to become known as Near East Relief, its growth made possible by donations from a number of prominent members of the American Jewish community.

Morgenthau's appeal had been heard by James Levy Barton (1855–1936), a thinker from a Quaker background who devoted his thoughts and writings to exploring the links between Christianity and Islam. Soon after going out to Harput as a missionary teacher in the 1890s, he had been forced to leave Turkey for the sake of his wife's health. In 1915, it was from the United States that he took practical action. By then, he was the international secretary of the American Board of Commissioners for Foreign Missions, and it was in this capacity that he set up a meeting with his friend Cleveland H. Dodge.

It was at this meeting that the American Committee on Armenian Atrocities was established, with Barton as president and officers including Charles R. Crane, Samuel T. Dutton, Stephen Wise, George A. Plimpton, Oscar S. Straus, David H. Greer, Isaac N. Seligman and Talcott Williams. Moving into premises in Dutton's offices on Fifth Avenue, the committee received the ardent support of President Woodrow Wilson. Dodge, for his part, undertook to cover all its costs and made regular and substantial contributions. At its inaugural meeting, the association—which was to prove unrelenting in its fundraising efforts—raised $100,000 for the relief of the deportees. Through the agency of American consuls and missionaries in the field, half of this sum was paid out to the deportees that very day.

Later on, the committee extended its activities to Russian Armenia, where many refugees were facing total destitution. In this way, it raised millions of dollars for Assyrian and Armenian refugees and was unchallenged as the leading force in their rescue. It is estimated that during the committee's lifetime, humanitarian aid to the refugees reached a total of over $100 million. These funds were used to provide the survivors with the basic necessities (food, clothing, medicines and shelter) and also to build hospitals and orphanages. The committee also rescued some 130,000 orphans, not only providing them with shelter and care, but also teaching them trades so as to give them the resources to look after themselves. In 1919, the American Committee on Armenian Atrocities was incorporated by act of Congress and renamed Near East Relief.

The efforts that led to the launch of the organization in 1915 constituted the first major national fundraising appeal of this kind to the American public, and it was unique in its use of sales points and in the support that it received from celebrities and volunteers as well as in the press. As these efforts spread, so they developed into what is now known as 'citizen philanthropy', the model currently used by most non-profit organizations around the world. Near East Relief also embodied the 'social gospel' movement, which believed that Christian spirituality should be accompanied by humanitarian and civic engagement, through which philanthropic entrepreneurs could use their skills to serve others. This unprecedented humanitarian impulse prompted the press to publish more about the tragic events that were tearing the Ottoman Empire apart. It is undoubtedly as a result of its efforts, in part, that so many articles about the genocide published in the American press are available to us today. Near East Relief was dissolved in July 1929 and renamed the Near East Foundation.

Sources and further reading

Sources

Chirinian, Michel (ed.), *Near East Relief: Secours au Proche-Orient* (bilingual edition) (foreword by Yves Ternon and Gérard Dédéyan), n.p.: Roquevaire, 1981.

Studies

Balakian, *Burning Tigris*, pp. 356–81.

Barton, James Levi, *The Story of Near East Relief (1915–1930): An Interpretation*, New York: Macmillan, 1930.

Donikian, Denis, 'Near East Relief Activities Report/Rapport d'activités de Near East Relief', in *Petite encyclopédie du génocide Arménien*.

'Near East Foundation', https://www.neareast.org/

Ternon, *La cause arménienne*, pp. 81–9.

63

ANTONY KRAFFT-BONNARD (1869–1945)

From humanitarian dedication to political commitment

Born on 15 June 1869 in Aigle, in the Swiss canton of Vaud, Pastor Antony Krafft-Bonnard centred his many works—which included writing campaigning pamphlets and initiatives such as setting up an orphanage—in his native region. But although he was rooted in his homeland, he was also acutely aware of world events and the upheavals of his time. A man of decision and a passionate believer in justice, he penned powerful indictments of political and diplomatic aberrations and was driven by his belief in justice, solidarity and morality to seek recognition for the rights of the Armenian people.

Role in the Swiss committees

In 1896, when he was twenty-seven and his attention had been drawn to the fate of the Armenians by articles in the press, he attended the Conference of Swiss Committees for the Relief of Armenians, presided over by Georges Godet. The aim of this Swiss-led initiative was to oversee projects being carried out in the field, but also to cooperate with the work of the American mission that was already long-established in Armenia, mostly in caring for orphans. Krafft-Bonnard's position as a pastor meant that his support of the various committees was a natural choice for him. First of all, he took over the running of the Swiss Society for the Immigration and Patronage of Armenian Orphans, which brought children to Switzerland and took care of all the necessary administrative processes. As president, he welcomed some thirty children and found homes for them with well-to-do families. Then, in December 1918, he became general secretary of the Federation of Swiss–Armenian Friendship Committees, working towards the establishment of a lasting structure for missionary activity in Armenia. This was at a time when there were still hopes for the recognition of an independent Armenia, as outlined in the treaties drawn up by the victorious powers in 1918. Finally, in 1921, he set up the 'Armenian Home' in Begnins, which like its counterpart in Geneva welcomed large numbers of refugees and orphans until 1930. This marked the beginning of a journey that was to continue until Krafft-Bonnard's death in 1945, a concrete personal involvement and constant investment in the Armenian cause.

What began as a humanitarian project for Krafft-Bonnard very quickly turned into a political issue. Initially, since Switzerland refused to either commit to the initiatives it had itself put in place or provide funding for them, he found himself obliged to look for patrons for his homes, and in order to do this he needed to raise public awareness of the Armenian question. To this end, he enlisted his literary and critical skills to denounce the abuses to which the Armenians arriving in Switzerland had been subjected. Once hopes of independence had been dashed, however, and faced with the ever-growing scale of the massacres, he soon realized that the funds invested in Armenia, by both American and Swiss organizations, were now useless for opposing the ruthless and oppressive policies of the Turks. Humanitarian initiatives were only practically possible if they were supported by a consistent approach at the political level. Hence in his pamphlets, essays and other writings, Krafft-Bonnard became the impassioned spokesperson for an ideal to which he would remain faithful to the end of his life.

He began his pamphlet *L'heure de l'Arménie*, published in Geneva in 1922 after the combined failings of European and American strategies had sealed the fate of the Armenian people, with an urgent appeal to the international community:

> It is to humankind that the voices of an entire people are raised in appeal. It is impossible not to lend them our ears. As a matter of urgency, the attention of all those who have any responsibility for the political direction of our world must be drawn to the ever more

intolerable fate of this martyred people, who for so many centuries have been subjected to such appalling oppression.

It was a manifesto in which he scrutinized treaty breaches point by point (such as Turkey's failure to ratify the Treaty of Sèvres); shone a spotlight on the consequences of the Entente powers' lack of political commitment, which allowed Russian, French and British diplomacy to carve up Armenian territory between themselves; and highlighted their refusal to take action against Mustafa Kemal's increasingly nationalistic and authoritarian regime. He denounced the consequences of America's refusal to give a mandate to the Armenian state in 1921 because of internal elections, and evoked Russian policy and the history of the provinces of Van, Bitlis, Erzurum and Trebizond, as well as the impotence of the League of Nations. Finally, he deconstructed Turkish government communiqués regarding the provinces in 1915, demystifying their diplomatic posturing and demanding reparations. At the same time, he reminded his readers of

> [t]he military loyalty of the Armenians to the Entente Powers, in a variety of ways and on every front, throughout the world war from its beginning to its end; the massacres and deportations that they have suffered in Turkey as a result; and the repeated promises made to Armenia by the Allied and Associated Governments.

In the name of the members of the Executive Committee of the League of Nations set up in Paris in 1920, he put forward concrete solutions for the creation of an Armenian national home, as proposed by Raymond Poincaré, president of France from 1913 to 1920 and president of the council and minister of foreign affairs from 1922 to 1924.

A prolific writer

Taken as a whole, Krafft-Bonnard's writings display a wide-ranging understanding of world politics and a profound involvement in the complex events of the period from 1918 to 1923. He was familiar with the legal position, treaties, political and economic geography, the influence of financial oligarchies in decision-making (particularly around the question of oil, to which he devoted a pamphlet), and the work carried out on the ground. Through a range of committees, he became the spokesperson for reparation work that went far beyond his responsibilities as a pastor—as could be seen, for example, in his reaction to the fate of stateless refugees at the Lausanne Conference in 1923. His universalist and idealistic interpretation of world events informed his precise and effective writing style and served as his guiding principle in commitments as diverse as the day-to-day running of an orphanage and the writing of manifestos, speeches, lectures and autobiographical works. He also wrote a series of pamphlets, the proceeds of which—following the American mission's withdrawal of funding in 1920 and the death of its benefactor Léopold Favre in 1922—went to support his orphanage.

Krafft-Bonnard published twenty-seven articles and some thirty pamphlets on behalf of the orphanages, on topics ranging from exile to tuberculosis, via education and of course politics. A selection of just a few of their titles indicates not only the range of his interests but also the wide variety of his target audience: *Suisse et Arménie, le passé et l'avenir de l'œuvre suisse en Arménie* (1919; translated into German); *L'heure de l'Arménie* (1922), with a preface by the Belgian senator H. La Fontaine (translated into German and Danish); *Arménie, Suisse et Société des Nations* (1924); *Le problème arménien: Comment il se pose aujourd'hui?* (1928), published in *Le Christianisme social*; *Arménie, justice et réparation* (1930; translated into German); *Faut-il abandonner?* (1933); *Au secours des grands blessés de la politique internationale* (1941; translated into German); and *Le problème des sans-patrie* (1942; translated into German).

The testimony of the Armenian Apostolic Church

On 25 September 2015, His Holiness Aram I, Catholicos of the Great House of Cilicia (Antelias), under the heading 'Half a Century in the Service of the Armenians', described Pastor Antony Krafft-Bonnard as

> a symbolic example of the Swiss people, who in his life and mission, with exemplary fidelity, embodied the authentic qualities and values of the Swiss people.
>
> In his person, the people of Switzerland heard the words of Christ, and they responded to this call to faith by giving eloquent expression to their love of God and for an oppressed and persecuted people.

ANTONY KRAFFT-BONNARD (1869–1945)

Krafft-Bonnard's redemptive work and his profound indignation in the face of the massacres of people who had earlier been rescued by the Armenian missions were grounded in a faith that was sincere and deeply held, as shown by his commitment to the children in the orphanage in Begnins. Far from confining himself to a single church or nation, however, he never ceased to pay tribute to all the humanitarian work undertaken by individuals for the common good, going above and beyond governments who were too often incapable of taking action, whether in the Caucasus, Mesopotamia, Turkey or Switzerland. The adjective 'charitable', a leitmotif in his writings, also sums up the motivations, outlook and character of this outstanding humanitarian and champion of the Armenian cause.

Sources and further reading

Sources

Krafft-Bonnard, Antony, 'L'Arménie à la conférence de Lausanne', Revue *Foi et Vie*, May 1923; Krafft-Bonnard, *L'Heure de l'Arménie*, Geneva: Société générale d'imprimerie, 1922; Krafft-Bonnard, *Pour le Droit de l'Arménie*, Paris: Le Christianisme social, 1922.

Studies

Association culturelle arménienne de Marne-la-Vallée, http://www.acam-france.org/bibliographie/auteur.php?cle=krafftbonnard-antony

Église arménienne de Cilicie, http://www.armenianorthodoxchurch.org/en/archives/13713

Haroutounian, Sévane, 'Le pasteur Antony Krafft-Bonnard: Un Suisse pour la défense des Arméniens', https://artzakank-echo.ch/2015/03/25/le-pasteur-anthony-krafft-bonnard-un-suisse-pour-la-defense-des-armeniens/

Kunth, Anouche, *Exils arméniens du Caucase à Paris, 1920–1945*, Paris: Belin, 2016.

64

JAMES BRYCE (1838–1922)

'Proof in hand': the reality of genocide

Academic career and discovery of the Armenians

James Bryce, 1st Viscount Bryce, son of a Presbyterian Church schoolmaster, was born in Belfast, on 10 May 1838, the son of a Presbyterian schoolteacher, and died in Sidmouth, England, on 22 January 1922. During his long career, he distinguished himself as an academic, jurist, historian and politician.

After studying at the universities of Glasgow, Heidelberg and Oxford, he was made a fellow of Oriel College, Oxford, in 1862, aged twenty-four; published a monograph entitled *The Holy Roman Empire* in 1864; and was called to the Bar in 1867. Three years later, he was appointed Regius Professor of Law at Oxford, a post he held concurrently with the chair of jurisprudence at Owens College, Manchester.

Bryce's love of travel, landscape and the Icelandic sagas took him to Iceland in 1872, while his passion for mountaineering led him to Armenia, which he immediately fell in love with. In 1876, he climbed Mount Ararat, and the following year he published an essay entitled *Transcaucasia and Ararat*, which contained valuable observations on the Armenians. In 1879, he founded and became first president of the Anglo-Armenian Society, supported by his friend William Gladstone, leader of the Liberal Party since 1865 and three times prime minister between 1868 and 1894; Garabed Papazian, a wealthy Armenian banker from Manchester; and Garabed Hagopian, chairman of the Armenian Patriotic Committee, founded in London in 1878.

In 1881, Professor Bryce addressed his American colleagues at Harvard on the Armenian question, and as a result ties were forged between the United Kingdom and the United States over Armenia. In 1888, he published *The American Commonwealth*, which received praise in academic circles, notably from Thomas Woodrow Wilson, future US president (1913–21) and founding father of the League of Nations, who was to play a crucial role in the defence of the Armenians.

British foreign policy and the Armenian question

Bryce was thus an early champion of the Armenians. In 1895, when the Hamidian massacres were at their height, he published an article entitled 'The Armenian Question' in the American *Century Illustrated Monthly Magazine*, which attracted a good deal of attention. In this article, he urged Americans to act to help the Armenians, denounced the Treaty of Berlin and the policies of the sultan, and argued that Turkey could never become part of Europe. In his view, the massacres of the Armenians demonstrated a deliberate determination to exterminate them. Abdul Hamid II reacted with fury, and a major diplomatic crisis blew up. In an effort to ease the ensuing tensions, the magazine published a glowing interview with Abdul Hamid by Alexander Watkins Terrell (a former judge who was at that time minister plenipotentiary to the Sublime Porte) in which, with barefaced hypocrisy, the despotic sultan paid tribute to the Armenians and laid the blame for the massacres at the door of the Armenian Revolutionary Committees.

By this time, Bryce was already established in his public career, having been elected as a Liberal MP in 1880. In 1885, he became under-secretary of state for foreign affairs under Gladstone, who was himself strongly committed to opposing Ottoman atrocities. Forced out of office later that year by the Liberals' electoral defeat, he remained close to Gladstone.

In 1897, he travelled to South Africa, on his return publishing his *Impressions of South Africa*, in which he went against public and political opinion to express fierce opposition to the British repression of the Boers in South Africa. Though he thus denounced the abuses of his own government, he was nevertheless appointed chief secretary for Ireland in 1905–6.

JAMES BRYCE (1838–1922)

Still a strong supporter of Armenia, in 1904 he was part of the movement led from Paris by the *Pro Armenia* journal. From 1907 to 1913, he was the British ambassador to Washington, where he helped to strengthen ties between the United States and Britain and built up a network of personal friends among American politicians.

In 1914, after retiring as ambassador, he was ennobled as Viscount Bryce and entered the House of Lords. Following the outbreak of war, he was commissioned by Prime Minister H. H. Asquith to draw up a report on German atrocities against civilians in occupied Belgium, which became known as the 'Bryce Report'. Although somewhat discredited after the war, it caused a considerable stir at the time, particularly in the United States, and contributed to the souring of relations between Germany and America.

Bryce and the 'Blue Book'

During the First World War, Asquith asked Bryce to lead an inquiry into the massacres of Armenians in the Ottoman Empire, and in July 1915 he became the first to raise the plight of the Armenians in the House of Lords. He was also involved in the creation of the British Armenian Red Cross and the setting up of a refugee fund. In 1916, with the distinguished historian Arnold Toynbee (author of the monumental twelve-volume *A Study of History*), he published *The Treatment of Armenians in the Ottoman Empire, 1915–1916*, his official report into the massacres that came to be known as the 'Blue Book'.

Bryce sent this collection of documents and testimonies, together forming one of the most important primary sources for the study of the Armenian genocide, to the British foreign secretary, Viscount Grey of Fallodon, with an accompanying letter in which he explained what had led him to collect these accounts, and the difficulties he had encountered in doing so:

> In the autumn of 1915 accounts of massacres and deportations of the Christian population of Asiatic Turkey began to reach Western Europe and the United States. Few and imperfect at first, for every effort was made by the Turkish Government to prevent them from passing out of the country, these accounts increased in number and fullness of detail, till in the beginning of 1916 it became possible to obtain a fairly accurate knowledge of what had happened. It then

struck me that, in the interest of historic truth, as well as with a view to the questions that must arise when the war ends, it had become necessary to try to complete these accounts, and test them by further evidence, so as to compile a general narrative of the events and estimate their significance. As materials were wanting or scanty in respect of some localities, I wrote to all the persons I could think of likely to possess or to be able to procure trustworthy data, begging them to favour me with such data.

On receiving the Blue Book, Viscount Grey replied:

It is a terrible mass of evidence; but I feel that it ought to be published and widely studied by all who have the broad interests of humanity at heart. It will be valuable, not only for the immediate information of public opinion as to the conduct of the Turkish Government towards this defenceless people, but also as a mine of information for historians in the future, and for the other purposes suggested in your letter.

In his July 1915 speech to the House of Lords, printed in the preface to Toynbee's *Armenian Atrocities: The Murder of a Nation*, published in the same year, Bryce summed up the magnitude of the crime and put it in perspective:

'There is no case in history, certainly not since the time of Tamerlane, in which any crime so hideous and upon so large a scale has been recorded.'

In his preface to the Blue Book, Bryce emphasized not only the horror but also the premeditated nature of the massacres and deportation, laying the blame squarely on the Young Turk government: 'There was no Moslem passion against the Armenian Christians. All was done by the will of the Government and done not from any religious fanaticism, but simply because they wished for reasons purely political to get rid of non-Moslem elements which impaired the homogeneity of the Empire.'

Bryce noted the systematic and organized nature of the massacres and, above all, exonerated the Armenians of the charge of rebellion that the Turks had raised against them as a pretext for unleashing the massacres, and that to this day remains one of the major untruths on which the denialist edifice of the Turkish state rests.

JAMES BRYCE (1838–1922)

The Blue Book, and the wealth of important details and evidence it contains, remains a thorn in the side of those who support denialist propaganda. In 2005, Turkish MPs sent a letter to the House of Commons asking them to acknowledge their claim that the Blue Book was a piece of British propaganda. The British ambassador to Turkey issued a diplomatically worded rejection of the Turkish position.

Last battles

In 1918, Bryce published an article entitled 'The Future of Armenia' in *The Contemporary Review*, in which he returned to the Hamidian massacres of 1894–6, the Cilician massacres of 1909, and the massacres and deportations of 1915.

Bryce also condemned the Kemalists who came after the Young Turks, delivering a speech in the House of Lords in February 1920 in which he spoke out against the massacres that had been unleashed once again in Cilicia.

Lord Bryce died in 1922, having devoted over forty years to championing the Armenians and coming to their aid. As his legacy, he left a body of work that has made a seminal contribution to the understanding and recognition of the Armenian genocide.

Sources and further reading

Sources

Bryce, Viscount, *The Treatment of the Armenians in the Ottoman Empire, 1915–16*, ed. Arnold J. Toynbee, London: HMSO, Sir Joseph Causton and Sons, 1916.
Chaliand and Ternon, *Armenians*, pp. 77–84.

Studies

Balakian, *Burning Tigris*, *passim*.
'James Bryce', Armenian Genocide Museum-Institute, http://www.genocide-museum.am/fr/10.03.2013.php
'James Bryce, Viscount Bryce', *Brittanica*, https://www.britannica.com/biography/James-Bryce-Viscount-Bryce
Kiuciukian, *Voci nel deserto*, pp. 120–37.
Prévost, Stéphanie, 'L'opinion publique britannique et la Question arménienne (1889–1896), Quelles archives pour quel récit?', *Études*

arméniennes contemporaines, 8 (2016), http://journals.openedition.org/eac/1170

Seeman, John T., *A Citizen of the World: The Life of James Bryce*, London, International Library of Historical Studies, 2006.

Steinberg, Oded Y. 'The Origins of the Armenian Question', *Journal of Levantine Studies* (Winter 2015), https://www.academia.edu/26438077/The_Origins_of_the_Armenian_Question_Journal_of_Levantine_Studies_Winter_2015_

Toynbee, Arnold and Viscount Bryce, *Armenian Atrocities: The Murder of a Nation*, new edition, Sacramento: Franklin Classics, 2018.

65

ANATOLE FRANCE (1844–1924)

The long struggle for human rights, the Armenian cause and peace

The Dreyfus Affair: the struggle against antisemitism

Above and beyond his outstanding literary gifts (he was awarded the Nobel Prize for Literature in 1921), Anatole France—born François-Anatole Thibault, the son of a Paris bookseller, in 1844—was a supporter of the Armenian cause. The enduring nature and depth of his commitment merit him a place among the people of conscience, or even among the Righteous, of the Armenian genocide.

France displayed constancy and courage in his support of major ethical principles. Elected to the Académie Française in 1896, he was the only one in the learned assembly to sign Émile Zola's open letter to Félix Faure, president of the Republic, published in January 1898 in *L'Aurore* (founded in 1897 and edited by Georges Clemenceau) under the bold headline *J'accuse!* He was also one of the prominent intellectuals to sign a petition accusing the French General Staff of adopting a defamatory attitude towards Captain Alfred Dreyfus and calling for a review of his trial. The Jewish officer had been falsely accused, based on a forgery, of having communicated secret documents to the German military attaché in Paris. In solidarity with Zola (he returned his Légion d'honneur after Zola was stripped of his) and in reaction to the condemnation of Dreyfus, France helped to establish the Ligue des droits de l'homme (Human Rights League), founded in 1898 by the right-wing but Dreyfus-supporting politician Ludovic Trarieux. In 1899, he left the *Écho de Paris*, which was opposed to a retrial, and joined

Le Figaro, which was conservative and Catholic, but also adopted a Dreyfusard stand. On 13 September of that year, the newspaper published an article by France in which—as cited by Marie-Claire Bancquart in her *Anatole France*—he offered an eloquent denunciation of the 'barbaric prejudice' of antisemitism.

France had meanwhile become a close associate of Jean Jaurès, contributing several articles to his openly socialist newspaper *L'Humanité*, founded in 1904 (the year in which France joined the central committee of the Ligue des droits de l'homme). He also joined the progressive group 'Clarté', set up by Henri Barbusse, and later signed the manifesto *Contre la paix injuste* (Against the unjust peace), published in *L'Humanité* on 22 July 1919. This denounced the signatories to the Versailles Peace Treaty on 28 June 1919 for paying lip service to the values of justice and peace, accusing them of disregarding the value of human life and democratic principles in favour of economic interests. Other signatories included Henri Barbusse, Roland Dorgelès, Georges Duhamel and Séverine, a libertarian journalist and co-founder of the Ligue des droits de l'homme who had denounced the Sassoun massacres in *Les massacres d'armor*, published in *La libre parole*.

Support for the Armenian cause

It comes as no surprise to discover that Anatole France—associate of Jean Jaurès and of Francis de Pressensé (Dreyfusard, second president of the Ligue des droits de l'homme and champion of the Armenians and Macedonians)—was a staunch champion of the Armenian cause. As early as 1900, he took part in what Vincent Duclert in *La France face au génocide des Arméniens* describes as the 'great conferences' organized by pro-Armenians (most of whom were also Dreyfus supporters) with the aim of drawing attention to the fate, suffering and culture of the Armenian people. He chaired the first large-scale conference organized by the Armenian community in Paris, held at the Théâtre du Vaudeville on 16 June 1900 under the patronage of the Ligue des droits de l'homme. On 15 February 1904, he attended the conference 'For Armenia and Macedonia' (Macedonia was under Ottoman rule from 1371 to 1913 and suffered massacres in retribution for the growth of a nationalist movement), the acts of which, including contributions from distinguished figures from France (Pierre Quillard, Georges Clemenceau, Antoine Meillet) and Britain (James Bryce), set out to offer a comprehensive overview of the 'Armenian question'. Unable to attend the London International Conference in support of Armenia and Macedonia, France sent an impassioned letter, read out on 29 June 1904, in which he denounced the attitude of a Europe that had fostered the 'Red Sultan', Abdul Hamid II, perpetrator of the massacres of 1894–6, accusing it of giving priority to 'economic and financial matters' in overlooking 'the slaughter of three hundred thousand of the Sultan's subjects'. He also expressed the hope that British pragmatism and dynamism would enable the Armenians to once again become 'what they once were, the most active agents of European civilisation in the East'.

Denunciation of the genocide and support for an Armenian national revival

It was the genocide of 1915–16 that mobilized Anatole France and other pro-Armenians, particularly at the 'Homage to Armenia' meeting held in the Sorbonne Grand Amphitheatre on 9 April 1916 (preceded on 16 January by a talk by Émile Doumergue, dean of the Free Protestant Faculty of Montauban, on the rescue of the resistance fighters of Musa Dagh), presided over by Paul Deschanel, president of the Chamber of Deputies. Deschanel argued that it was France's mission to defend justice, to mobilize in support of a people who were suffering a 'heroic martyrdom', and to denounce 'one of the greatest crimes in history'.

In his closing remarks, Anatole France declared: 'Armenia is dying, but it will be reborn. Its last drops of blood are precious blood from which a heroic posterity will emerge. A people that does not wish to die will not die.' He foresaw that 'after the victory of our armies fighting for justice and freedom', the 'great duties' that would fall to the Allies would include ensuring 'the security and independence of Armenia'. To the Armenian people, they would be able to say: 'Sister, arise! Suffer no more. Henceforth you are free to live according to your spirit and your faith.' Although himself an agnostic, France mounted a principled defence of the identity of the first country to adopt Christianity as its state religion, at the beginning of the fourth century.

THE RIGHTEOUS AND PEOPLE OF CONSCIENCE

When the League of Nations proved unable to give the Armenians 'a national home entirely independent of Ottoman dominion', since Kemalist forces had captured Cilicia and then the rest of Asia Minor in the early 1920s, Cardinal Louis-Ernest Dubois, archbishop of Paris, made an 'Appeal to Opinion' that has been analysed by Duclert. Dated November 1922 and published in 1923 in the *Revue des études arméniennes* (founded on 19 January 1920 by the linguist Antoine Meillet and the orientalist Frédéric Macler), the appeal highlighted the tradition of commitment to supporting the populations of the East among France's most distinguished representatives, who had come to 'champion the cause of the victims in the name of humanity'. The appeal was signed by the French intellectual, political, diplomatic and religious elite of the time, including Anatole France, then president of the Pro Armenia Committee.

Continuing his struggle in support of Armenia, less than two years before his death France subscribed to an 'Appeal for Armenia' launched on the initiative of Meillet, then a professor at the Collège de France and a specialist in comparative linguistics (who in 1903 had published a comparative grammar of classical Armenian). Sent on 8 December 1922 to the Lausanne Conference and published in the *Journal des débats* on the 17th, it too was signed by the intellectual, artistic and political elite, as though signifying the last stand of French pro-Armenians, or of the finest among the French people who still believed in justice and human rights.

The Treaty of Sèvres (signed on 10 August 1920, ending the First World War for the Ottoman Empire) had in fact provided for the creation of an independent Armenia (as well as an autonomous Kurdistan), but owing to Mustafa Kemal's victories over the Armenians in 1921 and the Greeks in 1922 and the absence of the Turkish parliament, it had not been ratified by France and other European powers. Against the advice of the government of the young Republic of Armenia, the Armenian delegation to the Paris Peace Conference in January 1919–August 1920 had presented to the victorious Allies a 'Memorandum of an Integrated Armenia', encompassing the eastern *vilayets* of the Ottoman Empire and the Republic of Armenia. This demand was practically endorsed in November 1920 by the arbitration of the American president Woodrow Wilson (although the US Senate had turned down a vote on Armenia). With the national home of Cilicia (1919–21) about to be evacuated by the French government following Mustafa Kemal's victories, the Armenian Republic, trapped between the Kemalist anvil and the Bolshevik hammer, renounced the Treaty of Sèvres and signed the Treaty of Alexandropol with the Turks on 2 December 1920, while a communist government was installed in Yerevan.

Despite this less than promising context, the signatories of the appeal recalled the promises made by the Allies:

> During the war, the Allies solemnly declared that the liberation of Turkish Armenia was one of the aims of the battle they were waging; Article 22 of the Covenant of the League of Nations and the decisions taken by the Allied governments after the victory enshrined this promise; the League of Nations, in several motions passed unanimously, confirmed the necessity of protecting the future of the Armenian race by the creation of the National Home that had been promised to it ... Humanity and justice, the honour of the Allies and the interests of the Turks themselves require that the martyrdom of Armenia be brought to an end and that the National Home be established without delay, so that these multitudes of refugees may be reunited and live there in security.

Stressing the necessity for ensuring the existence of a people 'who for centuries have rendered so many services to civilization', the signatories concluded, demonstrating a faith in humanity that was to prove wholly misplaced: 'We strongly hope that the delegates of France, and of all countries taking part in the Conference, will find the equitable solution that the conscience of humanity is unanimous in demanding for this question that is of the highest moral importance.'

Allied betrayal; Anatole France, prophet of wars to come

The Treaty of Lausanne, signed on 24 July 1923 at the conclusion of the Lausanne Conference (to which the Armenians were not invited), annulled the Treaty of Sèvres. There was now no longer any question of a 'national home' for the Armenians, nor of any restitution or compensation, but merely, as Claire Mouradian points out, the 'protection of minorities' (non-Muslims), since the genocide of the Armenians, Syriacs and Pontic Greeks meant that there were hardly any Christians left.

Allowing an exception for his visceral anti-clericalism (against all his expectations, the law of separation of Church and State did nothing to stem the growth of the Catholic Church), Anatole France's verdicts on events were often prophetic. Already in 1921 he was writing to a friend: 'At an age when I have no future left, I am starting to worry about the future. It seems to me that, in spite of the indifference of the public, a catastrophe is inevitable.' As Bancquart recalls in *Anatole France*, when he was awarded the Nobel Prize for Literature in December 1921, he was not afraid to offend some sensibilities in his solemn acceptance speech: 'The most terrible of wars was followed by a treaty that was not a peace treaty, but the continuation of war. If reason does not finally find a place in its decision-making, this will be the death of Europe.'

He also declared prophetically: 'This terrible war is the beginning of two or three equally terrible wars.' Although he refrained from taking sides during the split between socialists and communists at the Tours Congress of 25–30 December 1920, in 1923, a year before his death, he wrote that he had foreseen the rise of totalitarian ideologies, both fascism and Bolshevism. He had issued a warning to the Soviets as early as March 1922, at the time of the great show trials in Moscow, which led to his being fired from *L'Humanité*. He had written to them, as Bancquart recalls, 'in the name of humanity, in the name of the higher interests of humanity …'

It was the position that he consistently took in favour of the interests and flourishing of humanity—his magnificent humanism—that led Anatole France to become such an unflagging champion of the Armenians. And it is this commitment against all the odds that merits his inclusion as one of the Righteous.

Sources and further reading

Studies

Bancquart, Marie-Claire, *Anatole France: Un sceptique passionné*, Paris: Calmann-Lévy, 1984.

Duclert, *La France face au génocide des Arméniens*, pp. 184–5, 222–3, 291–3, 395–6.

ANATOLE FRANCE (1844–1924)

Khayadjian, Edmond, *Archag Tchobanian et le mouvement arménophile en France*, 2nd edn, Alfortville: SIGEST, 2001, part 1, chapter 14, 'Anatole France et Archag Tchobanian', pp. 97–116.

66

JACQUES DE MORGAN (1857–1924)

A dream of Eurasia, a passion for Armenia

Across Eurasia: the spirited career of a mining engineer turned archaeologist

Jacques de Morgan was a pioneering Western historian of Armenia. Born near Blois in 1857 and of aristocratic descent, de Morgan was an intrepid traveller and a distinguished mining engineer, geologist and above all archaeologist, who worked both in the Caucasus (where he spent three years) and in the Middle East. He was director of antiquities in Egypt from 1892 to 1897, and the excavations that he directed at Susa in Iran in the same period sealed his international reputation. He founded the French archaeological delegation in Iran, the forerunner of the present Institut Français de Recherche en Iran, and his remarkable work earned him two rooms in the Louvre dedicated to his collections.

De Morgan's interest in Armenia was triggered in the late 1880s. When he arrived in Armenia in 1886, with the palaeontologist, geologist and mining engineer Maurice Chaper, to exploit the mines of Akhtala in the north-west of the country, near the monastery-fortress of the same name, he was struck by the archaeological riches of the Transcaucasian region. He was soon forced to return to France, but on the strength of his initial observations he applied to the Ministry of Public Instruction to undertake an official scientific mission, and he set off on a two-year expedition in 1888–9. After dealing with teething problems with the local Russian administration, de Morgan excavated numerous necropolises in Armenia and Georgia; he established relevant dates and focused on metalwork and weapons, illustrating his descriptions with accomplished drawings. He also drew up an archaeological map of the region. At the end of the mission, he published the results of his research under the title *Mission scientifique au Caucase: Études archéologiques et historiques*.

Following this, he was awarded a grant by the Ministry of Public Instruction to explore Lankaran, in present-day Azerbaijan, where he carried out a study of necropolises and drew up an archaeological map in 1889–91.

The Montpellier Éclair and the Armenian cause

After retiring first to Paris and then to the Pyrenees for the sake of his health, and having been cast out by his family after his remarriage to a woman from a different social class, de Morgan nevertheless planned to spend the last years of his life in an independent Armenia. In association with Arshag Chobanian, co-founder with Pierre Quillard of the pro-Armenian movement in France, he embarked on a joint venture with the Montpellier-based newspaper *L'Éclair*, submitting articles on a regular basis from 1915 to 1921.

In these remarkable pieces, he provided comprehensive coverage of developments in the 'Armenian question'. His scope was both geographical, embracing Eastern Anatolia and the Southern Caucasus, and chronological, from the genocide of 1915–16 to the end of the First Republic of Armenia (1918–1920) and the national home of Cilicia (1919–21). On top of the death toll of the genocide, he also took into account Turkish reprisals in the Ottoman provinces recaptured from the Russians in 1918, as well as the massacres perpetrated by the Azeris in Baku and other Caucasian cities.

He also drew attention to the Armenian war effort during the First World War, highlighting the presence of 10,000 Armenian volunteers (the true figure was in fact 6,000) on the Caucasus front; the formation of a national army immediately after the creation of the Republic of Armenia; the resistance mounted against the Azeris by the Armenians in Baku; the fighting spirit of the Armenian–Assyrian forces; the Armenian presence in the Allied armies (which included over 10 per cent of the Armenians in France); and the actions of the Armenian Legion as a presence in Cilicia under the French mandate.

JACQUES DE MORGAN (1857–1924)

In de Morgan's view—echoing Georges Clemenceau in his description of Armenia as a 'valiant little ally'—the Armenians deserved to be included among the belligerent nations. The political project he supported was the creation of two Armenian states: Greater Armenia, stretching to Karabakh and the southern shores of Lake Van; and a contemporary heir to the kingdom of the French House of Lusignan in Cilicia. It would fall to France—not the United States—to press for the creation of these two states.

Historian of the Armenian question

Having already discussed the Armenian question in his *Essai sur les nationalités* (Paris, 1917) and *Contre les barbares de l'Orient* (Paris, 1918), de Morgan was persuaded by Chobanian—who would support him with documentary evidence—to write his *Histoire du peuple arménien depuis les temps les plus reculés jusqu'à nos jours* (Paris, 1919; translated into English as *The History of the Armenian People, from the Remotest Times to the Present Day*), published in the aftermath of the Armenian genocide and at a moment when the Republic of Armenia seemed to be on the verge of a promising future. Prefaced by the prominent historian Gustave Schlumberger, this valuable work of historiography was richly illustrated 'with 296 maps, plans and documentary drawings by the author', who once again displayed his exceptional skills as a draughtsman.

During his lifetime, de Morgan's multidisciplinary skills and vocation and his unconventional approach meant that his career and achievements did not receive the official recognition they deserved. Today, however, and especially since the archaeology exhibition entitled 'Jacques de Morgan (1857–1924), conquistador de l'archéologie', at Saint-Germaine en Laye in 2007, there is a renewed interest in and respect for his body of work, including his commitment both to Armenian culture and to the recognition of an Armenian state in the aftermath of the First World War. His words in *The History of the Armenian People* speak for themselves:

> As I have already said, the historian is not entitled to speak of the future. Whatever the outcome of this merciless war between the Armenian nation and its oppressors, the memory of this struggle

will remain one of the finest pages in the annals of the Haikian people. Her steadfastness, courage, and nameless woes have earned Armenia a glorious niche in the record of the World War.

Sources and further reading

Sources

de Morgan, Jacques, *Contre les barbares de l'Orient* ... [articles from *L'Éclair* and the *Revue de Paris*], Paris: n.p., 1918; Morgan, *Essai sur les nationalités*, Marseille: Académie de Marseille, 1982 (prefaced and edited by Francis J.-F. Chamant and Edmond Khayadjian) [Paris, 1917]; Morgan, *The History of the Armenian People: From the Remotest Times to the Present Day*, trans. Ernest F. Barry, Boston: Hairenick Associates, 1965; Morgan, *Mission scientifique au Caucase*, 2 vols, Paris: Ernest Leroux éditeur, 1889.

Jaunay, Andrée, *Mémoires de Jacques de Morgan 1857–1924: Souvenirs d'un archéologue*, Paris: L'Harmattan, 1997.

Studies

Borlo, Virginie, 'Le génocide arménien à travers la presse française de 1915 à 1920', 2 vols, MA thesis, Université Paul-Valéry Montpellier III, September 1996.

de Mecquenem, Roland, 'Biographie de Jacques de Morgan', *Bulletin de l'association des anciens élèves de l'École des Mines* (July–September 1924).

Khayadjian, *Archag Tchobanian et le mouvement arménophile*, part 2, chapter 7, 'Les écrits de Jacques de Morgan sur l'Arménie et la Question arménienne'.

Khayadjian, Edmond and Constant Vautravers, 'Preface', Jacques de Morgan, *Histoire du peuple arménien*, new edn, Marseille: Académie de Marseille, 1981, pp. v–liv.

Pottier, Edmond, 'Jacques de Morgan', *Syrie: Archéologie, art et histoire* (1924), pp. 373–80.

67

AHMET REFIK ALTINAY (1881–1937)

A passion for history and historic truth

Ahmet Refik, who adopted the name Altınay, came from a family who had close links with the Ottoman dynasty. His father had worked in the circles of Sultan Abdülaziz, the end of whose reign (1861–76) brought the period of the Tanzimat reforms to a close, before the accession of Abdul Hamid II, known as the 'Bloody Sultan'. In a military career in which he reached the rank of captain, Ahmet Refik began working as a teacher, mainly of history but also of geography and French (which, like many of the Ottoman intelligentsia, he spoke and wrote flawlessly), in the military colleges of Constantinople.

During the First World War, apparently with the protection of Enver Pasha, he remained in the capital because of a serious illness and served as a secret service officer in the intelligence branch of the War Ministry. Because of his familiarity with the Ottoman archives, in 1918 he was posted to Darülfünun—the precursor of Istanbul University, opened in Constantinople in 1869—where he became professor of Turkish history the following year. Sent to investigate in Anatolia during the trial of the Unionists that same year, he published *Two Committees, Two Massacres* (in Turkish, Istanbul, 1919), in which he wrote—as Taner Akçam writes in *A Shameful Act*—that the gangs of the Special Organization 'were composed of murderers and thieves who had been released from incarceration' and that during the Armenian atrocities it was 'these gangs who perpetrated the greatest crimes'. The Special Organization was indeed made up of criminals who had been released from prison and issued with army uniforms, who were then sent to the regions through which the deportation marches would pass, to mount ambushes intended to decimate them. As Ahmet Refik also noted, 'the annihilation of the Armenians had become one of the national objectives of the Unionists', who 'planned, by means of the annihilation policy, to avoid carrying out reforms in the six eastern provinces, and to solve the Armenian "problem" at its root'.

In 1925, two years after he proclaimed the Turkish Republic, Mustafa Kemal appointed Ahmet Refik as head of the Turkish History Committee, and in 1932 he took part in its first history conference. The following year, Kemal reorganized and officially transformed Darülfünun into the University of Istanbul, after the European model. Ahmet Refik was 'discharged' from his duties, probably because he would have found it impossible, on either a scholarly or an ethical level, to be part of the reinvention of the Turkish past that Atatürk had undertaken, from the creation of the Turkish History Institute in 1931 and the Turkish Language Institute in 1932.

As Hamit Bozarslan observes:

> After half a dozen history and language conferences, these two institutions were able to go further and construct the Turkish History Thesis and the Sun Language Theory, the former providing 'irrefutable proof' of the Turkish origins of humanity through all its civilizations, the latter asserting that all the world's languages were merely derivatives, necessarily corrupted, of the Turkish 'Sun' language.

Like a number of other academics at the time, who—as Bozarslan describes—lived in a kind of 'internal exile' and avoided academic conferences, or who did their best to work on relatively neutral subjects, Ahmet Refik had strong reservations about this rewriting of Turkish history. But when he found himself seated at the president's table, he was nonetheless obliged, in an ambience far removed from any scholarly ivory tower, to confess his 'ignorance' of history. This moment of weakness should be understood in the context of the enormous pressure that the new regime was putting on the intellectual elite of the new Turkey, and should not be allowed to obscure the courageous stand taken by Ahmet Refik. Impelled by love of his country and its history to oppose any form of falsification, however patriotic its intentions, he was forced to live out the rest of his life in modest circumstances, writing articles for various newspapers.

He leaves behind him the image of an impassioned historian who could write about the heyday of the Ottoman sultans with the greatest erudition but who was also able to share his passion through school textbooks and popular works. Through the honesty of his reporting and the integrity of his academic stance, Ahmet Refik Altınay may justifiably be described as a vector of the memory of the genocide and as one of the Righteous.

Sources and further reading

Studies

'Ahmet Refik Altinay', TDV, Islâm Ansiklopedisi, https://islamansiklopedisi.org.tr/ahmed-refik-altinay

Akçam, Taner, *A Shameful Act: The Armenian Genocide and the Question of Turkish Responsibility*, trans. Paul Bessemer, London: Constable, 2006, *passim*.

Bozarslan, Hamit, 'Le nationalisme kémaliste', in *Histoire de la Turquie contemporaine*, new edn, Paris: La Découverte, 2007, pp. 36–42.

Dadrian, Vahakn, *The History of the Armenian Genocide: Ethnic Conflict from the Balkans to Anatolia to the Caucasus*, Providence, RI: Berghahn Books, 1995, p. 392.

Gökman, Muzaffer, *L'homme qui aimait l'histoire* [in Turkish], Istanbul: n.p. 1978.

Tietze, Andreas, 'Ahmat Rafik', in Bearman et al., *Encyclopaedia of Islam*, 2nd edn, Leiden: Brill, 1991.

68

FRANZ WERFEL (1890–1945)

From Armenian resistance on Musa Dagh to Jewish resistance in the ghettos

Born into a Jewish family in Prague in 1890, Franz Werfel was drafted into the Austro-Hungarian army during the First World War. In 1917, he began an affair with Alma Mahler, widow of Gustav Mahler and wife of Walter Gropius, whom he would marry in 1929. After Hitler's annexation of Austria in the Anschluss of 1938, the couple fled Austria to seek refuge in France. There they lived in a fishing village near Marseille until 1940, when they escaped over the Pyrenees to Spain and Portugal before sailing to New York. On the way, they were given shelter in the pilgrimage town of Lourdes, and in gratitude he wrote *The Song of Bernadette*, which tells the story of the local girl Bernadette Soubirous, canonized in 1933. Published in 1941, and a year later in English translation, it was an immediate bestseller and was adapted into a hugely successful film by Henry King in 1943.

As the Israeli historian Yair Auron explains in his book *The Hundred Years of Musa Dagh*, originally published in Hebrew and in French translation in 2018, Werfel was one of a large group of German-Jewish artists and writers, writing in German, who were active in the period from 1875 to the late 1930s and played a crucial role in the flourishing of German culture. The rise of the Nazis put an end to this symbiotic relationship, in which outstanding intellectuals including Marx and Kafka, Freud and Einstein questioned the nature of their Jewishness.

According to Meyer Weisgal, the Zionist activist who conceived and directed *The Eternal Road*, an opera-drama tracing the

4,000-year history of the Jewish people, for which Kurt Weill wrote the music and Werfel the libretto, Werfel had confided to him in 1934 that the Armenians were his 'surrogate Jews' because of his questions about his own origins. From a mysticism close to Hasidism, Werfel did not in the end move towards Catholicism. At his death in 1945, his planned novel about the destiny of the Jews remained unwritten.

Werfel's first visit to Palestine in 1925 came as something of a shock: he distanced himself from his roots while at the same finding a deep interest in the Zionist experience. Alma meanwhile struggled to find anything of the ambience of life in Vienna, in which she played such a prominent part, in Eretz Yisrael (Mandatory Palestine). Werfel had earlier steeped himself in Jewish culture, but while acknowledging his Jewish humanity he called himself a Christian in spirit (his tragedy *Paul among the Jews* was published in 1926).

It was during a second journey to the Middle East, on a visit to a carpet factory in Damascus in March 1929, that Werfel was forcibly struck by the tragedy of the Armenian people and as a direct result conceived his great novel *The Forty Days of Musa Dagh*, as he wrote in the book's epilogue: 'The miserable sight of maimed and famished-looking refugee children, working in a carpet factory, gave me the final impulse to snatch the incomprehensible destiny of the Armenian people from the Hell of all that had taken place.'

In that year, Werfel was given a precious crucifix by Yeghishe Tourian, Armenian patriarch of Jerusalem, as a token of gratitude for his empathy with the Armenian tragedy. He kept it to the end of his life, and it is now preserved in the church of the Mekhitarist Congregation in Vienna, with whom Werfel spent several months in 1932 studying documents relating to the Armenian genocide.

Completed at a hectic pace, *The Forty Days of Musa Dagh* was published in 1933, when Hitler had just come to power as chancellor. According to Yair Auron, the official SS newspaper, *Der Schwarze Korps*, described Werfel as an enemy who had 'concocted atrocities committed by the Turks against the Armenians'. The book was banned in Germany, and in 1934 Werfel's works were burned. When *Forty Days* was published in the United States in that same year, it sold 34,000 copies within a fortnight. The following year, pressure from the Turkish government—which 'denounced' Werfel's Jewish background—forced the Hollywood film studio MGM to abandon plans to adapt the novel as a feature film. The first reference to the book in print came in an article written by the Armenian bishop of Bucharest and future Catholicos of All Armenians, Vazken I. Soon *The Forty Days of Musa Dagh* was to have a major impact on the Jewish youth of Eretz Yisrael, and on those in Europe who were about to be dragged into the inferno of the Holocaust.

Foreshadowing the fate of the ghettos of Europe, the novel appeared to have a prophetic quality. The following account is based largely on the work of Yair Auron.

The Forty Days of Musa Dagh tells the story of the Armenians who lived in villages on the slopes of Musa Dagh on the Gulf of Alexandretta, who fought back against the Young Turk government's plans to deport them—the true aim of which was their destruction, following the arrest of the Armenian elite of Constantinople on 24 April 1915. In July 1915, they took refuge, young and old, women and men, and mounted a desperate resistance on Musa Dagh (the Mountain of Moses). Against all the odds and repeated onslaughts from a Turkish army that was vastly superior in manpower and weaponry, they managed to resist for over forty days, until they were eventually rescued by the French fleet.

Behind Gabriel Bagradian, the hero of the novel and leader of the resistance, stands a real person, Movsês Der Kaloustian (1885–1984), a former officer in the Ottoman army, then a member of the Armenian Revolutionary Federation, who organized the self-defence of his compatriots. After their evacuation by the French navy, he served in the Légion d'Orient, later the Armenian Legion, was appointed district prefect in the *sanjak* of Alexandretta after the abandonment of the French mandate in Cilicia (1918–21) by the Henry Franklin-Bouillon government, and served again in the French army from 1939 to 1942. Elected to the Lebanese Parliament, Der Kaloustian worked on the development of the village of Anjar, in the Bekaa Valley in Lebanon, a community that he had founded for his fellow Armenians from Musa Dagh. He and his wife are buried there. The Armenians of Musa Dagh also had a spiritual leader, Pastor Dikran Andreassian, who left an account of the epic events in *Comment un drapeau sauva quatre mille Arméniens* (How a flag saved 4,000 Armenians; Paris, 1916).

It comes as a surprise to discover, as Auron points out, that in 1933, on the eve of the banning of *The Forty Days of Musa Dagh* and the burning of his books, Werfel was a candidate for the Nazi-supporting Writers' Union in Berlin. Did he take this step as a means of preserving his work, in particular *The Forty Days of Musa Dagh*, which could be read to suggest parallels between the Young Turk programme and Nazi ideology? Or, more shockingly, was he seeking to distance himself from Judaism? Given that the passion that burned within Werfel and fed his determination to publish his novel was to fan the flames of resistance among Jewish fighters in the ghettos ten years later, Auron argues persuasively for the former hypothesis.

Franz Werfel died in Los Angeles in 1945 and was buried there. In 1975, an American academic of Armenian heritage, Vartan Gregorian, together with a Jewish colleague at the University of Pennsylvania, Adolf Klarmann, arranged for his body to be repatriated to Vienna, where it was interred in the Central Cemetery. The grave was blessed by the Armenian bishop of Vienna.

Auron describes the reactions in Eretz Yisrael to the translation of *The Forty Days of Musa Dagh* into Hebrew—largely positive, owing to the parallels between the fates of the Armenians and the Jews, but also negative owing to their differences, in that the Jews were almost universally ostracized, while the Armenians were rejected only by the Ottomans. The fiercest criticism came only after the Holocaust, however, when Werfel was accused by some—wrongly, in Auron's view—of having become one of the 'enemies' of the Jews by distancing himself from them.

Nonetheless, Werfel's novel was to serve as an inspiration for Jews in their resistance to the Nazis, in Palestine and especially in Europe. In 1942, fearing a German invasion, which they planned to resist from Mount Carmel, Palestinian Jews devised a defence plan that they called the 'Carmel Plan', the 'Masada Plan' (in memory of the Jewish resistance to the Roman army in 70–3) or the 'Musa Dagh Plan', as they feared suffering the same fate as the Armenians in 1915. But it was in the ghettos of Central Europe, above all, that Werfel's novel fired the spirit of resistance. In 1943, a Jew in the Białystok ghetto in Poland declared: 'There is only one possibility left to us, to organize a collective resistance in the ghetto, whatever the price; to see the ghetto as our Musa Dagh.' And Pesya Mayevska described how in a ghetto in Belarus, 'Franz Werfel's book was circulating everywhere at that time, telling of the heroic uprising of a group of Armenians during the Turkish massacres.' The celebrated literary critic Marcel Ranicki, a survivor of the Warsaw ghetto, testified that Werfel's novel had been 'an unexpected success in the ghetto, where it was passed from hand to hand'. The book also influenced Jewish resistance movements in Western Europe. According to a 1997 study, the adult books that were most widely read in the ghettos were *The Forty Days of Musa Dagh* and Tolstoy's *War and Peace*. Werfel's novel was all the easier to read because it had been translated into Yiddish by 1938.

The memory of Musa Dagh was revived when the survivors of the Holocaust undertook the hazardous journey to Palestine, and their ships sailed across the Gulf of Alexandretta and past Musa Dagh. Yossi Harel, captain of the *Exodus* in 1947, was overwhelmed during an earlier mission in 1946, when through the winter night he made out the outline of Musa Dagh, which for him immediately evoked images of a visit he had made to Masada.

At a rally at the Armenian Memorial in Jerusalem in 2015, the Israeli minister of education, Yossi Sarid, was honoured to announce that *The Forty Days of Musa Dagh* would be included in the school curriculum. In doing this he risked his post, which he lost shortly afterwards, as the Israeli government chose to deny the Armenian genocide, thereby weakening the memory of the Holocaust, rather than compromise its relations with Turkey.

However, combining ethics with realism, on 4 November 2019 the *Jerusalem Post* declared that the time had finally come to give official recognition to the Armenian genocide, as Turkish–Israeli relations had deteriorated and the US House of Representatives had recently voted in favour of recognition of the genocide.

In his foreword to *Les cent ans du Musa Dagh*, Auron lays stress on the prophetic nature of *The Forty Days of Musa Dagh*:

> Although I was reading a book about the Armenian genocide, there were many passages where I had the impression that it was talking about the Jewish Holocaust. There were many ways in which I

found it hard to believe that this story was written before the Holocaust, rather than afterwards.

Sources and further reading

Studies

Auron, Yaïr, *Les cent ans du Musa Dagh: Découvertes et nouveaux regards sur l'ouvrage Les Quarante jours du Musa Dagh*, Paris: Éditions Sigest, 2018.

Jungk, Peter Stephan, *Franz Werfel: A Life in Prague, Vienna and Hollywood*, New York: Fromm International Publishing, 1991.

Kiuciukian, Pietro, 'Franz Werfel', in *Voci nel deserto*, pp. 42–65.

Lafon, Jean-Marc, 'Franz Werfel et le génocide arménien: Pertinence d'un regard, prophétie d'un discours', in Asso, Demirdjian and Louvier, *Exprimer le génocide des Arméniens*, pp. 101–11.

Malkhassian, Gérard, 'Interprétation d'une œuvre littéraire partagée, Les 40 jours du Moussa Dagh, de Franz Werfel', *Arméniens, Juifs vieilles connaissances, Israël, Arménie, le rendez-vous manqué, Résonamces*, special edition of *Nouvelles d'Arménie Magazine*, 3 (2021), pp. 68–73.

69

FRIDTJOF NANSEN (1861–1930)

Polymath who devoted his exceptional talents to aiding survivors of the genocide expelled by Turkey and all stateless peoples

The plight of the Armenian refugees

Born in Norway in 1861, Fridtjof Nansen initially gained renown as an intrepid Arctic explorer, record-breaking athlete and hugely gifted zoologist and research scientist. Later in life, he also played a key role in the fate of thousands of survivors of the Armenian genocide who had been left homeless, helpless and hopeless. In the 1920s, thousands of Armenians who had survived the deportation marches were still scattered in the countries around Turkey, including Russian Armenia, Iran and Syria, without any clear idea of where their future lay.

Outraged by their fate, Nansen, who in 1921 was appointed high commissioner for refugees by the League of Nations, did everything in his power to find legitimate ways to improve the conditions of the Armenian survivors of what he described as 'humanity's greatest tragedy'. In the preface to his book *Armenia and the Near East*, published in English in 1928, he declared that he could not imagine how anyone could remain unmoved by the fate of the Armenians:

> I feel sure that no one can study the story of this remarkable people without being profoundly moved by their tragic fate. In spite of a disheartening consciousness of the defects in my presentation of their case, I hope that the facts themselves will speak from these pages to the conscience of Europe and America.

THE RIGHTEOUS AND PEOPLE OF CONSCIENCE

Nansen occupies a special place in this period following the genocide: it is no coincidence that Armenia now has schools and streets named after him, for his courage and compassion remain a continuing source of inspiration for millions. A pioneer in many fields, Nansen left a significant mark on history.

Scientific training and exploration

Nansen's family background and education were clearly a formative influence on his worldview. His father, Baldur Nansen, was a lawyer and reporter to the Norwegian Supreme Court. His mother, Adelaide Wedel-Jarlsberg, was the niece of the Swedish king's Norwegian viceroy, who had helped draft the Norwegian Constitution of 1814. Fridtjof spent his childhood with his parents in rural Store Frøen and Christiania, later Oslo. As Roland Huntford observes in his biography of Nansen, the rural character of Store Frøen was a major influence on Nansen's childhood and his future choices. He excelled at sports and loved nature, while his studies took second place. It was a childhood that developed a marked degree of self-reliance in the young Fridtjof.

In 1881, Nansen enrolled at the Royal Frederick University in Christiania to study zoology. After working in the field in the Arctic seas, he chose to specialize in the relatively new field of neuroanatomy, and more specifically the study of the central nervous system of lower marine animals. Through his conclusions, published in a number of journals, Nansen became a co-founder of modern neuron theory. Like his compatriot and contemporary Roald Amundsen, who perished on a rescue mission in the Arctic in 1928, Nansen was a great and intrepid explorer: after crossing Greenland in 1888, he explored the Arctic by using polar drift in his specially constructed ship, *Fram*, setting off in 1893 and returning in triumph in 1895 after an epic polar trek by sledge to reach a record farthest north latitude.

Entry into political and diplomatic life

On his return from the *Fram* expedition, Nansen embarked on a brilliantly successful political and diplomatic career. From 1905, supported by the Norwegian people, he was involved in the separation of Norway from Sweden and held successful negotiations with Prince Charles of Denmark to persuade him to accept the throne of the newly independent Norway. This was to be the beginning of a career as diplomat and statesman, at a time of extreme tension on the eve of the First World War. From 1906 to 1908, Nansen worked with European ambassadors in London to draw up a treaty that would fully guarantee Norway's independent status under a monarchical regime, with Prince Charles of Denmark chosen by referendum as Haakon VII (1905–57).

High commissioner for refugees and Nobel laureate

After the war, the League of Nations (forerunner of the United Nations, which was established in 1945) was founded by the Paris Peace Conference on 10 January 1920 and was based in Geneva from 1920 to 1946. Nansen devoted his energies to the League from the outset, transforming the lives of thousands of people through his tireless work, and gaining the support of Norway and the other Scandinavian countries. That same year, the Norwegian government appointed Nansen as a delegate to the League, a position he held until his death in 1930. There can be no doubt that Nansen saw the organization as a new beacon of hope for humanity.

In 1921, Nansen was appointed the first high commissioner for refugees. Post-war Europe was about to find itself at a particularly difficult juncture, as it had to find a way to define the status of the 1.5 million Russians who had fled the Soviet regime after the October Revolution and whose nationality had been revoked by Lenin in 1922. To describe their predicament, jurists coined the term 'stateless'.

Under the 1922 decree, Russians living outside the country were required to recognize the new regime and register at a Soviet consulate within three months, failing which they would be stripped of their citizenship. This unprecedented move led to the first undocumented migrant problem in Europe. In addition to the tragic position of thousands of prisoners of war, the problems of Russians who had had their property confiscated and suffered persecution had to be dealt with—and all this amid the early stages of a famine that was to prove catastrophic.

THE RIGHTEOUS AND PEOPLE OF CONSCIENCE

The League of Nations chose Nansen to lead the rapid repatriation or resettlement of Russians living outside their homeland. Faced with the need to repatriate hundreds of thousands of refugees, Nansen sought to obtain a legal status for them that would not only ensure their protection but also enable them to support themselves. In his article 'Le passeport Nansen, première protection des réfugiés dans l'histoire du droit international' (The Nansen Passport, the first protection for refugees in the history of international law), Jean-Pierre Dubois argues that Nansen was the first to understand that one of the most pressing and very real issues for refugees was the fact that they had no internationally valid documents proving their identity or nationality, which meant they were unable to apply for asylum or cross national borders. As high commissioner for refugees for the League of Nations, Nansen led an inter-governmental conference on identity documents for Russian refugees who had been forced to flee their country after the civil war, and as part of this initiative he assembled a team of stateless Russian jurists to consider the rights and duties that should be attached to these documents.

In 1922, in recognition of this work, Nansen was awarded the Nobel Peace Prize. The citation referred to 'his work for the repatriation of the prisoners of war, his work for the Russian refugees, his work to bring succour to the millions of Russians afflicted by famine, and finally his present work for the refugees in Asia Minor and Thrace'.

The 'Nansen Passport'

Working with his team, Nansen created what would become known as the 'Nansen Passport', which for the first time provided international legal protection for stateless refugees and enabled them to cross borders. By as early as 1924, this document had received recognition from some forty states. Thanks to it, Russian refugees were able to travel to Paris, Berlin, New York and even Shanghai, where they presented themselves to Russian Refugee Committees with their 'passports', valid for one year and renewable for life.

Initially created for Russian refugees, the Nansen Passport was extended to include Armenians, among other groups, by the Geneva

Convention of 1933. After the genocide of 1915, the Armenians had been driven into the Syrian desert without any protection or support. Nansen had fiercely criticized Turkey on more than one occasion, notably in several passages in *Armenia and the Near East*:

> Then, in June 1915, the horrors began to which we know no parallel in history. From all the villages and towns of Cilicia, Anatolia, and Mesopotamia the Armenian Christians were driven forth on their death march; the work was done systematically, clearing out one district after another, whether the population happened to be near the scene of war or hundreds of kilometres away from it. There was to be a clean sweep of all Armenians.

Some 300,000 Armenian survivors of the massacres were left homeless and without any documentation. These refugees could not return to Turkey, nor did they have their own national state. Deeply concerned about the fate of the Armenians, Nansen was tireless in his efforts to find legitimate solutions to this crisis.

Arguing their cause with impassioned conviction, he initially sought to set up an irrigation system in the Mesopotamian desert to which the Armenians had been deported. At the Paris Peace Conference (January 1919–January 1920), the Armenian national delegation and the delegation of the Republic of Armenia (1918–20) demanded recognition, in a memorandum of 12 February 1919, of 'an independent Armenian State, formed by the union of the seven vilayets and Cilicia with the territories of the Republic of the Caucasus'.

The refugee settlement programme in Soviet Armenia

After the failure of the proposed American mandate on Armenia, Nansen's objective became the creation of a national home for refugees within the borders of the Republic of Armenia, where the Soviets had seized power in December 1920. As head of the commission for repatriation of the Armenians from 1925 to 1929, Nansen did everything possible to facilitate the return of refugees to what was now Soviet Armenia. He headed a visiting delegation to Armenia and, with the support of the Soviet authorities and the help of the International Red Cross and Near East Relief, was able to carry out an investigation in Yerevan. Thanks to the brilliant reputation he had earned through his scientific work, Nansen was welcomed to Armenia and shown the highest honours by the Soviet authorities. Wherever they went, the delegates were welcomed by Armenians of all social backgrounds with an extraordinary degree of hospitality, and Nansen was impressed by how they had managed to create order and even comfort out of chaos, poverty and hunger. But amid the magnificence of the landscapes and the generosity of the refugees he met, he was constantly aware of their sufferings, as he described in *Armenia and the Near East*:

> Away in the south Mount Ararat could be clearly seen in all its tremendous height, its broad cupola of snow shining brightly in the sunset. ... And past us trooped a never-ending pageant of the changing fortunes of bygone generations who lived on these self-same plains under the shadow of Ararat and Alagoz. So many wars and struggles, such dire straits, so much suffering and misery over and over again—and so seldom a victory. ... Has any people in any part of the world suffered as this one has done? And to what end?

On its return, the commission drew up a report that recommended the settlement in Yerevan of some 25,000 Armenian workers, mostly from Constantinople and with a minority from Greece. However, in order to put this plan into action, the report pointed out, the necessary funds would have to be raised. The Soviet government supported Nansen's proposal but insisted that since the country was still ravaged by the aftermath of revolution and civil war, it was essential that it should receive economic support. Nansen stressed this point in his report, pointing out that since so many promises around the Armenian question had not been honoured, it was the moral duty of European countries to provide material aid. He was convinced that, if aid was implemented in a rigorous fashion, Soviet Armenia would be able to take in some 25–30,000 refugees.

When the League of Nations refused to provide any financial aid, Nansen was scathing in his response:

> The nations of Europe and the statesmen of Europe are tired of the everlasting Armenian question. Of course. It has only brought them one defeat after another, the very mention of it recalling to their slumbering consciences a grim tale of broken or unfulfilled promises

which they have never in practice done anything to keep. And after all, it was only a massacred, but gifted little nation, with no oil-fields or gold-mines.

A fresh appeal by Nansen in 1927 elicited a more positive response from the member countries of the League of Nations. In 1928, he was able to settle 7,000 refugees in Armenia. But a 1929 agreement by which a further 12,000 Armenians were be settled in the country was eventually annulled, a bitter disappointment that drove Nansen to demand that the League should cease to take part in these repatriation operations. Already in Geneva in 1927 he had lamented that when it came to carrying out the promises made to the Armenian survivors, 'Nothing has been done, absolutely nothing.'

Nansen embarked on tours and wrote reports, not only to raise state funds but also to try to secure donations from private benefactors. In 1928, he embarked on a lecture tour of the United States, and in that year he managed to raise enough money to launch his modest project.

He also successfully petitioned the League of Nations to grant the Armenians the same rights to Nansen Passports as Russian stateless refugees. Since France had a mandate over regions—in particular Lebanon—that were home to thousands of Armenians, many of the survivors set sail for Marseille.

Nansen devoted numerous articles, reports and speeches to the Armenian people and Armenia, and in 1927 his book *Gjennem Armenia* was published in Norwegian and soon translated into English (as *Armenia and the Near East*), French and German. He continued to condemn the failures of Western governments:

> But the Young Turks have done what they set out to do; they have wiped out the Armenian population of Anatolia, and can say with Tala'at Pasha that the Armenian question *n'existe plus*. No European or American Government or statesman troubles now about what has happened; to them the everlasting Armenian problem seems finally and definitely obliterated in blood.

In conclusion, he offered a bitter lament: 'Woe to the Armenians, that they were ever drawn into European politics! It would have been better for them if the name of Armenia had never been uttered by any European diplomatist.'

THE RIGHTEOUS AND PEOPLE OF CONSCIENCE

After Nansen's death in 1930, the League of Nations established the Nansen International Office for Refugees in his honour, which in 1938 was awarded the Nobel Peace Prize. In 1954, the United Nations High Commissioner for Refugees established the Nansen Refugee Award, to be granted annually to 'those who have gone beyond the call of duty, who have demonstrated perseverance and courage, and who have personally, directly and significantly helped forcibly displaced people'. The award is bestowed by the governments of Norway and Switzerland, and laureates—the first of whom was Eleanor Roosevelt—receive the Nansen Medal and a prize of $150,000.

A great and faithful friend to the Armenian people, Nansen never gave up hope that the refugees would find a national home. Following the failure of his plan to return Armenian refugees to Soviet Armenia, he withdrew from the League of Nations. Despite this failure, he is still remembered in Armenia with the highest respect.

Fridtjof Nansen was awarded many honours and recognitions in his lifetime; in death, he was honoured with a state funeral.

Sources and further reading

Sources

Nansen, Fridtjof, *Armenia and the Near East*, London, George Allen & Unwin Ltd, 1931 [New York: J. C. & A. L. Fawcett, 1928].

'Scheme for the Settlement of Armenian Refugees: General Survey and Principal Documents', League of Nations, 1927.

Studies

Dubois, Jean-Pierre, 'Le "passeport Nansen", première protection des réfugiés dans l'histoire du droit international', *Après-demain*, 3, no. 39 (2016).

'Fridtjof Nansen (1861–1930)', Global Armenian Heritage, http://www.globalarmenianheritage-adic.fr/fr/6histoire/a_d/20_nansen.htm

Huntford, Roland, *Nansen: The Explorer as Hero*, London: Abacus, 2001.

Kévorkian, Raymond H., Lévon Nordiguian and Vahé Tachjian, *Les Arméniens, 1917–1939, la quête d'un refuge*, Beirut: Presses de l'Université Saint-Joseph, 2006.

FRIDTJOF NANSEN (1861–1930)

Kiuciukian, *Voci nel Deserto*, pp. 139–57.

Minassian, Anahide Ter, 'Le Sénat américain refuse un mandat sur l'Arménie', in *L'échiquier arménien entre guerres et révolutions, 1878–1920*, Paris: Karthala, 2015, pp. 213–24.

'Un Passeport pour les apatrides', http://aigueperse.spf63.org/pdf/histoire1922_Le_passeport_Nansen.pdf

Scott, J. M. *Fridtjof Nansen*, London: Heron Books, 1971.

Tachjian, Vahé, 'L'établissement définitif des réfugiés arméniens au Liban dans les années 1920 et 1930', in Aïda Boudjikanian (ed.), *Les Arméniens du Liban: Des Princesses et des Réfugiés du Passé à la Communauté contemporaine*, Beirut: Haigazian University and Armenian Heritage Press, 2009, pp. 59–76.

Willy, Nethanel, *Passeport Nansen*, n.p.: Culp Press, 2012.

EPILOGUE

THE RIGHTEOUS, AVENGERS AND BRINGERS OF JUSTICE

70

THE TRIALS OF THE YOUNG TURKS

In the immediate aftermath of the Great War, when many of the criminals among the Young Turks had fled and were on the run, debates on war crimes opened in the Ottoman Parliament. Now that the Ottoman Empire found itself on the losing side, Ottoman MPs were keen to dissociate the Turkish nation as a whole from the war criminals. The ministers of the Young Turk government who appeared before parliament attempted to exonerate themselves, to justify the crimes that had been committed and, if they had not been in office at the time, to cover up for their colleagues. By imperial decree of 21 November 1918, a commission of inquiry was set up, headed by Hasan Mazhar, one of the 'Righteous' whose courageous actions are discussed on pp. 99–103, to investigate the crimes that had been committed. The brief of the Mazhar Commission was to establish the extent of responsibility of civil servants and the government in the massacres of the Armenians. One hundred and thirty prosecution case files were duly drawn up and transmitted to the courts martial.

A series of trials was held in 1919–20, by imperial command, and some CUP leaders and ministers were arrested. Most of those responsible for the massacres of the Armenian people were already on the run, however, or on the island of Malta, where the British—fearing that the Turks could not be trusted to try their own or imprison them securely—had imprisoned them.

The trials took place in Constantinople. While some of the accused were acquitted, many others were found guilty and sentenced to exile, prison or death, often in absentia. Thus Talaat Pasha, Enver Pasha, Cemal Pasha and Dr Nazım, the chief instigators of the genocide, were sentenced to death in absentia by the Constantinople court, as were Cemal Azmi Bey, Nail Bey and the infamous Dr Şakir.

Most of the other sentences could not be carried out either, as the criminals had fled outside the borders of the Ottoman Empire. Thus while justice was served on a symbolic level, in practice the crimes went unpunished, especially as the new government failed to press for extradition of the criminals and subsequently even annulled some of the verdicts.

Nevertheless, the trials and the evidence presented at them occupy a place of critical importance in the historiography of the genocide, providing a fairly accurate picture and incontrovertible evidence of the extermination plan put in place by the CUP.

Sources and further reading

Studies

Akçam, *Shameful Act*, pp. 393–424.

de Garine, Marc, *Le recyclage des crimineles jeunes-turcs: Permanence des acteurs, persistance des sentiments hostiles et continuité des structures de l'Empire ottoman à la République de Turquie*, Paris: Éditions SIGEST, 2019.

Kévorkian, *Armenian Genocide*, pp. 885–975.

Nichanian, Mikaël, *Détruire les Arméniens*, Paris: PUF, 2014, pp. 206–25.

71

SOGHOMON TEHLIRIAN (1896–1960)

Avenger of the Armenians

A 'crime' absolved by German justice

On 5 March 1921, a twenty-one-year-old Armenian called Soghomon Tehlirian shot and killed a man in a Berlin street, in broad daylight and in front of numerous witnesses. The assassin made no attempt to escape and was arrested on the spot by the police. His victim proved to be carrying a Turkish passport in the name of Ali Salih Bey. But his real identity was soon revealed. This was Talaat Pasha, the former Ottoman grand vizier who had led the government of the Sublime Porte during the First World War, and the minister of the interior who in 1915 had been the chief architect of the Armenian genocide. This was the man who had boasted that he had 'done more to solve the Armenian problem in three months than Sultan Abdul Hamid in thirty years', and whom a court martial two years earlier had sentenced to death in absentia.

When Tehlirian was brought to trial a few months later, events took an unexpected turn. Instead of condemning the defendant, the court hearings established Talaat Pasha's guilt as instigator of the Armenian genocide. The trial was to prove of seminal importance, not only in gaining recognition for the atrocities committed at the instigation of the Young Turks, but also in the revolution it was to bring about in international law. What the courtroom did not know, however, was that Tehlirian was not the student he claimed to be.

THE RIGHTEOUS AND PEOPLE OF CONSCIENCE

Discovery of the genocide in the footsteps of the Russian army

An Ottoman subject, Soghomon Tehlirian was born on 2 April 1896 in the village of Nerkin Bagarij in the *vilayet* of Erzurum. Life was hard for his father Khatchadur and his mother, Henazant Katerdjian, daughter of a priest, Der Haroutioun, because of the scarcity of cultivable land for Armenian peasants. To survive, the men were forced to emigrate to the Balkans and work there for a few years, and his father and uncle duly left for Serbia. In 1913, a family friend, Sahag Boloyan, helped the rest of the family to move to the town of Yerznka (Erzincan), where Soghomon had attended the Protestant school in 1905–6, followed by the Central College until 1911.

In the autumn of 1913, aged seventeen, Soghomon went to join his father in Belgrade, where he continued his studies in mechanical engineering. But his studies were interrupted by the outbreak of war in 1914, when he went to Tiflis (Tbilisi), capital of Georgia.

In June 1915, the local Ottoman police in Yerznka ordered the deportation of all Armenians from the town. Unaware that his mother, three sisters, two brothers and other family members had been deported, Tehlirian would learn only later of the atrocities to which his family had been subjected.

When the Russian army recaptured Erzurum in 1916, some Armenian volunteers were able to go back there. It was in this period of confusion, when a few survivors of the genocide started to come back and put notices in newspapers in the hope of finding other survivors from their families, that Tehlirian—who was then working to help resettle orphans in the Caucasus during the Russian retreat—learned the truth of what had happened. From then on, the testimonies of survivors of the genocide would not cease to haunt him.

Now he also learned the details of the events of 24 April 1915 in Constantinople, when hundreds of Armenian intellectuals had been arrested, tortured and murdered. And in August of that year, the poets Daniel Varoujan, Rupen Sevag (who had published his *Red Book* after the Adana massacres) and Siamanto (Atom Yarchanian), whose work meant a great deal to him, had all been tortured and killed.

Tehlirian began to look for ways to go back to Yerznka to find his family. First he joined up with Andranik's volunteer battalion, then

SOGHOMON TEHLIRIAN (1896–1960)

he set off for Yerznka with some irregular Armenian troops. It was under the command of the famous Armenian military commander Sebouh (whose real name was Arshag Nersesian), that he reached Yerznka, there to discover the full extent of the crimes committed against the Armenians. The Armenian quarter where he had spent his childhood lay in ruins, and no trace remained of his family. The family house had been abandoned and converted into a barracks of sorts. It was there, in the devastated garden, that he experienced his first vision of the decapitated corpse of his mother and the dismembered remains of his brothers and sisters-in-law. The testimonies of the massacres that he heard were unbearable, and his health—both physical and emotional—was severely affected.

Between the village of Bagarij and the town of Yerznka, the Tehlirian family had numbered eighty-five members. After the genocide, with the exception of a handful of family members who were abroad, only his elder brother's daughter Armenouhi would be found alive, living with a Kurdish family. His mother, his two older brothers and their wives, and his brother Avedis—a medical student at the American University of Beirut who was home for the holidays—had all been massacred. Only his father and his brothers Missak and Setrak, who were living in Serbia, had survived.

'Operation Nemesis'

Tehlirian spent six weeks in Yerznka before going on to Tiflis, where he stayed for two years, until 1919. In February 1919, he left for Constantinople, where he stayed for two months before moving on to Salonika, then Serbia, then back to Salonika. In early 1920, he arrived in Paris, where he lived for ten months, before moving on to Geneva, where he obtained a visa to go to Berlin.

His nights were haunted by nightmares of the genocide, so vivid that it seemed to him that he had experienced it himself, although in fact he had left home before the war to study in Europe. At the same time, he was shocked to learn that the perpetrators and criminals behind the atrocities, including the main instigator, Talaat Pasha, had fled. Tried by court martial and sentenced to death in absentia, he and other organizers of the genocide had taken refuge abroad, aided by the Germans. Talaat was in hiding in Berlin, where—Tehlirian discovered—he was living at 4 Hardenbergstrasse under the name Ali Salih Bey.

Outraged by this impunity, the Armenian Revolutionary Federation (ARF) set up a 'special mission' for justice and organized a plan that it called 'Operation Nemesis', orchestrated by Shahan Natalie. The goal of this mission was to carry out the sentences of the Ottoman courts martial that had been handed down in absentia. Tehlirian, a member of the ARF, was assigned to the assassination of Talaat in Berlin. But before he could be entrusted with a mission of such importance, he had to prove his courage and determination by shooting an Armenian who had betrayed his own people. Haroutioun Meguerditchian had worked as an agent for Talaat Pasha, and it was he who had supplied the names of the Armenian intellectuals who would be arrested on 24 April 1915 and subsequently deported and executed.

After locating where Meguerditchian was living thanks to the young Yeranouhi Danielian, a schoolteacher he had met at the editorial offices of the Dashnak newspaper *Djagadamard* (Combat), Tehlirian staked out the building for several months before taking advantage of a party there to shoot Meguerditchian dead through a window.

From February to April 1919, Tehlirian was in Constantinople, where, following the Yozgat trial, Mehmet Kemal Bey was hanged on 10 April, and where he learned that Talaat Pasha had been condemned to death. It was by chance that he spotted Talaat in Berlin, five weeks before the murder, walking with two other men along the street leading to the zoological gardens. Tehlirian heard the three men talking in Turkish. Turning round, he recognized Talaat Pasha. He followed the three men to a cinema, where one of them left the other two, kissing Talaat's hand and addressing him as 'Pasha'. Under questioning at his trial, Tehlirian told the court that during this encounter the idea of killing Talaat had not occurred to him. He had felt unwell, and images of the massacre had flooded back to him. It was about two weeks before the murder that the idea took shape. Thus it was that, on 15 March 1921, Talaat Pasha, one of the most notorious criminals in history, was shot and killed in a Berlin street by Soghomon Tehlirian.

SOGHOMON TEHLIRIAN (1896–1960)

Towards a political trial

Tehlirian was not just meting out justice: he had willingly allowed himself to be arrested in order to draw attention to the genocide. He did not deny the facts, and the German jurors discovered that the motive for his crime was another crime that was even more terrible: the destruction of an entire people by their former Ottoman ally. As Claire Mouradian noted in an interview: 'The murder trial was immediately turned into a political trial: now it was the murder "victim", Talaat Pasha, who was found responsible for the death of more than a million people.'

As proceedings unfolded at the Berlin Court of Assizes on 2 and 3 June 1921, widely covered by the international press, the trial took on every appearance of a political tribunal, with the Young Turk regime in the dock. When Tehlirian said, 'I do not consider myself guilty, because my conscience is clear. I killed a man, but I am not a murderer,' his striking declaration was widely quoted in the press and came to symbolize his claim to innocence. General Gollnick, counsel for the prosecution, repeatedly took the line that Talaat's memory should be honoured and the German–Turkish alliance celebrated; to this, one of the lawyers in Tehlirian's defence team, the internationally renowned Dr Theodor Niemeyer, professor of law at Kiel University, replied: 'During the war, the military authorities, here at home and over there [in the Ottoman Empire], drew a veil of silence over and covered up the horrors perpetrated against the Armenians in a manner that bordered on assent.'

Grigoris Balakian, Armin T. Wegner and Johannes Lepsius give evidence

A succession of defence witnesses took the stand to describe the atrocities perpetrated during the genocide and to offer evidence of the direct involvement of Talaat Pasha. The Armenian priest Grigoris Balakian (future Armenian bishop of Marseille responsible for the building of the Cathedral of the Holy Translators there) travelled from Manchester to give evidence. He had been arrested in Constantinople in the round-up of the Armenian elite on 24 April 1915 and—like the composer and musicologist Komitas (Soghomon Soghomonian)—was one of the few survivors of the subsequent deportation convoys. In his evidence, Balakian quoted the confidences of the chief gendarme on his convoy, Shukri Bey, who (convinced that Balakian would not survive to repeat his remarks) had revealed to him chilling details of the violence, scale and premeditated nature of the slaughter.

A telegram sent by Talaat Pasha and other documents held by the journalist Aram Andonian were presented as further evidence of his major role in organizing the genocide.

In addition to the testimony of Armenians who had been victims of or witnesses to the massacres and other atrocities, special weight was given to the evidence of expert witnesses Armin T. Wegner and Johannes Lepsius. As a medical orderly in the German army, Wegner had secretly taken hundreds of photographs of Armenian deportees and the death camps, powerful images that provided irrefutable proof of the horrors to which the Armenians had been subjected.

The German pastor Johannes Lepsius was a witness to the massacres and had published *Armenia and Europe* in 1896, a *Secret Report on the Situation of the Armenian People in Turkey* in 1916, and a seminally important collection of diplomatic acts, *Germany and Armenia 1914–1918*, in 1919. His evidence therefore carried particular weight. His address to the court was powerfully moving but also coolly reasoned and closely argued; refusing to 'play the part of accuser, lawyer or judge', he declared that he could 'best serve the truth' by 'allowing the documentary evidence to speak for itself'.

The sum of evidence offered to the court—whether written from Lepsius, photographic from Wegner or verbal from the other witnesses—clearly had a strong bearing on the ultimate outcome. It was reported that Tehlirian was deeply moved by the fact that Lepsius, who was not an Armenian, should put up such a powerful defence of the Armenian cause. And Boghos Nubar, chairman of the Armenian delegation to the Paris Peace Conference, afterwards wrote to Lepsius to thank him: 'The acquittal of our compatriot has proved once again that there are judges in Berlin, and I have no doubt that your intervention helped to enlighten and stir the conscience of all those who absolved Tehlirian.'

The court chose to lay the blame for the frenzy of the Armenian genocide on one individual, when it was in fact, as Patrick Clervoy writes in *L'Effet Lucifer: Des bourreaux ordinaires*, 'the result of mass collective behaviour, inspired by an ideology constructed over several decades and perpetrated by thousands of individuals'.

The strategy adopted by the defence lawyers was intriguing but risky. It was clearly impossible to deny that the crime had been committed, which meant that—however monstrous the victim's deeds—the court could not let the murderer walk free. The only strategy available to them was to highlight the emotional and psychological trauma Tehlirian had suffered, to plead compassion for the victims, and to focus attention on the events that had led to Talaat's murder.

Without attempting to deny that Tehlirian had carried out the killing, the defence therefore laid stress on the effects that the genocide had had on his psychological state, arguing that they had caused him to lose control when he saw Talaat. They pleaded manslaughter.

When the presiding judge asked Tehlirian when he had conceived the idea of killing Talaat Pasha, he replied:

> About two weeks earlier: I felt unwell, and the image of the massacre swam back before my eyes. I saw my mother's corpse. The corpse stood up, came towards me and said: 'You have seen that Talaat is here and you do not care? You are no longer my son!'

To the question 'How did you come to do this?', Tehlirian replied: 'Because my mother commanded me to.'

Three of the five expert medical witnesses found that Tehlirian was not responsible for his actions at the time of the killing, while the other two considered that he was still in possession of his free will. The neurologist Professor Richard Cassirer testified:

> The accused is a major psychopath, but he became so as a result of the worst trauma to the human nervous system that could be imagined. His morbid state overcame the scruples of conscience that would have stopped any man whose mind was not unbalanced. This also leads me to conclude that it was indeed a sequence of well-founded arguments that inspired thoughts of vengeance in the accused.

The medical experts were unanimous in concluding that Tehlirian had suffered epileptic seizures and that the hallucinations he had experienced—including the slaughter of his entire family, which he believed he had witnessed—had caused a major trauma to his nervous system.

Acquittal

When, after just an hour of deliberations, the foreman of the jury pronounced a verdict of not guilty, the courtroom burst into applause. Reporting in the German press was generally positive, as the trial had culminated in the implicit conviction of the architects of the Armenian genocide. In finding Tehlirian not guilty of Talaat's murder, the twelve German jurors had not only given de facto recognition to the historical reality of the systematic extermination of the Armenian people, but they had also endorsed the reality of the psychological trauma inflicted on Tehlirian by the massacre of his family.

The success of Tehlirian's action lay in the fact that it transformed his trial into a tribunal of investigation into a historic event. At the heart of the trial lay the genocide. The journalists who were reporting on the proceedings observed that it was not possible to condemn the murderer of a single individual when those who had ordered the deaths of several hundred thousand others were living in freedom.

Whatever the interpretation of the trial—and there have been many—there can be no doubt that it was an event of singular importance, and one that shone a light on the events suffered by the Armenian people in 1915. So intense was the interest aroused by the defence case, as argued by two of the most prominent members of the Berlin bar and one of Germany's leading jurists, that most of the other lawyers working at the Court of Assizes abandoned their own affairs and crowded into the public gallery.

The Tehlirian trial was and remains an event of critical importance, a valuable test case both in the way in which the defence presented its case and in the verdict of acquittal, which was to become a point of reference for future generations.

At his trial, Tehlirian did not deny the killing of Talaat, of which he clearly realized the full significance; during questioning by the presiding judge, he declared: 'Still today, I am very satisfied with what I did. In both its political and its legal ramifications, this was indeed a trial of very great importance.'

SOGHOMON TEHLIRIAN (1896–1960)

The Tehlirian trial was to prove a catalyst for the thinking of Polish-Jewish jurist Raphael Lemkin. German justice had exonerated the accused on the grounds of a psychological disorder provoked by a massacre, but it had not incriminated the instigators of the massacre. Seeking a way to criminalize such actions, aimed at the intentional destruction of national groups based on their collective identity (the subject of his 1933 report to the International Conference for the Unification of Criminal Law in Madrid), Lemkin eventually coined the word 'genocide', from a hybrid of Greek and Latin roots. Introduced into international law in 1948, the crime of genocide falls under the umbrella term of crimes against humanity. The American-Jewish political scientist Hannah Arendt compared Tehlirian's execution of Talaat Pasha with that of the prominent Ukrainian politician Symon Petliura in Paris in 1926. Petliura denied having been involved in anti-Jewish pogroms, but at the subsequent trial his killer was also acquitted.

After his trial, Tehlirian moved to Cleveland, Ohio, then Marseille, then on to Serbia, where he married Anahit Tatikian, also from Yerznka, whose family had fled to Tbilisi in Georgia. They settled in Belgrade for the next thirty years or so and had two sons, Shahen and Zaven.

Forced to leave Yugoslavia around 1950, after Tito had come to power, Tehlirian went with Anahit to Morocco, where they were taken in by Azad and Berdjouhi Surmenian, with whom they stayed for several years. He then moved to Paris before spending his final years in San Francisco.

Soghomon Tehlirian died in 1960 and was buried in the Ararat Armenian Cemetery in Fresno, California. Thanks to a contribution from the Surmenians, among others, his grave was marked by an obelisk crowned with an eagle with outstretched wings crushing a snake in its talons. According to the sculptor, the eagle represents 'the arm of justice of the Armenian people extending their wrath onto Talaat Pasha'.

A bust of Tehlirian stands in Gyumri, Armenia, where a house-museum dedicated to him was recently inaugurated. In Marseille, a square is named after him. The remains of Talaat Pasha, meanwhile, were transferred to Turkey by the Nazis in 1943, where they were interred in the patriotic Monument of Liberty in Istanbul.

THE RIGHTEOUS AND PEOPLE OF CONSCIENCE

Sources and further reading

Sources

Carzou, Jean-Marie, *Un génocide exemplaire*, Paris: Flammarion, 1975, pp. 201–8.
Chaliand and Ternon, *Armenians*, pp. 121–34.

Studies

Akçam, *Talat Pasha's Telegrams*, pp. 83–4, 109–11.
Asso, Annick, *Le Théâtre du genocide: Shoah et génocides arménien, rwandais et bosniaque* (preface by Marie-Claude Hubert), Paris: Honoré Champion, 2013, pp. 216–24.
'Crimes against Humanity', United Nations, Office on Genocide Prevention and the Responsibility to Protect, https://www.un.org/en/genocideprevention/crimes-against-humanity.shtml
Derogy, Jacques, *Resistance and Revenge: The Armenian Assassination of the Turkish Leaders Responsible for the 1915 Massacres and Deportations*, trans. A. M. Berrett, New Brunswick: Transaction Publishers, 1990.
Donikian, Denis, 'Opération Némésis' and 'Justicier du génocide arménien: Le procès Tehlirian', in *Petite encyclopédie du génocide Arménien*, p. 512; p. 513.
Fisch, Marcus, *Justicier du génocide arménien: Le procès de Tehlirian*, Paris: Première, 1981.
Fisk, Robert, 'My Conversation with the Son of Soghomon Tehlirian, the Man Who Assassinated the Organiser of the Armenian Genocide', *Independent*, 20 June 2016, https://www.independent.co.uk/voices/robert-fisk-armenian-genocide-conversation-son-of-soghomon-tehlirian-mehmet-talaat-pasha-assasination-a7091951.html
Garibian, Sévane, 'Commanded by My Mother's Corpse: Talaat Pasha, or the Revenge Assassination of a Condemned Man', *Journal of Genocide Research*, 20, no. 2 (2018), pp. 220–35.
'Holocaust, Genocide, and Crimes against Humanity: Suggestions for Classroom Teachers', IHRA, www.holocausteducation.org.uk/wp-content/uploads/IHRA_Holocaust_genocide_and_crimes_against_humanity.pdf
Sands, Philippe, *East West Street: On the Origins of Genocide and Crimes against Humanity*, London: Weidenfeld & Nicolson, 2016
Ternon, *Enquête sur la négation d'un génocide*, pp. 50–4, 146, 207–9.

SOGHOMON TEHLIRIAN (1896–1960)

Vartabedian, Sarah, 'Commemoration of an Assassin: Representing the Armenian Genocide', MA thesis, University of North California at Chapel Hill, 2007.

CONCLUSION

The inspiration for these portraits of the 'Righteous and people of conscience', whether of individuals or of groups, lies—for the authors of the present work as for the heroes of 1915—in the concepts of 'justice' and 'righteousness': concepts that have evolved in different eras and different cultures down the centuries, intersecting, coalescing and cross-fertilizing each other.

Many great thinkers down the ages, from St Paul to Jean-Jacques Rousseau, have concurred in the belief that people are born with an innate conscience that inclines them towards the good. In the Epistle *to the Romans* (2:14), for instance, Paul stressed the crucial value of conscience and feelings of the heart:

> For when Gentiles, who do not have the law, by nature do what the law requires, they are a law to themselves, even though they do not have the law. They show that the work of the law is written on their hearts, while their conscience also bears witness, and their conflicting thoughts accuse or even excuse them.

While Rousseau declared in *Emile, or On Education*: 'Conscience! Conscience! Divine instinct, immortal voice from heaven; sure guide for a creature ignorant and finite indeed, yet intelligent and free; infallible judge of good and evil, making man like to God! In thee consists the excellence of man's nature and the morality of his actions.'

Freud might not agree; however, if aggression is inherent in human nature, as he claimed, might this not be a defensive form of aggression, an aggression of survival? Breaking away from Christian pacifism, some Latin theologians of the early Middle Ages—first and foremost among them St Augustine—developed the theory of the 'just war'.

Notions of 'justice' and 'righteousness' appeared at the time of the creation of the Persian Empire under Cyrus the Great (*c*.559–

530 BCE), who sought to respect the distinctive characteristics of the various peoples of his empire, and whom the contemporaneous Old Testament author of Deutero-Isaiah described as 'the Lord's anointed' for having put an end to the Babylonian Captivity and resettling the Jews in Jerusalem.

Old Testament notions of 'righteousness' and 'justice' are voiced by the prophet Isaiah (whose ministry in the kingdom of Judah lasted from 740 to 687 BCE), in the first song of the Servant of the Lord, a mysterious figure who may prefigure Christ. Yahweh says: 'Behold my servant, whom I uphold, my chosen, in whom my soul delights; I have put my Spirit upon him; he will bring forth justice to the nations' (Isaiah, 42:1). And he continues: 'He will not grow faint or be discouraged till he has established justice in the earth; and the coastlands wait for his law' (Isaiah, 42:4). And: 'I am the Lord; I have called you in righteousness' (Isaiah, 42:6).

Righteousness in the Old Testament is an attribute of God, as celebrated repeatedly in the Book of Psalms, traditionally attributed to David and now believed to be the work of several authors from the tenth to the fourth century BCE.

In the New Testament, the notion of righteousness appears in two very different contexts. Where we would be inclined to think of Joseph, husband of Mary, as a 'good' man, Matthew describes him as just, since before making an act of faith in Mary's innocence when she 'was found to be with child from the Holy Spirit', he, 'being a just man and unwilling to put her to shame, resolved to divorce her quietly' (Matthew 1:18–27), so sparing her the stoning foretold in Deuteronomy.

In a different context, Jesus of Nazareth could be described as an extreme example of righteousness—like others who, on a purely human level, have been faithful to the voice of their conscience, even to the point of sacrificing their lives.

Jesus is righteous because, he says, in order to be faithful to 'the will of him who sent me' (John 5:30), he is prepared to be defamed, tried and crucified at the hands of the Jewish authorities in Jerusalem.

Another martyr for his faith was the Persian Sunni mystic al-Hallaj, crucified by the Sunni authorities in Baghdad in 922 for violating the official interpretation of the Sharia and proclaiming the necessity of a direct relationship with God.

CONCLUSION

In Matthew's Gospel, the Beatitudes proclaim, 'Blessed are those who hunger and thirst for righteousness' (Matthew 5:6) and 'Blessed are those who are persecuted for righteousness' sake' (Matthew 5:10). During the trial of Jesus, Pontius Pilate's wife (unnamed in the Gospel but known in the Eastern Orthodox Church as St Procula), intercedes on his behalf, warning Pilate, 'Have nothing to do with that righteous man, for I have suffered much because of him today in a dream' (Matthew 27:19). More forcefully, according to Luke in the Acts of the Apostles Peter accuses the Jewish leaders of Jerusalem: 'But you denied the Holy and Righteous One, and asked for a murderer to be granted to you, and you killed the Author of life' (Acts 3:14–15).

For Greek philosophers such as Plato (427–347 BCE) and Aristotle (384–322 BCE), justice was first and foremost a harmony in the order of the universe, emanating from man and benefitting the city by ensuring that concord reigned (notwithstanding the position of women, peasants and slaves, who fell outside the parameters of Athenian democracy). Socrates (c.470–399 BCE), as portrayed in Plato's *Dialogues*, had the audacity to contravene the city's laws through his radical apology for beauty and goodness and the primacy he granted to the moral virtue of justice. Accused of offending the gods and corrupting the young, and refusing to recant, he was condemned to drink hemlock. Slightly earlier than Socrates, in *Antigone* in 442 Sophocles extolled his heroine, the daughter of Œdipus, who was condemned to death for preferring—in defiance of Creon, king of Thebes—the unwritten laws of moral conscience to the human laws of the city. Aristotle was to go further, describing the voice of conscience as a natural law inscribed in human nature.

In Rome, Cicero (106–43 BCE), who although perhaps the greatest lawyer of all time was not strictly speaking a jurist, sought to build the law on justice or righteousness, 'queen of all virtues', thus—as the legal historian Jean-Marie Carbasse points out—endowing law with a moral purpose. With admirable eloquence, Cicero emphasized in *The Republic* the importance of natural law, instilled in the conscience of all men by their creator:

> True law is right reason in agreement with nature; it is of universal application, unchanging and everlasting; it summons to duty by its

commands and averts from wrongdoing by its prohibitions. ... It is a sin to try to alter this law, nor is it allowable to attempt to repeal any part of it, and it is impossible to abolish it entirely. We cannot be freed from its obligations by senate or people, and we need not look outside ourselves for an expounder or interpreter of it. And there will not be different laws at Rome and at Athens, or different laws now and in the future, but one eternal and unchangeable law will be valid for all nations and all times. (*De Re Publica*, III, XXII)

According to Ulpian (d. *c.*225 CE), the greatest of all Roman jurists, justice was the 'art of the good and the just', a concept adopted by all European jurists of the medieval period and beyond.

Many Christian thinkers, beginning with St Ambrose, bishop of Milan (*c.*340–97) and St Augustine, bishop of Hippo (354–430), both Latin Fathers of the Church, offered their reflections on the Roman foundations of justice, even if the notions of 'righteousness' and 'justice' are difficult to identify clearly in the works of the Roman jurists, most of which have come down to us only through later compilations.

This is not the place for an exhaustive consideration of the Latin and Byzantine writers who considered ideas around justice and righteousness. Writings on law that were composed after the proclamation of Christianity as the state religion in 380, under Emperor Theodosius (ruled 379–95), naturally bear the stamp of Christianity. This was the case with the Theodosian Code, composed under Eastern Roman Emperor Theodosius II (whose reign influenced Christian dogma through the Council of Ephesus in 431) and promulgated in 438, which brought together the imperial constitutions since Constantine the Great (whose edict of Milan, in 313, only went as far as tolerating Christianity among other religions). After the collapse of the Western Roman Empire under attacks from barbarian tribes in 476, Byzantine Emperor Justinian I (ruled 527–65), who was deeply involved in the Christological matters that led him into conflict with the papacy, gave a Christian stamp to part of his vast legal system, from the *Code of Justinian* to the *Novels*. Under the Macedonian Byzantine emperors (from 867 to 1028)—who were in fact of Armenian descent—the expansion of large properties at the expense of more modest landowners conferred aspects of Christian socialism on some of the imperial 'novels'.

CONCLUSION

Roman-Byzantine law was subsequently transmitted to the West. Initially, mainly in the twelfth century (when Gratian brought together the whole of ancient law in his major work of canon law known as the *Decree*), it influenced the opposing aspirations of the Holy Roman Empire and the Roman papacy. It then passed to the kingdoms of the West. In early thirteenth-century France, under the influence of jurists during the reign of Philip the Fair, the ideology of absolute monarchy developed, guaranteeing the stability of the state and for the most part respecting the tenets of natural law, but largely failing to acknowledge the rights of the bourgeoisie and the common people—as the monarchy would be reminded by the French Revolution.

The Revolution went far beyond Thomas Aquinas's declaration in the thirteenth century that the rights of princes were necessarily limited by 'natural law'. On the night of 4 August 1789, the National Constituent Assembly voted for the abolition of feudalism and privileges. On 27 August, it voted for the *Déclaration des droits de l'homme et du citoyen* (Declaration of the Rights of Man and the Citizen). Adopted as the preamble to the Constitution of 1791, this unprecedented document, influenced by ideas drawn from members of the bourgeoisie, enshrined the inalienable and sacred rights of the individual and the collective, including freedom of speech and belief, and the political and social equality of all citizens. It was to inspire the Universal Declaration of Human Rights, proclaimed in 1948—following the violence and racism unleashed during the Second World War—by the General Assembly of the United Nations, which declared that 'recognition of the inherent dignity and of the equal and inalienable rights of all members of the human family is the foundation of freedom'. Thus the Universal Declaration of Human Rights returned to the concept of natural law and reinforced the idea of a universal conscience that would refuse to accept genocide, the most flagrant of all violations of natural law.

In France, the Ligue des droits de l'homme, established in 1898 in response to the Dreyfus Affair—which supported the Armenian cause at a time when most pro-Armenians also supported Dreyfus—was also founded on the 'principles of 1789'.

The starting point for this wave of rights and freedoms, beginning with the Declaration of the Rights of Man and the Citizen, was the philosophy of the Enlightenment and its consideration of the various forms of justice, as foreshadowed by Montesquieu in *L'Esprit des lois* of 1748. This work may be understood, as Till Hanisch has written, 'as a vast study of the conditions and forms of the fulfilment of justice, through his concern that justice should be done', through 'two closely related concepts, equity and moderation'. As Solange Jambon has observed, Rousseau (the philosopher who liked to dress in Armenian costume and a man wounded by life, as attested by his posthumously published *Confessions*), was deeply interested in notions of justice, denouncing private property in his *Discours sur l'origine et les fondements de l'inégalité parmi les hommes* (Discourse on the origin and foundations of inequality among men) of 1755 and the legal defence of such property in *The Social Contract* of 1762. In 1764, in the ninth of the *Lettres écrites de la montagne* (Letters written from the mountain), Rousseau wrote: 'All want equal conditions for all, and justice lies in this equality alone. The citizen wants only laws and the observance of laws. With leaders, it is another matter ..., they look for preferential treatment everywhere.'

Jorel François notes several different approaches to the notion of justice in the works of Voltaire, who was courageous in his denunciations of judicial scandals. The implacable legal crusader of the Calas Affair asserted in *Le philosophe ignorant* (1766) that without justice there was no possibility of community among men. In his *Poème sur la loi naturelle* (1756), he declared: 'To be just is enough; the rest is arbitrary'; and: 'From all corners of the world, it [natural law] cries: worship God, be just.' Twice imprisoned in the Bastille for attacking first the regent then the Chevalier de Rohan-Chabot, Voltaire was exiled several times as a consequence of the arbitrary justice that he saw prevailing in France. In *Candide, or Optimism* (1759), the character of the 'good dervish' (a Turk who follows, in principle, the asceticism of the Sufis, introduced to thirteenth-century Turkey by the Iranian mystic, poet and scholar Mevlana, better known as Rumi) is well highlighted. The eponymous hero of the philosophical tale *Zadig or Destiny* of 1747 (*Zadig* meaning Easter in Armenian), as minister to the king of Babylon in an Orient of the imagination, administers justice fairly.

We have already noted the role played by the concept of *adalet* (the Turkish form of the Arabic *'adâla*), in the Ottoman Empire.

CONCLUSION

The reforms of the Tanzimat era (1839–76)—in which the Armenian elite of Constantinople played an active part—produced the Mecelle, which came into force in 1876. This civil code of the Ottoman Empire codified part of the Sharia-based law of the Islamic state, combining the directives of the Napoleonic Code with the principles of Sharia law. In defining the '*adl* individual as a 'person of good moral character', it provided a model of conduct that the Young Turk rulers were to flout in flagrant fashion.

The Armenian jurist Krikor Odian was one of the chief architects of the Armenian National Constitution in 1863, introducing greater democracy to the workings of the Armenian community in the Ottoman Empire. He was influential as a member of the Council of State and advisor to the reformist grand vizier Midhat Pasha (between 1872 and 1877), who advocated a constitutional movement and was receptive to the principles of *adalet*. Odian also helped to draft the constitution of the Ottoman Empire in 1876, before being forced into exile in Paris in 1880 under the reign of the 'Red Sultan', Abdul Hamid II.

In Jewish reflections on the notion of 'the righteous' in the modern era, the Yiddish term *mensch*, as favoured by Yves Ternon and used from the eleventh century, became more generally adopted during the Jewish Enlightenment. Among other prominent figures of the Haskalah, the philosopher Moses Mendelssohn (a follower of Maimonides, the twelfth-century Sephardic Jewish philosopher in the Aristotelian tradition), who died in Berlin in 1786, initiated a process of conciliation between traditional Judaism and the educational, philosophical, scientific and literary advances of the modern world. This secularization of the rabbinical legacy, which transcended rather than abolishing the requirements of the *Torah*, made the *mensch* a harbinger of the messianic era, when, in its very fulfilment by the *mensch*, the Law would be abolished. 'A *mensch*,' Jacques Brafman concludes, 'is a man who behaves like a man in the community of men.' The concept of the *mensch*—in which righteousness (a concept no longer confined within the parameters of the *tzaddik* of rabbinical Law) is deployed in the full power of its potential—is framed by two religious references: its rabbinical roots and its messianic perspectives.

From this overview of the development and variations of the concepts of 'righteousness' and 'justice' down the centuries and in different cultures, we can conclude that 'the Righteous and people of conscience' described in these pages, whether individuals or groups, and whatever their religion, beliefs or philosophy, were responding first and foremost to the call of their conscience. It was a call that was explicitly rejected by the Turkish minister of the interior, Talaat Pasha, in the notorious telegram he sent to the Prefecture of Aleppo on 29 September 1915. Ordering Ottoman officials to carry out the policy of exterminating the Armenians, he enjoined them to do so 'without paying heed to any feelings of conscience'—an order that was in total violation of natural law.

Within the Ottoman Empire, the authentic heroes of the period of the genocide were the Muslim Righteous, who bring honour to Turkey, in stark contrast to the Three Pashas, Talaat, Enver and Cemal, the first two of whom are scandalously 'honoured' by the mausoleums erected half a century after the genocide that dominate the Armenian cemetery in the Şişli district of Istanbul, while the third is buried in Erzurum and in recent years has been radically disowned by his grandson, Hasan Cemal.

The association Gardens of the Righteous Worldwide, founded in Milan in 1999, pays due tribute to these heroes, as does the Museum-Institute of the Armenian Genocide, opened in 1995 near the Genocide Memorial Complex, in Tsitsernakaberd, on one of the hills of Yerevan.

With thanks to Professor Jean-Marie Carbasse.

INDEX

NB page numbers in **bold** indicate main entries

À la mémoire de Pierre Quillard
    (Chobanian), 25
Aaronsohn, Aaron, **279–86**
Aaronsohn, Alexander, **279–86**
Aaronsohn, Sarah, **279–86**
Abdülaziz, Ottoman Sultan, 68, 415
Abdul Hamid II, Ottoman Sultan, 2, 6, 19, 22–4, 31–2, 128, 289–91, 323, 398, 405, 415
    fall of, 351, 371–2,
    see also Hamidian massacres (1894–6)
Action Chrétienne en Orient (ACO), 197–8, 241–2
adalet / 'adâla, xvii, 67–8, 70–71, **153–62**, 456–7
Adana, Turkey, 3–6, 159
    massacres (1909), 2–6, 19–20, 43, 61–3, 168, 238–41, 258, 291–5, 351–2
Agha, Selim, 160
Aghassi (Garabed Toursarkissian), 19, 26
Aghpalian, Nigol, 222
Aharonian, Avedis, 44

Ahmed Izzet Pasha, xix, 100, 215
Ahmet Refik Altinay, **415–17**
Akbes, Turkey, 293
Akçam, Taner, 75, 155, 415
Akhond-Zadé, Mirza Feth-Ali, 51
Akin, Fatih, 325
al-Hallaj, 452
Aleppo, Syria, xix–xx, 9, 105–6, 144, 174, 196, 198, 224–7, 242–3, 259–61, 292–3, 333–8
Alevis/Alevism, xviii, **117–19**
Alexander II, Russian Tsar, 43
Alexandretta, Syria, 242–3, 357, 421
Alexandrian, Tourvanda, 168
Alexandropol (now Gyumri), Armenia, 266
Algeria, 197
Ali Kemal Bey, 101
Allenby, Edmund, 136–7, 174, 280, 283
Alliés sont en Arménie, Les (Altounian), 36
Alsace, 195–7
Altounian, Jean, 36
Ambassador Morgenthau's Story (Morgenthau), 303

INDEX

Armenian genocide (1915–16), 2–3, 7–11, 258–9, 290–91, 325, 369, 374–5, 381, 405
American Board of Commissioners for Foreign Missions, 185, 217, 250–51, 270, 387
American Committee on Armenian Atrocities, 387–8
American Commonwealth, The (Bryce), 398
American Physician in Turkey, An (Ussher), 201–2
Amundsen, Roald, 426
Anatole France (Bancquart), 404, 408
Anatolia, xvii, xix, 9–10, 49, 57, 100, 125, 137, 147–8, 167, 270, 308, 363, 412
Andonian, Aram, 338, 382, 444
Andranik, General, 133, 192, 440
Andreassian, Dikran, 354–5, 421–2
Andreievna, Sophia, 275
Anglo-Armenian Society, 397
Angora (Ankara), Turkey, xix, 167
  massacres, 99–101, 189, 366
Anjar, Lebanon, 421
Ankara *see* Angora
Anschluss (1938), 419
Antigone (Sophocles), 453
Antioch (Antakya), 105, 293
antisemitism *see* Jews/Judaism
L'Antisémitisme, son histoire et ses causes (Lazare), 30
'Appeal for Armenia', 406

Aqaba, Jordan, 136, 283
Aquinas, Thomas, 455
Arab Revolt (1916–18), 283
Aram I, Catholicos of the Great House of Cilicia, 394
Arapian, Armand, 155
Arapian, Armenak, 155–6
Arendt, Hannah, 447
Arif Ağa, 5
Aristotle, 453
Armenakan party, 289
Armenia/Armenians, 2, 24, 282–3
  Armenian independence (28 May 1918), 193, 283, 392
  Armenian National Constitution, 457
  decree of 26 June 1915, 316–17
  First Republic of Armenia (1918–20), 133, 192, 240, 298, 362, 375, 406–7, 412–13, 429
  genocide of 1915–16, 2–3, 7–11, 258–9, 290–91, 325, 369, 374–5, 381
  'national home' (1919–21), 363, 375, 393, 406–7, 412
  Russian Armenia, 6, 72, 388, 425
Armenia (Alexander Aaronsohn), 284
Armenia and Europe (Lepsius), 444
Armenia and the Near East (Nansen), 425, 429–31
Armenian Apostolic Church, 222

460

INDEX

Armenian Atrocities: The Murder of a Nation (Toynbee), 400
Armenian Catholic College, Pera, 22
Armenian Central College, Galata, 22
Armenian General Benevolent Union, 140
Armenian Genocide Museum-Institute, 266
Armenian Genocide, The (Kévorkian), 112
Armenian Legion, 283, 363, 412, 421
Armenian Memorial, Jerusalem, 423
Armenian Patriotic Committee, 397
'Armenian Question, The' (Bryce), 398
Armenian Revolutionary Federation (ARF), 6, 421, 442
Armenian Soviet Socialist Republic, 243
Arménie 1915: Un génocide exemplaire (Carzou), 41
Armenien und Europa (Lepsius), 270
Armenisches Hilfswerk, 270
Armistice of Mudros (1918), xxii, 137, 164, 362–3
Arpiarian, Arpiar, 22
Aslanian, Adom, 57
Asquith, H. H., 399
L'assassinat du Père Salvatore par les soldats turcs, (Aghassi), 26
Association Chrétienne en Orient, xxii
Astik Effendi, 80–81

Atatürk, Mustafa Kemal, 10, 75, 80, 90, 110, 118, 137, 251, 363, 406–7, 416
  proclamation of Turkish Republic (1923), 85, 102, 326, 357
  reinvention of the Turkish history, 416
Atif Bey, 99–100
Atkinson, Henry Herbert, xviii, **207–9**
Atkinson, Tacy, xviii, **207–9**
Auron, Yair, 279, 284, 419–20, 422–3
L'Aurore, 31–2, 34, 43, 403
Austria, 325, 419
Avetaranian, Johannes, 269
Axis Rule in Occupied Europe (Lemkin), 380–81
Ayntab (Gaziantep), 363–4
Azadamart newspaper, 9
Aziz Bey, 138
Azizoğlu, Mustafa, xix
Azmi Bey, 107

Baghdad, 324
Bahabanian, Gregory, 365
Bahri Pasha, 50
Balakian, Grigoris, 443–4
Balfour Declaration (1917), 284
Bancquart, Marie-Claire, 404, 408
barbarism, 380–81
Barbier de Meynard, Charles, 48
Barbusse, Henri, 404
Bardizag, Turkey, 163–5
Barnum, Emma M., 211
Barrows Ussher, Elizabeth, 202, 205

INDEX

Barton, James Levy, xxii, 387
Battle of Arara (1918), 137, 358
Battle of Bash Abaran (1918), 133
Battle of Sarıkamış (1914–15), 7, 76
Bauernfeind, Ernst, 112
Bayburt, Turkey, 153
Bayezid I, Ottoman Sultan, 149
Becker, Annette, 378–9, 381
Bedreddin, Ibrahim, 84
Bedrossian, Aaltoun, 24
Bedrossian, Khamo, 24
Begnins orphanage, 392, 395
Beirut, 198, 222, 235
Bell, Gertrude, 135, 137
Benedict XV, Pope, **187–94**, 299, 382
Benedictsen, Aage Meyer, 255–6
Bérard, Victor, xxii
Bergson, Henri, 39
Bericht über die Lage des armenischen Volkes in der Turkeï (Lepsius), 271, 280
Berlin-Charlottenburg, Germany, xxiii
Berlin, Germany, 441–2
Berlin–Baghdad Railway, 324, 333
Berliner Tageblatt, 344
Bernard, Victor, 22
Berron, Paul, xxii, **195–9**, 241
Beşir, Ahmed, 5
Beşiri, Turkey, 84
von Bethmann Hollweg, Theobald, 324, 333, 335–6
Bilemdjian, Agop, 143
Bilemdjian, Jean-Michel, 143–6

Bilemdjian, Ovhannes, **143–6**
Bilemdjian, Vartouhi, 143
Bilezikian, Vartan, 223
Biørn, Bodil Katharine, xxiii, **263–7**
'Birds' Nest' orphanage, Jbeil, 249–50
von Bismarck, Otto, 323
Bitlis, Turkey, xxiii, 9, 70, 76, 138
Bjornlund, Matthias, 251
Blair, Susan, 308
'Blue Book' (Bryce and Toynbee), xx, 399–401
Boghos Nubar Pasha, 281
Boloyan, Sahag, 440
Bond, Louise, 202
Boum, Hac Halil, 157
Boyer, Abbé Raymond, 362, 366
Bozarslan, Hamit, 416
Brafman, Jacques, 457
Brémond, Édouard, 136, 357
Breuning, Alice, 269
Britain/British *see* United Kingdom
British Armenian Red Cross, 399
de Brouckère, Charles, 375
Brunet de Coursou, Pierre, 357
Bruzy, Dominique, 48
Bryce, James, 1st Viscount Bryce, xx, xxii, **397–402**, 405
Bulgaria, xvii, xxii, 303–4
Büll, Anna Hedvig, xix, xxii, **237–44**
Byzantine Empire, 454–5

Cachin, Marcel, 44
Cahiers de la Quinzaine, 33–4

INDEX

Cahiers Jaurès, 41
Calvignac, Jean-Baptiste, 40
Cambon, Paul, xxii, 23, 41–2, 47, 49, 292
Campbell, George, 8th Duke of Argyll, 41
Candide, or Optimism (Voltaire), 456
Carbasse, Jean-Marie, 453
Carduchians *see* Kurds
Carmaux coal strikes (1892–5), 40
Carmaux glass-workers strike (1895), 40
Carnegie Foundation, 170
Carzou, Jean-Marie, 41
Cassirer, Richard, 445
Catholic Church, 26, 187–94, 316, 408
  Jesuits 192–3
Celal Bey, Mehmet, xix, 99, **105–10**, 224, 226, 334
Çelebi, Abdul Halim, **147–50**
Cemal Azmi Bey, 317, 319, 438
Cemal Pasha, 100, 102, 224–6, 284, 302, 323, 458
  trial, 437–8
Cemal, Hasan, 458
Central Committee for Armenian Refugees, 374
Central Powers, 189, 280
Century Illustrated Monthly Magazine, 398
Çermik, 84
Cevdet Bey, 8, 122, 203–4
Cevdet Pasha, 68
'Challenge of the Unprecedented, The' (Rabinbach), 383

Chaper, Maurice, 411
Chaperon, Abbé Jules, xxiii, **361–7**
Charmetant, Félix, xxii, 361
Chloyan, Serop, 160
Chobanian, Arshag, 19, 22, 25–7, 30, 36, 43, 374, 412–13
Christ, Hermann, 229–30
Christianity/Christians, 68, 70–72, 197–8, 220, 388, 405, 454
Christoffel, Ernst, 111
Cicero, 453
Çiftlik, Turkey, 113
Cilicia, 10, 19, 109–10, 238–40, 283, 290–92, 351–2, 361–3, 407
  as national home, 363, 375, 393, 406–7, 412
  French mandate in (1918–21), 3, 10, 109, 192, 243, 412, 421
  massacres (1909), 2–6, 19–20, 43, 61–3, 168, 238–41, 258, 291–5, 351–2
Cillière, Alphonse, 3, **47–53**, 55, 58–9, 289–92
'Clarté', 404
Clemenceau, Georges, xxi, 3, 26–7, 31, 39–40, 43, 283, 403, 405, 412
Clervoy, Patrick, 444
Cochin, Denys, xxi, 41
Comment un drapeau sauva quatre mille Arméniens (Andreassian), 422

INDEX

Commission for the Protection of Women and Children in the Near East, 259
Committee of Union and Progress (CUP), xvi, xxii, 9–10, 76, 80, 101–2, 148, 291, 295, 317–18
concentration camps, xvi–xvii, 10, 93, 144, 225, 342
Conference of Swiss Committees for the Relief of Armenians, 391
Confiscation des biens des réfugiés arméniens par le gouvernement turc (Mandelstam), 374
Constantine the Great, 454
Constantinople *see* Istanbul
Contemporary Review, The, 401
Contre la paix injuste, 404
Contre les barbares de l'Orient (de Morgan), 413
Coolidge, Calvin, 233
Cox, Percy, 135, 137
Crane, Charles R., 387
Crete, 42
Çüngüs, 212
Cut, The (film), 325
Cyprus, 41, 357
Cyrus the Great, 451–2

Dadrian, Vahakn, 99, 324
Dalbert, Georges, 36
Damascus, 136, 420
Damlamian family, **177–82**
Danielian, Yeranouhi, 442
Danish Friends of Armenians, 256
Dardanelles, 7, 76, 329

Darrieus, Gabriel, 355
Darülfünun (university), 415–16
Dashnak party, 27, 290
Dashnaktsutyun *see* Armenian Revolutionary Federation
Davis, Leslie A., xviii, 302, **307–14**
Daylam region, 125
Days of Tragedy in Armenia: Personal Experiences in Harpoot, 1915–1917 (Riggs), 211–16
De la réalité du monde sensible (Jaurès), 39
De Morgan, Jacques, **411–14**
Declaration of the Rights of Man and the Citizen (1789), 455
Delarue, Père, 290
Demirdjian, Haroutioun, 157–8
Demirdjian, Hayk, 157–8
Demirdjian, Yeghya, 157–8
Demlakian, Pierre, 355
Denison, Annie M., 211
Denmark, 250, 255–6
Dépêche de Toulouse, La (newspaper), 39–40, 42
Der Kalousdian, Movses, 356, 421
Der Zor, Syria, xvii, xx, 10, 12, 93, 95, 144, 225, 240, 337, 341
Derderian family, **173–5**
Derderian, Chaké, 163
Derderian, Ermine, 165
Derik, Turkey, 84
Dersim region, xviii, 117–18, 214
Deschanel, Paul, 405
Deutsch-Armenische Akademie, 273

INDEX

Deutsch-Armenische Gesellschaft (German–Armenian Society), 270
Deutsche Orient-Mission, 229, 256, 269–70
Deutsche-türkische Vereinigung (German-Turkish Association), 343
Deutscher Hülfsbund für christliches Liebeswerk im Orient, 196, 223
Devlet Hatun, 149
dhimmi (protected status), 68, 71–2, 118
Dialogues (Plato), 453
Digin Virginie: The Sufferings of an Armenian Woman (Petersen), 252
Discours sur l'origine et les fondements de l'inégalité parmi les hommes (Rousseau), 456
Diyarbekir region, xix, 9, 70, 76, 79–80, 83, 98, 212, 138–9
massacres, 79–81, 137–8
Djagadamard newspaper, 442
Djemal Pasha, xx
Documents officiels concernant les massacres arméniens (Andonian), 339
Dodd, William S., 108
Dodge, Cleveland H., 387
Dolci, Angelo Maria, xx, **187–94**, 297, 299
Dorfmann-Lazarev, Igor, 71
Dorgelès, Roland, 404
Doughty-Wylie, Charles, 6
Doumergue, Émile, 405
Drama, Greece, 174

Dreissig Jahre Dienst am Orient (Künzler), 235
Dreyfus, Alfred, xxi, 21, 27, 30, 43, 403–4
Dreyfus Affair, 403–4, 455
Dreyfus, Mathieu, xxi, 30
Drumond, Édouard, xxi, 29
Dubois, Louis-Ernest, 406
Duchesne, Louis, 29
Duclert, Vincent, 27, 35, 41, 44, 404, 406
Duhamel, Georges, 404
Dumont, Paul, 68
Dutton, Samuel T., 387

L'Éclair, 412
L'Effet Lucifer: Des bourreaux ordinaires (Clervoy), 445
Egoyan, Atom, 261
Egypt, 140, 192, 242, 281
1895, Massacres d'Arméniens (Cillière), 290
El-Ghusein, Faiz, **135–41**
Elbistan, 224
Eleanor of Bulgaria, 304
Emaus orphanage, Mezreh, 250
Enver Pasha, xx, 7, 97, 100, 102, 203, 271, 302–3, 323, 415, 458
trial, 437–8
Eretz Yisrael, 420–22
Erzberger, Matthias, 272
Erzurum, Turkey, 136, 202, 276, 290–92, 294, 313, 318, 440
massacres, 9, 290–94
Es-Süveydi, Ali Sabit, 80, **87**
Eskidjian, Hovhannes, 226
L'Esprit des lois (Montesquieu), 456

INDEX

Essad Bey, 52, **55–9**
Essai sur les nationalités (De Morgan), 413
Estonia, 237–8, 241, 243
Eternal Road, The (Weisgal), 419
European Pro-Armenia Congress (Brussels, 1902), 33
'Extermination of Ottoman Armenian Deportees, The (1915–1916)' (Kévorkian), 94

Fadil, Kaymakam Haci, 95
Faik Ali Bey, 11–12
Faik Ali Ozansoy, 97–8
Faisal I of Iraq, 174, 283
  as Prince, 136–7, 140–41
Faure, Félix, 43, 403
fedayeen (armed group), 143, 169
Fédération Suisse des Amis des Arméniens, 234, 392
Feinberg, Avshalom, 280
Fénéon, Félix, 36
Ferid Bey (Hamal Ferid), 109
Fille aux mains coupées, La (Quillard), 21
Findiklian, Carzouhie, 170
5th Conference for the Unification of Criminal Law, 380
Flotte française au secours des Arméniens en 1909 et 1915, La (Kévorkian), 351
Fool, The (Raffi) 122
Forty Days of Musa Dagh, The (Werfel), 35, 271, 358, 420–23
du Fournet, Louis Dartige, xxi, **351–9**

4th International Conference on the Unification of Criminal Law, 380
France, xxi–xxii, 19, 40–44, 49, 259–60, 283–4, 351–2, 355–7, 379, 403–6, 455
  French Navy, 355–6
  refugees and, 170, 197
  see also Triple Entente
France, Anatole, xxiii, 3, 19, 22, 27, 43, **403–9**
France face au génocide des Arméniens, La (Duclert), 404
Franco-Armenian committee, 30
François, Jorel, 456
Franklin-Bouillon, Henry, 421
Franz Ferdinand, Archduke of Austria, 75
Frederiksen, H. C., 255
Free Synagogue, 301
Freud, Sigmund, 451
Fumier de Job, Le (Lazare), 31
'Future of Armenia, The' (Bryce), 401

Gamat, Marguerite, 311
Gardens of the Righteous Worldwide (Gariwo), 458
Gauck, Joachim, 325
Geneva Convention (1933), 429
genocide
  definition of, xvii, 41, 377, 380–82, 447
  international recognition of, 325–6
  UN Convention (1948), xvii, 381–3
  see also Armenian genocide of 1915–16

INDEX

'Genocide: A Modern Crime' (Lemkin), 381
Georges-Picot, François, 282, 363
Gerçek, Burçin, 75
German–Ottoman alliance, 324–5, 329–32
Germany, 270–72, 280–82, 298, 304, **323–7**, 329–32, 342–6, 379, 420
Germany and Armenia 1914–1918 (Lepsius), 272, 444
Gevorg V Soureniants, 189
Gharman Sumbas, 5
Ghazarossian, Hovannes, 197
Ghazir, Lebanon, 233
Girou, Herman, 294
Giroux, Matthieu, 35
de Girs, Nikolay, 372
Gladstone, William, xxii, 3, 41, 397–8
Göçek, Fatma Müge, xvii, 70–71, 159
Godet, Georges, 391
Gökalp, Ziya, 79
Göksun, Turkey, 224
von der Goltz, Colmar, 323
Goltz, Hermann, 273
Gorrini, Giacomo, **297–9**
Gransault, Joannes, 192
Great Arab Revolt (1916–18), 136–7, 283
Greece, 164–5, 174, 182, 365, 375
Greek Orthodox church, 164, 167
Greer, David H., 387
Gregorian, Vartan, 422
Grey, Edward, 1st *Viscount Grey of Fallodon*, 399–400

Guichen (French battleship), 355, 357
Gulf of Alexandretta, 354–5

Haapsalu, Estonia, 237–8, 244
Haci Halil, 12
Haci Mohamed, 4
Hadjin (Haçin), Turkey, 4–5, 61–3, 363
Hagopian, Garabed, 397
Haïrenik Weekly, 382
Hajim Pasha, 260
Hakkari, Turkey, 90
Halebian, Hagop, 226
Halil, Haji, 155
Hamadiye (armed force), 23
Hamid Bey, xix, 57, **79–81**
Hamidian massacres (1894–6), xxi, 2–4, 6, 19–20, 23–8, 41, 100–102, 289–92, 371–2
   eyewitness accounts, 138, 289–90
   inquiry and trial, 100–102
Hanisch, Till, 456
Hanotaux, Gabriel, 23, 41
Hanum, Nejebe, 219
Harabanoğlu Mehmed Bey, 5
Harel, Yossi, 433
Harput, Turkey, 207, 211–15, 245–8, 250–51, 307–13
   massacres, 245–8, 250
Hasan Mazhar Bey, xix, xxiii, **99–103**, 437
Hayrénik' (Homeland) newspaper, 22
Hayri Bey, Sheikh-ul-Islam Mustafa, 71
Heizer, Oscar S., 302, **315–21**

INDEX

Herian, Rupen, 140
Herzl, Theodor, 30, 32
L'heure de l'Arménie, (Krafft-Bonnard), 392–3
Hijra (emigration), 72
Hilmi Bey, xix, 89–91
Hirdj (Köklü), Turkey, 8
Histoire du peuple arménien (De Morgan), 413–14
History of Pontic Armenia (Hovagimian), 316
Hitler, Adolf, 326, 345, 420
Hocazade Rasik Effendi, 98
Hoffmann, Hermann, 336–7
Holland, 198
Holocaust, 13, 345–9, 358, 421, 423
Holstein, Walter, 90
Holy Roman Empire, 455
Horton, George, 302
Höss, Rudolf, 326
Hotel Baron, Aleppo, 225
Hovagimian, Hovagim, 316
Hovhannessian, Karekin, 94
Hunchak party, 10, 23
Hundred Years of Musa Dagh, The (Auron), 419
Huntford, Roland, 426
L'Humanité newspaper, 43, 404, 408
Husni Effendi, 5
Hussein bin Ali, sharif of Mecca, 136–7, 141, 283

Iancu, Carol, 31–2, 34
Il Messaggero, 298
Im Lande des Blutes und der Tränen (Künzler), 229, 231–2

Indjeyan, Samuel, 169
Injarabian, Papken, 160
International Raoul Wallenberg Foundation, 75
International Red Cross, 429
Iran, 242
Iraq, 128, 135, 283
Islam *see* Muslims/Islam
Islamic State, 93, 457
Ismirlioglou, Stavros, 180–82
Israel, 279–80, 423
 see also Zionism
Israelian, Monsignor, 311
Istanbul, 110
 as Constantinople, xvii, 9, 19, 153, 188, 289, 329–31, 361–2, 364–5, 440, 457
 Istanbul Trials (1919–20), 325
 massacres in, 25
Italy, 298–9

J'accuse! (Zola), 21, 30, 43, 403
Jackson, Jesse B., xix, 224, 227, 302, 333
Jackson, Robert H., 380
Jacob, Max, 36
Jacobsen, Maria, xviii, xxii, 69, **245–53**
Jahangir Agha, 132
Jakhian, Grégoire, 85
Jambon, Solange, 456
Jarabulus, Syria, 232–3
Jaurès, Jean, xxi, 2–3, 19, 27, 33, **39–45**, 404
Jbeil orphanage, Lebanon, 221–2, 249
Jensen, Anna, 338
Jeppe, Karen, xix, xxiii, **255–62**, 270

468

INDEX

de Jerphanion, Guillaume, 192
Jerusalem, 269, 280
Jerusalem Post, 423
Jesus of Nazareth, 452
Jewish State, The (Herzl), 30
Jews/Judaism, 30–36, 68, 70–71, 279–82, 284, 301–2, 345, 378, 420–22, 457
    antisemitism, xxi, 27, 30, 302, 403–4
    Free Synagogue, 301
    Holocaust, 13, 345–9, 358, 421, 423
    mensch, 457
    Zionism, 30–32, 35, 279–82, 284, 420–22
    see also Dreyfus Affair
Job's Dungheap (Lazare), 34
Jobert, Henri, 356
John Paul II, Pope, 90
Journal des débats, 406
Jousselin, Gaston, 292
Jules Ferry (armoured cruiser), 352–3
justice/jurists, 369, 371–84, 451–8
    adalet/'adâla, xvii, 67–8, 70–71, **153–62**, 456–7
Justinian I, Byzantine Emperor, 454

Kadri Bey, 48–50, 52, 56, 58
Kaiser, Hilmar, 327
Kamal Bey, 98
Kâmil, Mahmud, 70
Karatchian, Mariam, 156
Karekin I Khachadourian, archbishop of Konya, 109
Kargel, Johann, 238
Kars, Turkey, 7
Katerdjian, Henazant, 440–41
Katma, Syria, 363
Kazarian family, **167–71**
Kazarian, Pierre, 167
Kemal Bey, Colonel, xx, 338
Kemal Pasha, 97
Kévonian, Dzovinar, 369
Kévorkian, Georges, 351, 355
Kévorkian, Raymond, 69, 94–5, 109, 139, 189, 316
Khachatrian, Taron, 156
Kharpert, Turkey, xviii–xix, 9
Khatanasian, Yervant, 222
Khayadjian, Edmond, 24–5
Kishinev pogrom (1903), 381
Klarmann, Adolf, 422
Klein, Elisabeth, 269
Kölnische Zeitung, 329
Kolvenbach, Peter Hans, 192
Konya, Turkey, 106–9, 147–9, 164, 324
    massacres, 147–8
Kowaliska, Irene, 345
Krafft-Bonnard, Antony, xxii, **391–5**
von Kressenstein, Kress, 326
Kuciukian, Pietro, 93, 122, 141
Kujumgian, Jean, 159
Künzler-Bender, Elizabeth, **228–35**
Künzler, Jakob, xix, xxii, **228–35**
Kurck, Sigrid, 246
Kurds, xvii, 23, **121–3**, 174–5, 214, 283, 290
    Yazidi Kurds, Sinjar, xviii, **127–9**

INDEX

Kütahya, Turkey, xix, 11, 97–8
Kvindelige Missions Arbejdere (KMA) (Women's Missionary Workers), 245–6, 249–51

Lambert, Rose, 5, **61–3**
Lammert, Norbert, 325
Landau, Lola, 344–5
Latour, Francis, 189
Launay, Marcel, 191
Lausanne Conference (1923), 394, 406–7
   Treaty of Lausanne (1923), 174, 365, 374–5, 407
Lavisse, Ernest, 24, 33
Lawrence, T. E., 136–7, 283
Lazare, Bernard, xxi, 21, 27, **29–37**
League of Nations, xxiii, 188, 192, 259, 261, 283–4, 380, 393, 398, 406–7, 425, 427–32
Lebanon, xx, xxii, 197–8, 242, 249–50, 284
Légion d'Orient, 192, 283, 357–8, 421
Lemkin, Raphael, xxiii, 102, 369, **377–84**, 447
Lepsius, Johannes, xx, xxii, 229, 232, 256, **269–74**, 280, 325, 339, 382–3, 444
Lepsius, Karl Richard, 269
Leroy-Beaulieu, Anatole, 33
'Letter to My Sons' (Stépan Damlamian), 177–82
Levonian, Adour, 221
Lice, Turkey, xix, 83–4
Liebknecht, Karl, 272
Ligue des droits de l'homme (Human Rights League), 22, 27, 30, 33, 403–4, 455
Lilli, Salvatore, 26
Longuet, Jean, 27, 43–4
Loris-Melikov, Jean, 27, 43
Loris-Melikov, Mikhail, 43
Loti, Pierre, 51
Lütfi Bey, 5, 62
Lwanga, Charles, 187

Macler, Frédéric, 406
Mahler, Alma, 419–20
Makriköy (now Bakırköy), Istanbul, 364–5
Malatya, Turkey, xix, 111–13
Malche Protestant mission, 238
Maloyan, Ignatius, 89–90, 189
Malta, 378, 437
Mamahatun (now Tercan), Turkey, 157
Mamoulian, Rouben, 169
Mamuret ul-Aziz, 70, 76, 311, 313
Mandelstam, André, xxiii, 369, **371–6**
Manoukian, Isgouhi, 219
Maraş region, xix, 223–4, 238, 263, 363
Marasco, Italy, 26
Mardin, Turkey, xix, 84, 89–90, 131–2
Margery, Louis, 21
Maronites, 284
Marsovan (now Merzifon), Turkey, xix, 217–20
von Martens, Friedrich Fromhold, 369
Martyred Armenia (El-Ghusein), 135, 138–9

INDEX

Martyrologe arménien (Charmetant), 361
Massacres d'Arménie, Les (Chobanian), 26
'Massacres des Sassounkh, Les' (Quillard), 23–4
Maurer, Henry, 5
Mayeur, Jean-Marie, 188
Mayevska, Pesya, 423
Mazhar Commission, 101–2, 437
McLaren, Grisell, 202
Medznakian, Zepur, 161
Meguerditchian, Haroutioun, 442
Mehmed Effendi, 4–5
Mehmed Reshad V, Ottoman Sultan, 148–9
Mehmet Kemal Bey, 442
Mehmet V, Ottoman Sultan, 71–2, 189–90, 323, 351
Mehmet VI, Ottoman Sultan, 100
Meillet, Antoine, 405–6
Memduh Bey, 79
Mémoires de Monseigneur Jean Naslian, Les, 382
Memoirs (Celal Bey), 106–7
Mémorial du génocide des Arméniens (Kévorkian), 94
Memorial to the Armenian Genocide, Tsitsernakaberd, 93, 141
Mendelssohn, Moses, 457
Menetchian, Assadour Hovsep, 159
Mercure de France magazine, 26
Mesdjian, Myriam, 156
Meskeneh concentration camp, 144

Metternich, Paul Wolff, 325
Mevlevi order, 147–9
Mezreh, Turkey, 245, 247, 250–51, 263–4
  massacres, 245, 247, 250
MGM, 421
Michelson, Alexander M., 373
Midhat Pasha, Ottoman Grand Vizier, 19, 128, 457
Midyat, Turkey, 84
Mikaelian, Sevart, 252
Mikayelian, Kristapor, 27
Mikhaël, Ephraïm, 29
Le Mintier de la Motte Basse, Christian, 355
Mirkin-Getzevich, Boris, 373
missionaries, 185, 195–286, 392
Moks, Armenia, 12, 122
Montesquieu, 456
Montpellier, France, 289, 293–4
de Morgan, Jacques, xxiii
Morgenthau, Henry, xx, 35, 297, **301–5**, 308–9, 317–18, 382–3, 387
Morley, Bertha B., xix, 69, **217–20**
Mount (Jabal) Sinjar, 127, 129, 131–2
Mount Ararat, 397, 430
Mount Varak, 8
Mouradian, Claire, 407, 443
Mouradian, Hagop Mourad, 157
Moussoyan, Kioulinia Dzerouni, 157
Muhtar, Said Ahmed, 320
de Mun, Albert, xxi, 40–42
Murad (Hunchak leader), 23
Murtula Beg, 122

INDEX

Muş, Turkey, xxiii, 264–5
Musa Dagh (Mount Moses), xxi, 153, 192, 271, 353–8, 421–3
  evacuation of (1915), 354–8
Musa Effendi, 5
Museum-Institute of the Armenian Genocide, 458
Muslims/Islam, **67–73**, 117, 159–60, 291
  '*adâla*, xvii, 67–8, 70–71, **153–62**, 456–7
  Alevism, xviii, **117–19**
  Sharia law, 140–41, 457
  Sufism, 128, 147–9
  Sunnism, 118, 127
  Yazidism, xviii, **127–9**, 131–3
Mustafa Agha Azizoğlu, **111–14**
Mutullah Bey, agha of Shatakh, 117
Mwanga, king of Buganda, 187

Nail Bey, 317–20, 438
Naim Bey, 339
Naki Bey, 95
Nansen, Fridtjof, xxiii, 266, **425–33**
  'Nansen Passport', xxiii, 428–9, 431
Nasim Mehmed, 113
Naslian, Jean, 149, 382
Natalie, Shahan, 442
Nathan, Edward I., 302
Nazarian, Elias Djerdji Nasri, 157
Nazim, Dr Mehmed, 102, 437
Nazism, 326, 422
Near East Foundation, 388
Near East Relief, xxii, 35, 140, 181, 221–2, 232–3, 249, 304, **387–9**, 429

Nesimî Bey, Hüseyin, xix, 80, **83–5**, 87
Nesimî, Abidin, 87
Neue Orient, Der, 343
New Testament, 452–3
Niemeyer, Theodor, 443
Niksar, Turkey, 178
NILI spy ring, 280, 284–6
Nolde, Boris, 369, 373
Norway, 426–7
Notre Jeunesse (Péguy), 34
Nottingham Evening Post, 354
Nubar Pasha, 281
Nubar, Boghos, 444
Nureddin Bey, 12, 95
Nuremberg Trials, 380
Nusret Bey, Mehmet, 153
Nyholm, Ivara, 261

Odian, Krikor, 19, 457
Odian, Yervant, 222
Odyssées arméniennes (Parcot), 165
Oeuvre missionnaire en Orient, Une (Berron), 198
Olchowik, Claude, 362
Old Testament, 452
Operation Nemesis, 385, 442
Osmaniye, Turkey, 5
L'Osservatore Romano, 189
Ottoman Empire, xvii, xx, xxii, 1–4, 6–7, 10, 41–3, 68, 70–72, 75–6, 251, 290–91
  antisemitism and, 301–2
  Armenian provinces, 76
  Germany and, 323–7
  judicial system, 372–4
  Mecelle (civil code), 68, 457
  Tanzimat, 68, 185

INDEX

Vilayets, 76
World War I and, 75–6, 137, 188–91
see also Young Turks
Ozanian, Andranik, 133, 192, 440
Ozansoy, Faik Ali, xix
Özdemir, Cem, 325

Pachalian, Lévon, 374
Pakaridj, Turkey, 173–4
Palestine, 32, 280–81, 283–4, 302, 358, 420, 422
von Pallavicini, Johann, 189
Panian, Karnig, 144–5, 221
Panpère, 197
Papazian, Garabed, 397
Parcot, Jean-Claude, 163, 165
Paris Peace Conference (1919– 20), xxii, 102, 406–7, 427, 429
Paul, Saint, 451
Pazarcık region, 224
Péguy, Charles, 21, 30, 33–5
Pera, Istanbul, 331
Petersen, Karen Marie, xxii– xxiii, xviii, **245–53**
Petliura, Symon, 378, 447
Pfade in grossen Wassern (Rohner), 228
Philip the Fair, King of France, 455
philosophe ignorant, Le (Voltaire), 456
photographic evidence, 342–3, 345, 444
Pinon, René, xxi, 281
Pisani, Abbé, 361
Pius XI, Pope, 187, 189–90

Pivet, Louis-Joseph, **351–9**
Plato, 453
Plimpton, George A., 387
Poème sur la loi naturelle (Voltaire), 456
Poidebard, Antoine, 192
Poincaré, Raymond, 393
Poland, 191, 422
Port Said, Egypt, 357
Portukalian, Mekertich, 289
Potoric (Haroutioun Damlamian), 177–82
Pour l'Arménie: Mémoire et dossier (Quillard), 21, 33
Poyrazoğlu Keussé, 5
de Pressensé, Francis, 27, 33, 43, 404
Pro Armenia Committee, 406
Pro Armenia journal, xxi, 3, 27–8, 32, 43, 289, 398
'Pro Armenia' (Aaron Aaronsohn), 282, 285
Protestants/Protestantism, 185, 195, 198, 217, 222, 223
Proust, Marcel, 41

Question d'Orient et la politique personnelle de M. Hanotaux, La (Quillard & Margery), 21
Quillard, Pierre, xxi, 3, **21–8**, 29–30, 32–3, 43, 405, 412

Rabinbach, Anson, 381, 383
Raffi (Hakob Melik Hakobian), 122
Rahman Pasha, Abdur, 59
Rakka, Syria, 10
Ranicki, Marcel, 433

473

INDEX

Rappaport, Emil, 380
Ras al-Ayn, Syria, xvii, xx, 10, 131
Rashid Bey, 113
Raynolds, G. C., 202
'Recording Death and Survival' (Bjornlund), 251
Red Book (Sevag), 440
refugees, xxiii, 197–8, 242–3, 261, 277, 375, 388, 425–32
  'Nansen Passport', xxiii, 428–9, 431
Reinach, Salomon, xxi
Republic, The (Cicero), 453–4
republicanism, 42–3
Reshid Bey, Mehmed, xix, 79–80, 83–5, 87, 89–90
Resisting Genocide: The Multiple Forms of Rescue (Göçek), 70–71
La Révolte, 29
La revue blanche, 35–6
Revue de France, 51
Revue de Paris, 23
Riggs, Henry H. (Harry), xviii–xix, 68, 154–5, **211–16**
de Roberty, Eugène, 27
Rogers, Daniel Miner, 5
Rogers, Gertrude, 202–3
Rohner, Beatrice, xx, 196, **223–8**, 239, 337–8
Roman Empire, 454–5
Romania, 31
Romieu, Louis, 137, 192, 283, 358
Roosevelt, Eleanor, 432
Roque-Ferrier, Fernand, 3, 50–51, **289–96**, 353
Roque-Ferrier, Fernand

Rössler, Walter, xix, 224, 327, **333–9**
de Rothschild, Edmond, 279
Rousseau, Jean-Jacques, 451, 456
Rumi, Jalal ad-Din Muhammad, 147, 149, 456
Russia/Russian Empire, 6–7, 42, 71, 275–7, 316, 372–3, 408, 412, 427–8
  October Revolution (1920), 277, 373, 427
Russian Armenia, 6, 72, 388, 475
Russkiye Vedomosti, 276
Ruyssen, Georges-Henri, 190

Sabah newspaper, 101
Sabit Bey, 212, 215
Sahak II, Catholicos of Cilicia, 222
Said Halim, 324
St Ambrose, bishop of Milan, 454
St Augustine, bishop of Hippo, 454
Saint Joseph orphanage, Constantinople, 362, 365
Sainte Marie, Flye, 363–4
Şakir, Dr Bahaddin, 76, *438*
Sakoyan family, **167–71**
Sakoyan, Éliane, 168
Salih Zeki, 93, 95
Samsun, Turkey, 177, 180–82
von Sanders, Otto Liman, 324
Sarah: The Flame of NILI (Alexander Aaronsohn), 284
Sarid, Yossi, 423
Sarıkamış (Sarikamish), Turkey, 7
Sarkissian, Greg, 155
Sarukhanyan, Tigran, 343
Sassoun (Sason), Turkey, 19

INDEX

massacres, 23–4, 49
Savur, Turkey, 84
Schäffer, Paula, 225–6
Schaufuss, Tatiana, 277
von Schellendorff, Fritz Bronsart, 324, 326
von Scheubner-Richter, Max Erwin, 326
Schlumberger, Gustave, 413
Schrei von Ararat, Der (Wegner), 344–5
Schwarzbard, Samuel 'Sholem', 378
Schwarze Korps, Der, 420
Sebouh (Arshag Nersesian), 441
Secret Report on the Situation of the Armenian People in Turkey (Lepsius), xx–xxi, 444
Seligman, Isaac N., 387
Semerdjian, Antranig, 158–9
Serengülian, Vartkes, 105–6
Sevag, Rupen, 440
Seven Pillars of Wisdom, The (Lawrence), 137
Séverine, xxi, 404
Shameful Act, A (Akçam), 155, 415
Sharia law, 140–41, 457
Shattuck, Corinna, 270
Sheikh Adi, 128–9, 131
Sheikh Hamu Shiru, **131–3**
Shukri Bey, 444
Siamanto (Atom Yarchanian), 440
Sick, Ingeborg Maria, 258
Silliman, Caroline, 202–3
Silvan, Turkey, 84
Sinjar region, xviii, 127–8, 131
Sis (now Kozan), Turkey, 4–5
Sivas, Turkey, 9, 70, 76

Slaughterhouse Province, The (Davis), 308
slavery, 140, 259
Smyrna, Turkey, xvii, 153, 156, 158, 320, 365
Social Contract, The (Rousseau), 456
Société des droits de l'homme, 42
Société des nations et les puissances devant le problème arménien, La (Mandelstam), 374
Socrates, 453
Somoundjian family, **163–5**
Song of Bernadette, The (Werfel), 419
Sonnenaufgang journal, 196
Sophocles, 453
Sort de l'Empire ottoman, Le (Mandelstam), 373
Soubirous, Bernadette, 419
Souchon, Wilhelm, 324
South Africa, 398
Souvenirs de jours sombres (Berron), 195
Soviet Armenia, 429–30, 432
Soviet Union, 128, 243
    see also Russia. Russian Empire
Special Organization (Teşkilât-i Mahsusa), xvi, xviii, 7–8, 72, 84, 168, 317–18, 415–16
    'butcher battalions', xvi
Stalin, Josef, 243
Strasbourg, France, 196, 198
Straus, Oscar S., 387
Stuermer, Harry, 327, **329–32**
Suad Bey, Ali, xx, **93–6**
Sublime Porte, 108, 439

INDEX

Süleyman Nazif, 97
Suppression des Arméniens: Méthode allemande; Travail turc, La (Pinon), xxi, 281
Sûriyya al-Fatât, 136
Surmenian, Azad and Berdjouhi, 447
Surp Garabed monastery, Halvor, 118
Survivre à la mort de ses enfants (Parcot), 165
Svazlian, Verjine, 155
Swiss Society for the Immigration and Patronage of Armenian Orphans, 391–2
Switzerland, 198, 231, 391–2
Sykes, Mark, 282–4
Sykes–Picot Agreement (1916), 137, 282–3, 362
Syria, xvii, xx, xxii, 197–8, 242–3, 259–60, 284
Syriacs, 72, 76, 408
Szawłowski, Ryszard, 380

Tachjian, Vahé, 140
Talaat Pasha, xx, 9–11, 97–8, 99–102, 106–8, 273, 301–3, 323, 325–6, 458
    assassination of, xxiii, 339, 344, 378–9, 381, 439, 441–7
    trial, 437–8
Tanzimat reforms (1839–76), 68, 185, 415, 457
Tashjian, Hovhannes, 233
Tatars (Azeris), 290
Tatikian, Anahit, 447
Tchachikian, Antranig, 158
Tchachikian, Archalouys, 158
Tehlirian, Khatchadur, 440–41
Tehlirian, Soghomon, xxiii, 11, 273, 339, 344, 378–9, **439–49**
    trial, 442–7
Tekeian, Diran, 357
Tekeyan, Vahan, 222
Temps nouveaux, Les 29
Ter Minassian, Anahide, 8
Ternon, Yves, 22, 30, 32, 34, 36, 327, 457
Terrell, Alexander Watkins, 398
Teşkilât-i Mahsusa *see* Special Organization
Testimonianze (Gorrini), 299
Tevosyan, Hasmik, 153
Tewfik Pasha, 100–101
Theodosius I, Roman Emperor, 454
Theodosius II, Roman Emperor, 454
Three Pashas *see* Cemal Pasha; Enver Pasha; Talaat Pasha
Todesgang des armenischen Volkes, Der (Lepsius), 271
Tolstoy, Alexandra, **275–8**
Tolstoy, Leo, 275, 277
Tossounian, Sarkis, 356
Totally Unofficial (Lemkin), 378–9
Tourian, Yeghishe, 63, 420
Tours Congress (1920), 408
Toursarkissian, Garabed *see* Aghassi
Toynbee, Arnold, xxi, 399
Tracy, Annie C., 211
Transcaucasia and Ararat (Bryce), 397

INDEX

Transjordan, 283
Trarieux, Ludovic, 30, 403
Travis, Ray, **221–2**
Treatment of Armenians in the Ottoman Empire, 1915–1916, The (Bryce and Toynbee), 399
Treaty of Alexandropol (1920), 407
Treaty of Ankara (1921), 362
Treaty of Berlin (1878), 31, 34, 41, 295, 398
Treaty of Brest-Litovsk (1918)
Treaty of Lausanne (1923), 174, 365, 374–5, 407
Treaty of San Stefano (1878), 19
Treaty of Sèvres (1920), 298, 362, 365, 375, 393, 406–7
Treaty of Versailles (1919), 192
Trebizond, Turkey, xviii, 9, 70, 76, 283, 292, 295, 297–8, 315–21
  massacres (1895), 47–52, 55–9, 188–9, 289–90
tribal clans, 115, 117–29
Triple Alliance (Germany, Austro–Hungary, Italy), 52, 107–8, 189, 298
Triple Entente (France, Britain, Russia), 6, 9, 202, 280, 282–4
Trowbridge, Stephen, 5–6
Tsitsernakaberd, Armenia, 141, 299, 458
Tunceli *see* Dersim
Turkey *see* Ottoman Empire
Turkish Historical Society, 102
Turkish History Committee, 416
Turkish Republic, proclamation of (1923), 85, 102, 326, 357, 416

'Turkish Rescuers' (Gerçek), 75
Türkoglu, Ömer, 75
Two Committees, Two Massacres (Ahmet Refik), 415
Tyan, Émile, 67–8

'Ugandan martyrs', 187
Ulpian, 454
Üngör, Ugur Ümit, 161
United Kingdom, 280–84, 398–401
United Nations, 427, 455
  Convention on Genocide (1948), xvii, 381–3
United States, 11, 188, 191–2, 202–4, 222, 233, 249, 284, 301–5, 380, 387–8, 398–9
Universal Declaration of Human Rights (1948), 455
Urfa, Turkey, xix, 228–32, 234, 256–9, 270, 363
Ussher, Clarence, **201–5**
Ussher, Eleanor, 202
Ussher, Neville, 204

Van, Turkey, xvii, 49, 70, 76, 153, 201–5, 276
  massacres, 8–9, 203–4
Var, France, 362
Varoujan, Daniel, 440
Vartan, Oovig, 24
Vazken I, Catholicos of All Armenians, 421
Veled Çelebi, 148–9
Veli Effendi, 5
Vêpres arméniennes (Cillière), 48, 51, 55
Vérité sur L'Affaire Dreyfus, La (Lazare), 30

INDEX

Versailles Peace Conference (1919), 281, 404
Versjin, Digin, 252–3
Vinaver, Maxim, 373
Völkischer Beobachter, 326
Voltaire, 456

von Wangenheim, Hans, 90, 324, 333
Warsaw Ghetto, 35, 433
Weg ohne Heimkehr, Der (Wegner), 344
Wegner, Armin T., xx, 327, **341–7**, 444
Weill, Kurt, 420
Weimar Republic, 325, 343, 345
Weisgal, Meyer, 419
Welt, Die, 30
Werfel, Franz, 35, 271, 358, **419–24**
whirling dervishes, 148
Wilhelm II, German Kaiser, 32, 270–71, 323, 343
Williams, Talcott, 387
Wilson, Woodrow, 188, 191–2, 194, 301, 304–5, 343–4, 362, 387, 398, 406
Wise, Rabbi Stephen, 301–2, 387
With the Turks in Palestine (Alexander Aaronsohn), 284
Women's Missionary Organization (WMO), 263
World Holocaust Remembrance Center, Yad Vashem, 345
World War I, xvi, xxii, 1, 6–7, 75–6, 188, 276–7, 280, 323, 381, 412
World War II, xiv, 198, 243, 381, 455

see also Hitler, Adolf; Nazism

Xenophon, 121

Yarrow, Ernest, 202–3, 276
Yarrow, Jane, 202
Yayian, Haroutioun, 226
Yazid ibn Muawiya, 128
Yazidis/Yazidism, xviii, **127–9**, 131–3
Yerevan, Armenia, 407, 430
Yerevan International Film Festival, 261
Yerznka (Erzincan), 440–41
Yoghonolook, 354
Yotnakhparian, Levon, 140
Young Turks, xvi, xxii, 2–7, 9, 19–20, 71, 97, 99, 106, 118, 168, 211, 215–16, 258, 272, 304
  Çelebi, conflict with 148–9
  decree of 26 June 1915, 316–17
  fall of, 100–101
  policies, 372–3
  religion and, 67–9, 80
  trials of (1919–20), **437–8**
  Young Turk revolution (1908), 290–91, 323, 351–2
Yozgat, 167–9, 442
Yusuf Khan, 117

Zadig or Destiny (Voltaire), 456
Zaven I Der Yeghiayan, 188
Zazas, **125**
Zeller, Maggie, 269
Zemstvo Union, 277
Zerahian, Esther Armine, 159
Zeytun, Turkey, 8, 224, 354

INDEX

Zia Bey, 94–5
Zichron Yaakov, Israel, 279, 285
Zionism *see* Jews/Judaism
Zionist Action Committee, 32
Zionist Congress, Basel
   1st (1897), 30
   2nd (1898), 32
   5th (1901), 32

Ziya Bey, Yusuf, xx, 93
Zohrab, Krikor, 105–6, 372
Zola, Émile, xxi, 3, 21, 30, 43, 403
Zoryan Institute, 155
Zouk Mikael, Lebanon, 249
Zwei Kriegsjahre in Konstantinopel 1915–16 (Stuermer), 329–32